THE SLOW LEARNER
IN THE CLASSROOM

NEWELL C. KEPHART

Glen Haven Achievement Center
Fort Collins, Colorado

THE SLOW LEARNER IN THE CLASSROOM

Second Edition

CHARLES E. MERRILL PUBLISHING COMPANY

A Bell & Howell Company   *Columbus, Ohio*

To MAK

THE SLOW LEARNER SERIES

Edited by Newell C. Kephart

Chapter opening illustrations by Janet Snyder

International Standard Book Number: 0-675-09196-9

Library of Congress Catalog Card Number: 77-158613

1 2 3 4 5 6 7 8 9 10 11 12 / 75 74 73 72 71

Printed in the United States of America

Preface

To most teachers, as well as parents, the slow learning child is a complete enigma. One day he learns the classroom material to perfection; the next he seems to have forgotten every bit of it. In one activity he excells all the other children; in the next he performs like a two-year-old. His behavior is unpredictable and almost violent in its intensity. He is happy to the point of euphoria but, the next moment, he is sad to the point of depression.

Too often these aberrant performances are attributed to willful misbehavior, stupidity or lack of interest. Actually, in many cases, the child's problems are not his fault. His central nervous system processes information in a little different way than that of other children. The organization among the items of information is disturbed, so that he does not see what we think we show him; he sees something different. He does not hear what we think we are saying to him. He does not make the connections as we do between bits of information which we think we are presenting in such a beautifully organized fashion. His central nervous system is treating these items in a different way.

It is almost impossible for us to imagine what the world is like for this child because our nervous system operates in the so-called normal manner. Whatever we can think of to show him or tell him is the product of this normal operation. We cannot conceive of how it could be otherwise or how these data could be torn apart or combined in some bizarre fashion. If we understand what the possibilities for aberrant processing are, we can guess at how it might be, but we cannot know for certain.

Obviously, to make the same classroom presentation over again is not going to help him. If the presentation was bizarre to him before, it will be bizarre again because it is being processed by the same deviant nervous system. Merely to go slower or to drill longer is not the answer. He requires a different kind of presentation, one in which the alterations in his processing will not interfere with the understanding of the material being presented.

It is apparent also that the deviation in the function of the nervous system will not be the same in all slow learning children. There will be as many variations as there are children and, hence, as many differences in learning as there are children. As a result, the presentation which works for one child will not work for the next. There is no "method" for teaching slow learners. There are hundreds of methods among which the teacher must select that one or ones which fit the needs of the child in question.

As a consequence, the teacher of the slow learner needs two basic competences: a rationale which permits consistent interpretation of the child's learning behavior and a repertory of techniques by which information can be presented in myriad ways. With a comprehensive rationale, the teacher can determine what type of presentation has the best chance of success. With a repertory of techniques, he can select and design presentations to maximize the chances of learning.

It is these two competencies to which the present volume addresses itself. In Part I a rationale for learning is presented. This rationale is based on two primary principles: development and generalization. In Part II a series of techniques related to successive steps in the rationale are described. It must be stressed that these are only illustrations and not a complete list of techniques. Taking these illustrations as a guide, the teacher must use creativity and ingenuity to augment and alter them to meet the needs of any given child.

NEWELL C. KEPHART

Fort Collins, Colorado
April, 1971

Contents

part I

Development and Achievement

chapter 1

The Course of Development

The human infant is born into a very complex universe composed of many objects, spaces and events. In spite of its extreme complexity, however, this universe is lawful. All of its operations and relations are strictly governed by law, be they the angles in a simple geometric form or the movements of the stars. This lawful structure of the universe is the principle tenet of all science, and it must be the basis of all theories of child development as well.

At the time of birth, however, the infant has no knowledge of the laws which govern this universe into which he has been thrust. He has certain responses which occur mechanically upon the occurrence of certain events in the environment and which serve to keep him alive until he learns more extensive responses. He is bombarded with sensory information from the environment but these data are global. They have no form and they have no parts; they supply only vague, ill-defined impressions rather then organized information.

The infant's task, which will take him a lifetime, is to discover the laws of the universe which surrounds him, and how to control his own behavior so that it will conform to the lawful complex of which it is a part. When such learning is successful, behavior, shaped by the same laws which control the whole of the environment, becomes appropriate when it is carried out in that environment. When such learning is incomplete or erroneous, behavior is inappropriate or unsatisfactory.

The organism which the infant uses for this learning task is admirably designed. It is designed with maximum flexibility so that its major operations and processes can be determined by learning. Only enough fixed responses are provided to insure survival. The rest are open to modification and fabrication through learning. (Wilcox, 1970.) The central nervous system is an intricate machine for learning. It allows for the collection and storage of data and their subsequent use to modify behavior. It permits the child to build a "little model of the universe" (Craik, 1952) within his own head and to shape his behavior on the basis of this model.

INNATE STAGE

REFLEX LEARNING

Traditionally, psychologists have described behavior in terms of the stimulus-response bond (S→R). Learning was originally conceived as the mere accumulation of numbers of S→R bonds.

The initial behaviors of the child can be quite well explained by this early concept. Such behaviors are largely reflexive, and reflexive behavior, although it is much more complicated than once thought, can be explained with relatively minor modifications of the S→R concept. A specific stimulus gives rise to a specific response with little or no modification or conscious processing in between.

These reflexive responses, however, are too specific to permit adaptive behavior. Although many of them are essential for survival, the resulting responses are too specific both on the stimulus end and on the response end to permit the child to interact with his universe and discover its laws, or to alter his behavior enough to solve the more complex problems which his environment presents to him. One of his earliest learning tasks is to increase the scope and flexibility of his initial reflex responses.

The learning necessary to this task takes three directions. *Chaining* is a process by which one reflex response is attached behind another. The response to reflex 1 becomes the stimulus for reflex 2, et cetera (A of Figure 1). The result is no longer a single reflex but a series of reflexes occurring in sequence. The initial reflexive responses

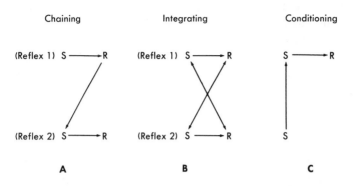

FIGURE 1.   The scope and flexibility of the reflex responses are increased through early learning.

have been expanded in time Chaining thus provides a temporal organization among reflexes.

Integrating is a process by which one reflex is tied to another so that a single stimulus gives rise to two or more reflex responses (B of Figure 1). Intermediate fibers lying between the phases of two or more reflex areas are activated so that a complex is developed. Although these fibers are anatomically present at birth, as Sherrington (1948) has pointed out, their anatomical presence does not insure their function. The child must learn, through experimentation and learning, how to use these fibers for the purpose of integrating reflexes into a complex of response. This process results in an intricate array of responses simultaneous in time. The scope of the initial response has been expanded in space.

Conditioning increases the flexibility of the stimulus. A second stimulus occurs frequently, contiguous in space and time with the initially adequate stimulus. When such contiguity has been experienced often enough, the second stimulus becomes adequate to elicit the response. Such a learning process is known as classical conditioning. The first stimulus is called the *adequate stimulus* and the new stimulus the *conditioned stimulus*. The classical experiment with this process was made by Ivan Pavlov in Russia (Pavlov, 1927).

Through these three processes, isolated reflexes are integrated into reflex systems. An example is the system known as the righting reflex. When balance is disturbed, a number of reflex responses occur in an effort to restore balance. Many parts of the body may move at the same time in coordinated balancing and counter-balancing activities. One such complex follows another until balance is regained. The entire procedure is a very complex assortment of movements, most of them reflexive, but all integrated into an organized totality.

Compare this mature response with that of the infant who is just learning to stand. One response or a very simple series of responses takes place and, when this is ineffective, he topples over. In the older child, the scope and flexibility, and hence the adaptability, of the response have been greatly increased through the integration of the initial reflex responses. Undoubtedly, some of this development has resulted from maturation. However, much of it must be attributed to learning. The variation in the final response system from child to child and the distortion of the development when learning is experimentally controlled (Fisher, Turner, 1970) attest to the significance of the learning factor.

Such complex behavior is difficult to explain with a simple S→R concept. On the one hand, one S gives rise to not one R but to many Rs. On the other hand any given R may be elicited by any of a number of Ss. The fixed relationship between S and R varies not only from individual to individual but within one individual from one situation to another. Apparently the S→R concept is too simple and too inflexible to permit adequate explanations of such complex behavior.

Recognizing this difficulty, psychologists sometime ago interposed a third term, the *organism,* between the stimulus and the response in the S→R bond, expanding it to S→O→R (Asher, 1946). This expansion implies that the organism acts on the stimulus and influences the response. The organism interposes between the stimulus and the response, manipulating both ends of the equation before the final response is exteriorized. Before behavior can be predicted, we must know not only the stimulus but also the nature and functioning of the organism. Insofar as the above kind of development is based on learning, the child has created his own "O" and has determined by his learning how many and how great the modifications of the initial S→R relationship will be.

MOVEMENT DIFFERENTIATION

At the same time that the reflexes are being integrated, there is another form of innate behavior which is undergoing development.

This second type of motor response is the generalized movement first described by Coghill (Coghill, 1929). Initially described in amblystoma, the generalized movement is a sweep of motion which begins at the head end of the organism, passes through its length without interruption, and exits from the tail. In amblystoma, which is a form of salamander, the movement throws the head to one side. As it passes through it twists the animal into an S shape. The movement then reverses, the head is thrown to the other side and, with the passage of this second phase, the S is reversed. This alternation of the S from one side to the other drives the animal through the water and provides the mechanism by which it swims.

The same type of behavior can be observed in the human infant. A wave of movement starts at the head, passes through the body, and comes out the feet. The head rears back, the back arches, and finally the feet come up. The various parts (arms, legs, et cetera) move as the wave passes by. However, they do not move as parts. They move only as a function of the wave, not purposefully, but as an attribute of the wave.

The generalized movement presents the opposite problem to that presented by the reflex response. This movement is too gross; it lacks detail. Whereas the reflex was too specific, the generalized movement is too general to permit adaptive behavior. The learning problem here is one of differentiation. The movement must be broken down so that the parts of the organism can move independently of the total sweep.

Such differentiation learning takes place according to two general developmental directions. The *cephalo-caudal* direction is the head-to-tail progression. According to this principle, the infant first learns to move the head and neck independent of the sweep. Later he learns to control the shoulders independently. Still later he differentiates the movements of the torso and hips. Finally the knees, ankles, and toes achieve independence in that order. When such differentiation has occurred, the differentiated part can be moved for itself alone, whereas formerly its movement had to await the arrival of the sweep; nor could the sweep be interrupted after the part had moved.

The *proximo-distal* direction is the inside-out progression. According to this principle, those parts which lie closest to the center of the organism are differentiated first and those which lie most peripheral are differentiated last. Thus, in the differentiation of the arm, the movement of the shoulder achieves independence first. Later the movement of the elbow is differentiated. Still later the independent movement of the wrist is possible. Finally the precise movements of the fingers, which are so important in classroom tasks, are achieved.

As a result of differentiation, parts can move independently. They can, therefore, perform their function as parts. They can be used to contact parts of the environment and to manipulate such contacts for the purpose of gathering information. They can move purposefully so that the child can determine what the nature of the environmental contact will be.

Children in whom the process of differentiation is not complete will be seen in the classroom. Asked to color a picture, such a child grasps the crayon in his stubby little fist and stabs away at the paper. The independent action of the fingers, which permits the thumb apposital grip, and their precise movement have not been differentiated out of the early generalized movement. Fine manipulations and precise responses cannot be properly taught until this differentiation process is completed.

It is, therefore, very important to the teacher and to the child that differentiation learning take place. Learning results from the interaction between the organism and its environment. Such interactions will be gross until the use of the parts of the body permits its refinement. Environmental interactions will be purposeless until the child can initiate and control his own movements and through such control determine for himself the nature of the contact.

It is also important that differentiation take place sequentially — that it follows the cephalo-caudal and the proximo-distal axes. It is possible, in response to outside pressures, for the child to differentiate specific movements of a given part without completing the progressive series of differentiations which would normally lead to such responses. The result is an isolated group of responses not firmly related to the activities of the rest of the organism.

Classroom practices frequently lead to such isolated responses. The kindergarten or first grade child is presented with a drawing or copying task. If the use of the fingers is not yet differentiated, he performs as described above. The teacher, however, "teaches" him how to draw. She pries his fingers apart and wraps them around the crayon in the prescribed manner. She then insists on a series of little

marks in a certain pattern. The child, unable to perform these movements in the context of his overall responses, "learns" this particular
task for itself alone. He learns to move his fingers in the prescribed
pattern to satisfy the demands of this specific task. Such learnings
have sometimes been called "splinter skills". They are isolated from
the child's body of learnings and are as specific as were the initial
reflexes (see Chapter 2).

Such specific, unelaborated responses result when differentiation
of certain movements has occurred out of sequence to meet specific
demands. They are fractionated and inefficient and bear little or no
relationship to any other activities of the organism. Bender (Bender,
1956) has described cases in which this splintering has gone so far
that the child conceives of the hand which is doing the writing as
being disembodied — floating free in space and unattached to the
rest of his body.

It is not only important, therefore, that differentiation take place
but that it take place in the proper sequence. It is through the sequential development of differentiation that the continuity between functions and responses is preserved.

SENSORY DIFFERENTIATION

The same kind of differentiation learning is taking place in the
sensory manipulations of the child. Initial sensory impressions are
vague and formless. Like the generalized movement, they are global
experiences which have no parts and are effective only *in toto*.
Reflexive responses serve to maximize their intensity (the fixation
reflex turns the eye toward an intense visual stimulus, a similar reflex turns the head toward the source of a sound, et cetera) but the
qualities necessary for interpretation are minimal.*

The qualities necessary for recognition and interpretation must
be sorted out of the initial mass and acquire their own identity so that
their relationships can be manipulated. In the visual field such qualities are the elements of form perception, lines, and angles (Hebb,
1949); in the auditory field they are pitch, tone, timber, and the
like which will be combined into integrated auditory impressions
such as speech and music.

---

*See the studies on the orienting response (Lynn, 1966).

Such information-carrying qualities of sensory impressions are identified through learning. They are differentiated, one by one, out of the initial global mass. Once separated, they are coordinated so that the whole is never lost, but a new whole emerges. This new whole is an integrated pattern of elements which carries within it a maximum of information, whereas the global whole carried a minimum of information (see Chaper 5).

This sensory differentiation will proceed as far as is necessary to permit the child to distinguish and recognize differences and similarities between sensory presentations. If the environment demands of the child many and precise sensory judgements, differentiation will proceed to extreme lengths, as in the musician who must recognize minute tonal differences or in the finish inspector in a manufacturing plant who must immediately identify tiny flaws in the product. If, on the other hand, the environment demands few such judgements, sensory differentiation will be limited and the individual will be able to differentiate only gross differences. Many speech problems in young children are due to lack of auditory differentiation. Certain reading problems are due to the inability of the child to see the difference between letters or words. Sensory differentiation has not proceeded far enough to meet the demands of these tasks.

Through such early learnings, reflex integration, motor and sensory integration, the tools for learning as it were, are refined and made functional. In the more complex learnings to follow, these initial achievements will be used as instruments for the manipulation of information from the environment and for the modification of behavior on the basis of such manipulations. Both ends of the learning equation have been refined so that they become useful in the learning process. Sensory differentiation has refined the stimulus while the motor learnings have refined the response. At the same time, the beginnings of a processing system, whereby outside information and internal response can be coordinated so that adaptive behavior can result, have been built into the organism.

THE DEVELOPMENT OF A PROCESSING PROGRAM

The following section is a hypothetical construct. The purpose of any such construct is to help one think in a clearer and more organized fashion about the principles involved and to draw meaningful hypotheses regarding everyday problems. If the reader finds the following discussion useful, he should use it. If he finds it confusing, he should disregard it.

The structure employed here is based upon a modification of the cell assembly theory of Hebb (Hebb, 1949). The principles derived, however, are inherent in many theoretical positions: reverberating circuits (Guyton, 1966), changes in the protein structure of cells (Katz, Halstead, 1950), the function of glial cells (Mountcastle, 1968) and others. The usefulness of the construct is not dependent upon the mechanics of the underlying theory. Neither is it dependent upon the exclusive validation of these mechanics. Many or all of the above mechanisms are probably operative in the processing of information in addition to the ones described below. Futhermore, when final analyses are made, the true mechanisms will undoubtedly be found somewhat different than described here. This too does not imperil the construct, since it is the principle and not the mechanics which makes any construct useful.

Some readers will be disturbed by the "neurologising" implied herein. Again, if this line of reasoning makes it easier to consider the problem, use it. If it does not, consider only the behavioral aspects of the description.

It is the common belief among students of behavior that the mind and the body are not independent entities. The functions of the former are militated by the operations of the latter. The central nervous system is the mechanism most closely related to behavior and to the processes we call mental which are related to behavior. Learning involves the modification of the operations of the nervous system so that alterations in behavior occur. The nervous system must contain mechanisms for the determination of behavior on the basis of incoming information. Mere accumulation of such simple mechanisms, however, cannot account for the complex alteration of behavior resulting from learning. A much more dynamic function of the nervous system must be postulated, at least in man. The basic functions of the system must be altered as learning proceeds.

The structural unit of the nervous system is the *neurone*. The neurone is a single cell characterized by two fibrous processes, one extending from each side of the cell body. The specialized function of the neurone is the development of a *neural impulse*.

The functional unit of the nervous system is the neural impulse. This impulse is a wave of negative electricity which passes without decrement from one end of a fiber process to the other (Eccles, 1953).

Neural fibers grow into close approximation to each other but do not make contact. Between each fiber and the next is an open space called the *synapse*. In order for a neural circuit to be established, the neural impulse must be transmitted across this synapse. The mechanism of synaptic transmission is a complex electrochemical process which need not concern us here.

Behavior results from the operation of a neural circuit. Figure 2 illustrates the simplest type of such neural circuit. The stimulus activates neuron "A," causing it to generate a neural impulse. This impulse is transmitted across synapse "a" to neurone "B," an interconnecting or internuncial neurone. It is thence transmitted across "b" to neurone "C," an effector or efferent neurone which transmits the impulse to a muscle and causes it to contract. Such a simple neural circuit can explain the simplest forms of behavior (for example, certain reflexive behaviors).

A number of such neural circuits, varying in complexity, are present at birth. Innate factors insure the transmission of the impulse along the proper neurones and across the appropriate synapses. A large portion of the nervous system, however, is so-called "free tissue" — in effect, a vast number of units in anatomical proximity which can be "wired together" into any type of circuits we wish. It is, as it were, an enormous computer with a multitude of relays which can be connected in any patterns which serve the purpose of the problem. The extirpation experiments of Penfield (Penfield and Roberts, 1959) are just beginning to reveal how much of the cerebral cortex in man represents such free tissue. The vast association areas

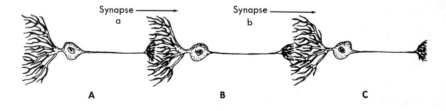

FIGURE 2.   The simplest neural circuit

appear to function in this way. Certainly much less of the nervous system has its function predetermined than was once thought.

The method of "wiring" a circuit involves a mechanism at the synapse. When an impulse is transmitted across a synapse, there develops on the tips of the fiber process of the post-synaptic neurone small tissue growths called synaptic knobs (Lorente de No, 1947). These growths are anatomical structures which result from the transmission of the impulse (Figure 3). Whenever a synapse is used, one or more such knobs develop. The more frequently a synapse is used, the larger and more numerous become the knobs. When a used synapse falls into disuse for any reason the knobs decrease in size but never completely disappear.

A general principle now becomes apparent: function alters structure. Since the synaptic knob is an anatomical structure, this alteration is anatomical. Since the knob is produced directly by the transmission of an impulse, the structural alteration is produced by function. Such alteration is progressive, since the knobs increase in number and size with increased use of the synapse, and it is permanent since the knobs never completely disappear thereafter.

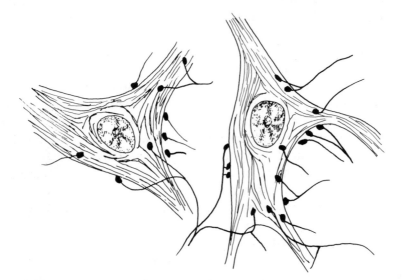

FIGURE 3. Synaptic knobs develop at a synaptic junction as a result of its use. (Reproduced from Strauss and Kephart [1955] as adapted from Lorente de No [1947].)

The effect of the synaptic knob is to lower the threshold at the synapse. Exactly by what mechanism this lowering is accomplished is not known. However, it does appear that the neural impulse is transmitted more easily across a synapse that has been thus modified than across a synapse which has not been so modified.\The mechanism of the synaptic knob can therefore be used to establish a neural circuit.

In Figure 2, if the synaptic function between neurone A and neurone B is used, synaptic knobs will develop on the fiber tips of neurone B and the threshold AB will be lowered. If the synaptic function between A and C has not been used, no such modification of the synapse AC will have taken place. If at a later date, neurone A is discharged, by the law of least resistance the impulse will be transmitted from A to B where the threshold has been lowered, rather than from A to C where the threshold is still high. A neural circuit has been established. Hereafter all impulses in A will tend to go in the direction AB rather than AC. Since the modifications at AB are progressive, this circuit will tend to become more firmly established at each subsequent use. Herein is the second phase of the general principle cited above: once function has altered structure, this alteration influences future function. By its own activities, therefore, the nervous system patterns its own function.

This patterning, however, is neither random nor haphazard. It rather tends to concentrate functionally formed circuits together and to relate new circuits to old. There are two reasons for this intensification of pattern. On the one hand, when a synapse is modified, it will tend to draw neural impulses toward itself since its threshold is lower; hence, energy will tend to flow through this lower threshold. Thus the operation of the system itself tends toward pattern. Experiences which are contiguous in space and time will tend to develop circuits having common synapses between them.

In the second place, the laws of the universe will tend to dictate patterns of circuits. By virtue of these laws, the environment of the child is an organized environment. It is not random. The environment, therefore, will tend to present to the child experiences which belong together contiguously in space and time. Because of this contiguity the circuits representing these experiences will tend to have synapses in common and to form a pattern of neural activity whose commonalities represent commonalities in the surrounding environment.

The patterns characteristic of reality tend to be reproduced in patterns of neural activity as a result of experience — that is, if adults do not interfere. If we put together and present to the child things which do not belong together in reality, these things get put together in the child's developing neural patterns because of their contiguity in space and time. The resulting neural patterns are often distorted or disrupted and do not conform to reality.

The so-called overstimulated child illustrates the problem. Indulgent relatives deluge him with toys and experiences which have no relationship to each other. This hodgepodge of experience is built into his learning pattern, which itself becomes a hodgepodge. His subsequent behavior is disrupted. He goes aimlessly from one thing to another without being able to sustain activity with anything. His behavior pattern is unstable because the stability which would have been given to his learning by the environment was interrupted and its continuity was shattered.

Because of the patterned nature of the modifications in the central nervous system and their effect upon future experience, the processing of information between stimulus and responses begins to become structured. Past experiences have left their effect upon the organism and effect present behavior in an indirect but none the less effective manner by virtue of their contribution to the pattern. The pattern, as it were, subtends all past experience, balanced and averaged out, as well as the various stimulus aspects of the present experience. The resulting behavior reflects the totality. It does so, however, all in one simultaneous operation. It is not necessary to catalog and call up in order the pertinent past experiences nor the significant aspects of the present stimulation. The pattern by its very nature supplies the overall significance of this collection of experience simultaneously.

This patterned structure in the central nervous system becomes the "organism" factor in the S→O→R formula. Incoming information is passed through this structure taking on in the process the characteristics of the pattern of the structure. This pattern is then translated into output terms (see Chapter Four) and is reflected in the overt behavior. The input no longer directly determines the behavior. The input is "processed" and this processing in turn determines the behavior.

It is a little like pouring sand through a sieve. If you drop a handful of sand on the floor, it falls in a formless glob. If, however, you drop it through a sieve, it falls in a series of little piles which reflect the number, size, and shape of the openings in the sieve. The sieve is a patterned structure. The sand was "processed" through the sieve and the resulting configuration reflects the pattern in the structure. Thus, the patterned structure in the central nervous system influences behavior. Unlike the sieve, which is a pattern imposed from outside, the central nervous system builds its own progressive pattern as a result of its own activities.

The patterned nature of the developing neural structure is of upmost importance. Whenever a pattern is completed, no matter in what medium, a new and unique quality emerges (Strauss and Kephart, 1955). Form perception offers a simple example. A square is composed of four lines and four angles. The quality of squareness, however, does not reside in any of the lines or the angles, nor in the mere accumulation of these elements. This unique quality derives from the relationship between these elements or from the pattern formed by them. Such emergence of unique qualities is inherent in the nature of pattern and, in like manner, pattern is necessary to this development.

In the patterned development of systems of neural circuits, similar unique qualities can be expected to emerge. They result from the interrelationships between circuits rather than from individual unique circuits. Since the neural system is dynamic (it is only evident where impulses are passing through it), its pattern is manifested as a procedure for processing data. Just as the sand is *processed* by the sieve and unique qualities are imposed upon it by this processing, so data are processed by the neural pattern and unique qualities are imposed upon them. The emergence of a new neural pattern is thus observed in behavior as a different (more complex or more efficient) method of data processing.

In the development of the child, such emergence of new processing procedures can be observed. There are two approaches to the study of child development current at the moment. The first of these is the *normative* approach. By this approach, the quantitative aspects of development are investigated. At each succeeding chronological age level, the child is seen to be able to perform more kinds of tasks and more complicated tasks. The tacit assumption is that the child is accumulating abilities, skills, and knowledge and that his progress follows a steadily increasing curve with no discernible breaks or points of inflection.

The second approach to development is that represented by Piaget (Phillips, 1969; Flavell, 1963). Piaget suggests that development occurs in a series of stages. He appears to conceive of these stages as essentially new methods for processing data involving a new principle. It is conceivable that such new principles could develop out of the patterned elaboration of neural circuits with their accompanying emergence of new qualities. If so, movement from one stage to another would be abrupt. When the structure has been elaborated sufficiently to permit the formation of a pattern, the new quality would emerge as an "aha" idea upon solidification of the pattern. Development would then occur as a series of step-like processes, the emergence of each new pattern resulting in a sudden change in the method of processing data for the purpose of problem solving.

It seems possible to combine these two approaches to development. Learning would then be seen to occur by accumulation according to the normative approach until a sufficient quantity of information had been amassed and had assumed a degree of continuity. At this point a new pattern would form and learning would jump up abruptly to a new stage (see Figure 4). The step-like process, resulting as it does from a new pattern in the structure through which data are processed, would result in two changes in the learning procedure. In the first place, all new data would be processed by the new method. In the second place, previous data would be immediately reprocessed, since they are now a part of a new pattern and must be interpreted in terms of the new pattern. Again take the square as an example; once the four lines have been seen as a square, they can no longer be seen as independent lines. Whenever a pattern forms, the elements are influenced by the emergent qualities from the pattern and take on new meaning.

According to such a view, development would be seen as a series of step-like processes with steep assents interspersed with accumulative processes with slow assents. If the step-like process is omitted, normative development continues. The end result, however, is limited development and an end which fails to achieve a true picture of the environment and the child's behavior within it. It is essential, therefore, that in teaching and learning, attention be given not only to the accumulative aspects of development but to the processing aspects as well. Both quantitative and qualitative factors must be considered.

The early motor and sensory differentiations of the child provide the units out of which the structured pattern is built. It is in the nature of pattern that it develops from inflected units. A mass with no units has cohesion but no pattern. Even its boundaries have no function until its contour is differentiated (Strauss and Kephart, 1955). Pattern results from the relationships between discernible units. Differentiation learning, therefore, is essential to structured processing by virtue of supplying the units.

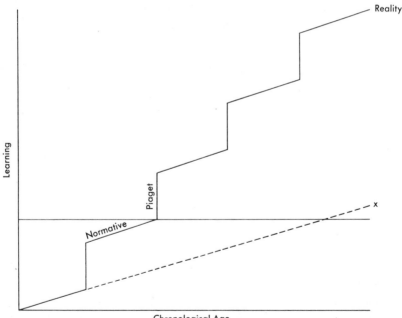

FIGURE 4.   The course of development. Periods of normative development (slow rising portions of curve) lead to next Piaget type stage (vertical rises). If normative development continues without the emergence of the next stage (dotted line), the final status ("x") is short of a true representation of the reality of the environment.

In the process of differentiation, however, the pattern is being built. It is important, therefore, that this differentiation be quantitatively adequate so that there will be enough units to supply a sufficiently extensive pattern. It is also important that the units develop systematically so that the pattern will have continuity. Thus the significance of orderly, sequential differentiation as stressed above.

When the units of a structure have been established, the learning process turns to the construction of increasingly complex patterns for processing data. The child writes, as it were, a series of programs to control his computer. These programs differ not only quantitatively but qualitatively as well. He learns not only how to process more data but also how to process it in different and more efficient ways.

PERCEPTUAL-MOTOR MATCH

The first processing patterns are devoted to collating preceptual data and motor data. Perception supplies the information upon which behavior is based. Motor responses supply the movements which are the overt aspects of the behavior. Unless these two functions can be related to each other, behavior has little or no relation to information. Perceptual information does not influence behavior but merely proliferates its own processes independent of the responses of the child.

The motor learning described above has resulted in a body of motor information. This body of information is concerned with what movements are possible, how you make them, and what are their results. Tactual and kinesthetic data are used to monitor the course of the movement and to provide knowledge of its results. Tactual and kinesthetic data are closely allied to (possibly inseparable from) movement, since they occur only in the presence of movement and since movement always produces one or the other or both. The body of motor information, therefore, is largely tactual and kinesthetic in nature. It is a body of action information, by and about movement.

Visual and auditory information, on the other hand, have initially no movement implication. They provide static information which needs no response for its fulfillment. Sometimes they trigger action, as in the signal qualities suggested by Werner (Werner 1948, 1957). Even such triggered responses, however, are only related to the perceptual data at the instant of inception. A continuing relationship to the perceptual data or modifications in the course of the response on the basis of such data do not occur.

Unless some relationship is established between the motor functions and the perceptual functions, the child builds up a body of perceptual information, resulting from the manipulation among themselves of the perceptual elements which he has differentiated, but this body of perceptual information will not be related to his motor information and hence will not influence it. An eight-year-old boy in a clinic read a passage about baseball. He correctly answered "comprehension" questions over the material which he had read. He was then given a ball and bat and asked to perform what he had just read.

Startled, he replied, "What are you talking about? What are these things?" He had no appreciation of what he had read in terms of actions or behaviors. He had merely manipulated words and perceptual relations.

Many children in the classroom are told what to do and indicate that they understand it. They then turn around and behave as though they had received no information at all. Frequently, such children have not established a correlation between perceptual information and motor information. As a result they cannot apply what they have been told to movement responses. Teachers frequently attack the problem by repeating the instructions; this is often followed by a repetition of the child's original behavior. What is needed is a translation of the instructions into response terms so that the child has a bridge between his perceptual function and his independent motor functions. Perceptual data and motor data become related through the perceptual-motor match. Perceptual information is matched to motor information so that both come to have the same meaning.

The development of eye-hand coordination illustrates the procedure. As Gesell has pointed out, the child first moves his hand and watches his hand as it moves. The hand is the actively exploring part and is producing the major part of the information. The eye follows the hand and its information is correlated with that of the hand. Thus, the eye is taught to see what the hand feels. "The eye learns under the tutelage of the active hand." (Gesell, et al, 1941). The first step in eye-hand coordination is *hand-eye*.

When the eye has learned, it begins to take the lead because it is more efficient. It can supply more information per unit of time and can move faster and more precisely than the hand. As the eye begins to lead, the hand follows along to confirm the result. In the event of trouble or confusion, reliance immediately returns to the hand for validation. As the eye becomes more adept, the hand is used less and less, until it is brought in to play only in complex situations. The second stage in eye-hand coordination is *eye-hand*.

The eye now begins to control the hand. It leads and directs the movements of the hand. At first this control is tight and rigorous, the eye moving a little ahead of the hand and the hand following closely; just as originally the child "kept his eye on his hand," now he "keeps his hand on his eye." As the perceptual information and the motor information become more closely correlated, however, the two types of information mean so nearly the same thing that one can be substituted for the other. Now the eye can monitor the hand. Rigid control is not necessary, but an occasional check keeps the hand moving properly.

Finally the eye can perform alone. It is now able to explore systematically as the hand did initially. Further, during such exploration, movement is implied so that, upon completion of the visual exploration, the hand can duplicate it either overtly or non-overtly. The perceptual data and the motor data are so closely matched that one can be translated into the other. The eye can explore and the hand can duplicate; the hand can explore and the eye can visualize.

Thus the perceptual-motor match is established. Perceptual data are matched to motor data so closely that the two forms of information come to have the same meaning. Perceptual data are enhanced with action components. Motor data acquire more efficient and more extensive sources of control. Such a matching is a very complex learning process. Many connections must be forged in the central nervous system, and the pattern of these connections is all important. It is no wonder that many children in the early school grades have not yet completed the process. Many of our classroom presentations for such children lack meaning because they exist in only one form, not in both. They fail to eventuate in changes in behavior because of the difficulty of the translations required. Initially the body of motor information provides the basis for the match. Perception is matched to motor, not the reverse. It is important that the match be made in the proper direction.

All preceptual data involve distortions. In the visual field, consider what happens when a disc is viewed from different orientations (Figure 5). If viewed "head on" the projection on the retina is a circle. If the disc is rotated slightly, the retinal image becomes an oval. If rotated 90 degrees, the image becomes a straight line. At all times, however, you continue to see a round disc. At an early age you manually manipulated similar objects in all sorts of ways, con-

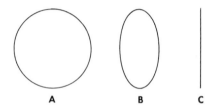

A   B   C

FIGURE 5.   Appearance of a disc as viewed (A) head on, (B) from a 45 degree angle and (C) from a 90 degree angle.

stantly changing the visual orientation as you explored. Your hand kept telling you, "This is round." Your eye kept telling you, "This is changing its shape." Your hand eventually won the argument and you matched the visual information to the motor information, altering the former to fit the latter. Thus you learned to "see" a round disc regardless of its orientation. The perceptual-motor match made in the proper direction resulted in form constancy.

Size offers another example of perceptual distortion. The more distant an object, the smaller its projected image on the retina. Yet you know that the person standing beside you is not a giant while the one across the street is not a pigmy. At an early age you locomoted toward a distant object and watched its image grow as you approached. Since the perceptual data were subjected to the motor data, the perceptual distortion was rectified and size constancy developed.

Particularly in our modern civilization, where we put so much stress on the early interpretation of perceptual data in books, pictures, and the like, children frequently make the perceptual-motor match in the wrong direction. They assign primary importance to perception and match motor data to perceptual data. Such children develop a very tight perceptual control of motor responses. These children are frequently seen in the classroom. If asked to draw a geometric form, the child keeps the eye exactly on the point of the pencil. Movements are tight and inflexible and follow the eye precisely. The child visually controls his movement, he does not visually monitor it. Through the entire task, he deals only with an infinitesimal part of the total form which is adjacent to the pencil point as it moves. He does not maintain awareness of the total form; he concentrates on the control of the immediate movement.

Such a reversed perceptual-motor match leaves the child at the mercy of the perceptual distortions. He has no basis for correcting these deviations and must warp his behavior to fit them with resulting error and confusion.

A fifteen-year-old boy with an I.Q. of 120 was asked to lay out a rectangular court on a playground. He was given an assistant who would place corner stakes where he told him they should go. The boy first laid out the line closest to him. He then laid out the side furthest from him and matched it to the near side in length. When he had finished, the far line was much longer than the near line.

He was then taken to the other side of the playground so that he viewed his court from the opposite direction. He now readily agreed that the rectangle was distorted. Asked to correct it, he had the assistant shorten the line nearest to him. He then matched the far line to it and asked the assistant to lengthen the line farthest from him. He thus had the same distortion as before, but in the opposite direction.

This youngster had matched motor data to perceptual data. He was slavishly adhering to the retinal image, expanding the far line until its image looked as long as that of the near line. He built this perceptual error into his behavior. Thus do the perceptual distortions influence responses when the perceptual-motor match is made in the wrong direction. When perceptual data are subjected to motor data in such matching, the more consistent motor data alter the perceptual impressions and produce more realistic information.

FIGURE-GROUND

The perceptual-motor match paves the way for perceptual control of motor responses. When accuracy and consistency of perceptual information has been assured, it can be used to determine and guide the overt responses of the child. Before control is possible, however, the activity or activities to be controlled must be isolated. These particular items must stand out from the rest of the environment, occupy and hold the focus of attention until the task is complete. Such selective attention is dependent upon the establishment of a *figure-ground relationship*. The pertinent aspects of the environment must become "figure," while the remaining aspects fade into ground but are not lost to consciousness.

The process of figure-ground development probably begins during the motor differentiation process described earlier. As the movement of an individual part is differentiated out of the mass and as this individual movement begins to be purposefully made, the muscular effort going into this movement is greater than that going into the rest of the musculature. This increased tonus in the muscles concerned with differentiated movement produces more intense kinesthetic information associated with this act than is associated with any other activities of the body. There is thus created a contrast between the kinesthetic stimulation from the purposeful movement and that from all other movements, which thereby recede into ground. The purposeful movement becomes a figure against a ground.

Attention can be directed specifically toward the figure movement since it now stands out against the ground. This early figure-ground relationship is, of course, dependent upon the nature and extent of the motor differentiation which the child has been able to learn. Without differentiation no specific kinesthetic pattern stands out from the rest. If differentiation is only partial, the figure movements are gross and their kinesthetic patterns are diffuse. Such diffuse patterns cannot direct attention sharply but rather leave it ill-defined and wavering.

There are two conditions which militate against the development of a kinesthetic figure-ground. Some children learn differentiation but, in doing so, they build up the energy level in all muscle groups in order to force out the voluntary movement. Whenever they move a part, the tonus of the whole body goes up so high that, even though the figure movement is made with maximum energy, its tonus is little higher than that of the ground. The figure-ground relationship does not appear because the level of the ground stimulation is too high.

Such children are hyperkinetic. They appear to be put together with springs. They are always under tension. Any movement is accompanied by excess tension throughout the entire musculature. They cannot confine increased muscle tone to those muscles essential to the task.

Hyperkinetic children concern the teacher because of their behavior. Their movements are quick, explosive, and uncontrolled. As a result they frequently destroy materials and supplies, break furniture or equipment, and appear clumsy and careless. Reprimands for such behavior have no effect. The child appears cowed by the teacher's wrath but immediately makes the same mistake again because he has not learned to attend to and control his specific movements. More important than his behavior, however, is the cause of the behavior and its effect on his achievement. He is unable to establish a figure-ground relationship in his movements and, hence, any classroom task (such as coloring, drawing, writing) which requires the figure-ground principle in the area of movement responses will be difficult or impossible for him.

The solution to the problem lies in reducing the level of the ground tone. Considerable success has been experienced with such children through the use of Jacobson's technique of progressive relaxation (Jacobson, 1938). By verbal suggestion, manipulation of the joints, and surface massage of the muscles, the child is induced to relax one part at a time. Beginning at the extremities, feet and hands, this relaxation is carried inward part by part. When the entire body is relaxed, a simple movement (such as a swing of the arm) is called for. Manipulation of all parts except the arm is continued to maintain relaxation in these parts while the arm is moving. The child is encouraged to note the feeling of low tonus and how it differs from movement tonus.

Especially in the early elementary grades, teachers frequently provide a "rest period" during which the children lie down on mats or blankets and remain quiet. During such a period the teacher could easily identify the hyperkinetic child and apply parts or all of the relaxation technique.*

The second problem in the development of kinesthetic figure-ground is that presented by the hypokinetic child. This child is characterized by a very low overall muscular tone. His muscles are limp and placid. He does not move unless he has to and, when he does, the voluntary movement is made with a minimum of energy. The term "limp rag syndrome" has sometimes been applied. In learning differentiation, he has kept all movement at a minimum and has performed the specific movement with as little energy as possible.

Such a child has difficulty establishing a kinesthetic figure-ground because the level of the figure movement is so low. Although all muscle tone remains low, the figure movement is performed with so little energy that the resulting kinesthetic information is too slight to provide a contrast.

Treatment for such a child requires raising the level of the figure movement. Such an increase can be accomplished by requiring a simple movement of the child (such as raising an arm) and providing a resistance to such movement. Resistance can be offered either through the teacher holding back or pushing against the movement, or it can be offered through mechanical means such as weights or springs. To overcome the resistance and perform the required movement, the child must increase the energy of the movement. Kinesthetic information from the specific movement is consequently increased while that from ground responses remains low.

---

*A series of films describing and illustrating the Jacobson techniques as applied to children is available from Learning Pathways, Inc., 1028 Acoma Street, Denver, Colorado.

A contrast between the figure movement and the ground is created from which a figure-ground relationship can develop.

As has been pointed out, kinesthetic figure-ground is essential to any learning activity of which the identification and control of overt movement is a part. In addition, it seems likely that this is the first figure-ground relationship which the child develops. As such, it would be expected to form the basis of and lay the ground work for later appearing figure-ground relationships such as visual figure-ground, auditory figure-ground, and the like. It would seem, therefore, that the problems of kinesthetic figure-ground relationships are deserving of a great deal more attention than they have received in the literature to date.

MOVEMENT CONTROL

When a figure-ground relationship has been established, there is available a basis for movement control. The child is able to isolate and attend to a particular movement on the one hand, and he can isolate and attend to a particular set of perceptual data related to the movement on the other. He can watch his hand as it draws or writes and can observe the visual stimuli created by the movement (the tracing left on the paper by the moving hand). By virtue of the figure-ground relationships he can focus attention on these two correlated sets of stimuli and can *eliminate all non related stimuli.* He can devote his attention, virtually exclusively, both motorically and perceptually, to the same activity. When such attentional isolation is possible, he can use the perceptual information to control the motor response.

In the development of movement control, however, a new method of processing data is required. Information about the nature and course of the movement must be available for control *while the movement is in process and while the data are being produced.* Such continuous or monitored control requires the establishment of a feedback mechanism (see Chapter Four).

Consider what happens when you draw a square. As the pencil starts to move, you observe the line being drawn and estimate its direction. As the line continues, you are continuously aware of direction and know at once if the direction starts to err. Corrections are made without stopping the movement on the basis of this continuous but largely subliminal information. As you approach a corner, you make repeated estimates of the length of the line you have drawn and slow down the movement as this length approaches the correct one. On the final side, you make repeated estimates of the location of the first side and continuously adjust the course of the movement to meet this side and accurately close the corner. Information generated by the process is continuously used to control the process. At no time, however, does the control take over and obliterate the impression of the total square form. If it did, you would forget what you were drawing.

Such continuous control requires feedback. The structure being built up in the central nervous system must provide for collating two or more separate patterns. Each pattern must be extensive enough to encompass all the required information. In addition, they must be integrated so that each can influence the other promptly and accurately. In the simple act of drawing a square, there is thus presented a picture of a vast, highly inflected pattern of neural activity involving large masses of the cortex performing in harmony. Failure of any piece or loss of synchrony between pieces can lead to breakdown. It is no wonder that many children experience difficulty in this extremely complex learning problem.

Difficulty in establishing an adequate feedback system is seen in failure to control movement. Such children move in bursts. They estimate the direction and extent of the movement required and then the movement explodes with maximum speed and force. This is control at its initiation and again at its termination, but there is no control during the course of the movement itself. Static control at the beginning and end may be accurate but, because of the lack of feedback, dynamic control during the movement itself is absent.

Such a child draws a square by rushing from corner to corner. Sometimes he locates dots at the corners ahead of time so that he can more easily control the termination of his movement. After his hand has started to move, he cannot alter this movement until it is completed. At each corner there is a marked pause while he reestablishes his static control.

The control of movement without feedback is similar to re-peated estimates from a series of still pictures. Movement control with feedback is similar to continuous estimates from a moving picture. Feedback permits movement responses to be *monitored*. Their control is accurate but general so that the primary concern can be the overall product rather than the control of the immediate movement. The significance of this difference for form perception will be discussed later.

SYSTEMATIC EXPLORATION

When feedback has established a correlation between two bodies of information, like any other correlation, the relationship works both ways. Perceptual data can be used to control motor response. On the other hand, any perceptual data generated or guided by motor activity takes on a continuity dictated by the motor activity. This continuity is preserved in the developing body of perceptual information.

When movement can be controlled, systematic exploration is possible. The hand no longer explores an object randomly. It moves systematically around the contour or among the elements of the object. This systematic movement generates perceptual informa-tion in a similar systematic form. The body of perceptual informa-tion takes on continuity. As the hand learns to move systematically, systematic information comes from the hand and, since the eye is now related to the hand, systematic visual exploration develops. Relationships between objects and among the elements within objects begin to appear, for these relationships depend upon con-tinuity and systematic exploration in producing continuity among perceptual data. This continuity will be reflected in all future pro-cessing of information, for relationships are now more significant to the child than elements. The square is now more important than its four lines.

Child development specialists have long stressed the vital sig-nificance of that point in child growth where systematic explora-tion first appears. It seems probable that the significance of this event is related to its contribution to consistency of information and the continuity of the body of information for which such consistency is so vital.

PERCEPTION

When the developing body of perceptual information begins to take on continuity, it can be manipulated within itself. Systematic exploration has revealed relationships among perceptual elements and these relationships have been structured into the body of information. Building upon these concretely learned relationships, other relationships can be derived by manipulating elements within the structure. Qualities which do not exist *per se* in the concrete world can be generated through such manipulations: the "something more" of constructive form perception (Strauss and Kephart, 1955). The squareness of a square form does not itself exist as a quality of any perception. It emerges from the manipulation in an orderly fashion of the elements (sides and angles) against each other within the perceptual structure. Once having emerged, it becomes an element itself and it is this emergent element, not the concrete elements, upon which we depend for recognition and meaningfulness.

When this new method of processing data has been achieved, the child becomes perceptual. Because his senses provide him so much more information per unit of time than does his motor exploration, and because his senses range over so much broader areas of his environment than does his hand, he comes to depend on these perceptual manipulations in his problem solving due to their greater efficiency. More and more he drops out motoric data gathering and depends upon perceptual data gathering processes, calling upon motor exploration only when extreme complexity among elements demands added help with continuity. Even as adults, when confronted with a very complex perceptual design or motif, we will trace over it or use our finger to "keep our place" as we analyze the complex series of elements.

At the perceptual stage, the child uses the emergent elements of perceptual manipulation to make comparisons of similarity or difference among objects or events. Note, however, that the success of such manipulations is dependent upon the continuity of the body of perceptual information. This continuity was achieved through systematic overt exploration. If such systematic exploration was faulty, the resulting perceptual manipulations will be confused, inconsistent, and unrealistic. The perceptual relationships will not conform to outside reality and, when used in problem solving, will dictate erroneous responses. Many difficulties in learning letter or word recognition skills are due to inconsistent or faulty manipulation of the relationships between the perceptual elements presented. The problem of perceptual development is discussed in greater detail in a future chapter.

When the child can process information perceptually, his environment is enormously expanded. No longer is he restricted to those data which he can manipulate with his hands. Information from many sources and from a wide range of environmental contacts can be brought to bear as a mass on the solution of any problem. The resulting response is made not to a single stimulus but to a broad and inclusive stimulus field. Chance stimuli are fitted into this overall stimulus field and, instead of becoming distractors and determinants of the child's behavior, produce only minor alterations in behavior since they are largely overweighted by the mass. The control of distractibility is largely dependent upon the extent and continuity of the body of perceptual information which the child is manipulating at the time.

INTERSENSORY INTEGRATION

The perceptual manipulations of the child are not limited to one sense avenue. They involve interrelationships between the data from all sense avenues. For such interrelationships to be meaningful, however, data from the various sense avenues must coincide. They must yield common information rather than each sense avenue possessing its own information without reference to that of others. In many children, data from one or more avenues may be independent or may conflict with the rest of the perceptual data.

The welding together of data from various senses is achieved through intersensory integration. Sensory data differ in their nature. Tactual, kinesthetic, and auditory data are extended over time.

Very little information is delivered through these senses in a single instant. If you speak a word, for example, the auditory stimulus flows through time. If you take a single exposure of one one-hundredth of a second out of this total stimulation, you have nothing, merely a single tone. To recognize the word, the brain retains and accumulates the stimuli from many such instants and integrates them into a total impression which is then appreciated as contained in our temporal instant. The temporally expanded auditory stimulation has been translated into an instantaneous stimulus with many variables.

Vision, on the other hand, is extended in space. All there is of a visual stimulus (if it lies within the limits of the visual field) can be received in a single hundredth of a second exposure. If you read a word on a page, you see the whole word at once. If it is a complex word, you may need to break it down syllable by syllable to analyze it before recognition takes place. The brain breaks up the complex visual impression into small pieces, each of which it deals with at a different point in time, but does not in the process ever lose the impression of the whole. The spatially expanded visual stimulus has been translated into a sequence of events in time. (See Strauss and Kephart, 1955, p. 50).

The translation from space to time and back again is of constant importance in the solution of everyday problems. The child is continually required to make such translations in his encounters with his environment. When the mechanism for such interchange is lacking or is disturbed, frequent problems arise in the child's interpretation of his environment and his achievement of the learning tasks presented to him.

It is the systematic, structured processing of stimulus data by the brain which makes such translations possible, both within a given sense avenue and between sense avenues. Within one sense avenue, the systematic exploration discussed above is essential. Between sense avenues, systematic exploration of *both* sets of sensory data is required and, in addition, it is necessary that the two sets of exploration be related to each other. The explorations in one sense avenue must parallel those in the other, and the resulting information must have the same meaning in either sense avenue.

In many children, this relationship between sense avenues is not established. The data from one sense avenue do not have the same meaning as do parallel data from another sense avenue. The result is confusion when both avenues are delivering sensations simultaneously. Such a child, for example, may be able to interpret what he sees rather well. Similarly, he can interpret what he hears rather well. But if he is required to react to both visual and auditory data at the same time, he becomes confused and both performances break down. Such a child is often seen in the classroom. He can read silently with considerable success (visual performance). He can recount what he has read accurately (auditory performance). When asked to read aloud, however, he can neither recognize the words nor pronounce them (visual and auditory performance).

In more severe cases, one sense avenue may block out another so that when the second avenue is operating, the first ceases to operate. Such a child can, for example, either see or hear but not both at the same time. Many children who close their eyes while listening to a story do so to eliminate the visual avenue since it either confuses or blocks the auditory avenue.

The relationship between data from various sense avenues is accomplished through intersensory integration (Johnson and Myklebust, 1967; Birch, 1964; Pimsleur and Bonkowski, 1961). Through this process two or more sensory systems become interrelated so that stimuli from all systems combine into one integrated whole which is responsive both to any single stimulation or to any combination of stimulation. As a result, an alteration in stimulation is interpreted not alone in terms of itself but also in terms of its interrelationship with all stimulation being received from all sense avenues at that moment. The child responds to a stimulus field rather than to an isolated stimulus.

Intersensory integration appears to become established through the statistical principle of a common factor. Developmentally, as was pointed out, the first systematic exploration is motor. Perceptual data from each of the senses are then matched to these motor data. The motor information thus becomes the unifying core which insures a relationship between all the variables.

In clinical practice, much success has been achieved through the use of this principle. Where vision and audition confuse each other, as in many cases of reading disability, the clinician first establishes a sound visual-motor match. He then establishes a sound auditory-motor match. When these two correlations have been established, he finds that vision and audition are also matched on the principle that two factors, each of which is highly correlated with a third factor, will be correlated with each other.

To simplify this process of integration, one sense avenue usually assumes the lead role. The bulk of the child's information is then garnered through this lead sense. Data from the other sense avenues become elaborative or confirmatory of the picture presented by the lead sense. Through the use of such a dominant sense, the child avoids the problem of integration for routine or immediate problems. When a problem demands instant solution, he can operate with his dominant sense, thus permitting immediate solution, and can elaborate with other sense data as time permits. When a problem is routine and needs no elaboration, he can respond at once on the data from the dominant sense without involving the integration problem at all. The use of a dominant sense avenue is thus a safety device on the one hand and an economy of effort on the other.

When a dominant sense avenue has been established, learning is easier and more efficient when the learning stimuli are organized around this core sense avenue. Education has long recognized the difference in learning styles between the audile child and the visile child. The audile child is one for whom the auditory sense is dominant in the intersensory integration. He learns more readily when school presentations are organized with auditory data predominant. The visile child is one for whom vision is the dominant sense avenue. He learns more readily when presentations are highly visual. The tactile child learns more readily when he can handle and explore manually concrete data. Where learning is difficult, as for the slow learner, attention to these differences in learning styles and reorganization of classroom presentations in terms of them, frequently provide a great aid to the achievement of the child.

CONCEPT

If the body of perceptual information is organized so that integrated forms emerge (see Chapter Five) and if the relationship between these forms is preserved through a space structure (see Chapter Six), this enhanced mass of data makes possible comparisons which were previously very difficult. When two things can be dealt with simultaneously, comparison is much simpler than when they must be dealt with successively. Thus, the body of perceptual information facilitates the observation of similarities and differences.

Similarities and differences form the basis for categorization. Those items which are similar tend to be grouped together. When this grouping has been achieved, the common elements which form the basis of the similarity stand out and occupy the center of attention. This isolation of the common elements leads to a grouping of the commonalties themselves. The first concept is born.

Initial concepts are perceptually based. They consist of a pattern of commonalties among perceptual elements. They represent categories of directly perceived objects. At the same time, the concept is more than the percept. Just as the integration of perceptual elements leads to an emergent quality in form perception, so the categorization of similarities among perceptions leads to an emergent quality in the concept. This emergent quality is what makes the concept real—something more than a mere collection of similar perceptions. The new quality differs from percept since it represents something which does not even exist concretely and hence cannot be perceived directly.

Consider your concept of a chair. It came from a number of concrete perceptual experiences with chairs. These perceptions varied widely: hard chairs, soft chairs, wooden chairs, arm chairs, et cetera. All these experiences had certain commonalties, the possibility of being sat upon. These commonalties were integrated into a consistent pattern and this pattern became your concept of a chair. It subtends a large number of specific chairs but is identical to none of them. It has a quality of its own, "chairness," which is more than any one specific chair. It permits you to perceive a new object which you have never experienced before and, on the basis of certain specific elements within it, to assign it to the classification, "chair." Once classification takes place, characteristics of the object and possibilities of behavior toward it appear which would have appeared only after extensive exploration and experimentation in the absence of the concept.

Thus does the concept increase the efficiency of data processing. Not only are a vast number of elements subtended at once, but additional elements, not immediately available in the stimulus pattern, are also available. The entire complex is held together and made cohesive by the pattern giving rise to the concept. It can all be effective at once in determining behavior through the use of the emergent quality representing the concept.

Such perceptually based concepts also display similarities and differences. Chairs are more like tables than they are like automobiles. There are similarities in both cases (you can sit in a chair and you can sit in an automobile). In any concrete example, similarities may be very close (my friend has constructed a chair out of an old automobile bucket seat). Nevertheless, the *class* chair is more like the *class* table than it is like the *class* automobile.

Herein lies the true abstraction of the advanced concept. Classes of objects or events are grouped into categories on the basis of similarities between the *classes* independent of the individuals within a class. The patterns representing the classes are compared. The advanced concept is thus a "pattern of patterns" (Strauss and Kephart, 1955).

With the achievement of such a concept, the child's data processing escapes the bounds of the concrete. He is now able to manipulate in terms of items for which no direct concrete example can be found. The concept "furniture," for example, has no concrete representation. You can point to a particular chair as an example of that class but you cannot point to a "furniture" as an example of this class. The advanced concept is truly abstract in that it has no concrete representative. It results from an organization among patterns which are themselves less complex abstractions. Like the integrated form and the perceptual-concept, this concept too generates an emergent quality through which all the myriad of data which have gone into it can be subtended in one psychological act. By the use of such concepts the child can respond directly to the patterns of the universe with only occasional confirmatory reference to the concrete units of which they are composed.

Consider what happens when you read a treatise on space travel. You juggle patterns about gravity, acceleration, velocity, thrust, et cetera against each other until you can solve the problem. Only occasionally does memory supply an appropriate concrete experience and, when it does, the concrete has only the attributes of an analogue. Just as such manipulations freed man from the earth, so concepts free the child from his concrete environment.

Abstract concepts, however, result from development. They do not arise full blown. The developmental stages described earlier are each essential to the concept. It is through these earlier stages that the patterns of the universe, which will be reflected in the concept, are discovered. If these earlier stages are incomplete, the concept will be restricted and barren. If the earlier stages are distorted, the concept will lack reality. Only when concepts are reality-oriented does the behavior based on conceptual manipulations "come out right" when it is exteriorized. Via conceptualization, the child builds up mentally a little model of the universe (as Craik states) which he can manipulate as though he were manipulating the universe itself. (Craik, 1952) Only insofar as this model is accurate, will the resulting manipulations lead to successful problem solving.

When the child becomes more efficient in conceptual manipulations, the pattern begins to come first and the details later. Thus concept begins to influence percept. When he glances at a piece of furniture, the first thing he sees is a chair. The details of its construction are observed afterward and are perceived within the context of "chair". It may be that this object is nothing more than a hodgepodge of bits and pieces: sticks and bits of fabric. However, once the concept "chair" has been aroused, he cannot see the bits and pieces as such; he can only see them as parts of a chair. The concept has determined what will be seen.

At this stage the child is able to predict. His concepts tell him what must be there and he needs only to catch one or two confirming elements to "see" what his concept told him he was going to see. Operating on abstract, disembodied patterns, he can reconstruct the universe as it "must" be and needs only refer to the concrete environment about him to maintain the reality of his constructs.

The influence of concept upon percept goes so far that we will distort the percept to fit the concept. We will omit elements which do not fit; we will add elements which seem to be missing; and we will distort elements to make them fit. Artists use this principle continuously. They present to us a strong clue to induce a concept. Then they omit elements which cannot be reproduced; they distort elements to fit a two-dimensional representation; they present elements without a complete context. They depend upon us to see not what is on the canvas, but what our concepts lead us to see.

At this final stage in development, the child deals primarily with relationships. Concrete elements are subjected to the pattern of relationships. Such a method of processing data is extremely complex. Not only is the child largely free of the concrete environment but, because of his ability to predict, he is also largely free of the present moment in time. He can anticipate what must happen and can concern himself with the ultimate outcome without getting bogged down in over-precise interpretations of present events. His problem solving can be projected in time and can encompass not only present events but past and future events as well. His behavior is no longer static; it has become dynamic. It is a flow of directed behavior over time rather than a discrete series of isolated problem solutions.

THE COURSE OF DEVELOPMENT

The development of the child is seen as a series of stages, each stage representing the emergence of a more complex method of processing data. The stages vary not only quantitatively in the number of data which can be handled, but qualitatively as well, as the processing procedure changes.

There are two ways of looking at development. The first is the normative approach (Gesell and Amatruda, 1947). In this context, development is seen as the ability to solve increasingly difficult problems. At each succeeding chronological age, the child is expected to solve more complex problems. No attention is paid to the method of solution, only to the correctness or error of the final answer.

The second point of view is represented by Piaget who feels that the method of attacking problems changes as the child develops and, although the same final answer may be forthcoming, the procedure by which the child arrives at the answer may change drastically. For example, the child who has only counting as an arithmetic procedure may arrive at the answer $2 + 2 = 4$ by holding up two fingers and then two more fingers and counting them. The child who has facility in the visual spatial processes of grouping may combine two groups of two and recognize immediately that the result is four. Both children arrive at the correct answer but one processes mathematical data much more efficiently than does the other.

If we combine these two points of view, we can conceive of development as a step-like process. With one method of processing, the child learns to solve a number of increasingly complex problems using the same processing in all solutions. When these experiences have become extensive enough and when they are properly related to each other, a new principle emerges. This new principle forms the basis of a different and more complex method of processing. The child now solves problems in a different manner; not only new problems but the previous problems are now transformed into the new format. The developmental sequence then begins again. The child applies the new processing method to increasingly complex problems until enough experience has been gained to permit the emergence of a third method.

By this view, development is seen as both quantitative and qualitative. It is quantitative (normative) within any one stage, but is qualitative between stages. It seems probable that the change from one stage to another is sharp and immediate. The emergence of a new stage is in the nature of an insight or an "aha" idea. Thus development within any one stage is gradual. Between stages it is precipitate (see Figure 4, p. 18).

Both the quantitative and the qualitative phases of development are important. In order to understand where a child is or the nature of his learning problems, we must know not only what problems he can solve but how he goes about solving them. We must ask ourselves not only "what answer did he give?" but also "how did he get it?"

If the step-like process is omitted, normative development continues, the child learning to solve ever more complex problems with the old method of processing. The demands of the environment, which do not stop because of his problems, force him to distort the direction of his development (dotted line in Figure 4). Through such distortion he comes, at a later age, to behave *as though* he were functioning on a higher stage (point x in Figure 4). At this point he takes on some of the characteristics of the higher stage and does the best he can to function at that point. However, since the step-like process was not achieved, his function is disrupted and his view of the environment is distorted. By this continuing but unmodified normative development, he may reach relatively high levels of performance; but he fails to achieve a true realistic picture of his world.

Seen in this light, the course of development is unidirectional. It can only go in the direction of greater complexity, never in the direction of lesser complexity. New functions result from the establishment of more extensive patterns in the central nervous system. These patterns are built up by accumulating and integrating additional circuits. Therefore, it follows that the pattern is becoming more complex all the time. To decrease the complexity would require erasing one or more elements. As has been pointed out, however, the functionally induced alterations in the nervous system, once established, are permanent. It is not, therefore, possible to reduce the pattern by subtraction. Development must always move forward. It can never back up nor can it stand still. Every learning experience of the child contributes to this development and adds to its complexity.

In the same way, development is irreversible. After the emergent quality which permits the new method of processing has been established, it too is built into the nervous system. Since this is a dynamic pattern and has to do with method of processing rather than manipulation of present data, all data from this point on will be processed by this new method. Since the processing pattern is also permanent, it cannot be removed and thus it is impossible to again process data by the methods which were used prior to the change.

Once the child has become perceptual, he can no longer see in terms of the isolated elements which characterized his earlier visual behavior. Once he has become conceptual, he can no longer see in terms of visual stimuli alone.

Look again at the chair. You may be able to remember a time when, at an early age, you saw some parts in certain relationships to each other. Now, however, you cannot see this purely visual display. You must see a "chair" and the visual characteristics come later. You cannot now ever see what you saw at the age of two or three years.

Each stage in the developmental process, once established, becomes compulsive. It determines how data will be processed. Earlier methods of processing drop out immediately and data previously processed are reprocessed in terms of the new program. Thus, once development has occurred, it cannot be erased. Development is not only unidirectional, it is also irreversible.

The question of regression is raised by the consideration of irreversability. Clinical cases appear to go back to less complex behaviors. They seem to have achieved a level of complexity in behavior at one point in time and then, at a subsequent point, show consistently less complex behavior responses. The phenomenon of hypnosis illustrates the condition. Under hypnotic suggestion an adult can be induced to behave like an infant (he will crawl instead of walk, he will cry instead of talk, et cetera) simply by suggesting to him that he has gone back through time to the age of twelve months. In such instances, it would seem that the later stages of development had dropped out and that the individual is not only behaving like an infant but also that he is thinking like an infant and is processing data in an infantile manner.

Close observation of so-called regressive behavior, however, would suggest that the simpler form of behavior has been achieved by the voluntary subtraction of elaborations. You can behave like a two-year-old. You do so by selecting from your complex repertory of behavior those actions which appear to be appropriate for age two and rejecting other behaviors. What you have done is take a complex system and reduce it. Your "two-year-old" behavior is only superficially like that of a two-year-old and differs significantly from the behavior of a true two-year-old. His behavior is simple because he has no complex behavior patterns. Yours is simple because you have reduced a complex pattern to simple terms.

In the clinical case, the same type of simplification can be postulated. In his case, however, the principles of the simplification are not conscious as they are with you. They are dictated largely by unconscious responses to emotionally dictated demands. It is for this reason that successful treatment of such cases does not take the form of teaching, establishing development through learning, as would be the case in the event of a true regression. Rather it takes the form of removing the emotional responses which dictate the over simplification. When these emotional problems have been solved, the more complex behaviors appear again "full blown" without the necessity for any intermediate learnings or relearnings.

DEVELOPMENT IN THE SLOW LEARNER

The slow learning child is one in whom progress through these stages of development has either broken down or is noticeably delayed. If progress appears to be normal but slow in its course, the condition is usually associated with borderline mental retardation or with cultural deprivation. If the progress is disrupted in its course, the condition is usually associated with diagnosed or assumed disturbances of neurological functioning. In either event, if the delay is sufficient or if the disturbance is severe enough, mental retardation will accompany the condition.

EDUCATING THE SLOW LEARNER

In educating the slow learner, the problem is to determine where, in the course of development, the child has broken down and, through teaching and/or therapeutic procedures, restore the course of development. Normal classroom presentations assume certain levels of development (at least the early perceptual stage by kindergarten and the early conceptual stage by second grade). The skills and abilities characteristic of this stage are an integral part of the design of the classroom presentation. If the child has not yet achieved this level of development, he will find it impossible to participate in the classroom learning presentation or to interact, for the purpose of learning, with the materials and events included therein. Classroom activities thus become meaningless to him and the learnings which they are designed to stimulate become impossible.

In kindergarten, for example, the child frequently is handed a mimeographed page which contains the outline of a picture. He is asked to color the different objects in the picture, indicating by the color he uses that he has meaningfully differentiated the objects, and by confining the coloring to the area within this contour, shows that he appreciates the figure-ground relationships involved. Such perceptual differentiations and manipulations, however, are well along in the developmental stages described earlier. Many children will not have achieved this advanced stage by age five. For such a child, the coloring exercises of kindergarten become meaningless.

He cannot color the apple red, because he can't find the apple. He is unable to differentiate this one form out of the conflicting maze of lines he sees on the paper. By the same token, since he cannot isolate the contour of the apple, he cannot use it as a guide for "coloring within the lines." The learning, interpretation of pictures for which the exercise was designed, and the information which we wish to relate to these pictures through verbal discussion, thus become meaningless. These educational objectives of the lesson can become effective only if the child can be brought to the level of development required by the task.

To determine where the child is in the developmental progression will require careful observation of his behavior and the manner in which he attacks problems. A certain amount of information is supplied by standardized tests. A useful battery of such tests employed in many schools consists of three test procedures, each focusing on a different area of development: the Purdue Perceptual-Motor Survey (Roach and Kephart, 1966) to measure the early stages of development; the Frostig Test of Visual Perception (Frostig, 1961) to measure the perceptual levels; and the Illinois Test of Psycholinguistic Abilities (Kirk and McCarthy, 1968) to measure the later stages of development. The Wepman Auditory Discrimination Test (Wepman, 1958) is frequently added when the child's auditory perceptual problems seem to be more severe.

Such test procedures yield evidence of areas of difficulty in the child's learning. They require refinement and augmentation through observation of learning behaviors in order to pinpoint the heart of the difficulty. The teacher should become acquainted with the types of problems displayed by children and their manifestations in learning behavior. The following chapters will describe a number of these behaviors. Test data can then be expanded with these direct observations to give a more precise picture of the status of an individual child.

When development is only *delayed* and is not complicated by the disruption resulting from neurological disturbance, the teaching problem is to supply experiences which will enhance development. Such a child behaves in a perfectly normal and predictable fashion except that his behavior is appropriate for a child of a lower chronological age. Observations of his behavior reveal that he performs quite well until a certain level is reached. After that point he shows a marked inability to perform. He has developed normally but he hasn't gone far enough.

This slow developing child can be expected to put together the appropriate processing programs if we can give him more data. He requires help with the quantitative aspect of development but has little difficulty with the qualitative aspect. The approach requires an enrichment program in which a wider range of stimulating learning experiences are provided.

Such an enrichment program, however, must be geared to the child's level of development. Frequently, we develop enriched programs in which learning experiences are broadened only on a level appropriate to his chronological age, not to his state of development. Thus at the kindergarten level we would provide him with more coloring of more pictures. Because of his lack of readiness, however, he cannot enter into any of these presentations. What is required is normal learning presentations at the level of visual figure-ground differentiation and contour development. The enrichment must be provided on the developmental level which the child has attained, not on some higher level which may be appropriate to his chronological age or to the group in which he has been placed.

When development is *disrupted*, the child has either skipped a stage in development or one or more of the stages has been incompletely achieved. His behavior reflects the disruption. He is very good in some tasks, very poor in others. He reads difficult words and then stumbles over an easy one or one he has just read correctly in the line above. He gets the right answer but does not know how he got it. He takes the most devious routes to solve a problem or, on the other hand, he responds to a single stimulus as though it were all there was. His attention span is short and he wanders away from his task.

With such a child, the problem is to restore the course of development. We must identify the stage or stages which have been omitted or which are incomplete and solidify them. Since the stages of development are sequential, each stage depends on the previous stages for its successful achievement. For example, if the child has not completed the stage of differentiation of visual sensations, he cannot identify the elements of the visual stimulus necessary for form perception. It will, therefore, usually be found that all stages beyond the one where disturbance first occurred will be impaired. When the initial impairment has been corrected, it will be necessary to move to each following successive stage in order and to solidify its pattern.

The crux of the problem is to teach development — to help the child achieve a developmental task rather than an academic task, to teach him how to learn rather than presenting him with facts to be learned. Teaching, through curriculum and subject matter presentations, presents the child with information organized in a manner which can be processed and hence learned easily by the normal child. The organization is external to the child and is a function of the subject matter, not of his functioning. It assumes he has mastered certain processing procedures. With the slow learner we must teach the processing procedures first. Otherwise it will be impossible for him to respond adequately to the subject matter.

The teaching of processing methods (development) is difficult for two reasons. In the first place, the child has particular trouble with this specific type of learning. If it were not so, he would have learned it in the normal course of events and at the normal time. At some point a disturbance interferred with this particular type of learning and caused him to break down. Therefore, traditional techniques will not work and unique types of presentation will be necessary to permit him to learn. We are, by definition, attempting to teach him in those areas which he has demonstrated are the most difficult for him. It would be expected that this teaching would be difficult.

The second reason why such teaching is difficult stems from the fact that, although the child's development has been interrupted, the environment does not stand still and wait for him to catch up. It continues to make demands for ever more complex methods of processing data. Thus the child is forced into stages of development for which he is not prepared. He must make some attempt to achieve, at least in part, the new processes. As has been pointed out, however, development is irreversible. Once a new stage has been achieved, no matter how poorly or how incompletely, it is impossible for the child to behave as he behaved at the earlier stage over again.

When an attempt is made to go back and fill in the earlier, unfinished developmental stage, the customary techniques and procedures appropriate to teaching at that earlier age do not work. They no longer mean the same thing they would have meant to him previously. Once the child has become conceptual, for example, he can no longer see the same things he saw when he was in the perceptual stage. Teaching, designed to promote perceptual skills, therefore, does not present the same learning situations that it does for the child who is in the perceptual stage for the first time.

When a gap in development is identified, it is not enough merely to go back and teach as one would teach a younger child. These earlier occurring learnings must be recast in terms of the highest developmental stage the child has achieved, even though this higher stage is very disturbed. Very frequently, for example, the child is seen whose visual perceptual skills are impossibly limited. He has limited ocular control, short visual attention span, and poor figure-ground relations. Nevertheless, he is completely dependent on this visual perception in his behavior. Any attempt to take away vision and ask him to perform on the purely motor exploratory level meets with marked resistance and an even greater deterioration in performance.

At first glance it would seem that the way to teach development would be to use kindergarten and nursery school techniques such as are used in the initial teaching of these skills. Such a procedure is used in many classrooms and clinics. Unfortunately, the task is not quite this simple. Although such techniques are still basically useful and are in fact still the principle teaching tools, they must be altered and revised in terms of the present status of the child. We must work backward so that, using his present processing, the child can piece together what went before and weld it into a solid, permanent structure.

If the interference with development is sufficiently extensive and if it disrupts certain kinds of activity, the child will be mentally retarded. Intelligence, as measured by intelligence tests, is essentially a quantitative concept. It tells us the number and difficulty level of tasks which the child can successfully accomplish. It does not tell us how he accomplishes them.

Intelligence sets the level at which teaching can be undertaken. It tells us the number and range of activities we can use in presenting learning situations. The disruption in development tells us the purpose of the teaching and determines the selection of activities to be used. The method of processing data is important on any level of functioning. It is, therefore, the over-riding teaching task. It can be adapted to any level of functioning within the school population and is equally significant regardless of the I.Q.

chapter 2

Generalization

The process of development involves the achievement of a series of increasingly complex generalizations. Each successive generalization permits more efficient processing of larger and larger quantities of data. Information from multiple sources is instantly summoned for application to the present problem. Responses learned in various situations and for various specific purposes provide alternate attacks upon the task of the moment.

Such a generalization involves the development of a pattern of function within the central nervous system. Information is not stored haphazardly. Things which belong together and which have elements or qualities in common are related to each other by the nature of the pattern. The pattern holds them together and provides the possibility of activating or partially activating all of them at once. Thus, many diverse kinds of data, all pertinent to the problem at hand, are summoned in one act of consciousness and applied to immediate behavior.

A few years ago I was driving my car through the hills of West Virginia. Roads in this region are characterized by many irregularities in both the lateral and vertical direction. There are many curves and many ups and downs, so that one rarely can see the road for more than a hundred yards ahead.

As I approached the crest of a small hill, there came over the crest toward me a slow moving farm truck. As the truck came over the hill and as I approached within a few feet of it, there came around the truck, and on my side of the road, a sporty, red, Ford hardtop. A problem was immediately presented for solution. Two objects were about to attempt to occupy the same space at the same time.

Past experiences with driving and traffic problems suggested a number of solutions. The first of these was the most common method of avoiding an accident: namely, to apply the brakes and stop. However, it was obvious that, as close as the Ford was and at the speed he was traveling, to stop would merely make me a sitting duck in the middle of the road. This solution was rejected.

The second solution suggested by past experience was to step on the accelerator, scoot through, and let the accident happen behind me. Such a solution is pertinent when conditions are heading toward an impasse but the way has not yet been fully closed. In the present situation, however, the impasse was already there. To increase speed, therefore, would only increase the violence of the impact. This solution was rejected.

A third solution involved driving off on the side of the road thus, in effect, increasing a two lane road to three or more lanes. Perceptual investigation of the terrain at the side of the road suggested that this solution was possible and, in fact, hopeful.

Just as I was about to pull to the side of the road, however, another piece of past experience was brought to bear on the problem. This man is coming over the crest of a hill on the wrong side of the road. He is, therefore, by definition, a nut. Such nuts, insofar as they are predictable at all, can be predicted to do the wrong thing. It is, therefore, highly likely that, if I pulled off to the side, he would pull off there too and we would have the accident in the ditch instead of on the road, a highly undesirable and not very productive alternative.

The solution to the problem appeared to lie in forcing him to commit himself. We were so close together and moving so fast that each of us would get only one move. I knew what my alternatives were. I did not know what he would do. If I could make him move first, I could take the other alternative.

Therefore, I slowed up to give as much time as possible but, more important, I blew my horn loudly to make him react. As predicted he veered off to the side of the road. With his response determined, I squeezed in between him and the truck with only inches to spare.

The point of this story is to illustrate the quantity of information which goes into the solution of our everyday problems. Past experience, present perceptual data, and response possibilities are all combined into one overall reservoir of pertinent information. We do not have to inventory this information bit by bit. The pattern of activity in the central nervous system presents it all simultaneously. If I had had to evaluate each phase of the driving problem item by item in the way in which it is presented above, I would have been killed trying to figure it out. The whole thing went off in one instant of time. Afterwards we can reflect upon the event and pull out the individual pieces of information which were significant. But at the time of the occurrence, they were all available and applied simultaneously.

Such integration is the function of pattern. It pulls together data acquired at different points in time and in different types of situations and presents them simultaneously. A generalization is such a pattern. When we respond on the basis of a generalization, we respond on the basis of overall qualities of the pattern rather than to the specific elements which make it up. With such generalized responses, transfer of information from one problem situation to another is possible; learned data and responses become available in many different problem-solving situations. The pattern pulls in the data on the basis of their similarities, not on the basis of the particular situation in which they were acquired.

Nor can this pattern, which represents the generalization, be static. It must be dynamic so that it can be entered at many points and function around this momentary point of concentration. Parents constantly say to teachers, "I do not see why he performs this task so poorly in school. He does it well at home." But the situation surrounding the task at school is different from what it is at home. The pattern of performance is there, but we stimulate it at a different point in school. On the one hand the pattern is too limited to include all the variables presented in the classroom; but, more important, it is too static. When it is stimulated from a little different angle it does not function. It is not sufficiently flexible to be available to the child under a large number of different situations.

One additional function of the pattern underlying the generalization is extremely significant. As it integrates pertinent information, it omits by this very process of selection, information which is not pertinent. It thus keeps out of consciousness, at the moment, irrelevant or distracting information. In the driving problem, I had in my head much valuable information about the statistical reliability of an average and its methods of computation. Fortunately, at that moment, nothing was further from my mind. The pattern kept out by elimination such non-pertinent information.

LEARNING DISABILITY

It is in the development of generalization in which the slow learning child frequently has his greatest difficulty. He learns facts and acquires specific skills with relative ease. His problem comes in integrating and organizing these data. They remain isolated and largely independent. They are called up only when a particular stimulus occurs. When he needs quantities of data to solve a problem, he must inventory his knowledge item by item, selecting and rejecting each in turn.

As a result, in any assigned task he is apt to overlook a fact or piece of information which he has been taught and knows well. He can read a word on a page at one moment and fail completely to recognize the same word at the next moment. His conversation is frequently a string of loosely related ideas which carries him further and further from the point. He puts together things which do not belong together, and composite wholes such as forms or words fall apart on him. His motor responses, both gross and fine, are jerky, explosive, and uncoordinated.

It is easy to see why the process of generalization would give such a child so much difficulty. In many cases his problem is due to a disturbance in the function of the central nervous system. One or more of the units in this system does not work. The patterns which underlie generalization are very extensive. They involve large masses of nervous tissue working in concert. When activity becomes this widespread and this intimately coordinated, the chances of encountering the non-functioning units is greatly increased. Consequently, even though the malfunction may be highly localized, the chances of its interfering are greatly increased when the scope of the pattern becomes greater.

In a computer, if one relay fails to function, the datum assigned to that relay is not computed. As the program of the computer becomes more complex, however, this relay not only contributes one datum but works in synchrony with the other relays to produce a pattern of data. Now the result of its failure is not only to omit one datum but also to destroy the pattern of data so that the whole answer is incorrect and meaningless. The more complex the program, the greater is the disrupting effect of the failure of this single relay.

It is similar with disturbances of the central nervous system. Even though the disturbance may be very limited and specific, its effect on the overall pattern of functioning may be very great. It is not the lack of individual data which creates the problem. It is, rather, the effect of this lack upon the integration of the body of data which disturbs behavior and learning.

Such disturbances are particularly disruptive during the early years when patterns of generalization are being formed. When a pattern is being developed but is not yet complete and a disturbance is encountered, the effect is to disrupt and make largely impossible the establishment of the pattern from that point onward. It is something like the weaver who is weaving a piece of cloth. If a thread breaks on the loom, the effect is not so much a hole in the cloth as it is the fact that the pattern of the fabric does not appear from the point of the broken thread throughout the rest of the piece. If the appeal of the weave is its overall pattern (as is true in the pattern underlying a generalization) the whole loom run is ruined. When the developing pattern of functioning encounters a disturbance in the central nervous system, a similar distruction of the pattern occurs. Since the overall pattern must be completed before the generalization can emerge to a useful degree, the result is devastating to the achievement of the generalization and the accompanying efficiency of learning and behavior.

In most cases, the disturbance in the central nervous system suffered by the slow learning child occurred at or near the time of birth. It, therefore, interfered with the achievement of generalizations from the earliest developmental period onward. Failures to generalize on all or a large number of developmental stages is to be expected. Herein lies the difference between the brain injured child and the individual who suffers an insult to the central nervous system in adulthood. The latter has already formed patterns. The insult, as it were, pokes a hole in it, but the overall pattern remains. Such individuals show bizarre behavior which is recognized by themselves as well as by the outside observer. Their overall behavior is normal but breaks down at specific points.

The child whose insult occurred near birth, on the other hand, found it difficult or impossible to build up patterns in the first place. His behavior is disrupted. It goes off in all directions. He is not aware of his errors, but acts as though he knew no other kind of behavior. Where he produces the wrong answer, he is told that he is in error. Within himself, however, he does not know what went wrong or why. He has not been able to achieve patterns of functioning which would lay out for him overall objectives for behavior or an overall picture of the nature of his response. He behaves in bits and pieces in the same way as his learning has failed to supply an integrated body of data.

CULTURAL DEPRIVATION

A second group of slow learning children have intact nervous systems. However, the learning experiences which have been presented to them are either very limited or so chaotic that they have not supplied the necessary information. These children are often called culturally deprived. Because they have intact nervous systems they form patterns and achieve generalizations as does the normal child. Because their learning experiences have been limited, however, these generalizations are limited in extent and are inflexible. The generalization is qualitatively adequate but it is based on too few data. They frequently fail because not enough information has gone into the solution of their problems.

At first sight, it would seem that all they require is a greater quantity of learning experience. It must be borne in mind, however, that patterns of generalization have already begun to form. Any additional learning experiences must expand and elaborate these patterns, not start new and independent patterns. Such additional experiences must, therefore, be related carefully to what has gone before so that they will expand the existing generalizations rather than constitute a new and separate body of information.

Whether the slow learning child suffers from a disruption of the central nervous system or whether he suffers from inadequate learning experiences, we must be concerned, in his teaching, with the development of generalization. It is easy to see why so frequently we have overlooked this requirement of teaching.

THE NORMAL LEARNER

The brain is built to be patterned. A mechanism is provided whereby generalizations develop automatically as a result of experience. Because of this fact we live with such patterns all the time. We do not know what it is like to be without them. When the mechanism of the brain is disturbed, however, this function which we take so much for granted does not occur. We are so accustomed to the results of the generalizing function in our daily lives that it does not occur to us that they can be lacking and what such lack might do to behavior and learning. We are apt to attribute the child's peculiar behavior to some other reason, such as laziness, lack of motivation, inattention, and the like, which we ourselves have more directly experienced.

Since we cannot directly experience the results of such lack of pattern, we can only analyze intellectually what our generalization does for us and then try to imagine what it would be like if it were not so. We cannot experience what a chair would look like if it appeared only as a collection of loose sticks. We can only guess at what would result if the words on the page broke apart and the letters would not hold together.

With the normal child, we have only to give him the data in some semblance of order and he will put them together and achieve the generalization, just because his intact brain works that way. With the slow learning child, however, we must learn to teach what we have always taken for granted. We must teach him how to generalize. If we fail to do so, the results of our teaching will be merely a collection of facts which cannot be marshalled and applied to a problem.

TEACHING GENERALIZATION

In order to teach for the development of generalization, it is necessary to know how generalizations develop normally (Vinacke, 1952). We can then consider how this normal process breaks down in the slow learning child and what modifications in teaching techniques might be instituted in an attempt to restore it. Generalizations develop in three stages: (1) initial datum, (2) elaboration, (3) integration.

INITIAL DATUM

Generalization begins with the acquisition of an initial datum. This is an individual piece of information: a simple motor response on the motor level of development, a perceptual element on the perceptual level, or an isolated fact on the conceptual level.

Because of its isolated nature, the initial datum involves only a very simple neurological process. The simple, unelaborated stimulus-response bond concept explains this type of learning quite adequately. No complex pattern of central nervous system activity is required and the learning can be accomplished with the use of only a very small part of the nervous tissue.

For this reason, the acquisition of an initial datum seldom gives the slow learning child any trouble. Sometimes the datum selected happens, by chance, to fall in that particular area where the disturbance is localized, as, for example, a task which requires reaching by a cerebral palsied child whose arm is spastic. In this event, the initial datum will not be learned. Such specific encounters with localized disturbances are very rare in such simple tasks and seldom interfere with the first stage of generalization. As we will see, when the pattern of learning becomes more complex, their interference becomes more marked.

The initial datum is similar to a rote memory learning. The slow learner is notoriously adept at this simple learning. Any classroom yields many examples of children who learn the addition and sub-traction facts by rote but cannot solve story problems or use these facts in arithmetic computations which have any degree of com-plexity. These children appear to have excellent rote memory abil-ities, but their rote memory information is very specific and cannot be manipulated. In fact, their rote memory is probably not as su-perior as it would appear. It is rather that this simple learning function is undisturbed. The child tries to do everything with single data because the more complex generalizations are so difficult for him. He is inclined to stop at the initial datum stage of generaliza-tion learning and try to expand this simple process, by summation, to solve all his problems. As the environmental demands become more complex, his technique becomes more inadequate and his fail-ures become more glaring.

ELABORATION

The second stage of generalization involves the elaboration of the initial datum by the addition of a large number of similar but not identical experiences. Now the process of developing a pattern begins. These elaborating experiences must be similar so that they belong together and the resulting pattern will be oriented in reality. They must not be identical so that they will develop into a pattern and not merely intensify the initial datum. They must be extensive so that the resulting pattern will be broad enough and dynamic enough to encompass all of the abstractions and manipulations of the data required by the problems of daily life (Harlow, 1951).

These elaborating experiences must hang together. They must be related to each other, not merely a collection of isolated events. The establishment of such a relationship between experiences is dependent upon the establishment of a pattern in neural functioning which will hold them together (Hebb, 1949). Here the slow learner begins to experience difficulty. As the pattern begins to involve more and more of the central nervous system, he soon runs into his dis-turbance and the developing pattern is disrupted. As a result, the relationship between the experiences is lost and they become a series of isolated data.

Where the developing pattern is not disrupted, as in the normal child, this elaboration occurs automatically. As indicated earlier, one aspect of pattern is the generation on the output end of alternative responses. Since the pattern is an organized and integrated structure, these alternative responses are not random but are related to each other. As such, they represent similar but not identical responses. The more elaborate the pattern becomes, the more numerous and more extensive become the alternative responses. Thus, the normally developing child has numerous alternative behaviors suggested to him by his developing pattern. He moves from one to another in the course of any activity, producing a slightly different response and hence a slightly different interaction with the environment at each move. Such alterations, by their very nature, produce learning and hence add to the pattern. At each such addition, the repertory of alternative responses is increased.

In behavior, these alternative responses are seen as variations in performance. The normal child constantly varies his activity. Given even the simplest task, he will perform it in a straightforward manner a few times and then start introducing variations. He will think of hundreds of different ways to perform this simple task. Watch young children on their way to school. They seldom merely walk. They run, hop, or skip; they step on all the cracks in the sidewalk or they painstakingly avoid all cracks; they walk with one foot on the curb and one foot in the gutter; they kick objects along ahead of them, and many other variations of the walking task. They are moving from one alternative response to another—all related to walking but each slightly different.

Since the developing patterns of the young child are not yet set and crystalized, as they become in the adult, his imagination is given free rein in such variation. Thus, the chair on which he sits is at one moment a place to rest; at the next moment it is a castle in which he barricades himself; at the next it is a mountain which he must climb, et cetera. Each of these responses is contributing information about the nature and functions of this object. Each is elaborating the extensive pattern which will eventually become the concept, "chair."

PLAY

Herein lies the value of free play to the young child. In play, he is free to experiment with all the suggested alternatives. He can try each one out and, by such experiments, determine which work and which do not. He generates a vast number of slightly new interactions with his environment out of which a greater extent and scope of pattern develops. Such play is a vital learning experience for the child.

It should be pointed out that such learnings develop from *free* play—activities in which free rein is given to experimentation and where no "right answer" is prescribed. Adults tend to "organize" play for children. Either by the rules of the game or by the nature of the materials, they reduce experimentation and emphasize one particular performance. Intricate toys are provided with which the the child pushes a button and watches the toy perform. How often have we seen children absorbed in playing with the box in which it was packed and ignoring the toy. Children are lined up on the playground and "coached" in how to run fast. Alternate methods are discouraged and the children are admonished to "stay in line." Such organized activities do not allow for the extensive learning provided by "free" play.

When the development of pattern is disrupted, as in the slow learner, this process of variation, which is so natural for the normal child, becomes difficult or impossible. Since his pattern is so limited, there are very few suggestions for alternative responses. As a result, free play becomes an endless repetition of one or two responses over and over. Instead of elaborating a pattern, this repetition merely intensifies the few isolated responses involved.

PROVIDING VARIATION

Where lack of pattern fails to suggest possible variation in performance to the child, the adult must supply these suggestions. *We* must create for him the variations which he is unable to create for himself. We must present and insist upon alterations in response which will elaborate the experience and contribute to the development of pattern rather than permitting the child to repeat the same response, thereby intensifying its specificity and thus impeding the development of pattern.

The creation and presentation of such variations for the slow learner is not an easy task. As adults we have already been through this stage of free experimentation. We have discovered certain efficient methods of procedure and have dropped out and forgotten about the inefficient methods. To go back and recreate those earlier responses is extremely difficult. To conceive of variation for the sake of variation without reference to efficiency or to the "right answer" is foreign to our thinking. To deliberately let a child make a mistake, let alone encourage him to do so, goes against all our previous teaching objectives. As adults we must change our thinking and deliberately reason out the required variations. Such an approach to the problem, through logic and calculated reasoning, challenges our ingenuity and our creativity.

The task becomes increasingly difficult by the nature of the variations which we develop through such a process of reasoning. Our patterns are established and hence influence our thinking. Any variation which we conceive, therefore, is a variation in terms of *our* pattern. Its relationship to the initial task, and its variation, is controlled by the nature of our pattern. When we present a variation to a slow learning child who lacks such a pattern, however, it may have a very different meaning to him than it does to us. Whereas, with pattern, the suggested activity may vary only slightly from the original task, without pattern, it may represent an entirely new task and have little or no relation to the initial task. This child, with no intervening pattern to tie the two together, may find our variation so different that it has for him no connection with the initial task. As a result, he learns the variation as though it were a new and specific problem. He does not use it to elaborate the initial experience, but rather acquires a new and independent initial datum.

SPLINTER SKILLS

Behavior learned in this manner has sometimes been called a splinter skill. A splinter skill is a performance learned in a specific manner to satisfy a specific need or demand. It is performed with high degrees of skill but with a minimum of flexibility. Attention is fixed on the end result, but the process by which the result is achieved may be highly distorted. Variations in performance are minimal and the same series of movements or manipulations is rigidly adhered to. Learning is confined to this specific series of maneuvers and there is little or no transfer to other similar activities.

A ten-year-old boy was asked to write his name on the chalk-board. He took the chalk between his fingers and placed his wrist against the surface of the board. He made the first stroke of the first letter, moved his wrist, made the next stroke, moved his wrist, and so on, until he had completed the task. Each stroke was independent and there was a noticeable pause between strokes. When he had finished, he turned to the teacher and said, "I can write my name, because I have memorized the movements."

Here is an example of splintering. To meet the demands of a classroom task, the child had learned a specific series of movements to accomplish a specific end. Very little variation was possible. Therefore, he placed his wrist on the board just as he placed his wrist on the desk top in the classroom. The process of the task was highly distorted. It was a series of independent movements. The end result was precise. The writing was legible. However, he could not write from dictation because he had only "learned" to write his name.

Such splintered performances often mislead us. Because of the child's concern for precision, the end product is often highly accurate and for this reason is judged excellent. The process by which this product was achieved, however, is very limited and very specific. Any alteration in the conditions surrounding the task or any shift which calls for the same task in a slightly different situation disrupts performance. The child is not dealing with the significant variables of the task (letter form, spelling, communications, and the like), he is dealing with a series of specifics (isolated movements of specific direction and length).

Splintering is frequently characteristic of the slow learner. The task frequently presents peculiar problems to him which the normal child does not even encouter. The movement problem in writing for the child who has little eye-hand control is an example. In addition, the slow learner has limited possibilities of variation and experimentation in learning. Therefore, he is very apt to reduce the learning problem to specifics with which he can deal, and achieve the task as a splinter skill.

Because of this tendency to cause splintering, classroom tasks frequently do not teach these children what they were designed to teach. The walking board is recommended frequently to teach balance. Indiscriminate use of this technique and overemphasis upon precision of performance often results in splintered learning. The child merely learns how to walk along a 2 x 4 without stepping off. He does not learn balance or adjustment to gravity. He merely learns a parlor trick with a 2 x 4. Vary the task; put him into another balance task and it is apparent he has not learned balance. He has converted a generalized learning situation into a specific learning task.

The teacher of the slow learner must be constantly on the look-out for such splintering. It cannot be assumed that this child will make the necessary variations and experiments to achieve the generalized learning which the presentation was designed to promote. The teacher must insure such variation through prescribing and demanding frequent alterations in the child's performance. She must look constantly at the processes the child is using to achieve a task, rather than concentrate on the end result.

RIGIDITY

The variations necessary to the development of a generalization are frequently impeded by the child's rigidity. Rigidity refers to the tendency of the child to resist a new activity and to prefer to repeat the old activity. Such children prefer to do the same thing in the same way over and over again. Whereas the normal child becomes easily bored and introduces a new activity or a variation of the present activity, the slow learning child is happy repeating the same act over and over. He is only disturbed when a change in the task is required.

There are probably two basic reasons for such rigidity in the behavior of the slow learning child. In the first place, as pointed out previously, the necessary variations are not suggested to him. Alterations can be undertaken by virtue of the fact that information pertinent to the task is organized and categorized so that all of it is partially available at all times. The generalization is developing as the child is performing. The integration inherent in the developing generalization serves to permit alterations. It is just this generalization, however, which is giving the slow learner so much trouble. Instead of having available an organized body of information surrounding the task, he has only a collection of isolated data with no connections between them so that he can move readily from one to another. Just as lack of pattern impeded elaboration of the initial datum, so the same lack of pattern keeps the child from undertaking a variation which has been suggested to him. Within a pattern, the child can move readily from one response to another. He merely goes back into the pattern, as it were, and comes out at another point. Since the entire pattern is activated at least partially all the time, such movement is easy. When pattern is lacking, however, there is no way to get from one response to another. The bridge between the initial task and the variation does not exist. He performs in the same way again because he cannot move to the new response. As adults, we sometimes experience problems similar to those of the slow learner. If you are engrossed in an activity and are suddenly interrupted by someone with a request very foreign to what you are doing, you have trouble shifting to the new orientation. You become annoyed and may even "blow your top" and tell the interrupter to "Get out and leave me alone." Because of the lack of similarity between the task and the interruption, you had difficulty moving to the new response. You had to build your bridges between these tasks before you could move. Because of the extensive nature of your patterns, both surrounding the original task and surrounding the interrupting task, you were able to do so, but with effort. You were annoyed by this demand for extra effort, may even have refused to expend it, and hence told the interrupter to "get out."

The slow learner faces a similar but much more intense problem. Because of the paucity of his patterns surrounding both of the tasks, he cannot bridge from the task to the variation. Therefore, it may be impossible for him to move to the new activity or, if it is possible, it requires a Herculean effort. He may be expected to refuse to spend so much effort and display his refusal in attempting the new task. Not only does he have greater difficulty in building bridges than you do, but he encounters this difficulty when the two activities are less disparate. His patterns are so minute that even very similar suggested activities represent major interruptions. He will therefore refuse your suggestion and repeat the initial task.

Rigidity differs from perseveration in the child's conscious refusal. Perseveration involves the repetition of the same response in the face of a new and contradictory stimulus. He appears not to be aware of the change in stimulus. Displaying rigidity, the child demonstrates that he is aware that a new response is called for but he refuses to make it. Perseveration probably results from a pattern so tight and so restricted that additional stimuli do not even reach consciousness or effect response at all. Rigidity reflects the difficulty of altering response but not a lack of awareness of the need to alter. In perseveration, the stimulus is ignored. In rigidity, the response is refused.

The slow learner has had a long history of failure. From this experience he has learned one thing: the best way to reduce the probability of failure is to never do anything new. When he changes or alters the task, his probability of failure goes up. Further, because of the nature of his problem, he cannot predict what the failure will be nor when it will occur. If he can find a task or modification of a task where he is successful, he is reluctant to give it up and risk the possibility of unpredictable failure. Therefore, he has a psychological reason for repeating the same act over and over and for resisting any change.

The concept of rigidity was introduced by Lewin (Lewin, 1936). In his classical experiment, he asked a group of children to draw moon faces. A stylized face consisting of a circle for the head, two dots for eyes, a vertical line for the nose and a horizontal line for the mouth was presented to two groups of children, one normal and one slow learning. Each child was given a large piece of paper and instructed to draw such faces until he got tired. When he was tired, he was to inform the experimenter and another task would be introduced. The normal children drew a few faces according to the instructions. Then they started varying the task. They would put the eyes in first and draw the head around them or they would draw a number of heads and then fill in the features, et cetera. A very large number of variations were introduced into the task. The slow learners, on the other hand, tended to draw in the same way time after time with little or no variation. Furthermore, the normal children tired and requested a new task much sooner than did the slow learners.

Lewin thought of the individual as a dynamic system composed of a number of regions. Each region involved certain types of psychological materials. He conceived of the slow learning individual as one whose system was differentiated into fewer regions than composed the normal individual. He also conceived of the boundaries between regions being less flexible in the slow learner than in the normal. It was this last consideration which led him to the concept of rigidity. He felt that the slow learning individual had more difficulty moving from one region to another because of the rigidity of the boundaries between regions.

In addition to clinical observations, Lewin based his hypothesis on studies of satiation. He responded that if the retarded child had more difficulty moving from Region A to Region B, he would remain in Region A longer, given a free choice, than would the normal child who moves freely from Region A to Region B.

Kounin (1962) offered experimental verification of Lewin's hypothesis. Kounin felt that rigidity was a "monotonic function of C.A." Therefore, he equated mental age among three groups of subjects: A group of mental retardates (adult), a group of young mental retardates, and a group of young normals. He then performed a series of five experiments on the rigidity hypothesis with these groups.

In this first experiment, he followed upon Lewin's satiation experiment. Kounin presented his groups with a stylized drawing of a cat. When they had drawn this figure until they were tired of the activity, they were permitted to draw a stylized figure of a bug. When they were satiated with this task, they were permitted to draw a turtle, and when they were satiated with this task, they were permitted to draw rabbits. The mentally retarded individuals drew longer on the second task following satiation of the first task than did normals. For each of the remaining tasks, the satiation time for the retarded was greater than for the normals. Kounin reasoned that by virtue of rigidity, satiation of one region (task) had little effect on satiation of adjacent regions (tasks). The normal child, being less rigid, showed a greater degree of such co-satiation.

In a second experiment, Kounin reasoned that by virtue of rigidity, there would be less transfer from a task in one region to a task in an adjacent region, and hence there would be less interference of the second task by the first. He presented his subjects with an apparatus which released marbles one at a time when a lever was either depressed or raised. In the first portion of the experiment, he taught the children to release the marbles by depressing the lever. In the second part of the experiment, he asked them to release marbles by raising the lever. As he had hypothesized, the retardates in the second part of the experiment made fewer errors (depressing the bar rather than raising it) than did the normals. With less communication between the two regions, there was less interference between the two tasks.

In a further series of experiments, Kounin asked his subjects to sort cards either on the basis of form or on the basis of color. The materials were so designed that both principles applied, and the task could be completed on either a form or color basis. The normal subjects evidenced the least difficulty in shifting from one principle of classification to the other, with the older retardates showing the greatest difficulty. The younger retardates fell between these two groups. Furthermore, the retardates resisted a suggestion of change in principle more intensely than did the normals.

Goldstein, although accepting the hypothesis that rigidity is an important symptom of retardation, disagreed with Kounin that rigidity was a positive monotonic function of chronological age. He also disagreed with both Kounin and Lewin on their conception of the nature of rigidity. Werner also considered that mental retardates are rigid; he took exception, however, to Kounin's concept of the nature of rigidity.

Plenderleith (1956) and Stevenson and Zigler (1957) failed to confirm the findings of Kounin regarding the rigidity hypothesis. Zigler prefers to explain the behavior noted in mental retardates on the basis of motivational factors. He points out particularly that the subjects used in earlier experiments were predominantly institutionalized retardates and children from low socio-economic environments.

In the classroom and in the clinic, behavior suggestive of Lewin's concept of rigidity is frequently seen. Slow learners tend to perform in a highly repetitive manner. Such repetition often leads to simplification of the task and to splintering of the learning. The child learns the specific actions necessary to success in the task, but does not expand these learnings to include other activities associated with the task. As a result, transfer of learning from one type of task to another is limited, and the development of a generalization which will permit such use of the learnings in similar but not identical situations is impeded.

RESISTANCE

In addition to his tendency to perform in the same manner, the slow learner shows an active resistance to any change in task or in the method of performing the task. This resistance is expressed through any of a number of specific behaviors which can be grouped into two basic categories: active and passive. Active resistance involves direct aggression toward the proposed change. The child refuses to change and indicates his refusal directly. If the task is more gross and the rigidity more intense, he may display tantrum behavior and active aggression. Passive resistance involves more subtle and indirect refusal. The child does nothing in response to the suggested change and simply does not heed the instructions for change. He may use one of a number of escape mechanisms varying from physical reasons for not changing (it would make him sick) to elaborate verbal justification for continuing with the old procedures.

If such resistance is successful, the child does not enter into the suggested variation, and the resulting effect upon the development of generalization is not achieved. In order to induce more extensive learning and produce elaboration, his resistance must be overcome. However, the child does not resist because he wants to. He resists because he has to. The poverty of his information and the lack of integration in its retention makes it very difficult or impossible for him to move into a new task or variation of a task. His only alternative is to resist the suggestion of such movement. Pressure against the resistance is therefore required before the child can move. He cannot overcome his own resistance because he does not have the alternatives which make this possible. Pressure must therefore be brought from outside to push him through his resistance and permit alteration in his performance. The teacher must break through the resistance since the child does not have the possibility of forcing himself through.

Kounin (1962) investigated the amount of "force" required to induce a child to change from one procedure to another. Children were given a set of cards to sort on the basis of color. When they had successfully sorted, using this color criterion, they were given a second set of cards which they were asked to sort on the basis of form. When they had successfully differentiated the forms, the experimental task was presented. This experimental task consisted of a set of cards which involved both form and color. This deck could therefore be sorted using either color or form as a criterion.

The child was permitted to sort the experimental deck according to whatever spontaneous classification he preferred. When he had completed the task, he was asked to sort the deck again. When he had completed the second sort, he was asked to do it a third time. If he continued to use the same criterion for classification with which he began, he was asked to sort it a fourth time with the instructions, "Put them together some other way." If he still did not change the method of grouping, the procedure was repeated with the instructions, "No, find a *different* way. See if you can find some *other* way that they belong together." This procedure was continued for a maximum of ten total trials.

Normal subjects shifted their method of classification quite readily after trial three and 100 per cent of them had changed by trial seven. Among slow learning subjects, only 60 per cent had shifted by trial ten. Older mentally retarded subjects shifted even more slowly and only 30 per cent of them had shifted by trial ten.

It would appear, therefore, that rigidity, in addition to inducing the child to continue an activity in which he is engaged, also acts to prevent his changing to a new activity. In order to get him to change, "force" must be used. The more rigid the individual, the greater the amount of force needed.

It should be emphasized that the resistance characteristic of rigidity is very specific. Although the child's aggression may be intense, it is directed specifically at the task. He does not resist the teacher, he does not resist the situation, he resists only the new task. Remove the task and the aggressive behavior ceases immediately. Restore the task and the aggressive behavior returns. The resistance is funneled, as it were, directly toward the task and its problem.

FRUSTRATION

There is another type of resistance which is not thus directed. This is the resistance characteristic of frustration. Frustration results when the new task is so difficult or so far removed from the previous task that the child has no possibility of success. His rigidity is so great and the new task requires such an extensive movement from one region to another (in Lewin's terms) that it is completely impossible for him to make the necessary shift.

The resistance characteristic of frustration is different. Now the behavior becomes fractionated. Whereas in rigidity the resistance was directed at the task, in frustration it goes off in all directions. The frustrated child resists the teacher, the surroundings, everything about the situation. His aggression shifts unpredictably from one item to another. His behavior splits and loses all semblance of continuity.

When the resistance grows out of rigidity, outside pressure must be applied to permit the child to move on and learn. When the resistance grows out of frustration, such outside pressure only makes matters worse. The child *cannot* move and hence additional pressure only increases his frustration.

The teacher's role in such behavior is tied into a long standing question in the field of education of the handicapped. One group of educators warns that slow learning children should not be pushed. They reason that the child has enough trouble with his handicap and that it should not be aggravated by the teacher pressing for performance. The other group replies that if you don't press, you will not get performance at all near the child's ability, and hence you will limit learning.

Both groups seem to have a point. The first group is concerned with frustration. It is certainly true that the frustrated child should not be pushed. Such pressure will only fractionate his behavior further and no learning can take place when behavior is disrupted. The second group, however, is concerned about rigidity. If no pressure is applied against rigidity, no further learning will occur since the child will merely repeat what he has already learned. The problem is to determine whether rigidity or frustration is involved.

Careful observation of the behavior will answer the question. If the resistance is directed specifically at the task in hand and if it rises and falls as the task is presented and removed, it is likely that the problem is rigidity. If the behavior is inconsistent and if the child seeks escape not only from the task but from the entire situation and continuity is lost, it is likely that the problem is one of frustration. If the former is true, the procedure is to press through the resistance. If the latter is true, the procedure is to alter or simplify the task so that the child has the possibility of success.

The teacher must, therefore, select variations of a task with great care. As pointed out above, the exact nature of the child's problem often is not clear and cannot be pinpointed exactly. As a result, what appears to be a very minor variation may be frustrating to the child. The teacher must expect rigidity and be ready to press through it. At the same time, he must be aware that unexpected frustrations may occur. When the behavior begins to suggest frustration, another variation or a modification of the present variation should be introduced. The lesson plan and teaching procedure must be flexible enough to allow for such alteration and for unpredictable responses on the part of the child.

OVERCOMING RIGIDITY

The rigid child appreciates the pressure which permits him to move out of his rigidity. He demonstrates this fact when, after the rigidity has been broken, he embraces the new task with as much enthusiasm as he formerly used to resist it. Now the new task gives him great pleasure and he enters into it readily. His joy in accomplishment is as great as that of a normal child who has solved a new problem. Furthermore, he will identify with the teacher who has pushed through with him rather than with the one who has not had the courage to press successfully against his resistance. Parents of slow learners are constantly relating how their children like the teacher who "is strict with them," and object to the teacher who "has no discipline." It is as though the child wanted to learn but was prevented by his rigidity. When a teacher successfully presses through his resistance, he helps the child to achieve his own ends. For such help, the child is grateful.

INTEGRATION

When the process of elaboration has gotten under way so that a collection of similar but not identical data exists, the problem of integration must be dealt with. Integration is the process by which the data from elaboration are tied together and knit into an inflected whole. The similarities necessary for association have been provided through variation on a central theme, and now these associations must be molded into a whole. This whole is not homogeneous but is composed of separate parts, each related to the other. The wholeness results from these relationships. The meaningfulness of the generalization emerges from this interrelationship (see the discussion of integrated visual form).

It is integration which gives the generalization its character and makes the individual data available simultaneously for the purpose of problem solving. Without such integration, the data remain isolated and are useful only when memory can call them up and present them. With integration, the characteristic of the whole subtends all the individual data and involves them by implication in any problem in which the generalization is involved. Through such generalization, the child responds to numerous data at the same time even though the isolated informations are not present individually in consciousness. Stimulation of any individual datum or limited group of data will activate the entire system, and hence data not directly presented by the stimulus will still become involved in the solution of the problem and the resulting response.

Integration is furthered by techniques which emphasize the similarities between data. Whenever numerous related data are activated simultaneously, integration is promoted. The core of information provided by elaboration is bombarded, as it were, from all sides at once. This bombardment serves to set off a number of individual data, and this activity welds together the pieces into a whole. To encourage integration, therefore, stimulation will be brought into the system from as many directions as possible at the same time.

The only way we know at present to provide such a bombardment is through the use of multi-sensory stimulation (MSS). Through MSS the developing system can be stimulated from a number of directions at the same time. This multi-directional input serves to activate many individual data simultaneously in an organized fashion. Out of such massive activity, the welding together can take place by virtue of the overall nature of the activity, involving as it does many areas of the system at once.

It is important to note that this effect is achieved only if the various sense avenues present the same information. That is to say, the information from each avenue must belong in the system and be directly related to the information provided by the other avenues. MSS has been used in education for a long time. We present reading by primarily visual avenues, history by lecture which is primarily auditory, writing by tactual and kinesthetic avenues. We use that sensory avenue which is most convenient for the presentation of the subject matter at hand. Such use of sense avenues does not promote integration of a generalization since the data from each sense feeds a different system. To promote generalization, MSS must be carefully planned so that the same information is presented by each avenue. This latter procedure has been called redundancy. The same information is presented in different ways. It is through redundancy that the bombardment required for the integration of the generalization is accomplished.

It is also important that the stimulation from the various sense avenues be presented *at the same time.* If visual information is presented at one time, the data primarily stimulated through vision are activated. If, at a later time, auditory stimulation is presented, other data stimulated primarly through audition are activated. The effect is a mere shift of activity from one locus in the system to another. Such shifting is little different from the serial stimulation of isolated data. To produce redundancy, the whole system, as nearly as possible, should be stimulated simultaneously. To accomplish this end the various sensory stimulations must be presented at the same time.

Frequently, the child presented with a multi-sensory stimulation attends first to one avenue, then to another. For example, a common technique is to ask the child to trace with his finger a form drawn on the chalkboard. Such a technique combines the tactual-kinesthetic stimulation of the tracing with the visual stimulation as he watches the figure. Often, however, the child is seen who looks away while he moves his hand. When he looks back, the hand ceases to move. He is using the tactual-kinesthetic information at one time and the visual at another. At no time, however, does he put these two together and use them simultaneously. For this child, a method must be devised to force him to attend to both types of stimulation at once, if the integration of the generalization is to be accomplished. One such method involves holding the child's head so that his eyes are pointed at the drawing. To be sure, we cannot be assured that because his eyes are pointed at the form, he is looking at it. However, strong inducement is provided for looking as he traces. Verbal encouragement, used to augment this technique, frequently results in the desired multi-sensory awareness.

MULTI-SENSORY STIMULATION

Multi-sensory stimulation is the magic word today in the teaching of the slow learner. This technique is employed more frequently than any other single method with this group. The early work of Fernald (1943) has been revived and has been elaborated through a number of alterations. (Gillingham and Stillman, 1956). Some form of MSS is used in almost all classes for the slow learner.

Although MSS is highly useful and frequently necessary in the education of such children, its use is fraught with problems and it cannot successfully be employed uncritically. The most important function of MSS is to promote integration. Prior to integration, however, must come elaboration. It is through elaboration that data are made available for integration. Before such elaboration, MSS can do no more than teach isolated skills just as any single sensory stimulation teaches an isolated skill. Before elaboration, MSS is something like a cafeteria where the child can select the avenue which is easiest for him based on the datum involved. The true function of MSS, however, is not achieved. Therefore, before MSS is introduced, elaboration must be carefully worked out.

Every individual has a sense avenue which is particularly efficient for him. Some people learn more readily through vision; some through audition; some through tactual-kinesthetic avenues. In like manner, every multi-sensory presentation has a core sensory avenue around which the other avenues are related. If the core avenue of the presentation is different from the most efficient avenue of the

child, the presentation may well confuse more than it helps. Therefore, no standard multi-sensory presentation can be developed, and
each presentation must be tailored to the individual child. Vision
must be made the core for the visual child; audition the core for the
auditory child, et cetera. Much failure has been experienced in the
use of MSS because of lack of attention to these differences in the
processing of data from the various senses by different children. To
be successful, the teacher must determine carefully what is the lead
sense in the particular child, and then adjust the presentation to
insure that its core is in this same sense avenue. Other sense avenue
data must then be utilized as auxiliary data, leaving the lead sense
predominant. Such considerations will lead to major alterations in
MSS presentations for different children.

   Johnson and Myklebust (1967) have pointed out that in some
children one sense avenue conflicts with or blocks out another sense
avenue. In this event, the addition of data from a second sense
avenue may serve only to confuse the data from the first. Rather
frequently, adults are seen who close their eyes while listening to
music or speech. For such persons, the visual data serves to confuse
the auditory data. With their eyes closed, they block out visual data
and concentrate entirely on auditory stimulation, thus avoiding the
confusion. Children also may find that one sense blocks another.
They can either see or hear, but not both together. When both
avenues are presenting data simultaneously, one is blocked out and
only the other is received.

   In either of these events, multi-sensory presentations are contraindicated. In the first case, they will only confuse the child. In the
second case, only one avenue will be effective in spite of the multiple presentation. It would appear from recent findings, such as
those of Birch and Belmont (1964), that more children with such
intersensory confusions exist than was formerly thought. It is, therefore, necessary to use MSS with some care. In the event of such
confusion, multi-sensory presentations should either be avoided altogether or should be delayed until the intersensory confusion is
eliminated.

REDUNDANCY VS. DRILL

   The difference between redundancy and drill is apparent. Redundancy means the presentation of the same material by different

means at the same point in time. Drill means presenting material by the same means at different points in time. Drill is thus the exact opposite of redundancy. Whereas in redundancy there is simultaneous presentation and variation in method, in drill there is serial presentation and identity of method.

For purposes of integrating a generalization, drill is contraindicated. At best, it serves through its repeated use of a single channel or limited set of channels to intensify an initial datum. At worse, it can produce a splintered learning. For generalization, variation in method and simultaneity in time is required.

There are certain facts in our body of educational information which must be learned in a rote memory fashion. The 100 addition facts in arithmetic are a case in point. The most efficient way to teach these facts, or for the child to learn them, is through drill. The arithmetic textbooks with their carefully designed drills indicate the efficiency of this method.

If these facts are drilled before the concepts of visual-spatial grouping basic to arithmetic are established, however, the child is in danger of learning a set of facts which he cannot use. He frequently finds himself competent in arithmetic computation but inadequate in arithmetic reasoning. He can complete the drill problems in the workbook with ease, but is lost when these same facts are embedded in story problems.

The basic grouping phenomena which are essential to the understanding of arithmetic concepts are in the nature of a generalization. Therefore, it is apparent that the generalization should be established first and the facts acquired through drill later. The establishment of the generalization requires elaboration and redundancy. Drill is contraindicated until such redundancy has led to the basic generalization. Drill, in its place, is necessary, but it should not be the only approach to arithmetic, nor should it be undertaken until the visual-spatial groupings are understood. What is true of the use of drill in arithmetic is also true of all other subject matter fields.

METHODS

An argument similar to the one for drill may be applied to teaching methods. The generalizations underlying any subject matter must be acquired first. These generalizations are best served through a variety of methods rather than a single educational approach.

Through the use of many methods, the elaboration necessary to the learning of the generalization is furthered. In addition, if methods are combined or manipulated, redundancy can often be produced, thus further aiding the generalization learning.

Instead of searching for a perfect method, the teacher should acquire skill in a number of methods. That method can then be used which best serves the purpose of the moment. If a number of methodological approaches are presented in the classroom at the same time, the best interests of each child can be served. What one child needs at a given time may be quite different from what a second child needs at that time. If multiple presentations are available, each child can receive the type of teaching he needs. If the teacher is restricted to a single method, one or more children will find the presentation confusing or meaningless.

Flexibility in classroom presentations and in methods is essential to the teaching of the slow learning child. Because these children display many kinds of atypical learning processes, no one method can serve the needs of all. Further, because of their problems with generalizing, they need a wide range of presentation of materials and a more rapid shift from one type of presentation to another than is the case in the normal child. Their greatest need is for flexibility in teaching and for classroom procedures which permit the additional elaboration and redundancy which they require.

TEACHING

Generalizations are of extreme importance in learning. They permit the child to handle groups of data simultaneously and eliminate the necessity for separate recall and attention to individual data. Through the emergent quality inherent in the generalization, all pertinent data can be subtended and can effect the response, even though each is not singly presented to consciousness. This efficiency in handling associated data makes learning much easier and more efficient. In addition, it lays the basis for transfer from one problem-solving situation to another similar problem-solving situation. It is through such transfer and its implications that learned behavior can become more than a collection of isolated responses useful only in the situation identical to the one in which they were learned. By interfering with generalization, the learning disability interferes with this more extensive product of learning and impairs its usefulness. The teacher must learn how to teach generalization as well as and in addition to subject matter.

It should be remembered that, with most slow learning children, the interference with learning occurred before the child reached school age. Therefore, the learning of basic generalizations in the readiness or preschool areas has also been effected. The teacher cannot concentrate wholly upon the conceptual and abstract language generalizations which we are accustomed to promoting in school curricula. Motor generalizations and perceptual generalizations are also disturbed. Frequently, these earlier developmental deficits must be attacked first, since they are assumed in the more complex generalizations of the concept level. The teacher must learn to teach not only verbal generalizations, but the more basic constructs as well. She must recognize when a concept is impeded because of the lack of earlier generalizations which go into it.

These earlier developmental learnings are true generalizations and must be taught in the same way that more complex generalizations are taught. The same stages of learning apply and the same methods are effective. Only the data are different. On whatever level the teaching is proceeding, its effectiveness is dependent upon the ability of the teacher to produce the necessary generalizations. Without them, learning becomes merely the accumulation of unrelated data, available to meet the requirements of the classroom task, but not useful in the solution of problems and not transferable to the accomplishment of similar tasks.

chapter 3

Motor Bases of Achievement

THE MUSCULAR BASIS OF BEHAVIOR

The early motor or muscular responses of the child, which are the earliest behavioral responses of the human organism, represent the beginnings of a long process of development and learning. Through these first motor explorations, the child begins to find out about himself and the world around him, and his motor experimentation and his motor learnings become the foundation upon which such knowledge is built. In early childhood, mental and physical activities are closely related (Jersild, 1960), and motor activities play a major role in intellectual development. To a large extent, so-called higher forms of behavior develop out of and have their roots in motor learning.

It is logical to assume that all behavior is basically motor, that the prerequisites of any kind of behavior are muscular and motor responses. Behavior develops out of muscular activity, and so-called higher forms of behavior are dependent upon lower forms of behavior, thus making even these higher activities dependent upon the basic structure of the muscular activity upon which they are built.

The situation is described by Sherrington as follows: "As we look along the scale of life, whether in time or in order of organization, muscle is there before nerve, and nerve is there before mind, 'recognizable mind.' It would seem to be the motor act under 'urge-to-live' which has been the cradle of mind. The motor act, mechanically integrating the individual, would seem to have started mind on its road to recognizability. The great collateral branch of life, the plants, despite all its variety and unexampled profusion of types, has never in any event developed an animal-like locomotory act, nor a muscle nor a nerve; it has likewise remained without recognizable mind. As motor integration proceeds, mind proceeds with it, the servant of an 'urge' seeking satisfaction" (Sherrington, 1951, p. 169).

MOVEMENT AND OVERT BEHAVIOR

In the case of certain gross behaviors where overt muscle activity takes place, the dependence of behavior upon movement can be easily seen. In such activities, the body or parts of the body move through space, and this movement through space can be observed. We can see directly how the behavior is based upon motor movement and how the efficiency of the behavior is conditioned by the efficiency of the motor patterns which are available to the individual.

MOVEMENT AND NON-OVERT BEHAVIOR

In other types of activity, non-overt activities, the relationship between movement and behavior is not so clear. In many activities, the organism is sitting quietly and, to all intents and purposes, not moving overtly while certain behavioral acts are certainly going on. Under this heading fall such processes as thinking and problem-solving, where the major portion of the behavior may occur before any overt muscle response is seen.

Muscular activity, however, also plays a significant role in these "pure thought" processes. Experimental evidence suggests that there are at least two kinds of such muscular activity: a general over-all increase in muscular tension involving the whole body, and localized increases in tension limited to particular muscle groups (Krech and Crutchfield, 1958, p. 487). General muscle tension in non-overt activities can be seen by an observable tensing of the postural mechanism, by occasional drumming with the finger or pacing across the floor. In addition, sensitive electrodes over the major muscle systems of the body will pick up impulses indicating that innervation has been sent to the major muscle systems and that they are under a higher state of tension than would be the case in relaxation. Localized tension during non-overt activity can also be shown by experiments designed to reveal changes in electrical activity of muscles. Sensitive electrodes placed over specific muscle systems will indicate that, during the thinking process, these more limited systems have also been innervated and that tension in particular systems, associated with the problem of its solution, are present (Woodworth and Schlosberg, 1954, p. 178).

Thus, it is logical to suppose that even in "pure thought" activities the muscular basis of behavior is not lost but still provides the foundation for these higher activities. Pure thought activities are based on the ability of the organism to respond muscularly just as the lower responses of simpler experimental tasks are based on motor abilities. There is evidence that the efficiency of the higher thought processes can be no better than the basic motor abilities upon which they are based.

POSTURE

The basic movement pattern out of which all other movement patterns must develop is that of posture. Posture is a positive neuromuscular act in which a series of muscle groups is innervated in pattern so that the position of the body with reference to its center of gravity is maintained (Dusser de Barenne, 1934). These postural adjustments are very basic and are among the most rigid in the organism.

THE SIGNIFICANCE OF POSTURE

There are perhaps two reasons for the significance of postural adjustment. In the first place, it is through posture that we are able to maintain a constant orientation to the earth's surface and to the environment which surrounds us. The zero point, or point of origin, for all directions and orientations in space is the gravitational axis of the body. If we cannot maintain a consistent relationship to this gravitational force, we cannot maintain a consistent orientation to the world around us. It is therefore essential to consistent relationships with the things around us that we maintain a consistent relationship to our center of gravity. This relationship is maintained through the postural mechanisms.

The second reason for the significance of the postural mechanism is safety. If we cannot maintain our relationship to the center of gravity and our relationship to the earth's surface, we are not in a position to move or to respond quickly and efficiently, and therefore we are in danger of harm from external sources. Just as we must have a zero point to establish directions in space, we must have a zero point for movement. This zero point is the posturing mechanism, or the upright posture in the case of the human organism.

POSTURE AND BEHAVIOR

The maintenance of postural adjustment is so important that, in the organism, it has been given a dominant place in the scheme of behavior. Posturing mechanisms are largely under the control of the cerebellum. The cerebellum is a mass of brain tissue located below the major mass of the brain and connecting directly with the brain stem and the nerve tracts leading to the major muscle groups. There is a feedback mechanism between the cerebellum and the higher centers of the cerebral cortex. Elaborated behavior patterns are worked out in the cerebral cortex, and the action patterns to muscles resulting from this intellectual problem-solving are sent down through the brain stem. As they pass through the brain stem, the influence of the cerebellum is exerted. If these behavioral patterns would interfere with postural adjustment, a veto is enforced at the brain stem level so that these behaviors are not permitted to eventuate in action. There is a "short-circuiting" mechanism by which these patterns can be returned to the cortex to be re-worked. An interaction of this type between cerebellum and cerebrum can also be seen in the experimental behavior of animals (Fulton, 1949, pp. 525 ff). Thus, nature assures that no behavior will pass through and eventuate in action if it is contrary to the very basic postural mechanisms. In this manner, we are preserved from injuring ourselves, from losing our orientation, and from losing the base or point of origin for our actions, by the dominance which the postural mechanisms exert over our behavior (Strauss and Kephart, 1955, p. 197).

You can observe the veto force of the posturing mechanisms by the following experiment. Stand about five feet away from a table. Now reach out and pick up an object from the table without moving your feet. At first you reach out without difficulty. Then you lean forward as you reach. Soon you are in danger of becoming over-balanced. Do not let this disturb you. Tell yourself how important this experiment is and that you can certainly reach the object since, if your entire body were extended laterally toward the table, your arm would surely reach. Now, having intellectualized the problem completely and having assured yourself on an intellectual (cortical) basis of the significance of continuing the forward movement, go right on leaning forward until you lose your balance and fall on your face. Such a response is impossible. The normal individual finds it impossible to continue leaning forward beyond the point where balance is threatened. Neurologically and muscularly, there is no reason why you cannot continue to lean forward until you fall. The response of the total organism, however, is such that this dangerous resolve cannot be carried out. The basic postural mechanisms in the so-called lower brain centers have vetoed your fine intellectual solution and their veto stands. No further overt action in the danger-ous direction is permitted. As a result, no further action can be performed. Thus, the mechanisms of posture dictate the final de-cision for action.

It follows from the discussion above that all movement patterns, and consequently all behavior, must develop out of the posturing mechanisms. Movement not in accord with basic posture cannot be performed. Learned movement patterns and learned responses can only result from the elaboration and reorganization of the basic posturing adjustments. This process assures that posture is main-tained and that it remains the core of the behavior pattern.

NEED FOR FLEXIBLE POSTURE

It can be seen that since posture forms the core of any behavioral activity it is desirable that the postural adjustments be flexible and operative over a range. If the posturing mechanism is stiff and inflexible, only a limited amount of elaboration can be accomplished without destroying the postural response. On the other hand, if posture is flexible, if it involves all muscle groups or a large proportion of the muscle groups of the body in a pattern, a certain range of movement is possible within which posture can be maintained. This flexibility permits much more elaboration and much more manipulation than could a rigid inflexible posture. Such flexibility would thus lead to an increased possibility of motor response and hence to an increased possibility of behavioral response.

The relationship between the flexibility of posture and the elaboration of behavior has been demonstrated in a study by Kagerer (1958). In this study, first-grade children were tested to determine their ability in activities involving flexibility of the posturing mechanism. These test scores were then correlated with achievement in school as measured by standardized school achievement tests. Substantial and consistent correlations were found between activities, designed to measure ability to move within a posture, and achievement in school. Those children whose posture was most flexible and had the widest range did better in first-grade classroom work than those whose posture was rigid and who were unable to perform activities which required flexibility in the posturing mechanism.

The objection may be raised at this point that previous studies comparing physical characteristics and capacities (including posture) with intellectual achievement have shown little relationship (Paterson, 1930). In like manner, the development of high degrees of motor skill through training, as in the sensory motor training of Itard (1932) and Seguin (1907), seems to have had relatively little effect upon intellectual competence.

Although we have been interested for some time in the relationship between motor ability and intellectual activities, only recently have we become concerned with the flexibility of motor activities. Previous studies have for the most part been concerned with the development of motor *skills* and the learning of a high degree of proficiency in a rather limited motor activity. Such studies have not consistently shown significant relationships between motor skills and intellectual activities (see Wellman, 1931). More recent research is beginning to be directed toward the problem of *flexibility* in motor control and the ability to perform a motor task without previous experience or the development of a high degree of skill.

Thus, early studies in the area of posture have investigated the postural adjustment of the child while he was not moving. Present studies investigate his posture during processes of movement. The emphasis has swung from highly specific motor skills (which can be learned as "splinter skills" and have limited relationship to the activities of the total organism) to investigations of general movement patterns and the ranges involved in these general patterns.

In like manner, we have been concerned with the existence of the machinery for movement responses and have paid relatively little attention to the learning processes required in operating this machinery. Thus, we have been concerned with problems of muscle pathology and pathology of the skeleton and have largely overlooked the fact that, given a perfect muscle system and a perfect skeleton, the child must still learn to use these parts. The process of innervating a muscle or system of muscles involves the development of a pattern of neurological impulses which can be sent down to this muscle group or muscle groups and result in a controlled and accurate movement. Our problem is not to move single muscles by single impulses, but to move muscles in pattern, by patterns of impulses. Thus, Fulton states "the central nervous system is organized not in terms of anatomical segments, but in movement patterns" (Fulton, 1949, p. 54). We must develop patterns of neurological activity which will produce appropriate muscle movement patterns rather than simply dispensing a single neurological impulse to a single muscle.

This process of innervating muscle groups is learned. It is the result of experience and experimentation with movement and patterns of movement. As Coghill (1929) and others have pointed out, the muscles develop first, the nerves develop second, and the functional activities by which the muscles are moved develop last. We have paid very little attention to this process of learning how to make muscles function. We have not realized to the fullest extent the learning problem involved, and therefore we have in many cases failed to develop the maximum function of muscle groups and movement patterns. Muscles develop function only as a result of use and the concomitant learning.

It is not enough that the functions of muscles be developed per se. Such activity results in the development of isolated skills which have little significance to the organism except as parlor tricks. It *is* desirable that the functions of muscle groups be developed for purposes of an overall usefulness so that they can contribute to the general behavior adjustment of the organism. For this reason, we are concerned not with the development of specific skills, but with the development of certain general activities in the organism. Chief among these are the development of laterality and directionality. Both of these functions depend upon movement patterns and the learning of postural and movement adjustments. We will want to foster the motor development of the child, but we will also want to guide it in the direction of these more general activities.

LATERALITY

There are no objective directions in space. The directions which we attribute to space (right, left, up, down, before, behind, etc.) are attributed to external space on the basis of activities which take place within the organism. We do not receive from outside our organism any direct information concerning direction. When a sharp instrument is applied to the skin, there is a direct experience of pain, but there is no similar direct experience of spatial relationships and direction. Spatial clues, visual or auditory, obtain their directionality through learning and through the projection onto external stimuli of internal experiences that result from the movement of the organism.

The first of these directions to develop appears to be that of laterality, right and left. The human organism is anatomically and neurologically designed to be an excellent right-left detector. Our body is bilaterally symmetrical. We have two eyes, two ears, two arms, two legs, etc. Neurologically, the nerve pathways innervating each of the sides of the body remain primarily separate. There is a minimum amount of crossing over, to permit feedback and matching, but essentially there are two relatively independent systems, one for the left and one for the right. All the nerve systems, for example, innervating the left side of the body are kept distinct, pass up through the spinal cord, cross in the brain stem, and enter the right hemisphere of the cortex. This anatomical and neurological differentiation makes of the organism an excellent device for detecting right and left.

LEARNING LATERALITY

Laterality must be learned. It is only by experimenting with the two sides of the body and their relationship to each other that we come to distinguish between the two systems. It is through experimenting with the movement of the two halves of the body, observing the differences between these movements, comparing these differences with differences in sensory impressions, and so forth, that we sort out the right side from the left and ascribe certain differentiating qualities to each (cf. the concept of "reciprocal interweaving," Gesell *et al.*, 1941). The primary pattern out of which this differentiation develops is that of balance. When experimenting with the balancing problem, the child must learn right and left, for he must learn how to innervate one side against the other, how to detect which side has to move, and how it has to move, in order to execute the appropriate compensatory movements as his balance varies from one side to another. Out of these and similar activities, he learns to differentiate the right from the left side.

AVOIDING LATERALITY

It is essential that this type of learning take place and that it be carried through to satisfactory completion. There are several stages in the process at which the child can be stopped and can still make responses which appear adequate. Two of these stages are of particular importance. The first is that in which the child learns that as long as all of his responses are bilaterally symmetrical he can avoid the problem of laterality. Thus, his movements and his responses will be organized so that both sides of the body are performing the same act at the same time. In such a child, we will see both sides of the body brought into play where only one is necessary, or we will see one side of the body performing while an abortive performance occurs on the other side. When writing on the chalkboard, this child uses one hand for the writing activity while the other hand and arm are noticeably tensed or are making small movements that are mirror images of those being made by the dominant side. Such a child has no need to differentiate the sides because they always perform the same movements.

The opposite problem is one in which the child becomes almost completely one-sided. In every activity, he performs with one side and merely drags the other side along. We see him frequently converting bilateral activities into unilateral activities. Where he must use both sides of his body, one side will definitely lead and the other side will follow without taking a positive part in the performance. When writing on the chalkboard, this child also writes with his dominant hand, but the opposite hand and arm hang limply at his side and appear almost paralyzed. This child has no need to differentiate the two sides because, in effect, only one is ever used.

In either of these two cases, the child restricts his movement patterns and restricts his learning. He does not gain an adequate appreciation of right and left and, confronted with problems of laterality in external space, he will reflect his difficulty by confusing the two directions.

LATERALITY *v.* HANDEDNESS

Laterality must be distinguished from handedness and from the naming of right and left. Laterality is an internal awareness of the two sides of the body and their difference. It is probable that when the child has learned the sides, he still has to solve the problem of keeping their relationships straight. It seems possible that he learns to do this by developing one side as the leading side and consistently leading with this dominant side. Such a learning process may lead to dominance and, among other things, handedness. In this connection, it is significant that studies of young children have shown that handedness *develops*. It is not innate, but appears somewhere around the age of two years. Gesell (1940) and others have noticed this phenomenon. Prior to this time, the child uses his hands alternately and appears to have no consistent choice.

LATERALITY *v.* NAMING OF SIDES

In like manner, laterality must be differentiated from the naming of sides. To ask the child to identify his right hand does not constitute a test of his laterality. The recognition of the right hand as opposed to the left hand can be based on external characteristics of the two parts. Thus, the left hand may be the hand on which he wears a ring. The child's differentiation is then not based on any concept of laterality, but on the observation of specific characteristics of the external parts themselves.

IMPORTANCE OF LATERALITY

The development of laterality is extremely important since it permits us to keep things straight in the world around us. The only difference between a *b* and a *d* is one of laterality. If there is no left and right inside the organism, there can be no projection of this left and right outside the organism, and consequently the directional characteristics of *b* and *d* disappear. In this connection, Lotz pointed out many years ago that if we had *only* visual impressions, the words *up, down, left, right* and so on could have no meaning. The visual field would be circular, but with no position either upright or inverted. It would be lacking anything else in consciousness with which to compare it. One cannot ascribe erectness, inverseness, or a slantwise orientation to the universe. Ascription of visual position can derive only from having each field point take its special place in a tactual kinesthetic space image. "Upper" in the visual field is what appears nearer the head and could be reached by a tactile member of the head. "Lower" is what appears nearer the feet and could be reached by lower tactile members. After learning the variable posture of the body, we can give independent meaning to the visual "up" and "down" by reducing our posture to an erect bodily position (Lotz, 1852).

DIRECTIONALITY

When the child has developed laterality within his own organism and is aware of the right and left sides of his own body, he is ready to project these directional concepts into external space. By experimenting with movement patterns directed toward objects in space, he learns that to reach an object he must make a movement, for example, to the right. He then reverses this deduction and develops the concept of an object to the right of himself. Through a number of such experiences, he learns to translate the right-left discrimination within himself into a right-left discrimination among objects outside himself.

Experimenters in the field of child development have consistently noted that spatial relationships and spatial directions develop first in relation to the child himself, and only later are objective relations developed between objects. Thus, early in his development a child locates two objects, each independently, in relation to himself. This has been called *egocentric localization*, or the development of *subjective space*. Later in development, he is able to conceive of one object to the right of another without the intervening step of locating each object with relation to himself. This later development has been called *objective localization*, or the development of *objective space*. Piaget (1956), Gesell (1940), and others have outlined this developmental sequence.

DIRECTIONALITY AND EYE CONTROL

One very important factor in the development of directionality is the control of the eyes. Since a great deal of our information concerning space and the location of objects in space comes to us through our eyes, it is necessary for us to develop a series of clues and matches by which this visual information can give us the same directional concept which we formerly received through kinesthetic activity. This is accomplished through the control of the eyes. The child learns that when his eyes are directed toward a given point, it means that the object lies in that same direction. In order to learn this, he must make a complicated series of matches between the position of his eyes and the position of his hand in contacting an object.

The control of the eyes is very intricate and highly precise. The eyes are moved by six extrinsic ocular muscles which must be innervated in patterns and which must be moved very accurately. The fovea is a narrow area (about two millimeters in diameter) at the back of the eyeball. For most efficient vision, the image must fall on this foveal area. In order to focus the image on this restricted area, the eye must be moved with extreme precision. For this reason, and because of the intricacy of the muscle system by which the eye is moved, the process of learning to control this movement is very difficult. When the child has learned this control, he matches the movement of his eye to a movement of his hand and thus transfers the directionality of information from the kinesthetic pattern in his hand and arm to the kinesthetic pattern in his eye. This is, of course, a very precise and very complex matching procedure, and a great deal of skill and learning is required to perfect it. When this matching has been perfected, the child can use his eyes as a projection device to determine directionality in space outside the reach of his hand.

DIRECTIONALITY AND THE MIDLINE

One further difficulty is encountered in the matching of kinesthetic information with information from outside which results in directionality. When the child is experimenting with basic movement patterns, he refers all movement to the center of his body as the zero point of origin. Thus, the young infant in his crib first moves his arms in a bilaterally symmetrical fashion toward the center of his body and away in circular motions. As one arm moves in (toward the center), the other moves in also. He therefore learns that this bilateral pattern is an "outside-in" movement. However, with his left hand, it is objectively a left-to-right movement, while with his right hand it is a right-to-left movement. Thus, one basic symmetrical movement pattern has two opposed objective directions. A little later, when he first moves his hand across the midline of his body, he must learn that the movement remains constant although it has crossed the midline and is now compared with the pattern on the opposite side. Thus, subjectively, the movement is first an "outside-in" pattern and, when it crosses the midline, becomes an "inside-out" pattern. He learns that the objective movement remains "right-to-left" even though it may begin as an "outside-in" movement and, at the midline, become an "inside-out" movement. The subjective direction must be reversed when the midline is crossed in order to maintain the constancy of the objective movement. Young children often show hesitancy and reluctance to move the hand across the midline and display confusion when it is on the opposite side. Many slow-learning children will be seen to show the same hesitancy and confusion at a later age.

The movement of a visual stimulus outside the body derives meaning by being matched to the kinesthetic patterns by which movement was first interpreted. Therefore, when a visual stimulus crosses the midline, the same problems of translation occur as when the hand crosses the midline. Unless the translation can be carried out accurately, confusion concerning the objective direction of movement of the visual stimulus results. Since the child follows the moving visual stimulus with his eyes, the movement of the eyes follows the same pattern as that previously followed by the hand. When the line of sight passes the midline, a reversal of visual-kinesthetic matching must be accomplished.

In order to maintain objective directions of movement without confusion, therefore, the child must learn three procedures with extreme precision: (1) he must learn where the midline of his body is; (2) he must learn how to reverse the translation at the midline without interrupting the continuous external movement; (3) he must learn to *always* reverse when the midline is crossed. This translation offers some children considerable difficulty. Their problem can be seen in indecision and loss of control when a movement crosses the midline of their bodies. In like manner, it can frequently be seen in eye movements where the child loses control and his following movements are rough and jerky as the target crosses the midline.

DIRECTIONALITY AND LATERALITY

It can be seen from the discussion above that directionality in space is the projection outside the organism of the laterality which the individual has developed inside the organism. Directionality thus depends upon laterality and, until good laterality has been developed, the elaborations and extensions necessary for the establishment of directionality in space will be limited and inaccurate.

The intermediary step in transferring laterality to directionality is supplied by the eye and its kinesthetic information. We project our visual images into space over the same band of light rays which brought them to our eyes. For this purpose, we must be able to locate accurately that band of light rays. To do so, we must be able to: (1) control the eye with accuracy; and (2) know accurately where the eye is pointed. Only then can we match the outside relations of space with the inside relations of space which are our only basis for valid projection.

Just as the child establishes the right-left directions by transferring laterality to space surrounding him, so he develops "up" and "down" by transferring the up and down direction within his own body into outside space. He develops a concept of up and down through isolating and observing the direction of the force of gravity through his body as a result of his learnings in balance and posture. He relates this vertical concept as perpendicular to the lateral coordinate which he has learned. The fore and aft direction is more complicated and will be discussed in the chapter on spatial relations.

It can now be seen that the primary directions of space and the coordinates of the spatial world are developed within the organism and projected outward into objective space. Orientation in space and the observation of relationships between objects in space becomes difficult if not impossible until these coordinates are established within the body itself. It is through motor activity and the observation of motor activity that these coordinates become established. It is therefore important that the child's motor learning be fostered and that it be directed toward the development of these coordinates. Specially devised activities and training procedures can aid the child in this learning process.

BODY IMAGE

As we have pointed out above, we do not have absolute clues to spatial relationships in the outside world. In all external information, we are dealing with relatives and relationships rather than with absolutes. For this reason, we must have a point of reference around which to organize the relative impressions which we receive so that we can impose some kind of order upon them and construct a coherent totality. We use our own bodies as this point of reference. Objects about us are referred to our body and oriented in space with reference to it. For this reason, it is important that the child have a clear, accurate, and complete picture of his own body and its position in space.

As a result of certain sensations which we receive, we form a picture in our minds which represents the way in which the body appears to us. We have tactile, temperature, and pain impressions from the surface of the body. There are sensations which come from the muscles indicating their state of contraction or relaxation. There are visual impressions of parts of the body. There are sensations arising from the viscera. All of these become welded into a unity which represents the body to us. Out of this, we build up a body scheme or *body image*. It is this body image which becomes the point of origin for all the spatial relationships among objects outside our body. (Bloom, *et al.*, 1970.)

IMPORTANCE OF BODY IMAGE

Schilder (1935) and Bender (1956) have emphasized the importance of the body image. They point out that it is necessary for the initiation of any movement. Thus, Schilder writes: "When the knowledge of our own body is incomplete and faulty, all actions for which this particular knowledge is necessary will be faulty too. We need the body image in order to start movements. We need it especially when actions are directed toward our own body. Every trouble in gnosia and in perception generally, will lead to a change in action. We have again and again emphasized the close relationship between the perceptive (efferent–impressive) side of our psychic life and the motor (afferent–expressive) activities. Consequently peripheral changes in the sensibility must lead to disturbances in actions. Central disturbances like agnosias will also be disturbances of action" (p. 45).

Schilder has also pointed out that a fault in the body image will be reflected in the perception of outside objects. "Experiences in pathology show clearly that when our orientation concerning left and right is lost, in regard to our own body, there is also a loss of orientation in regard to the bodies of other persons. The postural model of our own body is connected with the postural model of the body of others" (p. 16).

Knowing where your body is and how much space it needs are important early learnings. (Courtesy of A. Devaney, Inc.)

PROBLEMS OF THE BODY IMAGE

As indicated above, the body image is a learned concept resulting from the observation of movements of parts of the body and the relationship of the different parts of the body to each other and to external objects. Many children have difficulty with this learning process and the learning is incomplete. Such a child will display this difficulty when asked to select a space on the floor among furniture and other obstacles, which is sufficiently large to permit him to lie down and move his arms and feet freely. He will select a space that is too small and in which his arms and legs bump into the furniture when he moves them. On the other hand, he may demand much more space than he needs for his movements. Either error indicates an imperfect awareness of the space occupied by his body in various positions.

Children will also show imperceptions in body image in activities which require them to move various parts of the body upon command. Thus, a child may not be able to move one arm without moving the other arm as well. When lying on the floor, he may not be able to move his feet without abortive movements of the arms.

He is not sufficiently aware of the parts of his body and how to move them or what they can do. Particular difficulty is experienced in activities in which the child is required to move one member on one side and the other member on the other side, as when he is requested to move one leg and the opposite arm. Here he may show his difficulty by starting to move the other two members or by pausing and obviously considering which member is the one requested. He may have difficulty translating the visual impression, when you point to a part, into the kinesthetic impression resulting from moving the part. He must learn how to identify the parts of his body on the basis of various sets of clues and how to control the identified parts independently of other parts.

All of these problems are problems of the body image and indicate that the child has not developed a complete pattern of his own body and its movements. Since, as we stated above, this body is the zero point, or point of origin, for all movements and for all interpretations of outside relationships, these movements and relationships will be disturbed if the body image is disturbed.

INFLUENCE ON LATERALITY AND DIRECTIONALITY

We need to mention again the importance of laterality and directionality. These concepts are closely related to the body image and their development is dependent in large part upon the adequate development of the image of the child's own body. Only through a reliable and consistent body image can the child develop a reliable and consistent point of origin for either perceptions or motor responses. We should offer him motor activities and guide his motor development toward an awareness of his body in space and what it can do.

MOTOR GENERALIZATION

From the point of view of learning, the most significant aspect of motor activity in the child lies in its implications for gathering information about his environment. Such information gathering is dependent upon an interaction between the organism and the environment. Information develops only from an active engagement of the whole organism in response to impingements of the environment, and not through the sense organs alone. Any such engagement is dependent upon movement by the organism, overt in the early stages of learning, covert in the more advanced stages.

To explore and learn about his environment, the child must move about in his environment, and this movement must be *for the purpose* of contacting and interacting with the environment or parts of it. The more extensive the exploration demanded, the more comprehensive must be the possibilities of movement. The more intensive the exploration, the more precise must be the movements. To permit the type of exploration which the child needs to develop adequate information about the environment which surrounds him, four basic movement generalizations seem required (Dunsing and Kephart, 1965; Godfery and Kephart, 1969): (1) balance and posture, (2) locomotion, (3) contact, (4) receipt and propulsion.

BALANCE AND POSTURE

As has been pointed out above, the point of origin for all explorations is the force of gravity and the child's orientation to it. Gravity is the one constant in the spatial world which surrounds us (Einstein, 1955) and it, therefore, becomes the zero point for all spatial relationships and for all explorations of space. The child needs to develop an understanding of the constant nature of gravity, of its direction, and of its point of application relative to his body.

In order to serve as a point of origin for abstract mathematical spatial relations, gravity must become an abstraction for the child. It must satisfy the requirements of a mathematical point—having only location, no extension. It is for this reason that the refinements of laterality and body image are so important. The right-left gradient through the body resulting from laterality must have a zero point (the line of gravity) which is a true point, not an area. Similarly, through refinement of body image, the line of gravity through the body becomes a mathematical line, not a vague cylindrical area. It is only as such precision relative to gravity is learned that the mathematical functions of gravity as a basis for a spatial structure can be developed.

Exploration, however, demands movement around such a zero point. The child must reach out, as it were, and contact portions of his environment. He cannot remain rigid at a fixed posture for, if he does, he cannot come physically in contact with his environment for the purpose of interaction. Thus the importance of flexibility in posturing is apparent. It is this flexibility which permits freedom of movement and determines the scope of the exploratory movements open to the child. During such movement, however, the relationship to gravity must remain firm. If this relationship is lost, the exploration loses its systematic nature and becomes merely a collection of isolated interactions. Contacts are not related to each other and do not form a systematic body of information.

LOCOMOTION

It is through locomotion that the child explores the relationships *between* objects in space. Locomotion includes those activities which move the body through space, such as walking, running, skipping, jumping, rolling, et cetera. The child moves from one object to another for the purpose of exploring the relationships between the objects.

It is important that the child be able, in such exploration, to maintain his attention upon the information being generated. He must not be interrupted by the necessity of turning his attention to the question of how the movement is to be made. It is for this reason that the locomotor generalization must become a true generalization. The movements necessary to the exploration must take place automatically without attention from the child (Early, 1969b). If this does not happen, the child's attention must shift from the information to the movements.

In spatial exploration, consistency is essential. The relationships to be learned depend not upon the static condition of the moment but upon the events of the intervening time. Thus, if I explore by locomotion the distance from the door to my desk, the important information (distance) is dependent upon such things as time required to walk from door to desk, number and size of steps involved, changes in apparent size of the retinal image as I approach, et cetera. All of these essential informations are dependent upon orderly observations. If I encounter an obstacle during the walk and must shift my attention from the observations to the problem of how to get my feet around the obstacle, there is a gap in these orderly observations and the exploratory information suffers. The spatial exploration resulting from locomotion is dependent upon intervening observations and particularly upon consistency of such intervening observations. If locomotion is not a true generalization, such consistency is difficult to maintain.

Many slow learning children are seen in whom locomotion is not a generalization. It is a mere collection of locomotor skills. Such a child can walk, but his walking is inflexible and rigid. When an obstacle is encountered, he must stop and solve the movement problem presented by the obstacle before he can proceed. Such a child is restricted in his exploration of space and in his ability to develop a body of spatial information. What he needs is a more extensive repertory of locomotor movements and greater flexibility and interrelationship between them. When such elaborations have been achieved, his locomotor activities can become available for the purpose of gathering information.

CONTACT

Just as the locomotor generalization permitted the child to explore the relationships between objects in space, so the contact generalization permits him to explore the relations *within* objects. This generalization involves those movements related to the handling and manipulation of objects. In the human organism, they are principally hand skills. There are three aspects involved in these manipulative activities: *reach*—by which an object is touched and contact is made; *grasp*—by which contact is maintained while the exploration is taking place; *release*—by which the child lets go of one object so that he can go on to the next.

As with locomotion, contact must be a true generalization involving enough skills with enough precision to permit thorough exploration of the object. The movements must be sufficiently skilled so that the child's attention can be given to the exploration and not be diverted to the movement. Just as in exploration of space, so object exploration must be consistent since the relationship between the elements or parts is revealed through the intervening observations. Child development workers have long emphasized the importance of such systematic exploration.

Through these contact activities the child learns the nature of the objects which surround him. It is out of such knowledge that form perception and figure-ground concepts will emerge. As the eye explores with the hand, the perceptual-motor match is begun and eventually leads to the possibility of the generation of the necessary information through visual exploration alone.

RECEIPT AND PROPULSION

With systematic knowledge of the space between objects and of the relationships within objects, the child is equipped to deal with a static environment. However, the environment in which he lives involves movement. Things change their position with reference to him and also with reference to each other. He moves with relation to objects and he must distinguish between his movement and object movement. Therefore, he requires systematic information about movements in his environment. These data are supplied through the receipt and propulsion generalization.

Receipt involves those activities through which he makes contact with an object moving toward him. Catching, dodging, trapping, and the like are examples. Through such activities he learns to respond to a movement toward himself and to orient that movement in space with reference to himself.

Propulsion involves activities through which movement is imparted to an object. Throwing, batting, pushing, and the like are examples. It is through such activities that the child learns to respond to movements away from himself. Through a combination of the receipt activities and the propulsion activities, he learns to interpret movements which do not involve himself directly.

EXPLORATION THROUGH MOVEMENT

Through the following four basic generalizations, the child explores the environment which surrounds him. He begins to put the parts of objects together in space and construct integrated wholes. He relates objects to each other in space so that they remain stable and maintain a consistent order among themselves. He has begun to construct a world of space in which, eventually, everything in his environment will find its place in an orderly array which will encompass not only the concrete objects which he sees and touches but objects and spaces with which he can have no concrete experience as well. The relationship in space between New York and Chicago will be as meaningful as the distance between his chair and the door. All will be encompassed in an extensive, organized space structure.

These movement generalizations are identical with and are learned in the same way as other generalizations (see Chapter Two). The data for the movement generalizations are single movements or single motor skills. These units must be elaborated and integrated as are other data entering into generalizations. If the child has not been able to complete such learnings for himself, the teacher must aid him through the teaching of generalization. If he is left with simple motor skills, even though these be extensive, his basic fund of information regarding his environment will suffer.

MOTOR DEFICITS

The questions will be raised, "How about the child who has a motor deficiency (such as cerebral palsy), for whom certain movements are not possible? Does such a child find his overall learning disturbed through his inability to move extensively in his environment?" We all know cases in which movement is restricted by motor deficits but in which the child's learning does not seem to have been affected.

The important aspect of the motor learning stage in development is the establishment of generalization. Generalization can be learned in many ways. Numerous kinds of experiences go into the elaboration of the initial datum. No one of these experiences is, in and of itself, essential. It is the cluster of elaborations which is important. Therefore, if certain movements are impossible, others can be substituted. It is not the individual motor skill which facilitates learning, it is the movement generalization.

The child with a motor deficit can develop a generalization around the area of the deficit. It may, and probably will, involve a different set of movements than in the case of the child who is not handicapped motorically. However, the abstraction can emerge just as well, and it is this abstraction which, from the point of view of education, is required. Thus, a cerebral palsied child who cannot stand can develop the concept of gravity by experimenting with seated balance. Through a number of directed experiences in the seated position, he can abstract the same mathematical line of gravity that other children will develop in the standing position. The motor deficit is a specific defect, and specifics are expendable in the learning of the child. It is the generalizations which are essential.

MOTOR LEARNING

In general, the motor learning of the child will be found to follow certain steps. First will come the differentiation of single movements out of a global mass (Chaney and Kephart, 1968). Such differentiation will follow the cephalo-caudal and proximal-distal directions discussed in Chapter One. The child will learn how to move a part voluntarily and for a purpose.

Next, the child will isolate this movement from the movement of the rest of his body (kinesthetic figure-ground). He will learn to use only those muscle groups necessary for the movement and to relax and leave uninvolved any other muscle groups. These single movements will then be knit together into coordinated patterns with each separate motion synchronized with the total. The child has developed motor coordination. Numerous studies have demonstrated the relationship between such coordinated movements and educational achievement in the classroom (Ismail and Gruber, 1967; Dunsing, 1963). Such complex coordinated series of movements permit more complicated interactions with the environment and allow the child to explore more extensively. Out of these coordinated patterns, the basic motor generalizations develop.

In classroom activities and in physical education programs of motor learning, it is well to keep these steps in mind. It is fruitless to demand high degrees of coordination from a child in any activity when he is unable to separate from the mass the distinct movements required by the activity. To drill or practice under such circumstances will lead to the development of splinter skills which will look good but which will be limited to the particular activity which has been practiced. In like manner, to stop with the development of coordinated activities is to lose the contribution of motor exploration to the development of a more extensive body of information.

Programs of motor learning, as they are related to education, therefore, should start where the child is in the learning process and carry on through to the development of the major generalizations. The importance of space relationships in relation to these generalizations has been emphasized throughout the above discussion. It follows that, in teaching motor responses, the spatial aspects of the activity must be stressed and a spatial component must be introduced into the programs.

AUTOMATIZATION

As has been pointed out, when a motor generalization develops, the individual movements involved become automatized. Only insofar as the child can divert his attention from the problem of movement to the problem of exploration can such a generalization be used for the purpose of systematic exploration. The automation of specific movements and motor skills permits such selective attention (Early, 1969b). In teaching, therefore, it is well to direct the child's attention away from the movement and toward the goal of the movement as soon as possible.

Frequently, we impede the achievement of automation through our demands for excessive skill in movement. We like to see the child who can catch a ball with extreme accuracy. We place a premium on high degrees of skill in activities useful in sports programs. For our purposes here, however, high degrees of skill are not required. If the child has enough balance to identify the line of gravity, this is all he needs to establish the point of origin for the spatial dimensions. The degree of skill possessed by a tightrope walker adds nothing. It is, therefore, desirable that the child possess lower degrees of skill in a number of different movement activities rather than high degrees of skill in only a few. Where high degrees of skill are demanded, the child's attention is directed to the movement and its performance rather than to the goal of the movement. Automation is impeded when too much attention is directed toward the nature of the movement.

Both teachers and researchers are inclined to error in this regard. They assume that "if a little is good, a lot is better." Thus, teachers tend to continue programs of practice in an effort to produce precision of movement which is beyond the point of usefulness for education purposes. Researchers, using the same assumptions, measure the child's skill and, through correlational methods, assert that the child with the highest level of skill should show the most achievement. If this proves to be untrue, they assert that the theory is wrong.

MINIMUM REQUIREMENTS

The principle of minimum requirements applies to the learning of the child. Enough skill is necessary to produce the desired interaction with the environment. However, once this interaction has been accomplished, the related learning has occurred. The fact that the child may have had available much more skill means nothing, since he was not required to use it. Thus, there are minimum basic requirements for skill. The child whose skill level falls below this critical level is handicapped. It does not follow, however, that the child who has more skill than this has an advantage. The teacher should adjust her program to the requirements, not to some arbitrary standard of desirable skills. As soon as possible she should submerge this skill in a goal-oriented task so that the child can automatize the movement and proceed with the information-gathering process.

chapter 4

The Perceptual Process

Modern thinking and recent experimentation point toward the conclusion that a closed system, involving a feedback control, is operative in the perceptual process.

Figure 6 will help to make clear the type of system most commonly hypothesized. It should be pointed out that this diagram is not limited to investigations in perception. With minor modifications and additions, it is used extensively in discussions concerning speech pathology, endocrinology, communications, electrical engineering, et cetera. A model similar to the one used here has been found extremely useful in a large variety of fields.

INPUT

In perceptual theory, the input (as in the diagram) is thought of as activity in the sensory projection areas of the cerebral cortex. Some form of energy impinges upon the exterior of the organism. It strikes certain sensitive cells and (depending upon the nature of the energy and the nature of the cells) sets up a pattern of neural impulses resulting from the firing of a pattern of sensory cells located

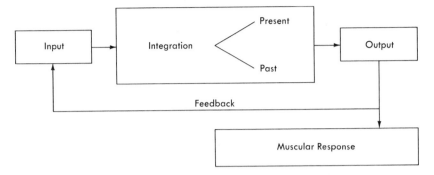

FIGURE 6.   Diagram of feedback mechanisms in perception.

on the surface of the body. This pattern of neural impulses is transmitted to the projection area of the cortex. There, an analogous pattern of neural impulses is set up through the action of internuncial neurones. It is this pattern of electrical impulses in the sensory projection areas which constitutes the input.

x Bear in mind that the input, as we understand it here, is a pattern of nervous impulses. These nervous impulses are generated within the organism as the result of firing by the organism's own cells. No outside energy enters the organism for the purpose of setting up perceptual activity. Perceptions result from activities of the organism itself, not from the transmission of outside energy into or through the organism. Our thinking often goes astray at this point. We consider that the stimulus enters the organism. We say, "I put such and such a stimulus into this organism." From the point of view of perception, no stimulus ever enters the organism. The stimulus is effective on sensory cells at or near the surface of the organism. The stimulation to which the organism responds is the pattern of neural impulses generated by the firing of these sensitive cells.

The input in our diagram, therefore, is input from the organism itself. Other things being equal, the preceptual input corresponds closely to the energy distribution impinging upon the organism. This correspondence, however (at least in any one sense field), is never perfect. Neither is the perceptual input a replication of the outside energy pattern. The perceptual input is a translation of outside energy into patterns of neural impulses.

When such an input has been generated in the sensory projection areas, its effects radiate through internuncial neurones into the surrounding association areas. It is here that the integrative process takes place.

INTEGRATION

The integrative process has proved to be one of the most mysterious of the organism's activities. We still know little about it, and there are many conflicting hypotheses and many alternate theories devised to explain its operation. There is, however, rather general agreement that two basic processes occur.

INTEGRATION OF SIMULTANEOUS INPUTS

In the first place, the integrative process is concerned with all of the sensory inputs operating in the organism at a given moment. Only in the most hypothetical of laboratory experiments is there ever a time when only one sensory input is present in the organism. Normally we are receiving information simultaneously from many sensory sources. Consider the stimulation which you are receiving at this moment. Dominant of course are the visual sensations from the printed page. However, these are by no means all of the sensations you are receiving. Noises of traffic on the street outside, kinesthetic sensations from the postural muscles, temperature sensations from the skin, tactual sensations from those parts of the body in contact with the chair, organic sensations from the digestive tract, all are present as you read. Furthermore, these various sensations do not occur separately; they are welded together into a total "stimulus situation." It is this stimulus situation of which you are aware and to which you are responding at this moment. Any reduction of the total stimulus situation resulting from removing some of these many simultaneous stimuli makes the situation seem unreal, makes you feel uncomfortable, and interferes with your responses. Our normal responses are responses to collections of sensory stimuli, all of which are active in the organism at the same time. We live in a world in which various forms of energy are impinging upon the organism at all times. These various forms of energy are setting up simultaneous input patterns in various sensory fields which are originating in various external areas of the body. The perception which results is based upon the net effect of all of these simultaneous stimulations, not upon one isolated input. It is in the integrative mechanism that all of these simultaneous inputs are integrated and organized so that a single response can be generated which will consider all of the outside energy in one act.

Into the association areas of the cortex, where integration takes place, fibers feed from all the sensory projection areas. As a result of the integrative process, a pattern of neural activity is aroused in the cortex which encompasses the contribution of all the senses into one overall pattern. Our response is geared to this overall pattern, not to the pattern in any one sensory area. It is essential that such an integrated pattern be used as the basis of behavior since only then can we efficiently consider all sensory information at one time. Only then can we balance one sense field against another for more complete and more accurate information.

Here again, our thinking frequently goes astray. We attempt to account for a perceptual response as though it were a response to a single stimulus in a single sensory field. Laboratory experimentation, in the interest of rigid scientific control, has frequently attempted to set up situations in which the latter condition held. These attempts have never been completely successful. Even under the most rigid controls yet devised, the organism receives multiple stimulation, not single stimulation. As recent experiments at McGill University have shown, if the organism comes too close to single stimulation, highly abnormal behavior results (Bexton, Heron, and Scott, 1954). Even under normal laboratory controls, the atypical reactions characteristic of the laboratory are notorious. No matter how interested we may become in a particular sensory stimulus, we must always keep in mind that this stimulus is only a part of the much larger stimulus field involving other sensory avenues; the response is made to this total stimulus field. (Compare with Gibson, 1950.) The integration of all of these inputs, so that a total response can obtain, is one of the functions of the integrative mechanism.

INTEGRATION OF PAST AND PRESENT EXPERIENCE

The second part of the integrative process involves the effects of past experiences of the organism. Here is involved the problem of memory and the memory trace. In this area again, there are numerous hypotheses. Modern thinking, however, conceives of at least a large part of the memory process as being a more or less permanent alteration of the organism. Any response of the organism involves not only the present stimulating activities, but effects of past activities as well. The further elaboration of the present stimulus situation by the addition of pertinent data from our past experience invests the present experience with "meaning." It is in the integrative mechanism that this synthesis of present and past experiences occurs.

We find, therefore, that, as a result of the integrative process, the original pattern of neural impulses which constituted input has been elaborated. This elaboration has involved the addition of all other stimulation present in the organism at the given moment and the alterations and modification of those input patterns resulting from modifications produced by the organism's past experiences. As a result, we have a vastly elaborated pattern of neural impulses.

SCANNING

This elaborated pattern is then processed by a scanning device and translated into an output pattern (Strauss and Kephart, 1955, pp. 9 f). It seems probable that this scanning mechanism is a simple translation from an association pattern to a motor pattern. Just as the scanning beam on a television camera translates the light gradients in the studio into a temporal series of electrical impulses, the scanning mechanism translates the afferent and association pattern in the integrative mechanism into a motor output pattern. Just as the television picture in your living room is an accurate model of the light distribution in the studio, the output pattern is an accurate model of the pattern existing in the integrative mechanism. Thus, we see the scanning mechanism as a simple translation device without alteration. The nature of the scanning device is not fully known.

However, it is thought to be related to the alpha rhythm of the cortex. The scanning rhythm appears to be about ten to twelve cycles per second (McCulloch, 1951, p. 100; Wiener, 1948, p. 32).

OUTPUT

As a result of the scanning operation, an output pattern is generated and we enter the output area as seen in Figure 6. This output process is again a pattern of neural impulses. However, this time it is a pattern in the motor area of the cortex which can be sent down to muscle and which will result in movement. Thus, the output pattern is a pattern of innervation to muscle.

It is generally considered that consciousness first occurs at this point in the perceptual process. We are first conscious of the stimulus when an output pattern has been generated. Thus, we cannot "see," as we think of this process in our everyday speech, until we have an output pattern.

FEEDBACK

When the output pattern has been generated, it is sent down the efferent nerves to muscles, and muscular response results. On the way to the muscle groups, however, a portion of the output pattern is drained off and is fed back into the system at the input end. The presence of feedback in the perceptual process makes the system a servomechanism (Brown and Campbell, 1948). Such feedback creates a closed system of control. Information from the output end of the system is oriented toward the input end and used for control. In such a system, the system becomes its own control.

The ordinary traffic light is an illustration of an open system of control. What the traffic does cannot affect the built-in timing mechanism which operates the light. Changes of traffic flow have no effect upon the system. In newer traffic lights, an electric eye senses the flow of traffic in each direction and, on the basis of this information, the timing of the traffic light is altered. These newer systems are closed systems of control. A part of the energy of output (the traffic) is fed back into the system at the input end (traffic light) where it is used to control the system.

The great advantage of closed systems is that they make possible a constant monitoring and continuous alteration of the system. In the older traffic lights, the control was periodic. It was established when an officer checked the system and reset the timing mechanism of the lights. The adequacy of the control was dependent upon how long it had been since the system was checked and what changes in traffic flow had taken place during that time. In the newer traffic lights, the system is constantly checked and the control is altered immediately when the check indicates that a change in timing would be more effective in controlling traffic flow. In the perceptual process, this feedback output pattern becomes in itself a part of input. As the feedback reenters on the input end of the system, it alters the input pattern and thereby calls for a new cycle of the perceptual process. Thus, each alteration of input resulting from the feedback calls for a new integration, a new output, and further feedback. This circular process will continue until the feedback exactly matches the input.

Thus, the preceptual process is not a static affair, not a straight-line process or one-time activity, but a continuing process that remains active until an exact adjustment occurs between feedback and input. Through the feedback mechanism, the process is perpetuated until an adequate response has been generated. The feedback is used as a control in a closed system which becomes self-monitoring.

It is of course apparent that the output pattern need not result in a muscular response on every cycle of the process. It is possible for us to generate an output pattern, drain most of it off in feedback for control purposes, and permit so little to continue to muscle response that no overt movement of the organism occurs. It is in this manner that we can engage in non-overt activities and can try out many possible solutions to a problem before committing ourselves to an overt movement. By this means, the perceptual process can be continued until an adequate matching of output and input has been achieved before muscular response occurs. It is of course apparent that much of our more important problem-solving goes on in this fashion.

PERCEPTION AND LEARNING

An appreciation of the feedback mechanism described above will indicate that all of the parts of the perceptual process operate together as a totality. After an input pattern has been elaborated through the integrative process, an output pattern is generated which becomes an additional input pattern because of the feedback. Owing to the cyclical nature of the process, we cannot consider one of these steps without considering all of the others. No area operates independently, but each is influenced by what transpires in the remaining areas and by its own modification of the activities in the remaining areas.

PERCEPTUAL-MOTOR

The fact that we cannot consider any aspect of the perceptual process without considering the total activity becomes particularly significant in the areas of input and output. We are accustomed to think of input as an independent process and output as another independent process. We speak of input activity and output activity as though they could be separated.

In periodicals and in our textbooks, we consistently make a distinction between input (sensory or perceptual activities) and output (motor or muscular activities). If you open a book on child psycholgy, you will find a chapter devoted to perceptual development and a separate chapter devoted to motor development. The implication is that these are two separate activities which can be studied apart from each other and which are only very tenuously connected, if at all. Similarly, if you open a book on psychology, you will find a section on sensory activities and a separate section on motor activities. If you are interested in experimental psychology, you will find a chapter on perception and a separate chapter on motor skills. Even in neurology you will find efferent processes discussed separately from afferent processes.

All of these approaches imply, if they do not actually state, that input and output are two separate entities which can be described independently. It is our thesis, of course, that such a division of thinking is impossible and can lead only to error. The input-output functions of the organism occur in a closed cycle. Anything which happens in one area affects all other areas. The input-output system is a closed system, and we cannot stop activities in one area while we investigate the effect of changes in the other. Therefore, we cannot speak of, or think of, input and output as two separate entities; we must think of the hyphenated term *input-output*. In like manner, we cannot think of perceptual activities and motor activities as two different items; we must think of the hyphenated term *perceptual-motor*.

Just as in our thinking we cannot separate what part of the child's activity in any task, such as copying a figure, is motor and what part is perceptual, in our teaching we cannot separate what parts of the activity are perceptual and what parts are motor. Many successful teaching programs have recognized this fact and have trained all aspects of the perceptual process at one time. If we think in these total-process terms, such activities as teaching a child to balance on a walking board in order to improve his perceptual performance no longer strike us as bizarre. In like manner, it will be obvious to us that attempting to teach in terms of input factors alone overlooks many valuable aids. The total perceptual-motor process should be considered in every learning activity which we set up for the child. Learning experiences should be designed for him in terms of this total process in order to obtain the desired results.

Teaching should be directed toward the total activity of the child in any given task. The total activity includes all four processes: input, integration, output, and feedback. If any of these processes are deficient, we may expect the child to experience difficulty. Classroom teaching, therefore, involves attention to both perception and motor ability, and especially to the very important feedback or matching between them, just as much as it involves attention to integration with its variables of experience and intelligence. Because of the cyclical nature of the process, physical education becomes a part of reading and the too frequent dichotomy between muscular or motor activities and intellectual activities becomes untenable. Since we cannot separate the perceptual and the motor in the processes of the child, we should not attempt to separate them in teaching him.

Eyes and hands must work together. When eyes give the signals, hands must cooperate. Neither can complete the task alone. (Courtesy of Hibbs from Monkmeyer).

MEMORY AND LEARNING

Just as we cannot separate input and output in the perceptual process, we cannot separate the integrative process from the total activity. We have pointed out that the integrative process involves the pulling together and organizing of all of the stimuli which are impinging on the organism at a given moment. In addition, it involves the process of tying together with the present stimulation experience variables retained from past activities of the organism. Many past activities are retained in the organism, not as separate pieces of information, not as independent data, but as alterations in the organism itself (Russell, 1956, pp. 25-26).

It seems probable that experiences which the organism undergoes leave more or less permanent alterations in the function of the neural units themselves (*boutons or synaptic knobs,* Hebb, 1949; Lorente de No, 1947). It is the effect of the accumulation of these alterations upon present perceptual processes which determines the nature of the elaboration of the input which will occur in the integrative process.[1]

Such a consideration makes of memory or learning something much more dynamic than a mere collection of pieces of information. We can stop thinking of memory as nothing more than a storehouse for ideas and data. Under our present thinking, memory and learning are dynamic processes as a result of which all future activities of the organism are modified. As Koffka (1951, p. 227) has pointed out, learning is a true development, not a mechanical addition of performances.

ROTE MEMORY

It is true that we have a type of learning which seems to result in mere storing of isolated pieces of information. We call this *rote memory*. It is the thorn in the flesh of every educator. It is possible, under certain conditions, to make a very restricted modification in the organism, influencing only very specific activities which are themselves as restricted as the modification itself. Thus, these rote memory items can exist in the organism and are called forth only

---

[1]Certain learning theories would not admit of memory as an alteration in the organism; others would ascribe to such alterations a minor role in learning. It would appear, however, that the point of view of Russell, Hebb, and others has sufficiently important implications for education to warrant serious attention.

by very specific stimulation. Their effect upon the total activities of the organism is extremely limited.

This rote memory type of learning, however, is inefficient and minimally useful. Any teacher can describe its problems in detail. Children who learn in this manner are the type who will sit in the class, read the textbook, pass back the information word for word on the tests and examinations, and then, when asked to solve a problem using this identical information, will be completely lost and have no idea of how to proceed.

LEARNING AS A DYNAMIC PROCESS

Opposite of the rote memory type of learning is the much more dynamic learning process which all teachers try to achieve. In this situation, much broader modifications of the organism result. Such learning results in usable knowledge in which large areas of the organism's activity are influenced. Such learning results, not in isolated bits of information, but in major alterations in the approach of the child to the solution of his problems.

It should be pointed out that all learning does not represent the dynamic process described above. Isolated facts are important and their learning by a rote memory process is often necessary. Remembering your telephone number and street address are important items although they cannot be expected to produce any major change in overall response. In like manner, many basic pieces of information must be "committed to memory" by a rote memory process. Many more learnings, however, are more generalized and are maximally useful when they contribute to a large number of behaviors. For example, the quantitative principles of arithmetic are general and, when learned, enter into and influence large areas of the individual's thinking. The basic addition and subtraction facts, on the other hand, are isolated bits of information best learned by rote memory process. They accomplish their purpose when they are integrated with and serve the general quantitative system. They have little use when they exist alone.

It should be obvious that the type of learning which results in broader modifications of the organism cannot be considered independently of the other activities in the perceptual cycle. Such learning is a very definite part of perceptual activity and every perceptual activity results, to some extent, in learning of this kind. We cannot think of learning as something which is turned on or turned off at specific times, as in a school classroom. Learning is a dynamic factor in every activity of the organism. Whenever the integrative mechanism is activated and whenever the feedback demands an alteration in this integrative process, learning occurs. Such learning will then influence subsequent activities of the organism. We cannot, therefore, separate learning and experience from the total perceptual cycle.

NEED FOR CONSISTENCY OF INPUT

It follows from this point of view regarding learning that the experiences of the child must occur in some kind of order. They must be integrated and capable of being combined in such a way that the structuring of the organism which results will produce a total pattern and will give rise to a logical output. From what we have said already, it is apparent that the output pattern can be no more adquate and can be no more generalized in its effectiveness than is the integrative pattern from which it is derived. Essential to the building up of a sound workable structure in the integrative mechanism is consistency of input. Experiences which are similar in nature must come into the organism through the input channel in a similar form. Two identical experiences must not leave different alterations in the organism. If the experiences aιe similar, their alterations must reinforce each other and not conflict with each other.

Illustrative of this problem are those conditions in which inconsistent or transient deficiencies involving the input mechanisms occur. Thus, one slow-learning child was found to have a problem in keeping both eyes working together. When he looked at an object which was beyond arm's length, his eyes worked together properly. As the object was moved in toward his face, somewhere near arm's length, his eyes would break apart and he would see a double image of the object. The distance at which the breakdown occurred was not always the same but depended upon fatigue and his general condition at the time. As a result, he sometimes saw single images and sometimes double. There was little predictability and he could not know which condition would dominate in a given situation or, when the breakdown occurred, which of the two images was the valid one. The result was continuous confusion, particularly in near-point tasks such as school work.

The problem in this case was not so much the defect itself as the inconsistency of the resulting information. Had the child's eyes been uncoordinated all the time, he merely could have learned to suppress vision in one eye and relatively less trouble would have resulted. It was the confusion resulting from the inconsistency which interfered most seriously with his performance. It is probably for this reason that clinicians have noted so frequently that minor defects of the input apparatus give the individual more trouble than a much more major defect appears to cause. The interference caused by the minor defect is transient and interferes with the consistency of the information. The interference from the major defect is always present and therefore can be compensated. (Oppenheimer, 1966).

When we consider the problem of consistency, it becomes apparent that one of the very important variables involved is the input pattern itself. The external sense organ and the control exerted by the child over this organ must be such that they give consistent input for similar experiential situations. Herein lies one of the most important considerations in the area of perception. How consistent is the input into the organism and how is the organism manipulating its sensory receptors to maintain this consistency? How is information from various sense fields collected and how is it matched with the fed-back data of output? Such questions are essential to readiness for school work. They may be of extreme importance in the case of the slow-learning child.

chapter 5

Development of
Form Perception

GLOBULAR FORM

Adults are thoroughly accustomed to seeing the world around them as a collection of distinguishable objects and shapes occupying positions in space relative to each other. We find it difficult therefore to imagine that the ability to perceive our surroundings in this fashion represents a very long and very complicated process of learning. In all probability, the infant organism does not see the world in this way. What the infant sees primarily are vague masses without distinct contour, without recognizable shape, and without definite location in space. In this connection, Harlow (1951) writes, "We would hazard that the only basic perceptual factors are size of differential brightness-hue areas in the perceptual field, steepness of gradients between the parts of the visual fields containing the differential areas, and total boundary extents." What Harlow is suggesting here is that the only things which the newborn infant sees are ill-defined masses which differ from one another only in area, intensity, and perhaps color. None of the aspects of objects which adults are so accustomed to dealing with (form, detail, shape, contour, etc.) are as yet a part of his perception.

It is this vague, ill-defined mass which has been called by Werner (Werner and Strauss, 1939) *globular* form. These masses are characterized by cohesiveness; that is to say, they hold together and appear different from their surroundings. They are not, however, sharply distinguished from the surroundings and do not stand out against it in the manner of a figure on a ground. Their chief characteristic is their cohesiveness. They are primarily undifferentiated and amorphous.

They are characterized by qualities of the whole, by which we mean that their wholeness, or cohesiveness, is their important characteristic. Individual aspects and details are not differentiated or sorted out, and the total form exists only as a totality with no parts or no relationships of parts. As a result, these forms can operate in one way and one way only. The quality of the whole is the only characteristic which they possess.

We have often likened this globular form to a "blob," which is the most descriptive term we have found. What a young child sees when he looks out on the world is probably nothing more than a series of ill-defined blobs having no qualities in and of themselves except their extension and intensity.

Gelb and Goldstein (1938) have recorded the case of an adult who suffered a severe brain damage. In describing the perceptual activity of this patient, they suggested that his visual impressions lacked all specific characteristic structure such as the normal individual is accustomed to experiencing. Instead, this patient's visual experiences were "blobs" from which he obtained only crude impressions, such as vague evidences of heighth, width, and their relationship. It would appear that the perceptual problems of this patient, who, as an adult, could give more direct evidence of his condition than could an infant, are in many respects similar to the visual impressions of the young infant before perceptual development and learning have taken place. Gelb and Goldstein agree with Harlow that such undifferentiated, primitive perceptions do occur. It is reasonable to assume that initial perceptions are thus undifferentiated and that more refined perceptual impressions must wait until learning and development occur.

SIGNAL QUALITIES

One can imagine how the child, looking about him, sees a series of these ill-defined "blobs." Perceptual learning with regard to these blobs begins very early, probably within the first few days of life. The child discovers that one of these blobs is such that the gradients of light which represent it present some characteristic aspect or element (perhaps a bright spot near the top which he will later know as a face or a moving protrusion which he will later know as an arm). The blob possessing this characteristic aspect can be expected to behave in certain ways. It will increase in size and the steepness of the gradient between it and the surrounding area will increase. When the size and steepness of the gradient have reached a maximum, suddenly food will appear in his mouth, certain pleasant sensations will occur from stroking the skin, and certain unpleasant sensations from wetness on portions of the anatomy will disappear. Thus, he learns to identify a characteristic detail in one of these blobs which he finds behaves in a characteristic manner and which is somewhat predictable. As a matter of fact, when he sees this characteristic detail, he can, to a certain extent, control the accompanying blob. If he makes certain noises, the blob can be expected to go through this characteristic set of stages, and all the pleasant sensations will result. He learns to exert this control very quickly, as all parents know.

He soon discovers that other blobs do not behave in this characteristic manner. He can scream his little lungs out, and nothing happens. He therefore differentiates from one of the masses certain characteristic elements which he recognizes as different and which can be used to identify this blob.

Werner (1948) calls the undifferentiated mass *syncretic form.* He refers to that detail which the child differentiates and which he uses for recognition as a *signal quality.* In early stages of learning, these signal qualities may be very limited and may represent only one or a limited number of the many details which we as adults perceive in the object. Shinn (1900) describes the behavior of a six-months-old infant who was given a round rattle one day after he had become accustomed to a square one. The infant accepted the toy and then tried in vain to find the corners on which he was accustomed to chew. The signal quality for "rattle" was present when the toy was handed him but the additional details which would permit him to distinguish this object from other similar objects had not yet been differentiated out of the primitive mass.

The element or elements used as signals for recognition may be any distinguishing characteristic of the mass, such as dark or light spots, sharp changes in contour, or protuberances. Hebb (1949) believes that the most characteristic elements for this purpose are lines and angles. At first, probably only one such element is distinguished, the remainder of the object being still only a blob. Later, more elements will be distinguished by the same process used in distinguishing the former until a large number of single elements characterizing the object has been distinguished. At this stage, we can imagine that these elements are not held together in an integrated fashion but are merely combined additively because of their proximity in the amorphous mass.

Gesell (1940) shows how the child in his early copying behavior reveals with pencil and paper how he is differentiating details one at a time out of a formless mass. Thus, when he attempts to copy a square, the three-year-old makes roughly circular marks which may or may not close. At four years, he may draw a circle or may produce a roughly circular form one side of which is straight, like a *D*. He may also execute one corner correctly, the remainder of the form being vague. At five years, he may draw three corners adequately, and at six years his square has four adequate sides and four adequate corners. He has been identifying and differentiating the details of the form little by little out of what was initially a vague mass.

This process of identifying characteristics of globular masses continues very rapidly. The child probably differentiates one element after another out of the globular form until he has built up a large number of elements characterizing a particular form. This differentiation of elements, or dimensions, or qualities, or characteristics, of globular forms does not occur suddenly but is acquired gradually as individual characteristics are attended to and differentiated out of the mass. It is this type of differentiation which has been stressed by Gibson and Gibson (Gibson, 1953; Gibson and

Gibson, 1955). They have pointed out the importance of this differentiation process and the extent of learning involved. This type of differentiation continues well into adult life and becomes increasingly intense as interest is settled on certain forms or on certain areas of forms.

This differentiation of perceptual elements out of the global whole will proceed to the extent that it is needed by the child. The purpose of the differentiation is to permit the child to identify and recognize the object. When he has differentiated a sufficient number of elements to permit such recognition, the process stops.

It follows, therefore, that, if the child's environment is complex and requires fine judgments between percepts, the differentiation process will be extensive. On the other hand, if the child's environment is sparse and the demands for recognition are limited, the differentiations will be minimal. It is desirable, therefore, to provide the child with a rich perceptual environment so that these environmental demands will motivate extensive differentiations.

There is evidence, however, that such differentiation on the basis of perceptual activity alone is very difficult. It is when the child responds actively to the stimuli through movement that differentiation is facilitated. Active motor exploration may well be required before the necessary differentiations are possible and before they result in valid perceptual elements which can serve as the units of a total form.

The demands of the classroom frequently involve very intricate and very precise perceptual differentiations. In reading, for example, the difference between letters or words is frequently dependent upon identification of minute differences between visual stimuli. Children whose visual perceptual differentiations are limited frequently cannot "see" these minute differences. In such an event, the process of reading may become impossible.

CONSTRUCTIVE FORM

Since the number of details involved in any form may be immense and since the importance of the form involves not only the details themselves but the relationship between these details, the differentiation process which we have described above becomes somewhat complicated. The child winds up with a mass of details about a particular form. To identify the form, he has in effect to sort through all of these details and check them off (present or absent) before he can make a valid judgment regarding the form. This is confusing, uneconomical, and time-consuming. For this reason, he learns to put together those elements which he has differentiated out of the globular mass into a new type of form. We have called this new product *integrated form* or *constructive form*, and it is the type of form perception discussed by Strauss and Lehtinen (1947) and later by Strauss and Kephart (1955). This constructive form is characterized by the organization of the details previously differentiated out of the globular form into an integrated, coordinated unit. When such an integration has been made, there emerges from the mass of detail a new quality which is characteristic of this form only.

Thus, if we are presented with a figure made up of four equal sides and four right angles, we call this a square. The squareness is a very definite quality of the figure which we can recognize at once and which we are very much aware of as a quality. Squareness is unique to this particular set of elements and especially to the relationships between these elements. There is, however, no squareness in any one of the parts. We have four equal lines and in no one of these lines does the quality exist. We have four right angles and in no one of these angles is there any quality of squareness. This quality is inherent in the relationship between the eight basic elements. As such, it is emergent when the elements are integrated in such a way that the relationships are preserved and unique. In the words of the Gestalt psychologist, it is "something more than the sum of the parts."

Similar stages in the development of perception have been stressed by Werner (1957), who lists (1) global, (2) analytic, and (3) synthetic. Russell (1956) speaks of perceptions as changing from "(1) a general, vague impression to (2) differentiation of parts, followed by (3) some sort of integration of the whole again."

If the child is able to put together the elements of a figure in such an integrated and coordinated fashion, he has a much more economical tool with which to manipulate the vast number of elements which he finds in the world about him. Since this emergent quality, this "something more than the sum of the parts," is unique to the square and is a single quality, it can be used to stand for the total figure and all of its parts. Thus, if we can identify a figure as square, this very identification presupposes four equal sides and four right angles. The unique quality of squareness presupposes the parts. Since squareness is a unitary quality, it can be handled psychologically as easily as can any one of the elements. Since it presupposes the direct number and relationship of elements, it can be used as a single act to handle all of the elements involved in this complex. Thus, integrated or constructive form is a highly economical method of dealing with large numbers of elements in our environment at one time.

GENERALIZATION

As has been pointed out, integrated form perception is in the nature of a generalization. The emergent quality of the form is the abstraction of the generalization. Constructive form perception must be taught as a generalization and, if it is learned, it must be learned as an abstraction.

Form recognition should not be confused with form perception. Frequently, we assume that, because a child can tell us that this □ is a square and this △ is a triangle, he is demonstrating form perception. Such simple recognitions, however, can be made solely on the basis of a single element or elements. Thus, if you are asked which of these ⊓, ∧ is a square and which is a triangle, you have no difficulty in making the proper judgment. Only a few elements are presented but, by comparison of these signal elements, you can "distinguish" between the forms even though you have not seen the entire percept.

Frequently, children in our classrooms behave as though they possessed form perception, whereas they are simply manipulating single elements or small groups of elements. It is for this reason that form reproduction is a better indicator of form perception than is form recognition. In the former, all elements of the form must be dealt with in order, whereas in the latter a comparison of elements permits the correct response.

Constructive form perception is a complex process and requires extensive and intricate learning. Care should, therefore, be taken to insure that the child is able to deal with the emergent qualities of form before complex academic tasks, such as reading, are attempted. Drill on recognition, such as flash cards and the like, is not sufficient to produce the necessary learning. The form perception problem should be attacked specifically and the generalization involved in its learning should be recognized. When the form generalization has been achieved, the manipulation of complex forms required in academic tasks becomes possible for the child, and his manipulations are meaningful rather than mere juxtapositions among elements.

LEARNING FORM PERCEPTION

Although the globular form characteristic of the initial stage of perception is innate, the constructive form characteristic of the final stage must be learned. We can obtain some information concerning this perceptual learning process from the studies of Senden (1932) and Riesen (1947). Senden compiled reports of a number of cases of individuals born blind who were given sight by surgical operation in early adulthood. Although these individuals had had contact with familiar objects and had probably built up certain concepts of form through tactual and kinesthetic information, their visual impressions of form were new. Some of these cases were able to see differences between two figures seen together, but in a number of instances, even this ability to identify differences was not possible. Thus, sometimes a patient saw the difference between a sphere and a cube and sometimes he did not. The use of single elements as identifying characteristics is illustrated by the patient who had been trained for a period of thirteen days in discriminating between a square and a triangle. At the end of this extensive learning program, he still could not report the form of these two objects without counting their corners. He had to pay attention specifically to the "signal qualities" he was using before he could identify the object.

Any alteration in the stimulus situation could destroy the recognition of form. Thus, a patient who had learned to discriminate between an egg, a potato, and a cube of sugar and could promptly name these objects could not recognize them when they were put into colored light. The cube of sugar could be named when it was seen on the table but was not recognized when it was suspended by a thread with a change in the background.

These adult patients were experiencing the same type of learning in the area of form perception which we have described in the young child. Their difficulties in the learning process illustrate the learning stages which we can hypothesize are necessary for the young child. It should be pointed out, however, that Senden's studies cannot be accepted uncritically. Adequate controls were not used in all cases and certain relevant observations were not made in a controlled fashion. Nevertheless, in spite of these weaknesses in the study, we can gain from Senden's observations some hints regarding the probable development of the perception of form.

Riesen's study is a report of the visual responses of chimpanzees who were raised in total darkness until an age when the normal animal would have definite visual response patterns. The results of Riesen's observations were very similar to those of Senden and tend to confirm the hypotheses of the former work. Here again, we cannot accept this study uncritically. There are many problems involved in reasoning from the performance of animals to the performance of human beings, and we must be very careful how we attribute characteristics observed in animals to human behavior. However, the study of Riesen also can give us some hints regarding the probable course of perceptual development.

As mentioned earlier, the quality of the whole stressed by Gestalt psychology attaches to both the globular form and the constructive form. In the case of globular form, however, the wholeness derives from its cohesiveness, the fact that it holds together in space. The emergent quality of constructive form derives from the articulation which the child has been able to make among the details. Globular form is characterized by maximum differentiation plus integration between the elements which have been differentiated.

We might be able to understand the difference between these two types of form perception if we use an analogy. Globular form is like a concrete wall. There is no differentiation of parts; it is a total homogeneous mass, possessing no internal characteristics except its cohesivensss. Constructive form is like a brick wall. It is composed of a large number of recognizable units articulated closely together. The concrete wall can be thought of only as a mass; its strength derives from its cohesiveness. The brick wall can either be thought of as a mass or can be analyzed into its units which can be manipulated individually or in groups. Its strength derives from its articulation. Both possess qualities of the whole: "wallness." In the concrete wall, however, this quality is limited to the totality. If we break up this wall, we have only a mass of rubble which cannot be reclaimed. If we break up the brick wall, however, we have a series of units which can be recombined either into the same wall again or into a different structure. The "wallness" emerges from the articulation or integration of the units, the bricks. Obviously, if we have need to construct and reconstruct (as we do in perception), the brick wall is more flexible.

Pieces fit together to form figures, but only if you have learned how to see a form, which is more than the sum of its parts. (Courtesy of H. Armstrong Roberts).

PROBLEMS IN LEARNING FORM PERCEPTION

The construction of an integrated or constructive form, as has been suggested, is a learning task and a very difficult one. Many children experience difficulty at the early stage of differentiating elements from the initial globular mass. They either do not or cannot attend to the details of this mass; hence, these details remain unrecognized. Many more children break down at the higher level where the details, having been differentiated, must be integrated into a constructive form. If this integration fails to take place, the child is unable to deal with a coherent figure in the manner in which we are accustomed to deal with it; instead, he is left with a mere mass of elements which he can manipulate only one at a time or in very small groups. Since he cannot perceive an integrated form, he does not respond to the totality of the elements in a figure but responds to only one or a limited number.

An illustration may make this procedure more clear. We once observed a sixteen-year-old brain-injured child at a summer camp. In connection with the camp activities, the children attended a campfire in the evening. This youngster announced that he would come to the campfire in disguise so that no one would know who he was. At the appropriate time, he appeared in his disguise. This consisted of an old felt hat pulled down over his forehead and a red bandana tied around the lower part of his face. Of course all of the children recognized him at once. He failed, however, to understand why the rest of the children could recognize him when he was disguised in this manner.

On the following evening, another campfire activity was scheduled. During the afternoon, this youngster announced that he was going to be disguised again and that this time no one would be able to recognize him. The time for the campfire arrived and the boy came in his disguise. It now consisted of an old felt hat pulled down over his forehead and a blue bandana across the lower part of his face. This night the children not only recognized him but perceived that this was the same disguise which he had worn the previous night and taunted him with the fact. The youngster was very disturbed. How could they recognize him and why did they think that this was the same disguise that he had worn last night?

He later discussed this problem with one of the staff members. "Why," the adult said, "would you think that the children would not recognize you when you wore the same hat and the same bandana tonight that you wore last night?" The child said, "Oh, no. I wore a red bandana last night and tonight I wore a blue bandana."

This child thought that whenever he changed an element in the situation, he changed the total situation. Unfortunately, in his case this was exactly true. He had not been able to construct an integrated form. He was bound by the elements of a figure, and from his viewpoint changing one of the elements would change the whole. He could not deal with all of the elements in a complicated form, such as the human figure, all at one time. He had to deal with them element by element. He became confused when an element was changed and he could not encompass the variation of minor elements within the total cluster.

The chief characteristic of the child who has been unable to construct an integrated form is his response to elements in a situation rather than to the situation as a whole. We are apt to speak of him as impulsive. In any given situation, he is apt to respond to one item where we would respond on the basis of a collection of items. We must not forget that for him this collection of items does not exist as it exists for us; only one item exists and it is this to which he responds. Since many of the items in the situation may be necessary to the solution of the problem, he will come out with the wrong answer. The modifications of his behavior which should be dictated by other elements in the situation do not take place. We describe him as distractable, impulsive, or uninhibited. All of these behaviors can well be the result of his inability to construct an adequate figure.

THE PROBLEM OF CONSTRUCTIVE FORM

It is very difficult for adults to realize the nature of the world in which such a child lives. For adults, form is so compulsive and so universal that they cannot imagine the situation if it did not exist. We deal with figure constantly. There is never any situation where we are not aware of a figure on a ground, or where we are not aware of numerous figures on numerous grounds. We constantly shift our figure-ground relationship as we change our attention from one point in the situation to another. We cannot imagine seeing four equal lines and four angles without seeing a square. This is why teaching is so difficult with children. We cannot see what they see; we cannot imagine the situation in which they are operating and, therefore, we have difficulty in constructing adequate learning situations to help them.

We can gain some insight into the problems of the child with inadequate form perception if we observe what happens to our own perceptions when the process of form is deliberately interfered with. Figure 7 is similar to items of the Street Gestalt Completion Test (Street, 1931). It presents the silhouette of a common figure. How-

FIGURE 7. Incomplete silhouette. Missing parts must be filled in perceptually and integrated with the parts presented before the form can be detected.

ever, certain parts of the total form have been randomly removed. As a result, it is difficult for us to generate perceptually the missing parts, integrate them with the existing parts, and "see" a dog. If the child has not adequately differentiated the parts of a figure and if the parts do not articulate closely together, he may have much the same type of difficulty with *all* forms which we have with this experimental form.

Note how, before you had the solution to Figure 7, you gave undue attention to the parts. You tried to "make something" out of one or more of the more predominant black areas by themselves. We have said that the child with poor form perception tends to respond to details. You next tried to use one of the predominant areas as a single clue to the whole figure (signal quality). The most difficult task of all was to integrate *all* the areas (plus what

had been omitted) into a total form. Yet it was only from this total
form that a *meaningful* figure emerged.

Figure 7 is only an exaggeration of a problem which confronts
us continually. Seldom do we have the time and opportunity to see
all the elements of a figure. Consider your behavior in reading this
page. You do not take time to see every letter, much less the parts
of each letter. Yet you construct the words from the relatively
small number of elements which you do see. It is similar with most
of our perceptions. We see pieces, as in Figure 7, which we integrate to produce meaningful forms. We can do this quickly and
efficiently because we have learned how to do it. For the child who
has trouble learning form perception, constructing the figure of the
chair across the room or the word on the page may be as difficult
as constructing Figure 7 was for you.

Another method of showing the problem of constructive form is
the "Hidden Figures" technique of Gottschaldt (1926). In Figure
8, the dollar sign with which we are all familiar has been hidden by
the addition of a number of irrelevant details. It is difficult for us
to hold together those elements which pertain to the familiar sign
and keep them separated from the additional elements. The figure
does not stand out from the background.

Here again, we have merely increased the difficulty of a problem
which is always present. Figures do not exist in a vacuum, nor are
they conveniently presented on homogeneous backgrounds. They
are embedded in backgrounds which are themselves collections of
elements. We must perform constantly the same task required in
Figure 8 to keep forms separated from their backgrounds. The child
who has had difficulty in learning form perception may well have
as much trouble with common everyday figure-ground problems as
we have with Figure 8. For this child, the elements of perceptual
figures, whether these be objects or printed symbols, become confused with the elements of the background and a meaningful figure
cannot be held. Of course it is only by holding the figure, well integrated and solid, that any of us keep it separated from the surrounding ground. Any weakness in the figure lets it slip easily and become
confused with the ground. It is often noticeable how frequently the
slow-learning child is disturbed by flaws or spots in the paper on
which he is working — minor background features which are not
even noticed by other children.

FIGURE 8. Hidden Figure. The addition of distracting elements makes it difficult to see a common figure within the pattern.

If we disturb the grouping of elements, we can create a difficulty in our own perception. In the sentence "se eSpo trun," it is difficult for us to recognize the all too familiar "see Spot run" of primer fame. Here we have merely regrouped the phonic elements. For the child, however, in whom difficulty has occurred in forming proper integration of phonic elements in the first place, we may in ordinary written or oral material all too frequently present him unsuspectingly with "se eSpo trun" and wonder why he does not respond. For us, the proper grouping of elements is compulsive; for him, it may frequently be only a matter of chance.

CONSTRUCTIVE FORM AND READING

Let us consider as an illustration the problem confronting a child with form perception problems when he begins to learn to read. In the kindergarten or first grade, he will probably be taught to read by the so-called "look and say" method. This method consists of having the child identify the word as a whole. Certain characteristics of the total word are discovered by the child or, if he has difficulty, may be pointed out to him by the teacher. Frequently, we draw a frame around the word so that these characteristics are shown up more forcefully. Thus, the word *toot* has an element which sticks up at the front of the word and another element which sticks up at the end of the word. By the "look and say" method, the child can identify this word by merely recognizing these characteristic elements. Actually, it is not necessary for him to see the remainder of the word at all. If he can recognize these characteristic elements, he can call the word adequately and pass the reading test.

This kind of task offers little difficulty for the child who is deficient in form perception. He has merely to differentiate out of the globular mass those particular elements which are characteristic of this word. He can then call the word off and nobody is aware that these particular elements are the only ones to which he has paid any attention. As a matter of fact, he is apt to be better at this type of activity than the child who has constructed an integrated form. He is not distracted or misled by any of the intervening elements in this word. Since the characteristic elements are the only ones he perceives, he is never confused by any of the other elements in the word.

A little later on, however, he is going to be taught to read by the "word analysis" method. In this method, he is taught to break the word down into its parts and to sound out the characteristic phonetic elements of each of the individual parts. But how can he break this word down into its parts if it does not have any parts to begin with?

Since there is no integration between these elements, if he pays attention to one, he loses all the rest. Thus, difficulty begins. In order to learn satisfactorily by the word analysis method, it is necessary that the child hold together in a pattern all of the elements of the word, that he pay attention to these elements in serial order but not lose the total pattern. Now our child who is weak in form perception has real difficulty. He is asked to break down into a serial order of parts a globular whole which for him has no parts. He is asked to integrate in time a series of elements which were presented to him integrated in space. But for him they had no integration in space, and therefore he cannot integrate them in time. He is in the predicament described by Vernon (1957, p. 15): "the implications of these studies for reading are that children (or, at least, some children) are less likely to see words as wholes than as meaningless jumbles of details with no apparent relationship between these. On the other hand, letters may perhaps be seen as unanalyzable wholes, and hence there is difficulty in differentiating their structure." Again, Vernon writes, "The one universal characteristic of non-readers suffering from specific reading disability is their complete failure to analyze word shapes and sounds systematically and associate them together correctly" (*op. cit.*, p. 74).

Not only must the child analyze the word form on the page into its parts, but he must associate these parts with the appropriate phonetic sound. Again, Vernon says, "We have no definite evidence as to the incapacity of such cases to perceive and analyze printed words, but it is quite clear that they often fail to recognize that a certain spatial orientation of the letters is essential, and also a particular order and arrangement of the letters within the word. Again, we have no definite evidence that they *cannot* hear the sounds of letters and words, though this may occur in some cases of mild hearing loss and high frequency deafness; but it is probable that many of them do not listen to, and hence do not hear, the separate phonetic units in the total word sound, and do not remember them in their exact order. This may often be due merely to inattention and lack of interest; but sometimes it seems as if they 'are like the deaf adder that stoppeth her ears, which refused to hear the voice of the charmer, charm he never so wisely!' The result is that they are unable to associate the visual and auditory units, because they are uncertain which correspond with which" (*op. cit.*, p. 188).

SENSORY-MOTOR SKILLS AND FORM PERCEPTION

The development of adequate form perception depends upon the adequate learning of basic sensory-motor skills such as we have discussed in earlier chapters. It is obvious from what we have said that constructive form is dependent in large part upon the relationship between elements. In visual perception, at least, these relationships are relationships in space. As we have pointed out earlier, the coordinates of space and hence the coordinates upon which the relationships of form must be built are learned. This learning begins with the development of laterality.

Our first information about form and about the spatial relationships involved in form is kinesthetic and tactual. We must learn kinesthetic laterality before we can proceed to visual form. This laterality must be projected outside of the body in terms of direc- tionality before we have a basis for maintaining the relationships involved in form. We have already discussed in this connection the importance of the control of ocular movements and the use of the eyes as a mediator of the projection of directionality onto visual stimuli. These basic skills are necessary in order to ensure that the relationships involved in a form are presented to the child and that he responds to them in a consistent manner.

His problem is to build up an integrated pattern which will represent the relationships within this figure. If those relationships do not come to him in a consistent fashion, if they vary from one presentation to another, it is obvious that he will experience difficulty in constructing a pattern within himself that will represent a consistent set of relationships. Such consistency in input is ensured by the basic sensory-motor skills which we have discussed in previous chapters.

RELATION OF FORM PERCEPTION TO ACHIEVEMENT

When we can be sure that the child has adequate basic sensory-motor skills, we will need to give him additional help in the development of form itself. It is at this level that such activities as peg-boards, drawing, copying, coloring, paper cutting and pasting, et cetera, become important.

In a study of some 1500 public school children in the first three grades, Lowder (1956) compared the ability to copy simple forms with achievement in school. He obtaind a correlation of .52. This correlation takes on considerable significance when we consider that it is almost identical to the co-efficient usually found when we correlate I.Q. against school achievement in the early grades.

Numerous other workers have observed a correlation between copying ability and achievement. Potter (1949) reported a correlation of .60 between a task of copying forms and reading achievement. When mental age was held constant, this value dropped to .18. Robinson *et al.* (1958) found correlations ranging from .38 to .44 when the Visual Achievement Forms were compared with the Chicago Reading Tests in first-grade children. Interestingly enough, her data revealed the correlation between the Kuhlmann-Anderson test of intelligence and the Chicago Reading Tests to be only .54. Small (1958) compared the developmental drawing performance of kindergarten children with their scores on the Metropolitan Readiness Test. His correlations ranged from .51 to .61. On the basis of these independent studies, it would appear that there is a significant relationship between form perception, insofar as this function is measured by copying performance, and reading achievement (Simpson, 1968).

In addition to these statistical studies, the work of Strauss and Lehtinen (1947) with brain-injured children has shown the importance of form perception. Their clinical studies as well as those of Strauss and Kephart (1955) reveal the relation of form perception to achievement in these children. Clinical evidence from these and other sources indicates that training programs designed to increase form perception ability can aid the child in increasing his achievement level.

chapter 6

Space Discrimination

THE CONCEPT OF SPACE

We have no direct information concerning spatial relationships in our environment. All of our information concerning spatial localization comes to us through some clue which must be interpreted to give us concepts of space. Our most direct information is in the field of kinesthesis or the muscle sense which tells us the degree of relaxation or tension in our muscles. Through this kinesthesis, we can estimate the amount of muscular movement required to make contact with an object. Through this estimate of amount of movement, we can guess the distance to the object. Only through the translation of movement into space, however, do we obtain knowledge of the distance to an object. It is so with all other considerations of space. We translate some other type of knowledge into knowledge of space. We calibrate changes in other sensory fields into scales by which we measure the distance to an object or the distance between objects.

Space is therefore essentially a concept developed in the brain (Craik, 1952, p. 61). It is not like brightness or color which are given to us through direct sensory activities. It is always a second-

143

order sensory datum. Although we think of space or a space world as a substantial, existent reality and although we behave as though we had direct information concerning it, we had in fact to build up this space world for ourselves through the interpretation of a myriad of sensory data none of which was directly connected with space itself.

This entails a serious difficulty. At one and the same time, we must learn to interpret sensory information in terms of space and build up the spatial concepts which make interpretations of these sensory data in spatial terms possible. Thus we have a circular probblem. We cannot develop a stable space world until we learn to interpret the information from our senses in terms of space. However, we can build up this space world only upon the basis of the spatial interpretations of sensory data. If either of these two poles were stable and fixed, we could use it to form the basis of a calibration for the other. Such, however, is not the case. We are required to build both ends simultaneously and in relation to each other. It is not surprising, therefore, that spatial localization and the development of a stable space world prove difficult for many children and even for many adults.

One of the clues to distance is size of the retinal image. The farther away an object lies, the smaller its image on the retina of the eye and, until we can make a spatial interpretation, the smaller it looks. Through learning, we develop, as it were, a scale by which apparent size of the image is translated into distance of the object from the eye. If we knew how far away the object was to begin with, we could calibrate the scale of image size with little difficulty. However, the only way we can know how far away the object is (if we consider, for illustrative purposes, that image size is our only clue to distance), is to observe the apparent size of the image. Thus, we are reduced to making a series of approximations in which the exact interpretation of neither the image size scale nor the distance scale is known. By repeating these approximations many times, we achieve a reasonable collation of the two scales. Both scales vary concomitantly. If one scale could be stabilized, the other could be compared to it and exact translations made. Since neither can be stabilized, only through a complicated observation of co-variance can they be equated. What is true of image size is true of all other clues to distance. The problem is further complicated by the fact that different clues must be matched to each other as well as to objective distance.

IMPORTANCE OF A STABLE SPACE WORLD

The importance of a stable space world can scarcely be overestimated. It is through space and spatial relationships that we observe the relationship between things or objects in our environment. We can only observe these relationships between things insofar as we can locate them in space and hold them in this spatial relationship while we make our observations. We cannot compare two objects unless we have an adequate space in which to put them while we make comparisons.

In an earlier chapter, we discussed the importance of form perception and the manner in which it serves to hold together the elements of a figure so that we can deal with them en masse and can observe the details within the figure for purposes of recognition or comparison. All of the relationships in which we are interested, however, do not occur within figures or objects. More of them occur between figures or objects. This latter type of observation is possible only if we have a space world in which we can place the figures in such a way that the relationships are maintained and can be adequately observed. Thus, space becomes as important as form and for the same reasons. It is through the preservation of relationships between objects in an adequate space world that we are able to observe similarities and differences and to handle the myriad of elements within groups of objects.

IMPORTANCE OF SPACE IN ARITHMETIC

The importance of space is particularly obvious in numbers or arithmetic. Arithmetic, as Strauss and Lehtinen (1947) have indicated, is a visual-spatial problem. Stern (1949) has devised a method of teaching arithmetic based in large part on the spatial concepts involved. Mathematics deals with groups of objects and the characteristics of groups and grouping phenomena. If the child has not developed an adequate space world, he will have difficulty in dealing with grouping phenomena, since groups can only exist in space. It is not surprising, therefore, that we find so many children who achieve adequately in school until they approach the problem of numbers. Here they fail miserably. Since stabilizing the space world is the most complicated of our readiness skills and since it develops last in the series of skills, we may expect to see many children who develop adequately until they reach this final stage and then, for some reason, fail to complete this most highly developed skill. It seems probable that this group of children represents many of the apparently specific arithmetic disabilities which we find in our schools. If Strauss and Lehtinen (1947) are correct, it seems likely that these children have developed adequately until they arrived at the problem of space. Here development failed to continue satisfactorily. They achieve adequately until they arrive at arithmetic where spatial knowledge is at a premium.

IMPORTANCE OF SPACE IN CONCEPTUALIZATION

Most specialists agree that concept formation rests upon a foundation of percept formation. Thus, Zuk (1958) states that we must recognize the close association between perceptualization and proper conceptualization. Perception and learning are not independent phenomena but must go hand in hand. Piaget and Inhelder (1956) point out how the abstractions of space (Euclidean geometry) grow upon the perception of space. Hurlock (1942, p. 285) relates the formation of concepts to the ability to perceive relationships between new and old situations. These are but a few examples of a rather general agreement concerning the importance of adequately organized percepts for the development of concepts and higher orders of thought. The observation of relationships is vital to more advanced thinking. In like manner, a space world in which these relationships between experiences can be preserved is vital to their observation.

The child who has difficulty with space is likely to have similar difficulties in thinking. As we have pointed out, we observe similarities and differences between objects by locating them firmly in space and then observing these characteristics. Such similarities and differences are very important to advanced thinking. Concepts, categorization, grouping on the basis of characteristics, and the like, all involve dealing primarily with similarities and differences. The importance of such categorizing in the thinking process has been repeatedly pointed out by various researchers (e.g., Vinacke, 1952; Welch, 1947). Unless we can compare the characteristics of different objects, we cannot make the judgments upon which categorization is based.

Concepts, which are so important in education, are in effect categorizations in which the common factors are elements within the objects. To develop such concepts, we need to compare many objects, selecting those in which the characteristics forming the basis of the concept are present, grouping these together, and extracting from the group the common characteristic which then becomes the concept. It is such categorization which leads to generalization and abstraction. Unless comparisons between objects can be made accurately, precisely, and in detail, the resulting concept will be weak. To make comparisons between objects, we need a stable and sufficiently extensive space world so that objects for comparison can be held in mind and observed while the relationships between them remain stable.

CLUES TO SPACE

Since the ability to manipulate space is so essential to learning, it is desirable that we look at the clues by which we locate objects in space and see how these are used to develop a space world. As we have said, the most direct clue to space is movement (see Bartley, 1958, p. 207). We move our hand until it comes in contact with an object. Through kinethesis, we estimate how far we had to move and, from this estimate, determine how far away the object is. For greater distances, we move our entire body. Thus, we walk to an object and, from the amount of movement involved, estimate how far away the object was.

Vision, however, is our most efficient indicator of space. Movement is too slow and, in many cases, too difficult to be depended upon for the many and precise estimates which we must make in everyday experience. If we had to make all our estimates of distance through the more direct data from overt movement, time would be too short for us to gather the information on which our behavior must be based. Vision, however, can give us rapid estimates of space and, if we have learned to use it, accurate estimates which we may substitute for those acquired more slowly through movement. Furthermore, vision can give us numerous estimates at once. We can look at a number of objects and locate them all in space simultaneously, whereas, if we depended upon kinesthesis, we would have to locate each object independently. Here again, time would be consumed and accuracy sacrificed to the magnitude of the task. As we will see later, this problem of locating a large number of objects simultaneously in space is a very important consideration in achievement. Vision, alone among the senses, is uniquely fitted for such space structuring.

As we have pointed out above, there is no direct information concerning space. Vision, however, gives us a number of clues which can be used to interpret distance and location in space.

PERSPECTIVE

Perhaps the most commonly considered visual clue to space is that of perspective. We encounter this clue in artists' products and photographs. Those who work with representational objects become adept at creating impressions of distance and depth through the use of this clue. There are certain characteristics of visual data which are related to distance. If an object appears to lie above another, the higher object is probably farther away. If an object overlaps another, the overlapping object is closer. Parallel lines continued into the distance appear to approach each other, and shadow and light distribution indicate depth and position. Any elementary text on sketching or drawing will outline in detail the rules of perspective (Abbott, 1950).

Through observation of these apparently impossible aspects of our visual picture, we come to ascribe different positions in space to the different objects involved. Thus, we learn to interpret perspective in terms of space and so assign each object its proper location in space in such a way that the perspective makes sense.

ACCOMMODATION

The lens of the eye is a marvelous organ. It has the power of changing its shape and thereby changing its refractive power when we are looking at objects at different distances. When you shift your gaze from a distant object to a close one, the lens of your eye changes its shape and its power so that the new object is as accurately focused on the back of the eyeball as was the former. You know that when you take a photograph, you have to adjust the camera lens for the distance to your subject. If you do not, the photograph will be out of focus. The same kind of adjustment must take place within your eye. But in the eye the adjustment is automatic. You have merely to shift your gaze and the new adjustment is made for you without your conscious effort.

This change in the power of the lens is accomplished by the action of the ciliary muscle which holds the lens in a kind of elastic bundle. By relaxing and contracting, the ciliary muscle can squeeze the lens into a thick, stubby shape or let it stretch to a long, flat shape. The thicker the lens, the more its power and, as a result, objects at a nearer distance come into focus.

In the ciliary muscle are sensitive end organs, called *proprioceptors,* which tell us how much tension there is in the muscle. The amount of tension on the ciliary muscle is (with certain exceptions in the case of refractive error) directly related to the distance of the object which is in focus. By observing the tension in the ciliary muscle, therefore, we can estimate the distance of the object. The process by which an object is brought into focus is called *accommodation.* We have, through the proprioceptive end organs in the ciliary muscle, an estimate of the amount of accommodation we are using. This information can therefore give us some idea of the distance to the object. Thus, we get a clue to space through accommodation (Woodworth and Schlosberg, 1954, p. 451).

CONVERGENCE

If we look at an object with both eyes, we must get the same picture in each eye. To do this, we must direct each eye toward the object. Since the eyes are set apart in the head, each eye must be directed differently from the other if it is to center on a particular object. The object, as it were, becomes the apex of a triangle of which the line between the right eye and the left eye is the base. The line of sight of each eye then becomes one of the sides of the triangle.

If an object is far away, the apex of the triangle will be far removed from the base. The sides of the triangle will be nearly parallel and the two eyes will have to point in a nearly parallel fashion to give us a single image of the object. However, if the object is near, the apex will be near the base of the triangle and the sides of the triangle will form a sharper angle with the base. The two eyes will have to point in toward each other to triangulate upon the object and give a single image. Thus, the parallelism between the two eyes alters with the distance of the object being seen.

The eyes are controlled by six muscles attached to the outside of the eyeball. It is through the operation of these muscles that we are able to move our eyes about in their sockets. In these extrinsic ocular muscles, as they are called, are sensitive end organs (more proprioceptors) which tell us how much tension is being placed on each of the muscles. Through the operation of these proprioceptors, we can tell the position of our eyes from the condition of the muscles controlling them. You know that this is true because if you shut your eyes and move them about, you know where they are pointed even though there is no image to tell you. You are receiving this information through the proprioceptive end organs in the extrinsic muscles. Just as we can know where the eyes as a team are pointed, we can know where each eye separately is pointed. Thus, we can tell whether they are nearly parallel or whether they are pointed in toward each other. In this way, we can estimate through these proprioceptive clues the distance of the object of regard.

The process by which we triangulate the two eyes upon an object is called *convergence*. Since we have information concerning the amount of convergence present at any time, we have through convergence a clue to the distance or location in space of an object (Woodworth and Schlosberg, 1954, p. 457).

IMAGE SIZE

The image of an object on the back of the eyeball (the retina) varies in size with the distance of the object. The further away an object is the smaller the size of its image. This is the same phenomenon we see in a camera. When you take a picture, objects which are close by are large on the photograph while objects which are far away are small. The size of the image is a function of the size of the object and of its distance.

Here we have another clue to distance. We learn to interpret the size of the image as a function of distance. If we did not, the man standing on the other side of the street would appear to be a pigmy while the man standing on this side of the street would appear to be a giant. So completely do we learn to make these adjustments that we reach the point where we are no longer aware of differences in the sizes of the images on the back of our eyeballs. Never do we see the man on the other side of the street as unusually small because we immediately correct his apparent size for the distance at which we see him. We must have our attention called to the difference in image sizes before we notice it. However, originally we had to learn this correction. Originally, things which were far away looked small and things which were near looked large. By experimentation and manipulation, we had to discover the relationship between apparent size and distance and to learn to correct size in terms of distance. We have become so adept at this that we omit the intermediate steps and automatically make the translation. We become so interested in keeping our images constant that we forget what we are doing in using image size as a clue to distance and are estimating distance from the apparent image size.

This phenomenon has been discussed in psychology as *constancy of image size* or *size constancy.* It is through the interpretation of inconsistent image sizes that we estimate distance, and thus image size becomes a clue to distance and to location of an object in space (see Bartley, 1958, pp. 215-16).

STEREOPSIS

As we pointed out above, when the eyes are focused upon an object they are not parallel in the head but are turned in toward each other. The further away the object the less they are turned in, and the nearer an object the more they are turned in. Such relative postures are necessary to give a single image of the object because the eyes are separated in the head by the nose. In a previous section, we discussed this posture under the term convergence and we saw how awareness of eye posture or convergence could give us a clue to distance.

There is, however, another effect of this posture of the two eyes. If the eyes are not strictly parallel, the image on the back of one eyeball falls at a slightly different position relative to the center of that eyeball than is the case in the other eye. When the eyes are exactly parallel, the image falls on the exact center of each eyeball. (Because of the shape of the eyeball, which is not a perfect sphere, this is not strictly true. However, the results of the phenomenon are the same, although a correction must be made for the shape of the orb.) When the eyes are not strictly parallel, the image in each eye is displaced slightly toward the outside of center. The more the eyes are turned in, the more this displacement will occur; the more nearly parallel, the less it will occur. As we have seen, the eyes are turned farther in when we are looking at a near object. It follows that, when we look at a near object, the displacement of the two images on the back of the two eyeballs will be greater also. We can interpret this displacement of images between the two eyes as a clue to the distance of the object. This phenomenon is called *stereopsis* (see Bartley, 1958, pp. 229-32).

Stereopsis is the clue to distance (or depth) which is manipulated in stereo photographs. Here two pictures are presented, one to each eye. Neither eye can see the picture meant for the other eye. The two eyes are kept separate either mechanically by a septum (as in the old hand stereoscope) or by polaroid or colored filters (as in stereo movies where the viewer wears special glasses). The two pictures are taken in such a way that the angle of photographing is changed in the way in which the images to the two eyes would be changed. In other words, the two pictures are taken on the sides of a triangle of which the object is the apex. When they are shown separately to each eye, the same type of image displacement is produced which we obtain normally from the triangulation of the two eyes. As a result, the composite single picture which we see appears to have depth.

Stereopsis as a clue to space has been given a great deal of attention experimentally. Tests have been devised, designed on the same basis as the stereoscope or depth photographs, to determine the accuracy of an individual's ability to interpret this phenomenon as a clue to distance. It is this type of test which is frequently referred to as a *depth test* in visual examinations. You may have encountered this kind of test in examinations given by the armed services or even in driver's license testing. Examples of these tests can be found in common testing instruments, such as the Keystone Telebinocular, the Bausch and Lomb Orthorater, or the American Optical Company Sitescreener.

Stereopsis is a very important clue to distance and to relative location in space. If you have looked through a stereoscope, you know the difference which the addition of this clue makes in viewing a picture. Surfaces and elements of figures stand out sharply in depth and the consciousness of three dimensions in space is greatly increased.

MOVEMENT PARALLAX

Another clue to distance which is of great importance has to do with the apparent movement of objects at different distances. Hold two pencils up before your eyes, one at twelve inches and the other at arm's length. Now move your head from side to side. Notice how the nearer pencil appears to move farther and faster than the pencil held at arm's length. This is the phenomenon called *movement parallax*. Whenever we move our head or the position of our eyes, the apparent speed and extent of the movement of objects in our field of vision vary with the distance of the objects. Near objects seem to move far and fast; distant objects seem to move little and slowly.

You may have noticed this phenomenon when driving in a car. As you watch a line of telephone poles down the road ahead of you, you can see that they seem to approach very slowly. As they come closer, they seem to move faster and faster until they rush by the side of the car. We can observe the phenomenon more extensively if, while riding in a car, we detach ourselves from the movement of the car itself and only pay attention to the movement of objects in our visual field. We will then see that a whole world of movement is taking place. Some objects are moving slowly, some are moving rapidly, some are moving to the right, some to the left, some up, and some down. An extremely complicated pattern of movements differing in speed and direction is taking place. If we can attend to the movement patterns only and forget about our own movement, the entire scene becomes unbelievably complicated and confusing. However, when we turn our attention to our own movement again, everything falls into place and makes perfect sense. We have learned to interpret this complicated series of movement patterns in outside objects as a clue to distance, and we use this complicated scheme to help us locate objects in space. For a further discussion of this topic, the reader is referred to Graham (1951), pages 877-82.

TEXTURE GRADIENT

Gibson (1950) has pointed out that any surface which displays texture shows a gradient of size among the texture elements as distance increases. Thus, the apparent size of the individual bricks in a brick sidewalk decreases as the distance increases. The texture of the surface appears coarse when we look at the near portion and fine when we look at the distant portion. Since nearly all surfaces have some kind of texture, this phenomenon, which Gibson has called the *texture gradient,* becomes an important factor in perception. We can use observations of this texture gradient to estimate distance. It becomes a very important factor since it provides us with a sort of scale upon which we can locate a number of objects at once. As we shall see later, the problem of simultaneous location of numerous objects is of great concern in space perception.

These are only a few of the clues to distance which we can obtain through our sense of vision. Many more could be mentioned: atmospheric haze, interpretation of known contours, et cetera. However, the clues discussed above will serve to illustrate our point. For a more complete discussion of space clues, the reader is referred to Graham (1951). There are three important points to note concerning all of these clues as well as those others which we have not mentioned. They are learned, none is adequate in itself, and they must be extrapolated.

LEARNED CLUES

As we have repeatedly stressed, the relationship between any of these clues and distance is a function of learning. Initially, we do not get information about distance directly from the clue; we had to learn to interpret the clue in terms of distance. Each of the clues is a variable in the visual data. That is to say, something in the visual datum changes, something is altered. It is this alteration or change which gives us the information about distance. Since space does not come to us directly but is inferred from changes in visual impressions which we must learn to interpret, any clue to distance or space is the result of a process of learning—learning to see changes in visual data as distances.

MULTIPLE CLUES

The second point of importance is the fact that no one of these clues is adequate in itself to give us accurate information about distance. Woodworth and Schlosberg (1954, p. 464) point out that any actual experience of depth involves several of these factors. The data from several clues are, so to speak, fed into a depth-perception computing machine. The final judgment is the result of a process in which the single factors are not merely added together but are weighed and balanced against each other. If we try to make our spatial judgments on the basis of only one clue, regardless of which one, we will be limited and inaccurate in our estimates. Any one clue suffers from two difficulties: it is limited in its extent, and it includes certain distortions over parts of its range. If we depend solely on a single clue or a simple addition of clues for our spatial judgment, we are at the mercy of these limitations and distortions.

We can see this fact most clearly perhaps in the case of perspective. We all know how artists and others trick us with false perspectives. Short objects can be made to look tall and wide objects to look thin by manipulating perspective. We can change the apparent distances of objects by changing the perspective and, in the case of illusions, we can even confuse the spatial relations by confusing the perspective. This perspective clue to space can be distorted, not only by outside manipulation, but in the natural course of events in our everyday life. If we depend on it alone for our estimates of space, we will often be deceived into making false judgments.

What is true of perspective is also true of all the other clues. Accommodation and convergence are limited. When an object lies somewhere beyond fourteen to twenty feet, our accommodative

mechanism is completely relaxed and no more clues from this phenomenon occur. In like manner, our convergence mechanism is
so nearly parallel beyond fourteen to twenty feet that no further
observable changes are present. Therefore, these clues are operative
only over a limited distance. Image size is variable. It does not
follow a straight line curve but the apparent changes alter at different
distances. Furthermore, the interpretation of image size is dependent upon knowledge of the object at which we are looking. After
all, the man on the other side of the street *may be* a pigmy. Used
alone, this clue can therefore distort our judgment and give us false
impressions. Stereopsis is another phenomenon which is operative
only over a limited distance (fourteen to twenty feet). Furthermore,
it is a phenomenon of two eyes and is useless whenever, for any
reason, one eye cannot see the target.

No one clue to distance is adequate in itself. We must combine
all these clues into one complicated total impression from which
we make our judgments. Through learning, we come to know how
to depend more on one clue in one situation and on another in
another situation. We discount the evidence of one clue at one time
and discount the evidence of another clue at another time. We
emphasize one clue now and discount it later. We *integrate* all this
information, sorting out the limitations and inaccuracies by weigh-
ing one clue against another and, from the total impression, form
a judgment. Our final judgment is based on a set of corrections and
summations resulting from all this evaluating and re-evaluating. The
accuracy of our final estimate depends on how well we can complete
this complicated process of integration of data.

EXTRAPOLATED CURVES

As we have mentioned earlier, our most direct clue to space is
movement, particularly that of the hand. In the process of learning
all the complicated relations between visual changes and distance
which we have been discussing, we can make direct comparisons
through that distance within which we can reach. In the case of
image size, for example, we can compare the apparent size of the
object with its known distance when we are holding it in our hand
and moving it away from us. When we reach arm's length, however,

we can no longer obtain direct information about distance. We can observe directly that the image gets smaller at a given rate as we move it further away until we reach arm's length. Beyond arm's length we see another image of the same object and it is smaller than any we have seen before. We assume that this is because it is still further away than the distance through which we can reach. However, we can have no direct evidence, and can get no direct confirmatory information.

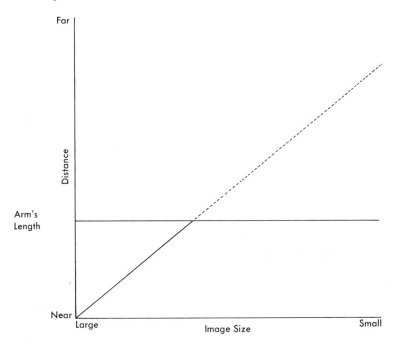

FIGURE 9. Extrapolation of a curve required to evaluate image size as a spatial clue beyond arm's length.

All we can do is project the curve of change in image size with distance, as we have been able to observe it directly within arm's length, to points beyond which direct investigation is possible.

In Figure 9, which is a schematic representation of this task, we can obtain the values on the vertical axis through hand activity up to arm's length. Beyond that point, we have no information about the values on the vertical axis. We can obtain the values on the horizontal axis through a much greater distance, but we cannot compare the two values beyond arm's length. What we must do, in effect, is to draw the curve through the distances where we have all the values (both vertical and horizontal axes) and then project the curve (dotted line of Figure 9) beyond this point. Mathematically, we call this *extrapolating a curve*. On the basis of complete knowledge over a part of the area, we construct the relationship and then project it beyond the point where information is complete.

Obviously, this process of extrapolation is relatively simple as long as the curve is a straight line as in Figure 9. However, as we have seen, many of the curves representing the relationship between visual changes and distance are not straight lines. As a result, a very extensive and exacting process of learning is necessary to make the proper extrapolations. Furthermore, in many of these clues there are other factors which enter the picture to distort the curves under certain circumstances. We are therefore faced with the necessity of making more than one extrapolation, using one under certain circumstances, another under other circumstances. Also remember what we have said about combinations of clues. It is necessary to evaluate the curves representing each of the clues together, since we must integrate all the information before making a final judgment.

The process of learning space localization is a very complicated one. It begins early in life and continues through adulthood. Even as adults we are still revising and re-evaluating our spatial judgments. Many of us give up and live in a limited spatial world. Our achievement is adversely affected as a result. It is not surprising that the young child has so much trouble with this complicated learning problem. He begins sorting out these clues as soon as he becomes mobile and can experiment with his hands. He continues to elaborate this learning actively for the rest of his life. There is evidence that one of the major learning problems of the kindergarten child has to do with this process of developing spatial localization for the objects and things around him.

SPACE STRUCTURE

The problem of spatial localization is further complicated by the fact that in daily life we are not confronted with a single object, but with a multiplicity of objects. Our space concept depends upon our ability to locate these many objects in space simultaneously in such a way as to preserve the relationships between them. In this manner, we develop for ourselves a space structure or *space lattice* in which we spot each of these objects in its proper relationship to ourselves and to each of the other objects. All of the complicated processes which we have described above must be carried out a large number of times, but it is not sufficient that we locate a single object and then forget it. To preserve the space structure, we must retain in the central nervous system the results of a given localization while we add to it additional localizations of other objects existing in our spatial milieu. None can be omitted, none can be added, and none can be replaced. If such errors occur, we will make similar errors in our behavior.

Bartley (1958, pp. 205-6) makes a similar point when he distinguishes two types of behavior in space. The first of these is encountered in animal behavior where the animal has to deal with items in space one at a time or in sequence. He must move about in space and find his way from place to place but does not need to react to all the items in his space world at once. This type of behavior deals only with restricted portions of space at any given time. The second type of behavior is that in which the organism responds to space as a whole. Bartley refers to such space perception as a *space domain*. The organism responds to space as a whole, to the extensional space domain as a domain, rather than to single bits of it.

DEVELOPING A SPACE STRUCTURE

Many slow-learning children reveal by their behavior an inability to respond on the basis of this total space domain. The young child arrives at a space structure through a process of development. First he locates objects singly with reference to himself and only later develops a system of objective coordinates by which he can handle numerous objects in space through a system of fixed directions (see Piaget and Inhelder, 1956). In estimating spatial relations, the child may be able to tell you how many steps it will take him to walk over to object a and how many to walk over to object b. However, he may have no idea of how many steps it would take to walk from a to b when he himself is located at a point removed from the two objects. Furthermore, he may have no idea of how to begin such an estimate except by walking over to one of the objects and thus putting himself in its position. In this manner, he changes the problem to the more simple one of estimating the distance from himself to the object. Such children have learned space localization but not space structure. They have not attained the space domain of which Bartley speaks.

Freeman (1916) suggests that the child first locates objects in space with reference to himself, then later with reference to a second object with whose location he is familiar, and finally by means of a system of fixed directions. It is only in the last stage that a space structure becomes possible. Many slow-learning children have found their development blocked before this last stage was reached. Their behavior, particularly in the area of abstraction and generalization, suffers as a result. They require special assistance to permit them to develop a stable space structure with which to stabilize the relationships which surround them.

If this space structure is to be maximally useful, it must be comprehensive and complete. It is not enough that we preserve localizations for the particular objects to which our attention is directed, but we must at the same time retain impressions of the localization of objects which are not at the moment in the focus of our attention. Thus, as I sit in a room and direct my attention to a table at the far wall, I must be able to localize this table with reference to myself, with reference to the far wall of the room, and with reference to the side walls, the ceiling, the floor, etc. At the same time, I must retain impressions of the desk before me and its location with reference to myself and with reference to the table which at the moment is the center of my attention. If I shift my attention from the table to the desk itself, I cannot permit my previous localization of the table to disappear and be finished. I must retain an impression of the table and its location while my attention is concerned with the desk and objects upon it. Thus, in order to develop an operative spatial structure, we must be able to shift the focus of sharp localization from one point to another as our attention is directed to one object after another, but it is very important that as our attention shifts in this manner, the localization of the remaining objects does not completely disappear. In other words, we must set up a complete spatial structure for any environment in which we find ourselves, simultaneously locating each object in relation to ourselves and in relation to every other object.

SPACE STRUCTURE AND FORM PERCEPTION

It can be seen that the problem of a space structure is similar to the earlier problem of form perception. Just as we had to learn to put the elements of a figure together into a constructive form, we must learn to put the objects around us together into a space structure. In this sense, space structure is a highly elaborated form. Just as we could deal more easily with elements by the use of form, we can deal more easily with objects through the use of space. Just as we use form to observe similarities and differences *within* objects, we use space to observe similarities and differences *between* objects.

PROBLEM OF COMPLETE SPACE STRUCTURE

This problem of spatial structure becomes particularly significant in respect to objects which lie behind us. In our everyday life, we are aware of the objects behind us and of their relationship to us and to each other, just as we are aware of the objects in front of us and their relative locations. We cannot, of course, see the objects behind us. We have very little information concerning their spatial relationships or even their existence. However, we know they are there and our space structure exists behind us in the same fashion that it exists in front of us. Through the use of this structure, we are able to turn around and still respond immediately to the objects behind us which we cannot see.

The young child, however, finds it difficult to build up this space structure behind him. If you have ever seen the toddler attempting to sit down on a footstool, you have seen the problem illustrated. He is not sure that there is anything behind him nor is he sure of its exact location. He cannot behave with certainty until he can feel the object on which he is attempting to sit. He also has difficulty in bringing his body into proper contact with this object after he has located it with his hands. The space behind him is not structured yet, and he cannot respond to objects and information behind him in the manner in which we adults, who have developed such a complete spatial structure, can respond. We see this problem very clearly in the case of certain retarded children who, at a later age and at a higher stage of general development, experience the same sorts of problems as the toddler trying to sit on the stool. Space behind them does not exist. When they turn their backs, objects and situations go out of existence for them.

THE EUCLIDEAN SPATIAL SYSTEM

The spatial system most frequently used is that of Euclid. It is a space of three dimensions: vertical, horizontal, and fore and aft. It should be pointed out that this is not the only possible system. Mathematicians deal with a space of n dimensions and Luneburg (1964) has described a space in which the dimensions are curved. However, the Euclidean system is the one most commonly employed and the one which forms the basis of the activities which we present in classrooms.

The first aspect of the spatial system is its point of origin. The only constant among all the relativities among objects in space is the force of gravity. This force, therefore, becomes the point of origin for the space system. This point of origin is represented geometrically by the point of intersection of the three planes representing the three dimensions of space. It is a mathematical point having only location, no extension.

The first learning problem for the child is that of locating this point of origin for the space system. This he achieves by abstracting from his learnings in balance, posture, and in body image the nature and location of the force of gravity. As we pointed out, gravity must become an abstraction for it is only through its abstract quality that it achieves the aspect of a mathematical point. If the child's concept of gravity is an area rather than a point, his space system will be vague since its point of origin is a variable. This explains our interest in the child's relationship to gravity because of its significance to his developing space system. Upon the generalization of this relationship and its constancy will depend the stability of that system.

The vertical dimension of space derives directly from the direction of the line of gravity. Its direction is toward the center of the earth. You will remember when, as a child, you were first told the earth was round and was revolving on its axis. You argued that this could not be, since, if it were, you would be upside down part of the time. The answer lies in the fact that the vertical is the direction of gravity, it is not an objective, outside direction.

We are therefore concerned that the child be able to identify the direction of gravity and that he appreciate the constancy of this direction. He should be aware that, when his body changes its relationship to the earth's surface, the direction of gravity remains the same even though its direction through his body has changed. He must be aware that his body has moved in relationship to gravity and that the vertical direction has remained constant. He must have the impression of his body turning, not the environment turning around him.

The direction of gravity must be abstracted as a line through his body. If it remains a vague cylindrical area encompassing the mass of his body within it, the vertical dimension will remain vague since the location of the vertical plane is variable through the distance represented by this mass. Through the refinement of body image, the force of gravity is abstracted so that it becomes a mathematical line through the body with a constant direction irrespective of the position of the body.

The horizontal dimension of space derives from the concept of laterality. The right-left gradient developed within the body is projected onto outside objects through directionality. The resulting projection becomes the horizontal dimension of space for the child. Such projection begins with spatial relationships within arm's length where the projection can be checked by kinesthetic information from the moving hand (Gesell, et. al. 1941). When the projection has been refined through such confirmation, visual data are used to project the same right-left gradient into space beyond arm's length where no such direct confirmation is possible.

The fore and aft dimension of space is provided through the clues to depth perception discussed above. These clues must be integrated so that the resulting synthesized information forms a continuum. This continuum provides the third dimension of space.

When the dimensions of space have been established, they are welded together into a spatial system in which the three planes intersect at a common point. Objects are now located not in a single dimension alone but in all three at once. It is only through such three-dimensional location that the stability of objects in space can be preserved. If one or more of the dimensions is unstable, the position of the object will seem to vary on this dimension. It cannot, therefore, be stabilized and maintain a fixed position.

When objects can be stabilized in space through a three-dimensional system, they can be stabilized in relation to each other. Each object is located and, since it becomes stable, can be maintained in space while the other object is located and stabilized. With both objects fixed, the difference between their positions can be observed. While either object is unstable, such relationships cannot easily appear.

When the spatial system has been expanded so that it encompasses a wide range of space, all the objects in the child's immediate environment can be located at one time. All are stable and all are fixed in relation to each other. Activities and learnings involving the relationships between objects now become possible. To the extent that the child's system is extensive and stable, such learnings can become comprehensive.

Most of the activities of the classroom are dependent upon manipulating the relationships between objects in space. The most obvious example is the field of numbers and arithmetic. "Threeness" is not inherent in objects themselves. It is inherent in the relationship between objects. Threeness is a grouping in space and is independent of any aspect of the objects except their spatial relationships. A group of people are three by virtue of the fact that they become related in some way in space. All other variables, age, sex, height, weight, color, et cetera, are irrelevant to this mathematical concept. It is this principle of grouping which makes arithmetic intelligible to the child. Without it, arithmetic is merely a series of rote memory facts. The difference between ability in arithmetic computation and arithmetic comprehension is frequently a function of the extent to which the child can understand the principles of spatial groupings. Without a stable space system, such groupings are difficult to construct or to maintain.

When the spatial system is adequate to handle the relationships within the child's immediate environment, it is abstracted to include relationships beyond his immediate perceptual awareness. Thus the distance from New York to Chicago becomes meaningful to the child and obtains its meaning from the same system with which he handles the distances within the room in which he sits. Out of such an extended system the principles of geometry and trigonometry and similar subjects can emerge. The system has generalized to include a much wider environment and to permit him not only to deal with the concrete objects which surround him but also to deal with his memories and past experiences, his abstract thoughts and concepts, within the same overriding system of space.

IMPORTANCE OF SPACE STRUCTURE

Obviously, the development of a spatial structure is a particularly difficult and complicated problem. In proportion to its difficulty and its complication, however, is its importance. As philosophers and scientists have pointed out, the only information which we get from the outside world is relative. We do not get absolute information through our sense organs about objects or events occurring outside us. Our only information is in terms of relationship (see Vernon, 1952, pp. 3 ff). We see and respond to objects in relation to other objects. We do not respond in terms of absolute values. For this reason, it is absolutely essential to the accuracy of our information about the physical universe that we be able to maintain at all times, and with great precision, the *relationships* between objects. These relationships are maintained through the development of a space structure and through the use of space structure maintain stable relationships between the objects which lie around us. Without such a space structure, we lose or distort many of these relationships and our behavior suffers from inadequate information.

OCULAR MECHANISMS

We have suggested in the discussions above that our localization of objects in space is the result of input signals on the basis of which an image of the object is generated in the cortex. This image is then projected out into space. In effect, we are putting things into space where they belong. Information concerning spatial localization is not direct information but is derived from the manipulation of sensory signals which come to us. The only way in which we can create impressions of objects in space is to project the elaborations of these sensory inputs into the space surrounding us. Most important in this process is the visual avenue. We do not, of course, get all of our sensory information through vision, but, as stated earlier, vision gives us the most efficient set of clues for spatial information and therefore the normal individual depends to a very great degree upon visual information for his spatial judgments.

The only way in which we can accurately project the visual images into space is to project the image along the same line of sight by which the input signals came to us. Visual input is carried along a light ray. We know that light rays travel in straight lines. We therefore determine the angle of the ray which brought the information to us and project the image along that same light ray. In this manner, we place the image accurately in space. Obviously, it is very important that we know with great accuracy the angle of the incident light which has brought us the visual information. As indicated earlier, the only zero point for localization of anything in space is our own body as the point of origin of the spatial coordinates. Unless we can know with accuracy the angle of incidence, with reference to our own body, along which the information came to us, we will be unable to project the image into its proper position since we will not be sure of the angle of projection.

This information concerning the source of light is given to us through the external ocular muscles. As we know, these muscles control the position of the eye in its socket and, through sensitive end organs in the muscles themselves, return to us information concerning the relative position of the eyeball. Through the operation of these muscles and their proprioceptive end organs, we know in what direction our eye is pointed. We have stressed earlier that learning to control these eyes is a very complicated and very exacting task. The degree of accuracy required is extreme. The young child has difficulty in learning to control the movements of his eyes. He is not able accurately to move the eyes to a position where he wants them. He does not have complete information concerning the direction in which they are pointed. He is not able to direct them accurately toward an object which has attracted his attention, nor is he able to keep them focused on a moving object. Instead of being smoothly and constantly under control, his eyes move in a jerky and uncontrolled fashion. The infant frequently displays a condition in which the eyes "wander about." This is not only true with reference to two eyes together, but may be true of either eye separately. We call this condition *strabismus*. In the infant, it is due to the fact that he has not yet learned how to direct his eyes purposefully toward an object or how to use these eyes to maintain an object in the focus of his vision. Slightly older children have learned to keep the eyes together and do not show such extreme deviations. However, many of these older children show inaccuracies and inadequate control when the visual demands are increased.

One result of inaccurate control of the eyes is insecurity in space. The child is not sure where his eye is pointed, and he is not confident of the location of an object in space, because he is not confident of the line of sight along which he is to project this image. Therefore, accurate and precise control of the extra-ocular muscles is essential to the development of spatial localization and particularly to the development of the space structure which we discussed earlier.

LEARNING OCULAR CONTROL

We frequently need to provide the child with additional help in the problem of learning ocular control. He must learn first to control the eyes themselves as an organ. He must learn to control each eye separately, and he must learn to put the two eyes together as a team. He must also learn to match the information about changes of eye position with the information which he gets from his hand about changes in motor movements. He must arrive at the point where he can substitute the movement of an eye for the movement of a hand and, because these are accurately matched, where he can obtain the same information from the eye movement that he previously obtained from the hand movement. As distances increase, he must learn to calculate the lateral distance subtended by a given angular movement of the eye and must be able to calculate this as a projection on the lateral movement of the hand in angular separations of lesser distance. He must learn to do with his eyes alone what formerly he did with his hand and arms and total body. This is possible only insofar as he matches precisely and accurately changes in the location of the eyes with changes resulting from movement of all of the other parts of his body. Obviously basic to this precise type of matching is highly accurate, highly precise, and highly efficient control of the eyes as an organ.

It must be stressed that the problem with which we are dealing here is one of learning to control a mechanism which is in perfect working order. There are certain pathological conditions in the eye and in the musculature of the eye which make it difficult or impossible for the child to make necessary eye movements. These conditions are medical problems and should be treated by medical techniques. Neither are we concerned here with weaknesses in eye muscles. These, too, are problems for the professional eye man. Our concern is with the child who has adequate ocular machinery but who has not learned to use it efficiently. The eye and its muscular attachments work adequately; what the child must learn is how to generate a pattern of neurological impulses which will control this mechanism with precision. This latter type of learning is a skill and can be taught in the same way as any other skill.

In like manner, we are not interested in teaching a neuromuscular skill for the sake of highly skilled performance alone. We are interested in ocular skills only in terms of the perceptual information which they can provide us. We must therefore teach control, not for its own sake, but by perceptual information for the sake of elaborating and standardizing this information.

chapter 7

The Time Dimension

The foregoing discussions have laid the foundation for the development of the three dimensions of Euclidian space. We have seen how the child's orientation to gravity provides the point of origin for the Euclidian system and how his awareness of the direction of gravity provides the vertical dimension. Laterality has been used to provide the lateral dimension and depth perception has completed the triaxial complex.

We then go to the mathematician and say "Have we not done well? We have provided the child with the three dimensions of space. We have helped him organize these into a space structure with which he can simultaneously account for all the relations between and within the objects in his environment. Is not our task now complete?"

"Not so," says the mathematician. He turns to the chalkboard and puts a dot in the center of it. "You have located this point," he says, "on the three axes of Euclidian space. You have constructed three planes, the intersection of which is a point which coincides with my dot. You have, therefore, defined the point in immediate space but you have not located it."

With this he turns and with one sweep of the eraser, removes the point. "You see," he says, "it is not there. You did not locate the point permanently. It was not there yesterday and it is not there now. To locate the point permanently, you must consider the variable of time.

"You must know, not only where the point is in terms of the three dimensions of space, but also where it is in time. In this sense, time is a fourth dimension of space and, before we can permanently locate any point, we must not only know where it is on the three Euclidian dimensions but also where it is on the time dimension.

"Before your child can systematize the relationships which surround him, you must give him a time dimension as well as the three spatial dimensions. The relationships which constitute the universe in which we live exist in four dimensions, not in three alone."

We turn, therefore, to the philosopher and raise the question, "What is time?" The philosopher produces many words but appears not quite ready to answer the question.

He describes two types of time: a static time involving relations of precedence and subsequence among events (McTaggart's B-series); and a dynamic time involving relations of pastness, presentness, and futurity among events (McTaggart's A-series) (McTaggart, 1927).

The first of these we might describe as historical time: a fixed sequence of events which have occurred. Historical time would appear to terminate at the present moment, since no fixed series can be known to us at any point future to the present moment. The present in historical time would seem to be a variable point. At any moment in the past, certain events in the historical sequence were past, some were present, and some were future. Thus, in 1790 the Revolutionary War was past but the Civil War was future. The pastness, presentness, or futurity of any event in the series is relative to the point which the observer chooses to call present.

The historical novelist arbitrarily selects such a relative point which will be the present in his story. He then develops his plot from this point, events assuming the characteristics of past, present, and future accordingly. Events subsequent to this present do not, at the moment of telling, exist. Once past, the order of events is fixed in historical time. When we experience historical time, we start with an arbitrary present. The true present is the termination of historical time.

The second type of time we might describe as experiential time. It is the "flow" of time whereby events of the future pass through the present and become past. In experiential time the present is fixed and the sequence of events is seen as extending in either direction from this fixed point. Those which are past are known; those which are future are unknown or may be predicted; those which are present are directly experienced. There is a continuous inexorable flow of events along this temporal direction which cannot be interrupted nor reversed.

The problem with experiential time lies in the fixed present. This present is a mathematical concept, like the mathematician's point in space, and hence has no extent. It can be divided into an infinite number of smaller and smaller units. Thus, the present has no finite existence and has caused some philosophers to suggest that it does not exist and, hence, only historical time has reality (McTaggart, 1927).

Attempts have been made to suggest a finite extension for the present moment. These have usually taken the duration of the sense impression as the basis for such extension (Mabbott, 1951). It would seem, however, that the experienced present is somewhat longer and more elaborate than the immediate sensory stimulation.

It is possible that the structuring of the central nervous system on the basis of experience may offer a solution to the dilemma. This structure subtends in one integrated system past events from memory pertinent to the present problem, an integrated array of present sensory information, and a series of alternate responses permitting prediction. When this elaborate system fires, we have past events, present stimulation, and future prediction present in consciousness at the same time. All are in an orderly array although the temporal sequence of the experiences involved is not necessarily preserved.

The activation of such a system might, therefore, be thought of as expanding the ephemeral present of the philosopher into a finite temporal interval (Figure 10). The experience at any instant of time welds together immediate past events as these are pertinent, the various displays of present information (which are not temporally finite), and anticipations of future events into one overall canvas which we know all at once and to which we react as a whole. We know where we have been, where we are, and where we are going.

In effect, we then wait for the future to happen and fulfill our predictions. If it does, we have a sense of familiarity (I have been here before). If it does not, we have a startled feeling which leads to a redistribution of the structure and a reprocessing of the data.

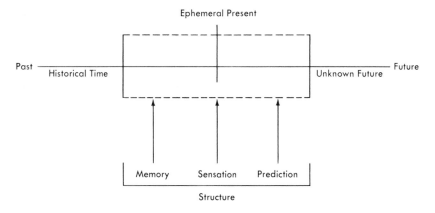

FIGURE 10. The ephemeral present of the philosopher is expanded through the learned structure into a finite range.

Within the limits of the structure, therefore, the present is an interval stretching from the most remote event encompassed by the structure to the most future event which can be predicted with certainty. The temporal present is created through the structure. The more elaborate the structure, the more extended the present. The more limited the structure the more instantaneous is the present.

The child who has built a limited central nervous system (CNS) structure usually has difficulty with time. Yesterday, today, and tomorrow are all the same to him. He cannot predict future events but asks us over and over, "When are we going to school?" He cannot recount events of the past but gets them all confused with present happenings. When he does recall, he mixes up the sequence of past events. He lives in the instant present where the immediate stimulus leads to the immediate response and is effected neither by the past nor the future. This is why he insists on a strict routine. He requires that *we* pattern temporal events for him since he cannot do it for himself. He is asking for an historical time sequence, which is projected into the future for him, because his experiential time is too ephemeral for him to grasp.

If the child is to manipulate this expanded present, he requires a temporal structure similar to the spatial structure discussed earlier. He needs to develop a temporal dimension similar to the spatial dimensions on which he can locate the series of events representing his present and which he can extrapolate backward into the past and forward into the future. As is the case of the spatial dimensions, the temporal dimension must not only provide for the location of an event in time but also it must provide for the preservation of the relationships between events in time. It must have the qualities of a structure so that temporal events can become stable.

SIMULTANEITY

The point of origin of the temporal dimension is *simultaneity*. We cannot appreciate temporal extent until we appreciate temporal simultaneity: events in which the temporal interval between them is zero. Therefore, the zero point on the temporal scale is simultaneity just as the zero point on the spatial scales was the center of gravity.

Simultaneity is first experienced motorically. Two movements are made *together*. Much activity in the infant is simultaneous. As he lies in the crib, his two arms or his two legs move together; both sides go off at once. This movement is contrasted with the sequential flow of activity resulting from the sweep of the generalized movement. Later, when he begins to sort out his two sides, contrasting simultaneous movement with alternate movements, he pounds the table with both hands together; then he pounds alternately with the right hand and the left. By contrasting the movement of parts *together* with their movement in succession, he develops the concept of simultaneity. The foundation for a temporal dimension has been laid. He can now go on to distinguish between auditory events or visual events which occur together and those which occur successively.

It is important that this zero point on the temporal scale become a true zero. Any time interval between events considered simultaneous must be infinitely small. Events considered simultaneous must truly happen *together*. Otherwise the temporal dimension will be loose and unstable just as the spatial dimensions were loose and unstable when the child's awareness of the center of gravity was not sharp and clear.

Many children have difficulty establishing a true simultaneity. When they jump with both feet together, one foot comes down ahead of the other. When they jump off of an object, they have trouble jumping with both sides together. They tend to step off rather than jump off. In the double circles task of the Purdue Perceptual-Motor Survey (Roach and Kephart, 1966), one hand moves faster than the other and finishes first. In "jumping jacks," the arms do not reach extension at the same time that the legs do. Such children frequently will be found to lack an awareness of temporal simultaneity.

The above can be considered a static form of simultaneity. The athlete demonstrates a more dynamic form of simultaneity which he calls "timing." As a movement is in progress, he institutes a response at a precise instant of this progress. In coming to a handstand on the parallel bars, he first performs a shoulder swing. At the exact top of the swing, he performs a "kip" which, if properly timed, brings him up onto his arms without the use of effort or strength. He has synchronized, through simultaneity, his response with a precise point in an on-going activity.

Coordination thus becomes important to the development of simultaneity. Attention to the synchrony in coordinated performances provides data for the concept of simultaneity. Activities designed to promote coordination can, therefore, be helpful in aiding the child in the learning of the first phase of time. As in so many other learnings it is the contrast between simultaneous movements and sequential movements in the coordinated performance which leads to a clear, sharp knowledge of simultaneity which can be abstracted and, as an abstraction, can form the basis of a temporal dimension.

RHYTHM

The unit of extension on the temporal scale is supplied by rhythm. Rhythm involves the awareness of equality among temporal intervals. A constant rhythm is a series of equal temporal intervals. Since these intervals are equal, they can become units on a temporal scale just as feet and inches, by virtue of their equality, become units on a spatial scale. The primary prerequisite is consistency from one unit to another. This consistency is supplied by rhythm.

We have taught rhythm in kindergartens and the elementary grades for many years. (Foster and Mattson, 1939; Cratty, 1964; Hall, 1960; Frostig, 1970; Andrews, 1954.) The principle concern has been its use in music, dance, and similar activities. Seldom has it been approached as a basic element in the development of a temporal dimension. The concern has been more for the teaching of complex rhythmic patterns (a temporal memory function) rather than the teaching of a stable constant rhythm (a temporal dimension function). Yet Carton (1963) and others have shown that among poor readers there is a very high percentage of problems with simple, constant rhythms.

No one knows what rhythm is. There have been numerous attempts to relate it to fundamental physiological rhythms, such as heart beat, respiratory rhythm, and even the alpha ryhthm of the Electroencephalogram. None of these explanations seem completely satisfactory. Although we do not know precisely what rhythm is, we can recognize its failure and can increase its effectiveness through educational activities.

Many children with learning disabilities lack a consistent rhythmic pattern. When asked to tap the table top with a constant beat, they start out but are unable to hold the pattern, and their performance soon becomes chaotic, the beats being irregular and inconsistent. Frequently they start out all right but, as the performance continues, they go faster and faster until they are tapping as fast as they possibly can. Such behavior can be seen as a breakdown in rhythm with a subsequent increase in pace in an attempt to take the temporal element out of the task altogether.

Rhythm occurs in various areas of behavior. *Motor rhythm* is the ability to perform a movement or series of movements with a consistent time interval. The tapping task described above requires a motor rhythm. Such rhythm is used in marching, running, the swing of the arms in walking, and many other everyday activities.

Motor rhythm involves not only the rhythmic movement of a single part but also the rhythmic coordination between parts. The good swimmer, for instance, moves his legs in the same rhythm that he moves his arms. The onset of fatigue can be seen when the rhythmic relation between the movement of the legs and that of the arms begins to break down.

Many children show their rhythm problems in such lack of coordination. In the jumping jack exercise, the arms go in one rhythm and the legs in another. If asked to continue the double circle task, so that each arm goes round and round in the circular pattern, the synchrony between the arms drops out and one or both begin to move irregularly. The child's rhythm concept is too limited. When the task becomes more complex, the child performs either without rhythm or in a series of different rhythms. In either event, the temporal unit is ill-defined and the temporal dimension lacks consistency.

Auditory rhythm involves the recognition of equal temporal intervals between auditory stimuli. It is particularly significant since audition is the distance receptor which is extended in time, whereas vision is the distance receptor which is extended in space. Where temporal relationships are of prime importance, audition is the primary source of information. It is for this reason that audition is so frequently used to pace movements or other rhythmic activities.

Auditory rhythm, however, is a receptive rhythm. Unless it is related to some response, some movement, awareness of its rhythmic quality does not appear. Unless there is a motor rhythm, therefore, the rhythmic aspect of auditory rhythm escapes the child. Identification of rhythm patterns (auditory memory) may exist, but the meaning of the pattern is limited and it cannot be used to influence behavior. It is for this reason that most classroom activities in auditory rhythm have a motor component: marching, simple dance steps, rhythm instruments played by the children, et cetera.

Visual rhythm involves the systematic exploration of a visual environment too extensive to be included in the visual field of a single fixation. It is through such rhythm that the various fixations required in the exploration are kept organized so that they can be integrated into a single visual impression. The temporal-spatial translation, to be discussed later, is largely dependent upon visual rhythm.

Little attention has been given to visual rhythm in education. It would seem, however, a very important function in the reading task. Many children read along, moving from one fixation to another until, at a given fixation, they do not pick up the clue or clues vital to the recognition of the word. At this point their eyes "freeze" to the page. Instead of visually moving back and forth until they encounter the critical clue, their gaze remains riveted on the point of breakdown and does not move either backward or forward. This type of performance is often characteristic of the poor reader or the remedial reader.

It is probable that the same difficulty happens to all of us. We all miss the critical clue on one or more fixations and do not recognize, or we miscall, the word. But our rhythm carries us on to the next fixation. Later we get the problem word from context or we come back and search in an orderly fashion for the critical clue. Where such visual rhythm is lacking, however, there is nothing to carry the child on and the entire process stops, frozen in its tracks.

It is not only desirable that these three types of rhythm exist and that each be consistent within itself, but it is equally important that they be consistent with each other. Watch any high school band on the first day of practice. You will see one or more youngsters who march in one time and play in another, while the rest of the band performs in yet a third. The various types of rhythm are not related to each other. The youngster has more than one temporal dimension in operation at the same time. The result is temporal confusion.

PACE

Temporal units must be consistent but there should also be provision for units of different length. Some temporal problems require short intervals, some long intervals, just as in space some problems require small units (inches), others require large units (miles). Whatever the size of the unit, consistency from one unit to the next is paramount.

Alteration in the size of the temporal unit is achieved through *pace*. A rapid pace utilizes small temporal units. A slow pace utilizes large temporal units. Rhythm maintains the consistency between units regardless of pace. We can shift readily from one pace to another as the task demands without losing this consistency.

Children will be seen who lack the ability to pace themselves. Everything which they do must be done at one standard pace. Regardless of the nature of the task, it is converted into the standard pace. If they are unable to make such a conversion, their rhythm breaks down at the new pace and performance falls apart. In the teaching of rhythm, various paces should be used. The child should be brought to appreciate the fact that rhythm is temporal consistency irrespective of pace.

SEQUENCE

When rhythm has produced a temporal scale with consistent units, the final problem is to organize events on this scale so that their temporal relationships are preserved. Such organization is accomplished through *sequence*. Sequence is the placement of events on a temporal scale so that the time relationships and the order of the events are apparent.

Sequence provides organization on the temporal dimension just as space structure provided organization on the spatial dimensions. It stabilizes and preserves the temporal relations of the environment as space structure did its spatial relationships (Bush and Giles 1969, pp 191-245).

The importance of sequence has long been recognized. The "Three Commands" task on the early Binet intelligence test (Binet and Simon, 1916) was a sequence problem which has been preserved in one form or another on all subsequent tests. The difficulty of the elementary teacher in teaching long division derives from the difficult sequence of computational units involved in the problem. Activities designed to aid the development of sequencing are a part of nearly all educational programs.

Needless to say, sequence depends upon the existence of a temporal scale. Until such a scale exists, there is nothing on which to organize events. The teaching of sequence frequently depends upon the possibility of establishing simultaneity and rhythm prior to the direct attack on the sequence problem itself.

The problem learner frequently reveals his sequence problem in everyday activities. One little boy, as a reward for good behavior, was permitted to pour the coffee for the staff in the school's dining hall. He invariably followed the same procedure: step 1, bring pot over cup; step 2, tilt pot forward; step 3, remove pot from over cup; step 4, tilt pot back up. His error in sequence resulted in many ruined tableclothes.

TEMPORAL-SPATIAL TRANSLATION

The temporal dimension for the child must become a true fourth dimension of space. He is required to deal with events and to solve problems which have both a spatial and a temporal extension. Unless these two extensions can be correlated so that events have the same meaning in either extension, and unless he can translate from one extension to the other with ease, constant confusion is encountered.

When the child looks at a picture, he is presented with a display in space. A number of elements are organized on the three spatial axes but are presented simultaneously in time. If required to study the picture carefully, however, he pays attention to first one detail and then the next. He constructs a series of events in time as he moves from detail to detail. This temporal series, however, must not be independent of the initial simultaneous presentation in space. If it is, he loses the meaning of the picture in the maze of the details. He cannot see the forest for the trees. Only when his temporal dimension is a fourth dimension of his spatial structure can he study the details of the picture within the context of the whole and thus refine and elaborate the total through his concentration on the details. He has translated from space to time.

Take language on the other hand. Speech and language are extended in time. Any one instant of speech is nothing but an isolated sound. The speech aspect derives from the relationship of these isolated sounds on the temporal dimension. The language aspect derives from the ability to expand on both the spatial and temporal dimensions at the same time.

If the child listens to the description of a scene, he first hears a series of isolated sounds extended in time. By organizing these stimuli on the temporal dimension he puts them together into recognizable words and phrases. These words and phrases give him, in succession, the details of the scene. He then combines the temporal and spatial axes and extends the details into a spatial array which gives him a mental image (visualization) of the scene described. He has translated from time to space.

The two great realities, space and time, are intricately interwoven in the child's environment. Some events are presented predominantly in one phase, some predominantly in the other. Seldom is an event limited to one phase. Even more, any manipulation of events always requires dealing with both phases simultaneously. When time is a true fourth dimension of space, the child can translate from space into time and back again with facility, since both phases are integrated in all his manipulations.

Most of our classroom tasks require the child to translate from space into time or the reverse. Consider the task of drawing a square. The child is presented with the shape to copy. This shape is a simultaneous presentation in space. If he continues to look at it, the presentation may be *prolonged* in time but it has no temporal *extension*. Each temporal event is identical with the preceding one. When he begins the task of copying, however, since he does not have four hands, he cannot produce all four of the lines simultaneously. He must, therefore, translate this simultaneous spatial presentation into a series of temporal events which will reproduce it, drawing one line at a time until the whole is constructed. He has had to translate the task from space into time.

When the child is taught word analysis, the opposite problem is illustrated. If we wish to teach him the word "constitution," we first break it down into parts. We then teach him to "sound out," on the basis of rules for word analysis, the separate parts: con—sti—tu—tion. We then teach him to put this together and say "constitution," or to recognize instantly from a flash card, the rapid fire fixation of context reading or other simultaneous spatial presentation, the word "constitution." He has had to translate from time to space.

When time is a fourth dimension for the child, he can make such translations with ease. He can go from time to space and back again as frequently as required and never lose one aspect while dealing with the other. When these two phases of reality are separate, or when one phase is too weak, the child is blocked. He can only do his best to convert one aspect into the other so that he can deal with that phase in which he is competent.

The child who is structured in space but weak in time is frequently a word caller. He can recognize the spatial relations on the page and identify the word. However, each word remains separate for him. He cannot integrate them in time so that the thought appears. Therefore, he has a poor understanding of the content although he reads fluently. He loves to read but hates to write, and his writing is illegible and full of errors. Writing is a complex sequential series of events in time, and in this his structure is weak.

When shown a shape, the child can recognize it but cannot reproduce it. His spelling is atrocious. What there is of it is phonetic, but there are frequent reversals, omissions, and additions.

The child who is organized in time but not in space talks a good line. He is often a poor reader, subvocalizes extensively and for an unusually long time, is over dependent on context, and frequently substitutes synonyms which preserve the context but do not reproduce what is on the page. When shown a complex form he will frequently be seen tracing with his finger in the air in an attempt to recognize or respond to it. He hates to read but picks up a vast body of information auditorily which he can manipulate with great facility. Complex sequences give him no trouble but simple visual displays frustrate him.

part II

Training Activities

chapter 8

The Training Process

EVALUATION

Training of the slow learning child begins with the determination of his learning problem and its effect upon his achievement. A careful evaluation is, therefore, necessary to arrive at an initial attack upon the problem and to plan a training program designed to alleviate the achievement lag. This evaluation should search out the earliest developmental stage at which a breakdown in learning occurred. It should indicate the nature of this breakdown and the nature of resulting compensations and distortions of learning. The training program should then be designed to restore development at this earliest stage and provide for the relearning of later stages on the basis of these new processes.

Such an evaluation begins with the use of standardized tests. Such tests are controlled samples of behavior. They select an area of learning which will be investigated and prescribe a series of tasks indicative of this learning. The presentation of these tasks is rigidly controlled as is the observation of the resulting behavior. The test, therefore, gives us a quantitative and qualitative picture of the child's performance in the area of learning investigated by the

187

test. Because of the rigid controls of both the test task and the observations of the behavior, these measures are much more constant and represent a more adequate sample of learning behavior than do uncontrolled observations in casual circumstances.

The nature of the information revealed by the test, however, is dependent upon the particular area of behavior selected for sampling. If the sample of behavior is very broad, as in an intelligence test, the resulting information is quite gross. It provides considerable data about the child's overall functioning but gives us little information about his specific problems or the particular nature of his learning difficulty. If, on the other hand, the sample included in the test is limited, as in the case of a reaction time test, the information from the test is restricted. It tells us a great deal about a very narrow bit of behavior but overlooks many areas in which problems may exist. In all cases, the nature and amount of information pertinent to the development of training procedures is a function of the behavior sample included in the test standardization.

The evaluation of the slow learning child involves a wide range of behavior extending throughout the developmental course. We therefore require a very broad sample of behavior. On the other hand, specific information is required at each stage of development. We therefore need intensive information at all points in this wide range. For this reason, it will probably be found that no one test will provide the necessary information. A battery of tests will be required so that intensive information can be obtained over a wide range of behaviors.

A suitable battery will be found to include: (1) The Purdue Perceptual-Motor Survey (Roach and Kephart, 1966); (2) The Marianne Frostig Developmental Test of Visual Perception (Frostig, 1961), or The Wepman Auditory Discrimination Test (Wepman, 1958); (3) The Illinois Test of Psycholinguistic Ability (Kirk et al., 1968).

These tests are basically similar in philosophy and purpose. All are concerned with the identification of learning problems. They differ in the particular areas of development with which the sampled behaviors are concerned. Thus, in terms of the developmental stages outlined in Chapter 1, the Perceptual-Motor Survey is particularly concerned with the early stages of development, the motor and perceptual-motor phases. The Frostig and Wepman are particularly concerned with the perceptual phases of development, Frostig with visual perception, Wepman with auditory perception. The ITPA is primarily concerned with the later stages of development, the perceptual-conceptual and conceptual stages. The three tests used as a battery cover the entire developmental range quite adequately.

CLINICAL EXPERIMENTATION

The results of such testing serve to deliniate an area within which the problem exists. They do not, however, indicate the exact nature of the problem. It is then necessary, within this general area, to determine the particular problem which is interfering with the child's achievement.

This pinpointing of the problem is achieved through clinical experimentation. Such experimentation consists of establishing an hypothesis derived from the test results and from an observation of performance on sub-test sections or individual items of the tests. This hypothesis is then verified through a controlled experiment. A situation is designed in such a way that, if the hypothesis is correct, a certain type of behavior will result; if the hypothesis is incorrect, another type of behavior will result. This controlled task is then presented to the child and his behavior is observed.

It should be pointed out that such experiments, although clinical in nature, are not uncontrolled observations of behavior. It is essential that an hypothesis be generated ahead of time and that the task be designed so that a test of the hypothesis results. The hypothesis must generate information which is pertinent to the training or teaching task. If we ask the question, "Is the child shy?" we generate no more information than we had before. If we hypothesize, "His apparent shyness is due to a delay in processing auditory information," we generate new information important to the design of training procedures.

In like manner, the test of the hypothesis must be controlled. If we merely observe that the child does not respond to verbal suggestions, we have no concrete information. If we set a task (raise your arm, stamp your foot) and a comparison task (raise your arm [five seconds delay], stamp your foot), a comparison of the child's behavior under these two situations can suggest a processing delay. Although the controls in such experiments cannot be as rigid as those in a laboratory experiment, they are the same kinds of controls and the more rigid they can be made, the more valid the resulting information.

ISOLATION OF THE PROBLEM

Through the clinical experimentation discussed above, the area of the child's difficulty can be narrowed down to a specific problem. This problem then becomes the point of departure for the development of a training program. A training procedure can be devised which will attack this particular problem and teach the child a more adequate performance.

It is only through the isolation of such specific problems that a basis for the beginning of training can be developed. As long as we talk in vague generalities about behavior and achievement, there can be no basis for the selection of a training procedure. When, on the other hand, we can isolate a particular problem or problems, we have a point of attack from which we can plan a training program.

INITIAL TRAINING PROCEDURES

As has been pointed out above, the initial training procedure will be designed to attack a specific problem. As such, the training activities will also be highly specific. Behavior in everyday life, however, is not specific; it is generalized. A specific skill or response is embedded in a collection of associated responses so that the child deals with a behavior situation rather than a specific behavior.

Therefore, the initial training procedures will be highly artificial. They will be pulled out of a situation and isolated for themselves alone. Consequently, the danger of developing "splinter skills" is very high. These initial procedures should be used only as long as necessary to permit the child to perform. Refinements or precision in performance should be undertaken in more natural activities.

It should be stressed in this connection that if such an initial procedure is going to work and permit the child to perform, it will do so relatively quickly. In theory, the child's lack of performance is due to a neurological interference. If our training procedure does not involve this particular neurological function, he will learn quickly. On the other hand, if he does not learn quickly, presumably our activity still demands the neurological process which is disrupted. In this event, no amount of repetition will permit him to perform, and an altered activity or a new task is required.

Long periods of drill in artificial activities are, therefore, contraindicated. Rather, the child's continued lack of performance would suggest that a new approach to the problem is required. Since we cannot know beforehand the exact nature of the interference, a repertory of approaches is needed rather than an intensive application of a single approach. Artificial training techniques to attack specific problems should be of short duration and more natural activities should be substituted as soon as possible.

GENERALIZATION

As soon as initial training techniques have permitted the child to perform, attention should be shifted to the generalization of the new learning. As has been pointed out above, such generalization is essential to the applicability of any learning. Therefore, the problem of generalization should be attacked as soon as any degree of performance has been attained.

Generalization involves the presentation of the newly learned skill in a large number of different situations. Out of such varied presentations the similar but not identical experiences necessary to the generalization develop. It is not necessary at this stage that the new skill be thoroughly learned or that it be refined to high degrees of precision. Variation, in the interest of generalization, should begin as soon as performance can be elicited. The development of precision, the overlearning required in some skills, and the like should be learned through these varied presentations rather than through long periods of practice on specific activities.

MAINTENANCE

When the generalization has been established, it is necessary to insure that it remains useful to the child. For some reason, the specific activities related to the problem were difficult for him to learn. It follows therefore that, left to his own devices, he will choose other activities which are easier for him and will avoid activities which involve his problem area. As a result, his new-found skill will deteriorate and his problem will return.

What is required is a program in which the new skill is demanded in the activities of his everyday life and where the use of his new skill is rewarding to him. No further specific training is required; he needs only a situation where the new skills are called for. Extracurricular activities of the school and community programs of recreation or crafts usually are available for this purpose. Attention should be given to enrolling the child in such programs so that the newly developed abilities are practiced and maintained, without direct attention, over a period of months or even years. Many excellent training procedures have broken down because no attention was given to the problem of maintenance of the results of the training.

TRAINING PROGRAMS

The procedure outlined above for evaluation and training is very neat and clean. However, children have a distressing habit of not developing neat, clean problems. They develop a number of problems at one time and produce intricate interrelationships between them. As a result it becomes impossible to ferret out a single problem for attack.

For this reason, the procedure outlined above will in almost all cases need to be undertaken repeatedly. Not one, but a number of problems need to be isolated and the relationships between them need to be investigated. The problem then becomes one of where to begin. Decisions must be made as to which of the problems identified should be attacked first and which must wait upon the solution of previous problems. Can any of the child's problems be attacked simultaneously? Can any be attacked together, working on each in relation to the other? Can any be attacked independently but at the same time?

Upon the answers to these and similar questions depends the program of training. Such a program will outline the various problems observed and the order of attack on each. This program should include a projection of anticipated results and future training needs. The teacher should estimate when a problem can reasonably be expected to be solved and what shall be the next step in the total program.

Indefinite periods of training with no check upon results are not desirable. Rather, a series of short range goals should be set up and periodic checks on the achievement of each should be carried out. In this way, the teacher is not training in the dark, so to speak, but has concrete objectives always ahead of her. The training program may need to be revised or altered from time to time but should always be laid out and organized with check points provided to insure knowledge of progress.

EVALUATION AND TRAINING

From what has been said above, it should be noted that the process of evaluation is one of increasing refinement. It moves from a general picture of the child's failures to a specific identification of a particular problem. The process of training, on the other hand, moves from specificity to generalization. Beginning with specific activities, procedures are provided to insure generalization and finally maintenance. Evaluation narrows down the problem; training broadens the learning. Both processes are essential to successful treatment. On the one hand, the problem must be operationally defined so that we can attack a deficit, not a vague, undefined essence. On the other hand, if our training remains specific, we are in danger of teaching only splinter skills.

VERIDICALITY

A performance is said to be veridical when it is dependent upon the fundamental laws of nature and when these natural laws provide a direct criterion of success. Opposed to a veridical performance is a valid performance. The latter is prescribed by the teacher or some other agency of society. It is a performance which *by agreement* is good and in which the criterion of success is social approval.

Balancing is a veridical performance. If the child does not maintain balance he falls down. Eating with a fork is a valid performance. If the child eats with his fingers, the fundamental needs of the organism for food are met just as adequately as they are when he eats with a fork. Social disapproval is the only criterion of error.

Veridical performances are related to natural laws with which the child must cope every day. His motivation for such performances is, therefore, high. Each learning increment represents something which he can use immediately and directly to increase his comfort or his well being. Valid performances have only a secondary motivation. If the child can convince himself that he does not care what people think, the motivation for the task is lost. His motivation then becomes limited to the interest created by the novelty of the task and, when this wears off, he is left with no motivation. If the task is extremely difficult, the social disapproval accompanying failure may well be less undesirable than the more veridical negative rewards generated by the effort required to perform.

In veridical tasks, the consequences of performance, be they success or failure, are immediate and unvarying. Since such tasks are related to natural laws, these same laws provide the consequences of the performance. Natural law is characterized by complete predictability. Nature does not "repeal" the law of gravity because its application would be inconvenient for the child or for the teacher. When balance is lost, the consequences are completely dependable.

The consequences of valid performances, on the other hand, are not thus predictable. They are dependent upon some external application by the teacher. Teachers, and all other social agents, are fallible. They sometimes fail to apply the consequences which they have set up or they permit "extenuating circumstances" to alter cases. Valid performances, therefore, have variable consequences. Learning is much easier and much more efficient when the consequences of the response are completely predictable. Veridical tasks lead to more efficient learning than do valid tasks.

Many classroom training activities are designed to be valid but not veridical. Emphasis is placed upon task performance rather than upon the purpose of the task. The walking board is a good example. Customarily the board is laid along the floor and the child is asked to walk across without stepping off. If he loses his balance, he merely steps off the board. The only consequence of such a response is disapproval by the teacher. He is not required to deal with the balance problem; he can avoid it merely by stepping off if he is willing to incur the teacher's disapproval.

If the board is raised 12 to 18 inches off the floor, however, the task now becomes veridical. If the child loses his balance, even though he can avoid falling by stepping off the board, he cannot avoid a balancing response required by the necessity of stepping down. This alteration of the walking board task insures that it will contribute to learning in the area of balance and posture rather than a splintered walking board response, and it takes advantage of the law of gravity to provide a predictable consequence for the performance.

Requiring the child to cut out a circle from colored paper is a valid task. The reward is the approbation of the teacher, "This is a very nice circle, Billy." This approbation sometimes comes when the circle is not too accurate. In like manner, it sometimes fails to come when, to Billy's eyes, the circle is very fine. He has difficulty identifying superior performance. If the task is redesigned so that the child is asked to cut out a circle which will later, along with circles from other children, be combined to form a caterpillar (Ebersole, et al, 1968, p. 116), the task becomes more veridical. Now Billy's circle is presented along with others in a veridical representation. If his circle is inaccurate, it is apparent both to Billy and others, since it shows up in the final product as different and destroys the overall effect. The teacher's approbation is not necessary since the laws of form present to the child the consequences of his performance.

Too frequently, classroom tasks are presented in forms which are non-veridical to the child. This is particularly true in special education where the child's deficiencies are so glaring and may be so annoying to us socially that learning of particular responses seems pre-eminent. There is then a tendency to isolate the child's failure and prescribe activities designed to remediate it. Such prescribed activities, however, by being removed from their natural context, frequently become artificial and hence, to the child, have little or no connection with the problem he is facing in trying to cope with his universe.

Redesign of such tasks is frequently possible so that they are less artificial and more closely related to the child's own needs and purposes. Such redesign can frequently lead to more extensive learning through increased motivation and a more consistent control of the consequences of learning behavior. Training activities then become truly educational rather than a mere adjunct which may later serve an educational function. Whenever possible, specialized remedial activities should be embedded in an overall educational effort and not divorced either from the child's immediate educational needs nor from his long range educational program.

Not only is it desirable that individual training activities be veridical, it is also important that the curriculum be veridical. Curricula are designed to present a certain scope of information in a predetermined sequence. When the child faces a learning problem, either the scope or the sequence or both may become unrealistic. In this event, the curriculum loses its purposefulness and becomes non-veridical. The customary environmental demands upon which motivation depends no longer obtain and daily classroom activities become highly artificial and unrelated to the child's needs.

The so-called tool subjects, particularly reading, frequently give the most trouble. The normal child is introduced to reading through the home or similar experiences where reading is used for the purpose of obtaining information. He quickly absorbs the rudiments of the reading process so that he can imagine himself using the skill for a purpose. Although reading in and of itself is non-veridical, he can foresee the time when it will serve a veridical purpose. The gap between the non-veridical aspect and the more veridical function is comprehensible. The anticipation of future satisfaction motivates the present skill learning.

If the child has a learning difficulty, however, the initial experiences with reading may be so overwhelming that he cannot conceive of this procedure as a method whereby he can gain information. If reading is taught as a skill, this child will lack motivation since he cannot see the possibility of a useful function to follow. Whereas the normal child recognizes that the present non-veridical learning will become veridical, the slow learner has no such anticipation.

The basic reading competencies can be taught as a function rather than as a skill. Instead of teaching word recognition in the regular manner, the child may be taught to recognize the labels on cans in the grocery store. Many examples are cited in the literature to indicate that slow learners frequently learn a sight vocabulary by this procedure whereas they had been unable to learn it through normal primer materials. It is customary to account for this learning by sighting the reduction of scope of the reading task and the added clues from the format of the label. May it not be, however, that in addition to these considerations the increased veridicality of these tasks aided the learning? To recognize a label on a can is an everyday problem for the child. His learning is rewarded immediately by fewer errors, which is of significance to him.

In a similar manner, frequently it is difficult to teach the principles of measurement in the abstract context of arithmetic or numbers instruction. These same concepts, however, can be taught with relative ease if they are embedded in a construction project where measurement is essential to the success of the building project.

Such illustrations would suggest that the sequence of the curriculum might profitably be altered when the child has a learning problem. Such alterations should probably be directed toward drawing the sequence of learning more closely out of the veridical problems faced by the child. Delaying veridical functions while skills are taught with some degree of thoroughness may involve a delay in arriving at a functional use of learning which the child who is already experiencing difficulty in solving his day-to-day problems cannot tolerate.

SCOPE OF THE CURRICULUM

The problem of the slow learner also effects the scope of the curriculum. It can be anticipated that he will not learn as much or as fast as other children. He requires a curriculum reduced in scope to accommodate the reduced quantity of his learning.

In general, curricula are designed with the future needs of the child for information in mind. In planning its scope the curriculum designers are concerned with college requirements and vocational needs. The curriculum is, therefore, broad in scope and designed as a sort of a forerunner of professional level competence in the various areas of study. Relatively little attention is given to the child's informational needs today; most of the material will become functional in the far distant future.

When the scope of curriculum is reduced to accommodate the slow learner, the tendency is to simply reduce the overall quantity of material. The same subject matter is used and the same orientation within the subject matter field is maintained. There is just less of it; it is not altered, but merely reduced.

It seems possible, however, that the slow learner requires a true alteration of curriculum. If less overall learning will occur, it becomes increasingly important to insure that those learnings which he does acquire are maximally useful. His need for information is as great as that of any other child; his ability to absorb this required information is limited. The requirement for efficiency in the selection of the information to be presented then becomes critical. Whereas the normal child, with his relatively high rate of absorption, can afford to spend time on material which will not prove maximally useful to him at any time, the slow learner must be assured that every item of the limited store of information he acquires is essential to his everyday needs.

The curriculum for the slow learner should not be a watered down model of the normal curriculum. It should be especially designed to present only essential information. The informational needs of these children should be carefully analyzed. First of all, the needs of his own chronological age within his own social and operational sphere should be investigated. These immediate informational needs should be given first consideration in developing his curriculum. Because of his difficulties in gaining information, he already shows a lack of knowledge when he enters school. The first task of the school is to relieve this knowledge lack and, as far as possible, supply the information required immediately to permit him to achieve an adequate adjustment as a child in his environment.

When his immediate needs have been supplied, the curriculum should turn to his probable future needs. Here, again, a careful analysis of these probable future needs is required. Curriculum builders have, in general, proceeded on the assumption that all children should be directed toward the same goal, and that when differences occur they represent drop-outs who stop short of the goal for one reason or another, either within the child or within his environment. The goal of a conventional college education has been set for all children and the curriculum from kindergarten through high school has tended to reflect this universal goal. Insofar as changes are made, they are made with reluctance (as in vocational education), or they are made as necessary substitutes (such as business arithmetic instead of algebra) designed to remove the child as little as possible from the universal college preparatory orientation. "Diplomas" received for such substitute plans are considered second rate documents and a certain stigma attaches to them.

There are many children for whom the conventional college education with its marathon absorption of loosely classified information is neither necessary nor desirable. Enormous contributions have and will continue to be made to the social and economic life of their community by individuals who possess a lesser quantity of information and academic skill but a more useful body of selected information and ability. For effective functioning, however, such reduced bodies of skills, attitudes, and knowledges must be carefully selected. The selection must be based upon the applicability of the knowledge to the problems which the child can be expected to face.

Curriculum builders should consider carefully the living and working situations available to the slow learner in our society. New curricula should then be devised incorporating the *essential* learnings pertinent to these situations. The child would then be educated to the life which he will lead rather than, as is so often the case, being educated to a life which he cannot live and hence, when he fails and drops out, being left to his own devices to pick up the knowledge necessary to the life which he must live.

Such alterations in curriculum should be recognized as increased selectivity of subject matter, not qualitative changes. Frequently the problem is approached by simply omitting subject matter areas. The slow learner has as much need for mathematics as does the normal learner. To omit all mathematics from his curriculum robs him. His mathematics must be shorn of embellishments and concentrate on the mathematical essentials. Within this context, his needs are acute.

Frequently, also, curriculum revision for the slow learner leads to an increased emphasis on informational detail at the expense of generalization. As has been pointed out elsewhere, such a shift of emphasis is directly contraindicated. The development of generalization is a more important educational problem with the slow learner than with his normal peer. Care must be taken to insure that the basic quality of education is not altered when the quantity of the curriculum is manipulated to accommodate the child whose learning is atypical.

The development of such a curriculum involves many thorny questions to which definite answers are not now available. How much can the child be expected to learn? What economic and social adjustments are open to him? What are the minimum needs of these adjustments for learning? What alternative adjustments are possible or may become possible? What needs does he have for self fulfillment other than social and economic? These and other questions will require intensive research before the questions of scope and sequence can even be attacked. The time has come, however, when education must examine and plan for the child whose educational needs are non-conventional.

LENGTH AND PACE

Not only is the slow learner limited in quantity, he is limited in rate. Thus a second problem of the curriculum is raised. How long should the educational career be for such children? The public school customarily completes its educational responsibility in twelve years. There is, however, no magic in this figure. If a child learns more slowly, it may be that the public school's responsibility for his education should be expanded to fourteen, sixteen, or twenty years. If he is continuing to progress educationally within the scope of the public school curriculum, it is logical to assume that the public school's responsibility is not yet complete regardless of his age.

The temporal rigidity of the curriculum leads to two problems. For some children the best educational results might be expected if they were removed from the conventional school environment for a period of time while intensive therapeutic attacks on their basic learning disabilities were undertaken. Upon the successful completion of such therapy, they could be returned to classroom routine.

If such a program is followed, however, the child will return to his class some months behind. He must then either progress faster than normal to catch up or finish later. The problem is not too intense if the therapeutic intervention is relatively short. However, if therapy requires three or four years, the procedure frequently becomes unrealistic.

The second problem concerns the pace of the curriculum. Frequently, either as a result of therapy or of his natural pace, a child learns well but slowly. The requirement of a curriculum to cover a given amount of material in a given time demands that the teacher force learning upon him faster than he can accommodate it. The result is frequently a breakdown in the learning process, frustration, the development of emotional maladjustments, and the like.

One slow learner for six years religiously followed a schedule which involved an hour and one-half of tutoring and two hours of supervised homework daily. Such forced feeding got him through high school at the appointed age. However, it sacrificed all recreation and normal peer contact; it gave rise to various physical symptoms such as nausea, upper respiratory infections, and the like; and it robbed him of his childhood.

Attempts have been made to adjust the pace of the curriculum through track systems, ungraded rooms, and the like. Such developments need to be expanded and improved. More flexibility must be developed within which the pace of the curriculum can be adjusted to the learning pace of the child. At the same time, the overall period of education needs to be reevaluated to permit educational careers of varying lengths for children with varying learning capacities and educational needs.

PROSTHESIS

Although remediation is the overriding goal in most cases of learning disorder, there are certain situations where this approach is not immediately feasible. In the first place, there are some conditions which do not yield to remedial attempts either because the condition is irremediable or because remedial techniques are not sufficiently advanced to deal adequately with the problem.

In the second place, excessive delay may be involved in the treatment. Remedial approaches take time, sometimes excessive time. There is the single severe problem which may require a long series of treatments before useable performance can be obtained. There is also the child who shows a number of relatively minor problems but for whom each of these problems must be solved before a noticeable effect on achievement can be observed. Instead of a single remedial effort, he requires several remedial efforts, some of which can be attempted simultaneously, but others of which are dependent upon each other and must be approached successively. Remediation in such a case can be expected to be an extended process for which two or three years is a realistic projection. In the meantime, learning demands are continuing and increasing in both quantity and intensity. The child, since remediation has not yet equipped him to meet these demands, falls further and further behind. Remediation becomes largely self-defeating because of the excessive delay involved in its application.

A third problem with remedial activities concerns interference which sometimes precludes their success. A problem which must be attacked relatively late in the remedial process may so disrupt the child's response that the learnings involved in earlier procedures cannot be accomplished. Probably the most common example of this problem is excessive distractibility. The remedial approach to distractibility involves teaching the child to structure both the stimulus field and the response complex. It is, therefore, one of the last symptoms to be attacked and to yield to remedial attempts. Less complex problems, such as eye-hand coordination, for example, require the child to maintain attention to a task in order that he can learn from that task the eye-hand relationships involved. The distractibility prevents such sustained attention and thus prevents the prescribed learning. Unless the distractibility can be temporarily controlled, no learning can occur in the eye-hand activities. The distractibility, which cannot be attacked immediately, prevents the success of those initial remedial treatments which, if they could be successful, would eventually contribute to the solution of the distractibility.

In these circumstances, a somewhat artificial process is needed which will permit the child to successfully accomplish an end, even though the method by which he accomplishes this end may be artificial and atypical. The end, for the moment, is more important than the means. Such processes or the devices which make them possible can be thought of as *prosthesis*. They are "crutches" which permit the child to make certain essential responses or to avoid certain self-defeating responses. Just as an orthopedic crutch permits the child to locomote even though he cannot walk, so these learning crutches permit the child to perform even though his performance is abnormal and in the long run undesirable. They are useful where the activity which they make possible is essential to the child.

A number of such prosthetic procedures have been described in the literature and have been used successfully in treatment. They appear to fall into three general areas based on the type of activity they are designed to aid.

LEARNING PROSTHESIS

The majority of such devices have been developed to permit the child to perform some academic process in the face of an unresolved learning disability. The child with inadequate space structure or poor ocular control is frequently permitted or even taught to point with his finger as he reads, following with his eyes the progress of his finger across the page. This procedure permits the finger to provide a crutch for the eyes until such time as visual perception is able to sustain this function unaided. In the meantime, the essential reading functions can be performed (Strauss and Lehtinen, 1947, p. 180). When the prosthetic aid is no longer needed, it is anticipated that it will be dropped by the child or will be taken away from him.

It is in the nature of prosthetic devices that they provide methods of performance which are less efficient than the normal method. Therefore, whenever the child can perform without it, he will voluntarily give up the prosthetic aid. In the case of pointing with the finger while reading, as soon as the child can follow the line of print with his eye, he finds that the finger slows him down. At first he will eliminate the finger on easy passages and use it again on difficult passages. Eventually, as he is able, he will eliminate it altogther.

The question of when to remove the prosthetic aid frequently bothers the teacher or therapist. All that is necessary to answer this question is to follow the lead of the child. If dependence on the aid is prolonged, it is probable that remediation is either not attacking the right problem, that the process for which the aid is used cannot be attacked until later in the remedial program, or that remediation is not proving successful. As soon, however, as remediation begins to solve the basic problem for the child, he will begin to dispense with the prosthetic aid. He is the one who provides the answer to the question of how long to use this aid.

Counting boards have been devised for the child who cannot proceed in an orderly fashion through a series of items (Strauss and Lehtinen, 1947, p. 155). Various color codes to aid the child who has difficulty sorting out the task item among a cluster of items have been used (Bannatyne, 1964). Variations of spacing and of positioning of items on the page serve the same purpose.

Such procedures permit the child to perform certain academic tasks along with his classmates. They are not in themselves primarily teaching devices. Their purpose is to circumvent a learning problem to allow performances which are not disturbed to be used, and to accomplish an end result which would normally require a performance which is disturbed. Thus pointing with the finger permits the child to "read." He can use his symbol recognition and interpretation processes (which are not disturbed) but need not use spatial structuring (which is disturbed). Obviously, the stategy will not work if the underlying processes of symbol recognition and interpretation are also disturbed. Only when there are enough basic abilities in the activity area to permit performance can prosthesis help. In like manner, if the ability compensated by the prosthetic device is essential to the task, prosthesis will not help. No prosthetic device, for example, could compensate lack of symbol interpretation since this is a fundamental ability in reading. When prosthesis is applied in the area of learning, it can compensate only auxiliary abilities presented by the task, not fundamental abilities.

SOCIAL PROSTHESIS

The child with learning disorders is frequently confused by complex or conflicting stimulus situations. The most complex of these situations are activities involving other persons. Not only does the child have to deal with a multitude of objects but he must also deal with frequent changes in the relationships between these objects, in view of the fact that people move frequently and their movements may be inconstant and difficult to predict. The child may, therefore, need to be protected from such complex occurrences until he has developed sufficient structure to deal with them adequately.

The most common prosthetic device in social situations is physical restriction of the size of the group. Thus, these children are usually taught in small classes and frequently in sub-groups within these small classes. Their schedules are arranged so that less stimulating activities are substituted for more confusing special events such as parties, field trips, school picnics, and the like.

Too frequently such alterations are seen as restrictions. The child is *deprived* of some stimulating activity. We do not, however, do the child a favor when we thrust him into an activity with which he cannot cope without losing control of his behavior. Such forcing of complex participation can only lead to confusion which is as uncomfortable for the child as it is for the adult. Protection from such events is as essential to the child with learning disorders as is the brace or splint to the child with a bone difficulty.

Once the child with learning disorders has adapted to an activity, he has difficulty changing to a new activity. Therefore, he becomes easily confused when activities change frequently or unpredictably. A well structured and rigid routine is frequently demanded to help him organize his day or his classroom session. The development of such classroom routines serves a prosthetic purpose in helping the child to participate in group classroom activities. Ebersole, Kephart, and Ebersole (1968) recommend that, when this routine must be broken, time be taken well ahead of the event to explain to the child what is going to happen and what he can expect. Such a procedure helps him to predict and to structure ahead of time in anticipation of the unusual event. The description to the child must be sufficiently accurate and sufficiently detailed to permit his predictions to be valid.

BEHAVIOR PROSTHESIS

The child with learning disorders frequently presents behavior disturbances which interfere with his learning. Chief among these are distractibility and hyperactivity. Until such time as remediation can supply the child with a control of these behaviors, a prosthetic control may be needed to permit the child to enter learning activities and profit from them. The major prosthetic devices in the area of behavior control are partial isolation and drug therapy.

Partial isolation is achieved through the use of cubicles in which the child's desk is placed and where work requiring concentration and resistance to distraction is done. Many variations of the cubicle are in use but the principle involves a limited space within which as many distractors as possible are eliminated. The walls are painted a pastel shade and are free of decorations. Furniture consists only of the child's desk and chair. The only material present is that needed specifically in the performance of the task. The child may be assigned to the cubicle when the teacher notes that distraction is interferring with his work, or he may be left free to work there when he feels he needs it. Practice has shown that children quickly come to welcome such protection and ask to be permitted to work in such isolation (Cruickshank and Johnson, 1958, p. 273-ff).

By thus partially isolating the child, distracting stimuli are reduced to a minimum. Frequently the child can then learn in spite of his distractibility. The distractibility still exists but, because the stimuli are reduced, it is less apparent and interferes less with the learning activity. Carefully planned learning activities can then be used to develop structure within the child which will control his distraction. When such structuring has been accomplished, the cubicle no longer serves a necessary purpose and it can be eliminated.

For the child whose hyperactivity makes it impossible for him to work on a task, drug therapy is frequently useful. The drug serves to depress overall activity in the organism or to depress areas of activity. Among the specific activities thus affected will be some hyperactive responses interferring with learning. Also affected, however, may be some specific activities necessary to learning. No drug at the moment appears to be able to depress undesirable activity selectively while leaving desirable activity unaffected. Frequently, however, the undesirable responses of the child are so disruptive that work with desirable responses becomes impossible. In such an event, the effect of the drug on the hyperactive responses may be essential even though some minor diminution of active learning responses may be associated with it.

The use of drugs for this purpose is a medical problem and must be undertaken only under the advice and direction of a physician. The therapy, however, may be a prosthetic aid for education. The drug does not teach nor does it solve the behavior problem. It may well permit the child, however, to engage in controlled learning situations which can teach structure and hence can attack the behavior problem.

USE OF PROSTHETICS

The use of a prosthetic aid to learning is indicated in situations where (1) the success of remediation is doubtful, (2) the effects of remediation upon essential function will be delayed for a long period of time, (3) temporary control of a disruptive symptom is necessary to make remediation possible. The prosthetic aid does not in and of itself solve the problem but it may be essential *to* the solution of the problem.

In practice, remedial programs should first be considered and evaluated. The necessity for prosthetic aid should then be examined. A suitable aid to accomplish the required purpose can then be sought and applied. Continued attempts at the direct solution of the problem through remedial work should be pursued, looking toward the eventual abridgment or elimination of the prosthetic aid. A prosthetic aid may be considered as a permanent solution to the problem only when the possibility of successful remediation seems remote. Too frequently the success of prosthesis leads to a cessation of active treatment, since the child is now performing. It should be remembered, however, that the *best* prosthetic device is less efficient than the normal method of performance. The child should be left with a permanent prosthetic aid only as a last resort.

chapter 9

Perceptual-Motor Training

THE WALKING BOARD

We have previously discussed the walking board as a method of observing the behavior of the child. This device may also be used as a training device. By adapting many of the activities described in our earlier discussion of the walking board, we can provide experiences which will aid the child in the development of dynamic balance and contribute to the learning of laterality and directionality. The walking board has been used for many years in kindergarten and elementary school activities (see Jones, Morgan and Stevens, 1957, pp. 60, 64). We must remember, however, that the contribution of the walking board results from its implications for teaching balance and laterality rather than in the development of skill on the walking board itself. As with so many other activities, the child must be helped to generalize rather than merely to acquire a specific skill. Thus, from our point of view, the child who walks across the board and does not lose his balance is not learning from the activity. Only when he loses his balance and is required to correct it, does he learn.

The walking board is a section of two-by-four measuring eight to twelve feet in length. Each end of the board is fitted into a bracket which serves as a brace and prevents the board from tipping over. When fitted into place, the board is raised approximately two inches off the floor. Each bracket has a combination fitting so that the board can either be set in flat with the wide surface up or be set on its edge with the narrow surface up.

The walking board technique is a modification of walking a fence or walking railroad ties, activities which were common in our childhood. The child is asked to start at one end of the board and walk slowly to the other. For beginners or those having difficulty, the four-inch surface is used. As the child becomes more adept, the board is turned on edge and the two-inch surface is used. For the child who has extreme difficulty, a two-by-six or even larger board can be substituted. When the task is difficult, the adult should help the child by holding onto one hand. The child should be encouraged to dispense with this help as soon as he is able. However, he should not be forced, since he may develop a fear reaction which will interfere with further training.

WALKING FORWARD

The child first learns to walk the board forward. Care must be taken to see that he walks slowly and maintains balance at all times. By running across the board, he may be able to perform the task without the necessity for balance. Since balance is the function being trained by the technique, we must see that he does not avoid the problem by running or otherwise changing the procedure. He should place each foot squarely on the board so that both toe and heel make contact at each step.

WALKING BACKWARD

After the child has learned to walk the board forward, he learns to walk it backward. At this point, he will probably need help from the adult. As before, he is encouraged to dispense with this help as soon as possible. He is allowed to look back to see where the next step should be, but is encouraged to learn where the board is behind him without having to look. He will soon find that the task becomes more difficult when he has to look and is easier if he can keep his eyes ahead while walking backward. He may have to explore with his toe before each step to locate the board behind him. He is allowed to do this but is encouraged to learn the direction "straight back" so that such preliminary explorations will no longer be necessary.

WALKING SIDEWISE

The child can now learn to walk the board sidewise. To do this, he stands with feet together facing across the board and on the left end. He then moves his right foot out, shifts his weight, and moves his left foot until his feet are together again. This sequence is repeated until he has crossed the board. After each step, the feet are brought together again. When he returns from right to left across the board, the sequence of actions is reversed. Again, care must be taken to see that he moves slowly and maintains balance at all times.

TURNING AND BOUNCING

When he has learned these three basic procedures, the child can be taught to turn on the board. He is asked to walk across the board and, without stepping off, to turn and walk back sidewise. When he has mastered this half turn, he can be asked to walk forward across, turn, and return walking forward. The most difficult task is to walk backward across the board, turn, and return walking backward. This latter task requires maintaining the difficult backward directionality while turning. Variations and combinations of these routines can be introduced to maintain interest and also to reduce anticipation. Thus, he learns to maintain balance under conditions which cannot be completely foreseen.

The ability to maintain balance under conditions which are not predictable can be further cultivated by asking the child to walk to the center of the board, turn, and walk back. All combinations of direction and turn can be repeated in the center of the board. Under these conditions, the spring of the board becomes an additional factor which must be considered in maintaining balance. The child should be encouraged to experience this spring and the resulting sensations. Allow him to "bounce" on the board and discover how it feels to be on a springy surface. Help him, if necessary, but encouarge him to learn to maintain balance under conditions that, for him, are unusual.

For childen in whom number concepts are beginning to develop, elementary concepts in this area can be combined with balance training. Maximum spring is experienced at the center of the board. When the child is asked to walk out *halfway* on the board, this springing sensation can reinforce the visual and other clues to "halfway." He can be asked to count the steps required to walk across the board, then the steps required to walk halfway across, halfway across and back, etc. The child can be aided to a fuller understanding of quantitative concepts by the use of the total body in this demonstration.

LATERALITY AND DIRECTIONALITY

The primary purpose of the walking board is to aid in teaching the child balance and postural responses. Maintaining balance on the board requires an accurate knowledge of the difference between the right side of the body and the left. The technique thus aids in the development of laterality. As we have seen, laterality is necessary in such activities as reading and writing (where a left-to-right progression across the line of print must be sustained). It is probable that many reversals of words or letters are due to inadequate laterality.

The board also aids the development of directionality. Added to the experiences of right and left in maintaining balance are the experiences of forward and backward in progress across the board. Lateral direction is separated from fore-and-aft direction. The former is used in balance, while the latter figures in the goal of the activity. When the spring of the board is added to the activity, the directions "up" and "down" are also added.

SPECIAL ADAPTATIONS

For the child who is having exceptional difficulty, the task of walking the two-by-four may prove too difficult. For such a child, we may have to decrease the difficulty of the task. As mentioned above, we can use a two-by-six or two-by-eight instead of the narrower two-by-four. In some cases, however, even these boards may be too difficult. We may need to start with a paper alley, constructed by laying a strip of wrapping paper along the floor, or a "street," marked out by two parallel paper strips placed along the floor with the width between them adjusted to the needs of the child. The child is then required only to walk within the alley or "street" without getting off. In this manner, we teach the child to control the gross direction of his movement before we introduce more complicated concepts of balance.

When the child has learned control under these rather simple demands, we can begin to increase the demands by reducing the width of the "street." As he is able to perform, he can then be asked to perform on the boards, beginning with the two-by-eight and proceeding to the two-by-six and finally the two-by-four.

Children displaying such gross lack of control will be found to be apprehensive of any task requiring more refined control. Thus, they will require the presence and support of the teacher. They may wish, for example, to hold his hand (see Bender, 1956). The teacher should offer such support and be very careful of requiring greater control than the child possesses. At the same time, he should encourage the child to dispense with such support as soon as his control develops to the point where he no longer needs it.

For the same reason, such children may fear the height of the two-by-four, even though it is only two or three inches off the floor. For such children, it is desirable to start with activities where there is no height from the floor. Thus, a four-inch strip of paper may be substituted for the board. In like manner, the child can be started with the board flat on the floor and only later be introduced to the board off the floor on the braces.

THE BALANCE BOARD

Another device which will be found useful in helping the child to learn balance and accompanying skills is the balance board. With this device, we can help him to pinpoint the center of gravity of his body and, through requiring him to maintain both fore-and-aft and left-to-right balance, we can offer him a more dynamic problem than in the case of the walking board. It will usually be found desirable to develop relatively adequate ability with the walking board before attempting the balance board, since performing on the latter is a somewhat more difficult task.

The balance board is a square platform sixteen by sixteen inches. Underneath and in the middle of the board is a balance post three inches in height. Three sizes of balance posts are provided: three by three inches, four by four inches, and five by five inches. These posts can be interchanged by means of a simple wing nut so that the task can be made easier for the child who is having greater difficulty. Some children may have to begin with the board flat on the floor with no post at all until they become accustomed to the task and to the idea of being off the floor.

Start the child with the largest post and, when he can balance without difficulty, change to the middle post. When he can use the middle post with ease, change to the smallest post. If the child has difficulty, pin up a picture or other visual target at his eye level and several feet in front of him. Ask him to keep looking at the picture while balancing on the board. The task is easier if the eyes are held still. Encourage the child to rock the board both in the right-left direction and in the fore-aft direction. Let him experience a shift of weight and of the center of gravity and observe how such shifts are accomplished and controlled. It will be found that children enjoy such experimentation in situations like this where there is no danger.

SPECIAL TASKS

When the child has achieved skill in the simple balancing performance, ask him to perform other neuro-muscular tasks while balancing on the board. Let him bounce a rubber ball on the floor in front of him and catch it. Begin with a large beach ball and decrease the size until he can use a tennis ball. Let him bounce and catch the ball with both hands, then with the right hand, then with the left.

While the child is balancing on the board, ask him to throw objects at a target (bean bag, ring toss, et cetera). Suspend a ball by a string from the ceiling so that it swings in front of him like a pendulum about arm's reach away. Ask him to strike out and touch it with his finger as it swings past.

A balance board helps develop a flexible postural adjustment (Courtesy Highland School, Lafayette, Indiana. Photographer: Howard R. Knaus).

Ask the child to perform simple calesthenics while balancing on the board. Some children are even able to jump rope on the board. Use the board to help increase awareness of the body and its parts. While he is balanced on the board, ask the child to touch his shoulders, hips, knees, ankles, toes. Gross identification can be aided by commands such as "Touch your left knee with your right hand." Combining maintenance of balance with movements of identification helps to create body image.

TRAMPOLINE

One of the most helpful training devices in the area of coordination and muscular control is the trampoline. This device is a sturdily constructed metal frame within which a heavy canvas is attached by means of springs. The canvas serves as a performing surface. When the child jumps on the trampoline, the spring of the canvas surface throws him into the air and permits him to be free of the earth for a few seconds by counteracting the forces of gravity. This freedom and this new orientation to his own body and its activities can be experienced without danger and provides a most exhilarating sensation for the child.

LEARNING DYNAMIC BALANCE

One of the most important contributions of the trampoline is the development of total bodily coordination throughout the gross muscle systems. When standing on a firm surface, the child can

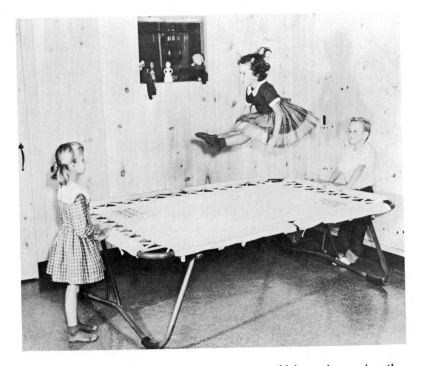

The trampoline helps develop motor patterns which can be used as the basis for future learning (Courtesy Nissen Trampoline Company, Cedar Rapids, Iowa).

avoid the problems of dynamic balance by distributing the weight masses of his body around the center of gravity and making only minimum necessary adjustments. As he rises into the air from the surface of the trampoline, such minimum balancing adjustments are not adequate. His body is free of the ground and he must locate the center of gravity under unfamiliar and much less stable circumstances. He must then maintain a dynamic coordination of all of the major muscle groups around this center of gravity in order to maintain balance. If he is unable to maintain such a dynamic balance, either he falls harmlessly on the canvas or the spring of the canvas is snubbed and the activity is reduced.

LEARNING COORDINATION

Not only must the child learn a dynamic relationship to the center of gravity and maintain a dynamic balance, but he must maintain these coordinations under changing relationships. In addition, the changes in these relationships are not the result of his own efforts directly but are dependent in large part on the trampoline and its functions. Thus, the timing and rhythm of his activity are dictated by the spring of the trampoline rather than directly determined by his own movements. Here is another important teaching aspect of this device. In activities on the ground, the child can adjust his movements to the rhythm patterns of his muscles. Thus, if the neurological innervation to one or more muscle groups loses its rhythm, he merely adjusts his movement to this change. On the trampoline, such adjustment is not possible since the rhythm is dictated by the device. Therefore, he must learn to maintain adequate and constant rhythms in his neuro-muscular coordination which are demanded in few other activities.

DISCOVERING INADEQUACIES

Very frequently such experiences serve to teach the child that his neuro-muscular rhythm is inadequate and to point out to him the situations and activities in which his rhythm becomes distorted. Thus, when a child seven years of age demonstrated a neuro-muscular problem in the right leg, the trampoline helped him to appreciate the problem. As he was bouncing, this leg would go out of phase and its rhythm would display a faster rate than that of the rest of his body. This alteration in rhythm on one side would stop the trampoline and interfere with his performance. In walking and similar situations, he would merely adjust to this change in rhythm by limping and would not be completely aware of when the alteration occurred or the nature of the alteration. The trampoline, through its insistence on the maintenance of a prescribed rhythm, pointed out to him these difficulties which he had not been able to appreciate fully in more normal activities.

DEVELOPING BODY IMAGE

When the child is thrown clear of the canvas, he must learn to balance not only in a right-and-left direction but also in a fore-and-aft direction. The former of these balancing problems is closely related to the problem of laterality which we have discussed previously. The latter is closely related to directionality and to appreciation of a third dimensional axis through the body. Thus, the mere activity of bouncing on the trampoline contributes to body image and spatial relationships within the body. These relationships are further emphasized in more complicated trampoline stunts such as the seat drop, the knee drop, or the back drop. These more advanced activities help to teach the child the location of various portions of his body and their relationship to each other both in the upright position and in less customary positions. Certain relationships can be observed which are very difficult to observe under more normal conditions. Thus, in the seat drop the relationship of height between his seat and his feet can be observed through the difference in timing between bouncing on his seat and bouncing on his feet. In like manner, the height from the ground to the shoulders or the back can be observed in trampoline activities.

Simple activities on the trampoline are suitable for young children. If an adult is present to watch the child and if certain simple rules are followed, there is no danger in this equipment. The teacher will find that, for the most part, children will not attempt activities which are beyond their ability.

BOUNCING

The simplest activity on the trampoline is straight bouncing. The child stands in the center of the canvas and jumps up and down, permitting the canvas to add to the force of his jump and therefore lift him higher off the surface (LaDue and Norman, 1956). The child should stand on the canvas with his feet about shoulder width apart. As he rises from the canvas, his legs should be kept straight and, if better form is desired, his feet should be brought together. As the child descends toward the canvas, his knees should be slightly bent to cushion the shock and his feet should return to the shoulder width position. The child should anticipate contact with the canvas and begin preparations for his next jump as he descends.

Stress should be placed upon controlled bouncing in one spot. Do not permit the child to inch forward or backward but encourage him to jump in the same spot. For this purpose, most trampolines are equipped with an X mark in the center of the canvas to indicate the target of the jump.

In early stages of training, it will be found desirable to hold the child's hands as he jumps. This support gives him additional confidence and, perhaps more important, gives him a clue to his center of gravity and the relationship of his body to it. Do not try for height or form in the early phases of bouncing. It is important that the child get the feel of being unsupported and recognize the dynamic factors of balance involved.

When the child can bounce easily for a series of jumps without support, ask him to bounce on one foot only. This alteration in procedure alters the requirements for balance in much the same way that standing on one foot on the floor altered the requirement in some of our earlier activities. He should learn to bounce on the right foot alone and also on the left foot alone.

When the child has learned to bounce on each foot alone, ask him to alternate feet (to jump once on the left foot, once on the right foot, once on the left foot, etc.). When he has learned this simple alternation, ask him to try more complicated patterns, such as jumping twice on the left foot, twice on the right foot, twice on the left foot, etc. When he has accomplished these symmetrical patterns, we can introduce asymmetrical patterns such as those described in the jumping activities of the examination sequence.

When the child has learned straight bouncing, activities can be introduced in which he is asked to turn in the air while he is bouncing. Thus, we can ask him to jump up, turn 90 degrees, and land. It can be seen that such activities make rather severe demands on the child's control and orientation. He must change his balance relationships while in the air, and at the same time he must maintain his orientation to the ground and to the trampoline. When he has learned to turn through 90 degrees, we can ask him to turn through 180 degrees and, when he has learned this, we can introduce intermediate angles between these coordinates.

During all the bouncing activities, the child's attention should be called to the rhythm which is demanded. We can do this by asking him to count his jumps. Be sure that his counting is related to the activity of jumping and is not a purely independent counting task. He must count as he hits the canvas of the trampoline. At a somewhat later stage, we can ask him to count a certain number of jumps and then stop. Such activities can help him to estimate time and to anticipate events in time.

TRAMPOLINE STUNTS

Seat Drop. One of the easiest stunts on the trampoline is the seat drop. The child lands on the canvas in a sitting position with his legs fully extended forward so that the entire backs of the legs contact the canvas simultaneously. The trunk is slightly inclined backward from the vertical. Hands are flat on the bed six to eight inches in back of the hips. The fingers are pointed toward the feet and the arms are slightly bent. The child bounces once or twice and then performs the seat drop, springing back into the standing position.

Knee Drop. The child lands on the canvas in a kneeling position with the contact point being the knees, shins, and instep. He is instructed to keep the body directly above the knees when landing in the knee-drop position. He then springs back to a standing position.

Back Drop. The child lands on the canvas in a supine position with legs straight and vertically inclined. He places his hands either on the outsides and fronts of the legs just above the knees or free of the legs, semi-extended forward and upward. He is instructed to keep his chin on the chest throughout this trick. Attempt the stunt first from a standing position. Raise one leg and fall backward to the backdrop position. After he lands on his back, the child springs back to a standing position.

Front Drop. Land on the canvas in a prone position. Extend the arms forward with the elbows extended sideward and palms of the hands downward. The following contact points should land simultaneously: palms, forearms, abdomen, and thighs.

Other Stunts. A kit of materials describing the trampoline and activities with which it may be used may be obtained from the Nissen Trampoline Company, Cedar Rapids, Iowa. The simple stunts described above, and particularly straight bouncing, will be found most useful with elementary school children. Most of the learnings in which we are particularly interested can be fostered by these very simple activities. As we have mentioned above, the motivational value of the trampoline is very high and some of the children will be interested in learning more complicated tricks. These stunts and methods of teaching them are described in the kit.

BEDSPRINGS AND MATTRESS

In the absence of a trampoline, many of the learning situations described above can be provided by the use of bedsprings. Obtain a set of bedsprings and a mattress which are highly resilient. Tie the mattress to the springs so that it will not slip off. Many of the stunts described above can be performed on this bedspring apparatus. Since the resiliency of the bedsprings is not as great as that of the trampoline, the same degree of activity cannot be obtained. However, many of the desired experiences can be presented to the child with this equipment. It is highly desirable that the child be permitted to experience the sensation of bouncing and being free of gravity. For this reason, some type of equipment which permits such experience will be found very useful in training.

ANGELS-IN-THE-SNOW

This technique is a modification of the childhood game of the same name. The child lies down in the snow and moves his arms and legs. He then gets up and looks at the pattern created in the snow as a result of his movements. This old game has many elements which can be used to aid the child's development. The original game has been modified for use indoors but the activities required of the child remain basically unchanged. We have previously described the use of this activity as a testing technique. It will also be found highly useful as a training method.

BILATERAL MOVEMENTS

The child lies flat on his back on the floor with his arms at his sides and his feet together. He is then asked to move his feet apart as far as he can, keeping his knees stiff. He is then asked to move his arms along the floor until his hands come together above his head, keeping his elbows stiff. Encourage the child to press against the floor with his heels as he moves his legs and with his hands and wrists as he moves his arms. He should be aware of his hands and feet and their positions at all times during the exercise. The tactual sensation from contact with the floor will increase this awareness.

Children may be found who are unable to make these simple movements or who can move one side at a time but not both together. Other children may be able to make the movements but cannot change time — "move fast" and then "move slow." In these cases, the adult may have to help the child by moving the arm or leg with his hands. The child should be encouraged, however, to learn to perform the movement without help as soon as possible.

When the child brings his feet together, encourage him to "click his heels." When he brings his arms down to his sides, encourage him to slap his sides. By this means, awareness of body parts can be increased through the addition of tactual stimulation. Also, awareness of the difference between a body-body contact and a body-outside object contact can be heightened.

When he has learned to make bilateral leg and arm movements easily and smoothly and equally on each side, ask him to combine the leg and arm movements. In this phase, he is asked to move his legs apart and at the same time move his arms over his head. He then moves his legs together and at the same time brings his arms down to his sides. He is asked to coordinate these two movement patterns so that his legs are apart *at the same time* that his hands come together above his head. His heels touch *at the same time* his hands touch his sides. He is thus asked to time each pattern so that it is synchronized with the others. Both leg and arm movements must be smooth and the arm movement must take as long as, and no longer than, the leg movements. Be sure he keeps his movements smooth. He may try to avoid the problem of the exercise by moving one limb or pair of limbs independently and then "catching-up" with the others.

UNILATERAL AND CROSS-LATERAL MOVEMENTS

When the child has learned how to make these bilateral movements and has become aware of his body in the various positions, introduce unilateral and cross-lateral movements. Ask the child to move his right leg only to the extended position. Then ask him to return it. Always stop at the end of any movement to allow him to appreciate the new posture. Then ask him to do the same with his left leg only, then his right arm only, then his left arm only.

Some children will have difficulty moving one leg or one arm without moving the other. In this case, hold one foot down while the other leg is being moved. It is desirable to hold the foot in a firm grip so that the child maintains tactual awareness of this limb while he moves the other. Encourage the child to complete the single movement without help as soon as possible. Pressing the non-moving foot against the floor will increase tactual stimulation and help him make the transition.

Some children will not be able to identify the leg or arm to be moved if we merely point to it. They cannot make the translation from a visual awareness to a tactual-kinesthetic awareness of the limb so that movement can be initiated. These children will need the additional help that results from the teacher's touching the limb to be moved. Press firmly against the selected limb so that a strong tactual stimulus is provided upon which to base a choice. As a result of this tactual stimulus, the translation from visual to tactual-kinesthetic is made unnecessary. However, encourage the child to make the translation and to initiate the movement on the basis of the visual stimulus alone as soon as possible. Such encouragement can be provided by being sure that the child has awareness of the visual stimulus before the tactual is added. For this reason, point to the limb and stop, waiting for him to become fully aware of the visual stimulus and to attempt to initiate the movement. Add the tactual stimulus only if he has trouble or makes an error. The intensity of the tactual stimulus can be gradually decreased by using a lighter and lighter touch as he progresses.

When the child has mastered these simple unilateral movements, introduce more complicated unilateral movements. Ask the child to move his right leg and right arm together. Next ask him to move his left leg and left arm.

When he has mastered these movements, introduce cross-lateral movements. Ask him to move his left leg and right arm together. Then ask him to move his right leg and left arm. In all of these exercises, timing and the synchronization of timing are important and must be given constant attention.

ALTERING TIME AND POSITION

When these basic movements have been completed, alter the time factor itself. Ask the child to move fast, then slow, then in rhythm to a beat or count. All the types of movement discussed above should be repeated with this timing factor added.

Ask the child to turn over face-down on the floor and repeat all the exercises in this new position. Then place a hassock or pillow under his abdomen so that by raising his shoulders and legs he can be free of the floor except for the pivot provided by the support. The entire series of exercises should be repeated in this position. Now he has an added anti-gravity factor which requires a greater muscle tonus throughout all the muscle systems involved in posturing. The child is required to perform all the former tasks while maintaining this increased tonus of the postural muscles. Do not forget that this position is *very tiring*. Therefore, the periods of practice in this posture should be short. Do not ask the child to maintain this posture continuously for more than one or two minutes at the outside.

PURPOSE OF EXERCISE

This exercise is designed to help the child learn laterality and to increase his awareness of his body image. It can assist him in discovering his extremities and becoming aware of their position in space relative to his body. Movements directed toward the two sides of the body develop an awareness of laterality and teach him to use this awareness in directing activities. Asking him to make movements in time sequence or rhythms helps him to gain good bilateral control in which each side maintains its independence but is integrated with the other. Timed movements also help him to translate spatial changes into temporal sequences of action. He can see his response both as a sequence in time and as a change in space and he learns the relationships between these two methods of seeing the same act. Body image is increased since individual identification and control of limbs alone and in combination are required.

STUNTS AND GAMES

Certain stunts and games used in elementary physical education classes will be found useful in aiding the child to develop body image and motor control. Many of these stunts require the child to reverse normal patterns of movement so that the resulting overall movement takes place in unusual directions or in unusual positions. Thus, the duck walk or rabbit hop require the child to move forward through space but with motor patterns somewhat different from those normally used in walking or running. By the use of such stunts, the child can be taught variations in movement patterns and elaborations of his customary patterns. Laterality and directionality are required to carry out the task and must be maintained while the usual postural and balance relationships are altered.

Parts of the body are required to assume different relative positions and different functions during these stunts. This alteration of the customary body schema can be used to point out more strongly to the child the location and functions of the various limbs. By this means, his body image may be strengthened.

Since these stunts and games are discussed in textbooks on elementary physical education (Neilson, 1956), only a few examples will be described here. The reader is referred to such texts for further materials.

Duck Walk. Ask the child to place his hands on his knees and perform a deep knee bend. In this position, ask him to walk forward.

He may also place his hands behind his back with his palms together and his fingers pointing backward in imitation of a duck's tail.

Rabbit Hop. Ask the child to place his hands on the floor and perform a deep knee bend. Have him move his hands forward and, keeping his hands on the floor, bring his feet forward between his hands with a jump. He then moves his hands forward again and repeats the process as he progresses across the room.

Crab Walk. Ask the child to squat down reaching backward and putting both hands flat on the floor behind him without sitting down. Ask him to walk or run in this position. He should keep his head, neck, and body in a straight line.

Measuring Worm. Ask the child to place his hands on the floor in front of him and about shoulder width apart. His legs should be stretched out straight behind him with the weight of the body supported on the arms and toes. The arms should be kept straight and the body should be straight from head to heels. Keeping his hands stationary and knees straight, he should bring his feet up by little steps until they are as close to his hands as possible. Next, keeping his feet stationary, he should move his hands forward with little steps until he has reached the starting position again. This series of movements is repeated as the child progresses forward across the room.

Elephant Walk. Two children are required for this game. The first child grasps the second at the hips. The second child then jumps upward and locks his legs high around the hips of the first. He then drops backward and works his head, shoulders, and arms between the legs of the first child. The first child then drops forward onto his hands keeping his arms and legs stiff. Both children hold these positions while the first child walks forward.

RHYTHM

Many of the problems of form perception and of figure-ground relationships which have been investigated over a number of years in the field of visual perception exist also in other areas. The investigation of form perception in the past has been largely concerned with spatial relationships and with foreground-background relationships in space. It seems probable that similar types of relationships exist in time. When figure-ground for form is encountered in the dimension of time, we know it as rhythm. Rhythm is important in kinesthetic and tactual problems since much of the information which we obtain from the senses is probably aided and militated by ability to establish and maintain rhythm relationships. In the auditory field, information is kept classified and organized through the imposition of rhythm upon auditory stimuli.

It is felt that many of the problems of auditory span, temporal order in series information and the like, may be related to weaknesses in ability to establish and/or maintain rhythm patterns. As in all other perceptual activities, rhythm in various sensory-motor areas must be integrated so that the child has a concept of rhythm in the total organism. Kinesthetic rhythms must be integrated with tactual rhythms and with auditory rhythms. In any complex task, all of the rhythmic relationships in all of the areas must coincide and the same rhythm pattern must be dominant throughout.

RHYTHMS ON ONE SIDE OF THE BODY ONLY

Many children find it difficult to maintain a rhythm pattern when the rhythmical activities alternate from one side of the body to the other. They are able to establish a rhythm when they are required to beat it out with one hand, for example, but encounter difficulty when two hands must be used and movement of the rhythm must pass from one hand to the other and back again. Therefore, in beginning training in the area of rhythm, it is desirable to start with rhythms on one side of the body only.

Obtain a set of bongo drums or similar objects which, when struck with the hand, produce a strong characteristic sound. (For the present activities, only one such instrument is necessary, but for later techniques it will be desirable to have pairs in which the tone produced by each instrument is distinctively different.) Two sets of these objects are desirable, one for the child and one for the teacher.

Give the child one of the drums while you take the other. Beat out a constant rhythm pattern in which all of the beats are of equal length and equally spaced (*da-da-da-da*). Ask the child to repeat on his drum what you have produced.

In the early stages of training, permit the child to watch you and to beat his drum along with you. In this way, you afford him visual information concerning rhythm as well as auditory, kinesthetic, and tactual information. Alter the rhythm pattern by increasing or decreasing the overall rate; that is to say, beat a fast constant rhythm, then beat a slow constant rhythm, et cetera. When the child is able to identify the rhythm and to reproduce it while watching you, ask him to close his eyes and listen to your beat and then reproduce it. In this activity, we are asking him to recognize and establish a rhythm pattern on the basis of auditory information alone.

When he is able to recognize and establish simple constant rhythm patterns of the type described above, we can move on to more complex rhythms. Present next a simple two-beat rhythm (*da-dit, da-dit, da-dit*). Again vary the speed of the overall rhythm and begin by permitting him to watch as well as listen until he is able to pick up the rhythm from the auditory clues alone.

We can next go to three-stage rhythms (*da-dit-dit-da-dit-dit*). These three-beat rhythms can be altered in various combinations of two items taken three at a time (thus, *dit-da-dit, dit-da-dit, dit-da-dit*). As the child is able to master these three-beat rhythms, we can move on to four-beat, five-beat, six-beat, etc.

In all these rhythm exercises, be sure that the child establishes a smooth rhythmic flow. In three, four, and greater numbers of beats, we have a rhythm imposed upon a rhythm. Thus, *da-dit-dit, da-dit-dit, da-dit-dit* is a series of triads. The child must learn to establish not only the rhythm within the triad (*da-dit-dit*) but the overall rhythm among the triads (*da-dit-dit, da-dit-dit, da-dit-dit*).

In order to learn to generalize these rhythm patterns, the child should produce them in various ways. Thus, in addition to beating the drum with his dominant hand, he should learn to produce the same rhythm by beating with the non-dominant hand. Then he should learn to establish the same rhythm with both hands together. He should also beat the rhythm with his feet, produce it with his vocal cords by a series of vocal sounds, etc. We want him to generalize the concept of these rhythms so that any activities of his organism which can be grouped in time may be used to produce the same rhythm.

BILATERAL RHYTHMS

When the child has learned to establish rhythm patterns on one side of the body and with one part of the body alone, he must learn to establish the same type of rhythm pattern when both sides of the body are used or when the part used to produce the rhythm alternates from one side to the other. Thus, we will want him to learn to beat out rhythm patterns with both hands, with both feet, etc.

For this bilateral activity, pairs of bongo drums are used. Give the child one pair of drums while you take the other pair. Beat out a simple alternating rhythm in which the beats are of equal length and are equally spaced: thus, *R-L-R-L*. The rhythm should alternate regularly from right to left. Ask the child to reproduce this rhythm pattern.

In the early stages of training, let him watch you as well as listen to you. In this way, he can make use of maximum clues (visual, auditory, kinesthetic, tactual) in establishing his rhythm. When he has been able to establish the rhythm on the basis of all of these clues, ask him to close his eyes and develop the rhythm on the basis of the auditory information alone. Vary the overall speed of the rhythm: sometimes beat a fast rhythm, sometimes a slow rhythm, et cetera. Be sure that the child flows smoothly from the right to the left so that the rhythm is smooth and constant, not jerky or accented. Be sure that the flow between the sides of the body is back and forth, not split up into a flow in one direction only (thus, we want *R-L-R-L*, not *RL-RL-RL*).

When the simple *R-L-R* alternation has been mastered, present rhythms in which two beats with each hand are alternated: thus, *R-R-L-L-R-R*. Again, be sure that the flow of the rhythm is smooth and that the rhythmic pattern is not interrupted when it crosses from one side of the body to the other. When the double alternation has been mastered, present alternating series of three (*R-R-R-L-L-L*), four (*R-R-R-R-L-L-L-L*), and five. Whenever the child has difficulty, permit him to watch you as well as listen. However, as soon as he is able to do so, ask him to develop the rhythm pattern on the basis of the auditory stimuli alone. Do not present single series (*R-R-L-L*) but present continuous series of sufficient length to be sure that the child has established the cross-body flow (*R-R-L-L-R-R-L-L*, et cetera).

When these regular rhythms have been mastered, we can present irregular rhythms (*R-R-L-R-R-L*). These irregular patterns can be altered in all combinations of two items taken three at a time. When simple irregular rhythms have been established, we can move on to irregularities involving four beats, five beats, six beats, etc. It is desirable that the child learn to establish these rhythm patterns up to as many as ten or twelve beats, both in the previous activity where all of the rhythm was on one side and in the present activity where the rhythm alternates from one side to the other.

Here again, we want the child to generalize the rhythm to all types of bodily activity. Thus, we will ask him to beat it out with his feet, either using the drums or tapping out the rhythm on the floor. We will ask him to beat with the right hand and the right foot and also with the left hand and the left foot. In like manner, we will ask him to beat with the right hand and the left foot and with the left hand and the right foot.

chapter 10

The Perceptual-Motor Match

TRAINING PERCEPTUAL-MOTOR MATCH

As has been pointed out earlier, when the child has developed a body of motor information he begins to match the perceptual information which he receives to this earlier motor information. In the early stages of such matching, motor activities play the lead role. Since the perceptual information at this point is primarily meaningless, the child uses his motor response to the environment for the purpose of attaching meaning to the incoming perceptual information. As development progresses the perceptual data are gradually used to guide the motor response. Because of the extreme efficiency of perceptual data, this information eventually assumes the major role and the child now responds to perceptual data. It is important to note that in the initial stages the motor response controls the perceptual awareness. The child attends only to those perceptual data which fit in with his motor response and are related to it. In the later stages of development the child modifies his motor response in terms of the perceptual information. Training in the area of perceptual motor matching, therefore, begins with activities in which perceptual data are used to initiate motor responses, and

233

in which the child's attention is called to perceptual information which is being generated as his motor response proceeds. The motor response, however, is the function which is under control and which is determining the activity. The child is encouraged to note the relationship between his motor response and the accompanying perceptual information. Only when this stage has been mastered can training move on to activities in which perceptual information is used to modify motor response or to control motor response.

Initial activities will thus set up a controlled motor response with accompanying perceptual information. At a little later stage, simple perceptual data will be provided and the child will be asked to alter his motor response in terms of these perceptual data. Finally a continuous series of perceptual data will be provided which the child will be asked to use to monitor his motor performance. In this final stage there is a continuous and constant modification or control of motor response in terms of perceptual information.

GROSS MOTOR ACTIVITIES

Training in perceptual motor matching begins with gross motor activities in which the entire body, or major segments of the body, are controlled in terms of perceptual information. In such activities both the motor response and the perceptual data are quite gross. The precision of control demanded for finer motor activities is not required. The child will normally learn these more gross controls before he learns the more precise controls required by fine motor activities such as writing. If the learning begins with overall body activities and is refined to the more precise movements, the perceptual motor control remains related to the response of the total organism. If fine motor control is learned before or without gross motor control, such precise control may develop as a splinter skill and may come to be detached from the overall activities of the organism. It is, therefore, well to insure that the child has learned the gross perceptual-motor match in terms of his entire body or before proceeding to demands for precise control of the hands and fingers.

WALKING AND RUNNING

The most common gross motor activities of the child are walking and running. These activities, therefore, provide a convenient place to start the teaching of perceptual control.

Ask the child to walk to a goal and stop when he reaches it, using perceptual information to determine the stopping. Initially the goal should be a solid object such as a wall or a piece of furniture. In this case, if the child fails to use the perceptual information to influence the activity, the walking will be stopped by the goal itself. The child's attention can then be called to the perceptual information which he failed to use. He can be encouraged on the next trial to use the perceptual information, to which his attention has been called, to stop walking before he is physically stopped by the goal. Thus he can be asked to walk to the wall, stop before he runs into it, and when he is close enough reach out and touch it. In this type of task a gross motor activity has been set in operation. The child's attention is called to the accompanying perceptual information and he is encouraged to attend to these perceptual data.

Such training is best used in connection with simple games. Thus, tag games in which the child is "safe" when he is in contact with a base can be used. Children run across the room from one wall to another while the one who is "it" attempts to catch them. "It" can catch a child only when he is not in contact with either of the walls. This game can be varied by giving "it" a soft ball. Upon a signal, children run from one wall to the other. "It" catches a child by hitting him with the ball while he is running across the room. A child cannot be caught when he is in contact with the wall.

In the next stage the child is asked to control his walking or running by perceptual information alone. In this case the goal is no longer a concrete object but is a perceptual element. Thus the child might be asked to walk to a line but to stop before he steps over it. Here he is asked to alter his activity, in this case to cease it, on the basis of perceptual information.

This type of training can also best be used in connection with games. The same tag games that are described above can be used at this stage in training. Now, however, the base will not be a concrete object such as a wall, but instead an area marked out by lines on the floor or similar visual clues. Thus the child will be "safe" when he is behind a line drawn on the floor or when he is within a circular area mapped out on it.

The same type of training is provided by relay races in which the child runs to a line, turns, and returns. He can also be asked to run around an object or an area mapped out on the floor and return. He is required to come back and start over if he touches the goal or steps into the marked off area.

In the last stage of training, perceptual information is used to monitor or continuously control the activity. In this task, the child is asked to walk along a line. If the child's coordination is adequate, a line can be drawn on the floor with chalk or laid out with masking tape. The child is asked to walk along the line without stepping off. If the child's coordination is less adequate, an alley can be devised by laying two strips of masking tape along the floor. The width of this alley can be adjusted to the coordination of the child. He is asked to walk down the alley without stepping out.

OTHER TOTAL BODY TASKS

Jumping is also a common activity with children which involves the total body. The child can be asked to jump with both feet or he can be asked to jump with one foot alone. A jump such as the running broad jump, in which the body is propelled with one foot and lands on the other foot, is a modification of walking or running and is probably less useful in the present context than the simpler forms of jumping. The child can be asked to control the length and direction of his jump on the basis of perceptual data.

Lay out or ask the child to lay out on the floor a circular pattern using a short length of rope such as a jump rope. When the circle has been formed, ask the child to stand in the circle and jump out of it by jumping over the rope. Then ask him to turn around and jump into the circle. In the former task he is merely asked to perform the motor activity of jumping attending to the perceptual data as he does. In the latter task he is asked to modify his jumping performance in both direction and extent on the basis of the perceptual information.

Lay out an alley on the floor with masking tape. Ask the child to jump over the alley. Encourage him to jump only as far as is necessary to clear the alley, not to jump as far as he can in the hope that he will clear the alley. Here the perceptual information is being used to control the extent of the motor activity. The alterations required by the perceptual demands can be varied by altering the width of the alley.

A vertical jump can be related to perceptual information with similar activities. In this case a light stick similar to that used in high jumping is held horizontally at a small distance above the floor. The child is asked to jump over the stick. Again he is encouraged just to clear the stick, not to jump as high as he can. The influence of the perceptual data on the jumping activity can be altered by varying the height of the stick above the floor.

A similar activity involves jumping off of or on to a raised step or platform. Ask the child to stand in front of the platform and jump onto it. Encourage him just to clear the step so that he lands lightly, rather than landing with a "thud" because he has jumped too high. Pieces of playground apparatus, stairs, curbs, and the like can be used as platforms for such tasks.

During the swimming period the child can be asked to jump from the side of the pool into an innertube floating on the surface. He is encouraged to jump into the middle of the tube so that his body passes through it without touching. Here perceptual information is used to determine the extent and the direction of the motor activity.

The child can also be asked to jump into prescribed areas successively. A ladder can be laid down on the floor. The child is asked to jump from the space between two rungs into the space between the next two rungs and so on. Modifications of the game of hopscotch can be used in the same fashion. For many children the customary hopscotch pattern will be too complex. For such children the activity can be simplified by reducing the number of areas laid out in the pattern and the complexity of the series of movements required.

Perceptual data are used to determine the activity or position of the total body in many normal classroom routines. Thus, when the children are asked to form a line, perceptual motor matching may be involved. In the initial stages the children may be asked to line up along a line on the floor. In this task each child places his body in position in terms of the perceptual information from the line on the floor. His attention is also called to the perceptual data represented by the group of children, each of whom is lined up with the line on the floor. At a later stage the children can be asked to form a line without the added clue of the line on the floor. Here the child is asked to place his body in position with reference to the perceptual information provided by the total group of children. This is a more difficult task and requires more complex use of perceptual data. If the child is "out of line" in such an activity, do not put him back in line but rather ask him to put himself in line. Call his attention to the perceptual data which he needs to use to accomplish the task and permit him to experiment with the use of these data to control his body and his movements. Staying in line while walking or marching involves a continuous monitoring of the motor activity with perceptual data. Such activities represent the later stages of perceptual motor matching in gross motor activities.

ARM AND HAND ACTIVITIES

Intermediate between the activities of the total body and the precise eye-hand coordination so frequently required in classroom activities are activities of the arm and hand. These activities involve tasks in which the hand operates as a part of the arm and in which the movement involves hand, arm, and shoulder. Perceptual control of such large movements is encouraged when a target is added to the task and the child is asked to direct the movement toward the target.

Most common of such tasks are throwing activities involving throwing a ball or similar item toward a target. Such tasks involve the coordinated movement of the arm and the integrated grasp and release of the hand. When a target is introduced, the perceptual data serve to determine the direction of the movement. Various objects of playground equipment or classroom supplies may be used as the targets. The size of the target should be graded to the coordination displayed by the child. Since high degrees of precision are not the object of this activity, the target should not be so small as to make the task frustrating for the child. On the other hand, if the target is too large, the child can successfully complete the task with little or no perceptual guidance of the movement. Targets should be placed in various orientations toward the child. Thus, some should be placed on the floor, some on the wall at approximately shoulder height, and some above his head, such as a basketball backstop or a basketball hoop. They should be placed in front and also to the side of him so that he has practice in controlling his arm in various directions. The child also needs to learn the control of various throwing motions. Therefore, he should throw sometimes with a large ball which he propells with both hands, sometimes with a small ball which he throws with his right hand, and sometimes with a ball he throws with his left hand.

When the target is placed horizontal to the child, the perceptual information serves to control both the direction and the force of the throw. Set a waste basket in front of the child. Give him a bean bag and ask him to throw it into the waste basket. He is now encouraged to control both the direction and the force of the throw in terms of the visual information received from the waste basket. Set the waste basket in various orientations, sometimes straight ahead, sometimes to the right, and sometimes to the left. Alter the distance between the child and the basket so that he has an opportunity to control various forces of movement. In this activity, as in throwing at a target, high degrees of precision are not the object of the task. Therefore, the size of the waste basket and the distance from the child should be graded to the child's ability. Grade the tasks so that it will challenge the child to control his movement perceptually, but will not prove frustrating to him.

Another similar activity involves rolling a ball at a target. Set up a plastic bowling pin in front of the child. Give the child a ball and ask him to roll it along the floor and knock the pin down. Encourage the child to watch the ball as it rolls toward the pin. Such observation encourages him to remain aware of the perceptual data over a period of time. It further provides him with continuous information concerning the adequacy of his control. Since the rolling ball moves more slowly than the thrown ball, such continuous observation is possible. By encouraging the child to be aware of such continuous perceptual information, we can lay the groundwork for the final stage in which he will use perceptual data to *monitor* the movement of the arm and the hand. Similarly, groundwork can be laid for later training in the area of ocular control by such continuous observation.

Continuous perceptual control can be encouraged by tasks which require the child to push an object along a path. Give the child a toy wheelbarrow with the wheel far enough in front of the frame so that it can be seen when he pushes it. Ask the child to push the wheelbarrow, keeping the wheel on a line which is drawn on the floor with chalk or laid out with masking tape. The difficulty of this task can be graded to the ability of the child by increasing or decreasing the width of the line. In such tasks, the child is required to attend continuously to the perceptual data and to use this information for a continuous control of the movement. This activity can be varied by using dollies, toy cars, wands, and similar devices which can be guided along a line. The path should be laid out on the floor rather than on a desk or table top so that the entire arm and shoulder and not just the hand will be involved in the guiding.

The use of perceptual information in the initiation of a movement as well as its guidance and termination is provided in batting activities. Toss a ball toward the child and ask him to bat with his hand. The perceptual information must now be used to determine not only the direction of the movement but its timing as well. Initially, the child should be asked to bat the ball with his hand since this part is most directly controlled. Later he can be given extensions of his hand in the form of various types of bats and rackets. The control of these devices, however, is less direct and more difficult than the control of the hand itself. When bats or rackets are used, bimanual as well as unimanual control can be practiced.

One of the difficulties with batting as an activity is the amount of time required to reclaim the ball after it has been batted or missed. There is also a problem of controlling the ball in limited spaces or in spaces filled with equipment which can be damaged or broken if hit with the ball. These problems can be avoided by the use of a tether ball in which the ball is attached to a post by a rope.

A more flexible method of controlling the ball involves the teacher holding the rope in his hand. Attach a rope to a plastic ball such as a practice ball. Hold the free end of the rope above your head. Swing the ball, by the rope, in a complete circle around you. The child stands just outside the arc of the ball and bats it as it swings past. By varying the length of the rope, the speed of the ball and the extent of the arc can be altered.

Normal classroom tasks and chores can frequently be used to provide experiences in perceptual-motor matching. Returning equipment to its storage area frequently requires pushing or sliding large objects through doors and into confined spaces. Such activity is similar to that of pushing objects along a line as described above. Putting away materials frequently involves placing smaller objects in terms of perceptual information. Thus, packing building blocks into the container, stacking books on the shelf, and returning boxes to the storage cabinet are activities in which the arm and hand are guided by perceptual data. Such activities have the great advantage that they represent real tasks rather than contrived exercises.

FINE MOTOR ACTIVITIES

It is probable that the normal activities of the classroom make greater demands upon the fine motor coordination of the child than upon any other activity of the organism. He is required to perform a large number of highly precise movements of the fingers and hands. Coloring, drawing and copying and, finally, writing make heavy demands for extremely precise fine motor coordination.

As has been suggested earlier, it is well to delay direct attention to these fine motor activities until a certain degree of facility has been established in the more gross movements. If too great a premium is placed on fine motor coordination too early in the development of the child, a splinter skill frequently develops through which the child performs these precise activities without being able to maintain an awareness of their relationship to the rest of the activities of his body. As a result, these fine motor skills exist isolated and alone. Their usefulness is limited to those situations for which they were specifically developed; they frequently create confusion and there is conflict between what the hand is doing and what the rest of the body is doing.

Since the classroom situation places such great demand upon precise movement of the hand and fingers, it is particularly important that these eye-hand skills remain related to the activities of the arm and shoulder. Following the proximo-distal gradient, activities of the shoulder are differentiated first, activities of the elbow are differentiated next, and finally activities of the hand and fingers are differentiated. In establishing the perceptual-motor match in the precise activities of the classroom, therefore, it is well to give attention to this match as its exists in the more gross activities of the arm and shoulder through the exercises described above. Watch the child's performance: if, when he is writing or drawing, the shoulder and arm are stiff and rigid; or the reverse, limp and without tonus; if a minor variation of the activity, such as shifting from paper to chalkboard, where arm and hand are required, markedly breaks down the performance; if the size of the product cannot be altered without altering its accuracy. These are indications that the fine motor activity may not be adequately integrated with the total activity of the organism. In this event it would be well to stress temporarily the fine motor performance less and stress the gross motor performance more until a balance between these two types of activity can be achieved.

Many years ago, penmanship was taught by the Palmer Method. This method stressed the relationship between the fingers, the hand, wrist, the elbow, and the shoulder in the writing task. Writing movements were taught which involved all of these parts, and writing skills which involve the fingers alone were discouraged. This method proved quite cumbersome for the majority of children in the classroom and hence fell into disuse. For the majority of children in the classroom, however, the coordination of finger activities with activities of the hand, wrist, arm, and shoulder could be assumed. The normal differentiation and subsequent integration of these movements had occurred. For children with learning disorders, however, in many of whom difficulties in these normal developmental processes have occurred, methods similar to the Palmer method may be found very useful because of their emphasis on the integration of these precise writing movements with other movement patterns of the organism.

HAND-EYE ACTIVITIES

Developmentally, motor learning came before perceptual learning. Therefore, in the perceptual-motor match perceptual information is matched to motor information. In the development of eye-hand coordination, the initial stage involves teaching the eye to follow the hand. The control of the process is in the hand, the hand is the part of the system which is under control, and the eye follows the activity of the hand. The child first learns how to make the eye follow the hand, keeping visual contact with it throughout a movement or series of movements. He pays attention to the perceptual information involved in this process and begins the matching of this information to his body of motor information.

Eye-hand coordination, therefore, begins with activities in which the movement of the hand is controlled and the child follows this controlled movement of the hand with the eye, matching the movement of the eye to the movement of the hand. Initial training activities, therefore, involve tasks in which the hand moves in a controlled fashion and the child is encouraged to watch the hand as it moves. Emphasis is placed on maintaining consistent visual contact with the hand.

In some children, the control of the hand itself will be inadequate. In still others the hand, which may be under control when visual information is not present, may become confused when visual information is added. Thus the addition of visual information may disrupt the control of the motor movement. Such a child performs more accurately when he does not watch his hand than when he does watch his hand. The visual information confuses and disrupts the motor process. For such children it may be desirable to use devices in which the movement of the hand is controlled by exterior means.

With such devices the movement of the hand is prescribed. If the perceptual information confuses the motor control, the direction and extent of the movement are insured by the nature of the device. Obviously, such devices must be designed so that the force involved in the movement is supplied by the child. Simply grasping the child's hand and moving it in a particular direction is not sufficient since the entire process would be external to the child. He has not generated the motor pattern and, therefore, has nothing to which to match the perceptual information. The situation must be designed so that the child makes the movement and it is his movement, but its nature and direction are guided so that if he cannot control his own movement it is controlled for him.

The simplest of such devices is a board with a groove cut in it. A peg or handle fits vertically into the groove. The groove is flanged at the bottom so that a washer attached to the bottom of the handle moves in it. Thus, the handle can be moved down the groove but cannot be removed from it. The child grasps the handle and moves it back and forth across the board in the groove. Should the child loose control of the movement of his hand, the device prevents the hand from moving in an unwanted direction and restores the nature and direction of the movement. We are thus assured that the hand will move in a prescribed fashion. The child is then encouraged to watch his hand as he moves the handle back and forth across the board. To increase the visual stimulation, it is possible to paste a brightly colored sticker on the back of the child's hand or on the top of the handle. Such a sticker provides a strong visual target and helps the child maintain visual contact with the moving hand (Early, F., 1969).

Slightly more complex models of this device can be constructed. These variants involve simple forms (circle, square, triangle) grooved into a plywood base with a handle which slides in the groove but cannot be removed. The child can then move around the periphery of a form in a controlled fashion and is encouraged to watch his hand as it moves. Such devices have implication not only for the basic eye-hand match but, at a little later stage in training, for the introduction of form perception.

If the control of the hand is somewhat better, so that the child needs only slight guidance, certain commercial toys may be appropriate. Model trains in which a model locomotive is pushed around a track of metal or wood, the wheels of the locomotive being flanged to fit the track, can be useful. Also avilable are toys in which a model of an automobile is pushed around a grooved track cut into a wood base. Unfortunately for fathers who are eager to buy electric trains for their children, at this stage the toy cannot be mechanical. It must be pushed by the child since it is only through his own motor response that he forms the basis for the eye-hand match.

In the media of pencil and paper, scribbling serves somewhat the same purpose. In scribbling the child performs a movement. The pencil leaves on the paper a record of this movement. Thus the perceptual information generated by the movement, which is itself ethereal in time, remains behind and becomes permanent in time. The child is encouraged to watch his hand and attend to the perceptual information as it is being generated. He is then encouraged to examine the trace left behind by the movement and attend to this same perceptual information which now lasts over time and can be examined at leisure and more completely. Scribbling can thus provide an excellent bridge between a simple perceptual-motor match, in which the eye follows the hand, and more complex perceptual activities in which the child deals with the results of such simple matching.

It is desirable that scribbling begin with large movements. The chalkboard provides an excellent medium for scribbling with large movements of the arm. If paper and pencil or crayon are desired, large sheets of newsprint should be provided so that similar large movements can be executed with the arm and hand. Beginning with such large movements again emphasizes the relationship between the fine motor activities of the fingers and hands and the overall motor activities of the body. It also serves to emphasize the matching of perceptual data, not only to the fine movements of the fingers but to the overall movement patterns of the total body.

In the beginning stages, scribbling should not emphasize production, but rather the process of production. Attention should be called to maintaining visual contact with what the hand is doing. Frequently, attention is called to the production, and the marks on the paper are interpreted as representations of common objects or symbols. Thus, after the child has scribbled, we say to him, "Look, you have drawn a tree" or "See, you have made a picture of a dog." If attention is drawn to such production before the child is aware of what it is he has done, again we frequently create confusion. The child can only assume that something magical has happened. He has done something, he knows not what, which has resulted in this applauded production, he knows not how. If on the other hand, we first draw his attention to what he is doing by emphasizing continuous visual awareness of his movement and attention to the perceptual data generated by it, we preserve an awareness of *how* the production was accomplished. We maintain an intimate relationship between the movement and the production, and we preserve the relationship between the perceptual information and the motor information. If this is done, the child is not only aware of how the production came to be but he can reproduce it again. He can translate perceptual information into an appropriate motor response and can predict the perceptual information which will result from his motor response. Scribbling is thus a very important activity both in furthering the perceptual-motor match and, through the motor match, in making meaningful the perceptual information provided by pictures and later by symbolic materials.

Another device which is useful for encouraging the eye to follow the hand is a streamer. To a piece of ¾″ dowel 12″ to 18″ long, attach a narrow streamer of crepe paper or ribbon. Streamers approximately 1″ wide and from 30″ to 36″ long will be found most effective. The child grasps the dowel and moves his hand in a circular or other curving pattern. The streamer follows the pattern of the movement and sets up a similar pattern as it moves through the air. Since the streamer provides an intense visual stimulus, the child's attention is drawn to the movement of his hand and, since this movement is preserved for a limited period of time, to the perceptual nature of the movement and its result.

One hand-eye difficulty frequently encountered in children with learning disorders involves the movement of the wrist. Although the child may learn to move the wrist in a vertical or horizontal direction, he has difficulty learning the twisting movement of the wrist and particularly its purpose and results. Thus, if the child is asked to draw a circle on the chalkboard, he does not turn the wrist during the performance but maintains a rigid position of his hand with reference to the forearm. The result is a very stiff and inflexible drawing performance, and frequently an inaccurate one.

The problem of the turning motion of the wrist can be attacked through a device in which nuts must be screwed onto bolts. A board is drilled with holes through which bolts of various sizes are inserted and permanently attached so that they will not turn. Nuts in sizes to fit the bolts are provided. The child is required to screw the nuts onto the bolts or to unscrew them from the bolts. Thus, a clockwise turn of the wrist is required in screwing the nuts on, a counterclockwise movement in unscrewing them. The child should be encouraged in using a wrist motion in assembling or disassembling the nuts and bolts. He should be discouraged from turning the arm at the shoulder. Bolts of various sizes are provided so that the turning motion of the wrist can be practiced and also, in the case of the smaller bolts, a turning motion of the fingers. This device also helps to train size judgments and size matching.

EYE-HAND ACTIVITY

When the eye has learned to follow the hand and the child has learned to obtain consistent information from his eye, the next stage in development is reached. Because of the greater efficiency of the eye and because of the larger amount of information per unit of time supplied by it, the eye begins to assume the dominant role in the perceptual-motor match. Now the eye takes over and begins to guide the hand. To aid the transition to these eye-hand controls, activities are required in which the movement of the hand is less rigidly controlled and the child is encouraged to substitute visual information for these more rigid controls. Eventually, the hand will be guided almost entirely by the eye and by the information which the eye is supplying.

The control of the hand can be reduced but not entirely eliminated by the use of a template. A template is a pattern cut out of cardboard or similar material. Simple forms (circle, square, triangle, rectangle) are most frequently used. The form is cut out of the sheet of cardboard. The template is then the cardboard sheet with a cut out portion in its center. The child inserts his finger, a pencil, or chalk in the cutout and runs it around the boundaries of the form. The cut out portion also can become a template. For this portion the child runs his finger or his pencil around the outside edge of the form.

Templates offer an external guide and a tactual-kinesthetic cue for the hand. The movement of the hand is controlled in one direction from its path but not in the other. Thus, the child is required to establish visual control for half the errors, the other half being controlled externally by the device. In like manner a non-visual clue to the location of the correct path is provided in the event the visual control breaks down. These templates, therefore, provide a good intermediate step between hand-eye activity and eye-hand activity.

For this particular purpose, the interest is in the movement of the hand and its control, not in the form which is being produced. Therefore, the teacher should call the child's attention to what his hand is doing and encourage him to develop more visual control of the hand's activity. Attention to the nature of the form represented by the template will come when form perception is being trained.

It is important to stop here and point out that the template is an illustration of a device which can be used for more than one aspect of training. In the present context, it is being used to train eye-hand coordination. In another context it will be used to train form perception. The use made of the device is different in the two situations, and the method of its use is different. In the present instance, attention is on the control of the movement. Only one part of the template, such as one side of the square, may be used. In training form perception, less attention will be paid to the control of the movement and attention will be directed to the overall figure. Inaccuracies in movements used to produce the form will be largely overlooked in the interest of attention to the whole qualities of the form. Thus, one pice of equipment may be used in two entirely different ways for two entirely different purposes. One might say that the template is psychologically a different device when used for different purposes. The teacher should be aware of the skills and functions involved in performance with a piece of equipment. She should be ready to use any piece of equipment available which illustrates the function which she is attempting to train irrespective of the principle involved in the original design of the equipment or the uses which she may have made of the equipment in the past. Such flexibility in the teacher's relationship to her material makes available to her many more training opportunities than can be provided by specially designed equipment to solve each problem which she may face.

For the present purpose, the template is attached to the chalkboard or to a sheet of paper. The child is asked to run his finger or pencil around the periphery of the template or a portion of this periphery. His attention is drawn to the movement of his hand. He is encouraged to control this movement visually and to use the template as little as possible. He is asked to draw close to the edge of the template but not touch it. For this purpose a broad heavy line may be drawn close to the periphery of the template. Thus the teacher will draw a form slightly smaller than the template in the case of the inside template and slightly larger in the case of the outside template. The template is then laid so that it just touches this figure. The child is now asked to trace the figure, using the template only when necessary.

The next stage in training involves activities in which the opening clue to the control of the movement of the hand is a visual one. The most common example of such activity is tracing. Tracing should begin with very gross tasks in which the precision required in hand control is limited. Thus a strip an inch to an inch and one-half wide can be drawn on the chalkboard or on a sheet of newsprint. The child is told that this is a road. He is given a toy car and is asked to "drive it down the road without getting into the ditch." The child's attention is drawn to his hand, and he is encouraged to "keep the car on the road." (If the road is extended and the child is stationed in the middle so that the hand crosses the midline, directionality is involved. If the road is long the relationship between the hand, arm, and shoulder as described above is also involved.)

When the child is able to maneuver a straight road in both a vertical and a horizontal direction, curves can be introduced. When he is able to handle roads in a diagonal direction, a combination of curves and straight lines can be used. Now the patterns can be quite complex and the tracing task can become quite difficult. At this stage, however, the roads should not cross each other as this involves a figure-ground problem which the child is probably not yet ready to handle.

After these more gross activities, the child can be introduced to more conventional tracing tasks. These tasks should involve simple pictures and forms drawn with broad lines outlining the periphery so that the degree of precision required is limited. The child is given a crayon in a color contrasting with that of the outline to be traced. He traces over the outline, keeping his crayon on the line. As he learns to use this visual clue to control the movement of his hand, the task can be increased in difficulty by decreasing the width of the line to be traced. When sufficient control has been developed, tissue paper or other transparent materials can be placed over the picture and the child can trace on the transparent paper. After the tracing has been completed, the transparent paper can be removed and the child can observe his product independent of the original copy.

Such activities are important, since his figure is thus lifted off of the original figure. Such manipulation leads him to a consideration of the figure-ground problem.

A number of devices are available for testing or training eye-hand coordination. In general these are known as steadiness testing devices. One such device involves a groove in a piece of wood. The child is given a stylus which he is asked to move down the groove without touching the sides. The groove becomes increasingly narrow as he moves down. The sides of the groove are lined with metal and his stylus is metal. Whenever he touches the side an electrical contact is made and a bell rings. He is thus given an auditory signal when he has made an error. He attempts to move the stylus the length of the groove without ringing the ball.

Another such device involves a series of holes drilled in a metal plate. The child is given a metal stylus which he is to insert in the hole without touching the side. If he touches the side an electrical contact is made and a bell rings or a light flashes. The holes begin large and decrease in size as the child proceeds down the plates. He is asked to see how far he can go, inserting the stylus in each hole, without touching the edges and ringing the bell.

Such mechanical devices are useful in refining the eye-hand coordination. It is important to note that this coordination must be established and the eye-hand relationship must be learned before it can be refined with such devices. Therefore, the more gross activities outlined above should be completed before these more complex tasks are used. Refinement of eye-hand coordination after its establishment, however, can be aided by these devices since they provide additional clues in the event of error, and they consistently and automatically recall the child's attention to the task when his control is not adequate. If stories and other motivating devices are built around these instruments, the child becomes highly motivated for the task and enjoys the activity.

VISUALIZATION

The primary purpose of the perceptual-motor match is to match perceptual information to motor information. When this match has been made, perceptual data and motor data should yield the same information. In like manner, perceptual information resulting from motor activity (tactual and kinesthetic information) should be the same as visual information. The child should then be able to translate from tactual-kinesthetic to visual, and the reverse. Frequently, however, his attention needs to be called to the similarity between these bodies of information through activities designed to emphasize the match.

The most common task for this purpose is the blind bag. Place a group of common objects such as model cars, doll furniture, et cetera, and classroom objects such as chalk, pencil, eraser, et cetera in a paper sack. Lay out in front of the child a group of objects exactly matching those in the bag. The child reaches into the bag, selects an object, and manipulates it without looking at it. He is then asked to point to the object on the table which is the same as the one he has in his hand. This decision involves the comparison of tactual-kinesthetic information on the one hand with visual information on the other. The child then removes the object from the bag and compares it with the one he has selected to check his match. This check involves the comparison of visual information with visual information.

The task should begin with objects in the bag between which the differentiation is very gross. As the child becomes more able, objects can be included which are very similar to each other. When such similar objects are included, the demands for accuracy in matching the two avenues of information are increased. Obviously, care should be taken to select objects in which tactual information and visual information are parallel. Thus, the selection within the bag between two objects which differ only visually, such as in color, is impossible. In like manner, tactual differentiations which are overshadowed in the visual avenue by more intense visual stimuli, such as a slight indentation in the surface of a picture, should be avoided. The aim in this task is not to refine differentiation in either the tactual-kinesthetic area or the visual area, but to emphasize the relationship between these two areas. Therefore, the qualities on which differentiation is based should have parallels in the two sensory areas and this parallelism should be emphasized during the task.

When the child has shown some facility in the recognition of concrete objects under these conditions, more symbolic stimuli can be presented. Thus, cut out letters or figures can be placed in the bag and the child can be asked to recognize the similar figure from among a group of letters or figures.

The task, in this form, emphasizes the comparison of tactual-kinesthetic perceptual information with visual perceptual information. The relationship between these perceptual data and motor response can be emphasized by asking the child to reproduce the object which he investigates. In this case, a single object is placed in the bag. The child reaches in and, without looking, manipulates the object until he has developed an awareness of it. He is then asked to draw a picture of this object. When the task is used in this form, the child is first asked to use tactual-kinesthetic perceptual information to develop a motor pattern. He is then asked to reproduce the motor pattern, controlling it by visual information. Finally, he is asked to recognize the visual pattern which he has created. The task has required, on the one hand, a tactual-motor match and, on the other hand, a visual-motor match. These two functions have been kept separate so that the child must depend upon his ability to match, and no direct comparison is permitted until the end of the task, when the child checks his production by removing the object from the bag and comparing it with his reproduction. In such a task, motor activities are used as a common intermediary between two perceptual bodies of information. Only insofar as perceptual-motor matching is accurate in both avenues, can the task be completed successfully.

A similar task involving more symbolic materials uses tactual forms. These are figures (circle, square, triangle, rectangle) routed out of a wood base. The wood base containing the form is placed behind a screen or curtain. The child reaches under the screen or curtain and runs his finger around the form without looking at it. He is then asked either to recognize this form from a group of visual forms which are presented to him or to reproduce it on paper.

These tactual forms frequently are produced by indenting them into a surface as described above. They can also be produced by raising the figure above the surface. The latter is usually preferable because it parallels more closely the normal figure-ground relationship. Such forms can be produced by nailing narrow strips of wood over a base. They can also be produced within the classroom situation. Prepare a mixture of wallpaper paste and place it in a cake decorator. On a piece of porous paper draw out the form with the cake decorator. When the paste has dried, it will harden and adhere to the paper so that the child can run his finger over the form and investigate it.

VISUAL-MOTOR TRANSLATION

Closely related to the problem of visualization is the problem of visual-motor translation. Upon being presented with a visual stimulus, the child should be able to develop a pattern of movement which will reproduce this stimulus. In the early stages of development, the child's attempts to reproduce involve a great deal of motor exploration and overt trial and error to correct mistakes. As the child gains more facility in perceptual-motor matching, the visual stimuli set up an image of the motor pattern required for their reproduction. This motor pattern can be manipulated and corrected within the central system before it eventuates as an overt response. This ability to translate a visual stimulus into its motor counterpart and the reverse, the ability to anticipate the perceptual data resulting from motor activity, helps the child to maintain the consistency of perceptual-motor data. At all times, he is dealing with a perceptual-motor body of information rather than dealing with one of these functions alone. Through such ability to translate, the motor response remains always closely related to the perceptual stimulus and vice versa.

Experimentation with such visual-motor translation begins with imitative activites. The child imitates movements which are presented to him and attempts to reproduce movements demonstrated by others. Therefore, all sorts of imitative tasks provide practice in such translations.

Particularly applicable in the classroom situation are many of the imitative games found in books of children's activities. Thus, the singing game in which certain activities are prescribed by the song and the child either reproduces the movement from the verbal description or by the imitating of a leader can be used. The song game

"Did you ever see a laddie (lassie)" places the emphasis on imitation of movement. The song asks "Did you ever see a laddie go this way and that?" The child is then asked to perform a movement which the other children are required to imitate. At the next verse, another child becomes the leader and so on. These tasks may be used for the development of body image and variability in movement. In the present context, however, the emphasis is on the ability of the child to reproduce the prescribed movement. Therefore, the child's attention should now be directed to the accuracy of his reproduction. He should be encouraged to correct his response until it matches the model presented. He should be especially encouraged to consider his response before he performs so that corrections and alterations are made before the pattern is exteriorized in overt performance. Through this prior consideration of what his movement is going to look like, the visual-motor translation is encouraged.

Obviously, a large variety of movements must be presented to serve this purpose. If a single, well practiced movement pattern is used over and over, the visual stimulus does not lead to a translation into a motor pattern but rather serves only as a trigger for an already established pattern. The pattern is, therefore, performed as it has previously been learned, with little or no reference to the perceptual information during the performance. Games such as "Did you ever see a laddie" are particularly useful because they present many variations in movement rather than a number of repetitions of the same movement.

Such games involve the direct presentations of movement to the child. As such, the visual stimuli are transient in time. Some children may have difficulty because they do not have sufficient time to check their response against the perceptual model which was presented. The game of "statues" can be used to minimize this problem. In this game the leader assumes and maintains a certain pose. The children are required to imitate his pose. Since the leader holds his pose over time, the children have an opportunity to check and double check their response. In such a task, however, the child should be encouraged to assume the required pose immediately with as little correction and alteration as possible. The visual-motor translation involves the development of a motor pattern on the basis of the initial perceptual information. The checking of this pattern, however, involves a comparison of perceptual information against perceptual information. The child compares what he sees of his pose with what he sees of the leader's pose. This is a vision-to-vision match rather than a visual-motor match. The child who has problems with visual-motor translation may attempt to minimize his problems by a successive series of vision-to-vision checks. Thus he may check and correct, check and correct, and so on, depending upon the visual checks to produce a correct response, rather than monitoring the response through a perceptual-motor translation. This type of behavior is discouraged when the child is requested to assume the modeled position directly with as little correction as possible after the response has become overt.

The same type of imitative activity can be provided for the hands and arms. In this case the children are seated in a circle. The first child is given an object and asked to pass it to the second child. The second child must pass it on with the same movement which the first child used in delivering it to him. The object then passes around the circle, each child imitating the movement of the leader. On the second round, the next child becomes leader and each must imitate him in turn. The same visual-motor translation is involved in this task as was involved in the previous task. Because of its nature, more emphasis is placed on the activities of the hands and arms than was the case in the more gross activities of the earlier games.

The child should be encouraged to think of how he is going to move before he performs. In the event of an error, he should not be corrected directly but should be encouraged to observe what he did wrong and then to determine how he could change his performance. Overt experimentation with movements should be discouraged as soon as possible, and the child should be encouraged to plan his movement pattern before he responds.

Following these directly imitative activities, the child is ready to translate a less concrete visual presentation into a pattern of movement which will reproduce it. Thus, he can look at the drawing of a square and develop the series of movements necessary to make one like it. As with the previous concrete activities, the square suggests the motor patterns required in its reproduction. Representational and symbolic materials are now closely related to their motor counterparts, and his response to such visual presentations is perceptual-motor. The importance of such a close relationship between the perceptual data and the motor data in such classroom activities as coloring, drawing, writing, and the like, is obvious. Activities designed to promote the development of this more abstract type of visual-motor matching are discussed under *activities in drawing and copying.*

OTHER BODY PARTS

Because so much use is made of eye-hand coordination in ordinary classroom activities, we frequently pay little or no attention to perceptual-motor functions in areas other than the eye-hand process. Such over-concentration on eye-hand coordination sometimes leads to a restriction of the perceptual-motor generalization. The child develops eye-hand coordination but does not develop the perceptual-motor function in other areas or, if he does, these other functions are not seen as related to the basic eye-hand coordination. Thus, the perceptual-motor function in walking and similar activities may come to be different than those in which the hand is the major performer. If this lack of relationship between functions develops, confusion results and the child must approach his environment differently, depending upon the function which is involved. Where there is a difficulty in the development of a perceptual-motor match, such splitting off of the eye-hand function is more likely. Therefore, with such children, it is desirable to pay attention to the problem of perceptual-motor matching in a broader area than eye-hand coordination alone.

The most common of such perceptual-motor functions is eye-foot coordination. The eye is used to guide the foot in the same way that it was used previously to guide the hand. It is probable that eye-foot coordination develops in the same fashion as eye-hand coordination. First the movement of the foot is controlled and the eye follows the foot. As this process becomes more highly developed, the eye takes over and assumes the lead. Now the eye guides the foot and determines the nature and extent of the movements. Such eye-foot functions are particularly important because of their close relationship to the locomotor activities. The fact that the child must be cautioned so frequently to "Look where you are walking," is an indication of weakness in the eye-foot coordination. The child receives either inadequate perceptual information or confusing perceptual information which makes it difficult for him to use perceptual data to control motor activity.

Training in eye-foot coordination begins with activities in which the movement or position of the foot is controlled and the child's visual attention is drawn to it. One device for this purpose involves the use of stepping boxes. The stepping box is an oblong open box slightly larger than the child's foot. The sides of the box are approximately 2" high. The overall dimensions will vary somewhat with the size of the child but for young children a box 4" by 6" is probably about right.

Begin with one such box placed on the floor. The child stands a short distance from the box so that he can step easily into it. Ask him to put his foot in the box. The sides of the box now provide an external control for the position of the foot. The child is encouraged to look at his foot and to attend to the perceptual information about its location.

When the child can use one such box with some ease, introduce a number of boxes. These should be placed on the floor in an irregular pattern spaced approximately equal to the child's stride. The child steps from one box to the next. At each step be sure that he looks at his foot and that his visual attention is drawn to what has happened. Encourage the child to watch his foot as he is putting it in the box. He is thus encouraged to depend primarily on perceptual control and to use the external control only when necessary.

Frequently, a similar type of training can be provided by the use of the ladder. The ladder is laid flat on the floor. The child begins at one end and steps in the space between each rung. If a ladder is used in which the rungs are relatively close together, an external control of the foot similar to that provided by the stepping boxes can be achieved.

When the child has less need of the external control of the foot, stepping stones can be introduced. Stepping stones are 6" squares cut from cardboard and pasted to or drawn with chalk on the floor. These squares are placed on the floor in an irregular pattern and the child is required to step from one to the next. Be sure that the space between the squares is varied so that sometimes a long stride, sometimes a short stride is required. Be sure that the position of the squares is varied so that sometimes the child steps straight ahead, sometimes to his right, sometimes to his left. Arrange some of the squares so that one foot is required to cross over the other in stepping from one square to the next. In these activities, the external control of the position of the foot has been removed. Only visual stimuli as to the correct positioning are available. This activity, therefore, requires a greater degree of eye-foot coordination than did the stepping boxes.

The child can be given practice with either foot or with any combination of the feet by determining which foot he shall use at each step. This can be determined either verbally or visually. In the event of verbal control, he is told which foot to use for the next step. In the event of visual control, the stepping stones are color coded, one color for the right foot, another color for the left foot. The child then puts the appropriate foot on each square. If he has difficulty distinguishing between right and left, colored ribbons matching the colors of the squares can be tied to his feet. He is then required to put the foot of the matching color on each square.

As with the stepping boxes, at each step the child's attention should be drawn to the position of his foot and what has happened. He should be encouraged to watch his foot as he is placing it on the square so that more continuous eye-foot control is encouraged.

In both the stepping boxes and stepping stones the visual control of the foot required by the task is sporadic. Each step is an isolated task, and the child is required to control his foot only when it makes contact with the target. Between these critical periods little or no control is required. When he has learned this sporadic control, it is desirable that he move on to more continuous eye-foot coordination.

This more continuous monitoring can be encouraged by the use of a path or alley. Lay out a path along the floor with paper strips or chalk marks. The width of the path should be graded to the ability of the child and can be made narrower as he becomes more proficient. The child starts at one end of the path and is asked to walk to the other end without stepping off. At first the path should be straight, but corners and curves can be introduced as the child becomes more able.

Direct the child's visual attention not only to the placement of his foot in the individual step but also to the path ahead of him. By this means he is encouraged to anticipate the eye-foot control which will be demanded. If he pays attention only to the next step, this task is similar to the stepping stone task. If, however, his attention is directed beyond the next step, he is encouraged to establish a more continuous eye-foot control.

The present activity can be combined with balance and posturing activities by using a walking board instead of a path. In this event the child's visual attention is called to the board which projects in front of him. When balance alone is being trained, the child's visual attention is either disregarded or is directed straight ahead. When eye-foot control is being trained in addition to balance, the child's visual attention is directed toward his feet and toward the board itself.

Eye-foot coordination is involved in many playground games and activities. Kickball and kick-the-can are common examples. Tag games can be used in which an object is kicked off a base. The runners are "safe" until "it" has recovered the object and restored it to the base. Modifications of the game of "catch" can be used in which the ball is kicked from one player to the next instead of thrown. Circle games can be modified so that a ball is kicked or lifted with the feet from child to child around the circle rather than tossed or passed. Such games are useful both for their motivational value and because the child is required to establish eye-foot control quickly. In such activities as stepping stones he has all the time he needs to match the perceptual and motor data. However, in these playground games, the time factor stresses the performance and places a greater premium on facility in eye-foot coordination. The fact that the eye-foot performance is integrated with many other performances in the game task encourages later generalization in the performance and a more complete integration of this function with other functions of the organism.

In order to insure the overall relationship between all the parts of the body, it is desirable that the foot be used for more representational and symbolic activities. By such means these representational and symbolic activities are generalized beyond the eye-hand area. Activities involving the use of the foot in drawing, copying, and similar tasks are described elsewhere.

AUDITORY-MOTOR MATCH

Because of the nature of most classroom activities, a great deal of attention is given to visual-motor matching and particularly to eye-hand matching. Although other sense avenues are used for the presentation of classroom information, relatively little attention is given to the relationship between this perceptual information and motor response. We have discussed the use of tactual and kinesthetic information and its relationship to motor activities as well as the relationship between such information and visual information. Auditory information is also related to motor activity and this relationship needs to be established in the child. Just as in some children visual information appears to exist independent of the activities and responses of the organism, so in some children auditory information seems to be separated from the activities of the rest of the organism. It is probable, however, that in the normal child, auditory stimuli are as intimately related to motor responses as are visual stimuli.

It would, therefore, seem that the child needs to develop an auditory-motor match in the same fashion that he develops a visual-motor match. Since auditory stimuli are extended in the time dimension, such a match is particularly important in motor responses which extend over time.

Practice in auditory-motor matching begins with objects which emit a sound when manipulated. A baby's rattle probably serves this purpose in the development of the normal child. With the older child, rhythm band instruments such as maracas, clappers, and the like can be used. For a more continuous sound, a barrel or drum filled with pebbles and mounted on a crank can be used. As the child turns the crank, the pebbles rolling about in the drum produce a sound.

The child should experiment with devices in which his activity serves to alter the sound in various ways. Thus, volume is related to effort. For this purpose, horns and similar instruments can be used. The harder the child blows, the louder the sound. In like manner, drums and instruments which can be beaten serve the same purpose. The harder they are hit, the louder the sound. Rhythm is related to the pace of movement. Again the drum can be used to illustrate this relationship. If it is beaten rapidly, a rapid series of sounds is produced. If it is beaten slowly, a slow series is produced. Pitch is related to the location of movement. This relationship can be illustrated with a toy xylophone in which the pitch of the sound is related to the position in which the instrument is struck. Whistles and toy instruments that change pitch as a plunger is slid back and forth through a cylinder also illustrate the relationship between pitch and the position of a movement.

The child should be encouraged to imitate vocally the sounds which he is producing because of their relationship to speech. Thus, when he changes the volume of a sound, he should imitate the change with his voice, emitting sounds which are now loud, now soft. Similarly, with rhythm he should duplicate the rhythm with some vocal expression. He should attempt to reproduce different pitches of sounds, imitating with his voice the alterations in pitch which he is producing with instruments or devices.

When the child has developed a relationship between auditory stimuli and bodily movement, he should learn to use these auditory data to control or direct a movement. He should learn to begin an activity or cease an activity in response to an auditory signal. Games such as musical chairs are useful for this purpose. In such games, the child begins an activity when the auditory stimulation begins. When the auditory stimulation ceases, he uses this clue to either stop his activity or change it in some prescribed way. Many modifications of this basic game are possible. Thus, the children can be asked to walk or run while the music is playing, and stand while the music is silent.

The child should learn to control the intensity of his activity on the basis of auditory stimuli produced. He should learn to walk softly or walk stamping his feet. He should learn to clap softly or clap loudly with his hands, and he should learn to speak softly or speak loudly. Activities providing practice in this type of control are frequently incorporated into stories or musical games on phonograph records. In such material, the story describes and illustrates intense activity versus less intense activity. The child is asked to imitate these illustrations and to perform with the proper degree of intensity in subsequent story situations.

The child should learn to time or pace his action in response to an auditory stimulus. Such activities as marching to a drum beat or to music provide practice in such pacing. The child is asked to alter the normal pace of a repetitive activity, such as walking, on the basis of the rhythm presented by the auditory stimulus. Such tasks should provide a wide variety of rhythms so that the principle of pacing on the basis of auditory stimuli may become generalized.

INTERSENSORY INTEGRATION

As has been pointed out above, some children show disturbances in the relationship between the sense avenues. Thus, one sense may block out another, or one sense may confuse another. In the former case, data from a given sense avenue may be adequate as long as the second sense avenue is delivering a minimum of information. When the second sense becomes active, however, the information from the first sense avenue is greatly reduced. Either sense is adequate alone, but the two together result in blocking. In the latter case, the quantity of information is not affected so much as the organization of the information. In the event of information from two sense avenues, one or both of the perceptual inputs becomes confused or loses its meaningfulness. An example is the child who can see or hear with consistency and meaning but cannot do both together. Such a child becomes uncomfortable and confused when the second sense avenue is active.

In the above discussion of the perceptual-motor match, we have dealt first with a kinesthetic-motor match, then with a visual-motor match, and finally with an auditory-motor match. It may be that in this progression lies the key to an attack on the problems of the child whose intersensory integration is disturbed. The information from each sensory avenue has been correlated with the motor response. A consistent, meaningful body of motor information has been assured before these matches were attempted. If this correlation is reasonably complete, the consistent motor response becomes a common factor in a matrix of correlations. When two variables are each correlated with a common variable, they will be correlated with each other. It is, therefore, possible that intersensory integration can be achieved by using the motor response as a common correlating factor through the perceptual-motor match. Clinical observations have indicated that such may often be the case.

chapter 11

Training Ocular Control

In the interaction between the child and his environment, control of the organism's response is established through motor learning. The child learns what responses are available to him and how to initiate and control these responses. The resulting body of motor information serves to stabilize one aspect of the organism-environment interaction. One aspect of the function, thereby, becomes stable and predictable. It can then be used as the basis, through the perceptual-motor match, of stabilizing the other aspect of the function and the interrelationships between these two aspects.

Although the environment exists outside the child and cannot therefore be directly controlled, a certain amount of control can be instituted through selection of the data from the environment which will be stimulating to the organism. Such control is exerted through selective attention to certain aspects of the environment or through selective processing of environmental information. Among all the stimuli which are arising from the environment, certain ones are selected and become the focus of attention. Other data are neglected or are processed in much less detail. Through such procedures, those aspects of incoming information considered to be important in the determination of response are given increased weight in determining the nature and extent of the interaction which will occur. Through such procedures a systematic exploration of the environment becomes possible. Environmental stimulations can be selected not only on the basis of their relative stimulus strengths, but also on the basis of their contribution to the response in question or to their contribution to the developing body of information about the surrounding environment. Thus, just as in motor learning a consistent exploration of objects becomes possible, now the same type of consistency among all environmental stimulation becomes possible. To a large extent, the child is no longer at the mercy of the chance combinations of stimuli which impinge upon his organism, but he can exert some control over these stimuli in the interest of consistency and system. Using this systematic input, he can build up an integrated and organized body of information about his total environment.

One of the major aids to such development is control of the external sense organ. In most of the sense organs there is at least a certain amount of control of the stimulation which will be received. Thus, we can turn our ear towards the source of a sound and intensify one portion of the auditory stimulation. In like manner, we can determine the tactual information that will be received by controlling the part of the environment which our skin will contact. Taste sensations can be controlled by determining what substances will enter the mouth, and the nose can be pointed toward the source of an odor. Although such control of input information is far from complete, these manipulations of the external sense organs can serve to statistically increase the quantity of information arising from one part of the environment as compared with other parts of the environment. Thus, a statistical concentration of information can be arranged relating to that part of the environment which at the moment is under most intensive investigation. By controlled manipulation of these areas of intensity, orderly information suitable for the development of an integrated body of information can be produced.

For most individuals, the most important source of input information is the eye. The eye gives us more information, and particularly more spatial information, per unit of time, than does any other sense organ. This superiority of vision is due largely to two major considerations. In the first place the concentration of sensory cells in the eye is very intense. Retinal tissue is more similar to brain tissue than any tissue in the body outside the central nervous system itself. These retinal cells have very direct connections with the brain. The amount of cortical energy generated through the optic nerve is therefore extensive. In the second place the projection area in the cortex devoted to the receipt of visual information is more extensive than the projection area from all the other sense avenues combined. Thus the amount of information received by the brain for processing, but originating in the retina of the eye, is very extensive. In addition to these anatomical and physiological factors, the psychological significance of the eye as the primary distance receptor and as the sense avenue which ranges widely over the environment and thus produces a very wide range of information contributes to its importance in the development of the body of environmental information. Although any sense avenue can be used as a basis of this body of information, because of its extreme efficiency, vision will occupy this central position for the majority of individuals, the other sensory information being matched to and organized around it. Only when the visual sense displays a specific defect, as in the case of the blind or the partially sighted, is the central role assigned to another sense avenue. Even when the visual process is markedly disrupted, as in visual perceptual problems, it continues to occupy the central position because of its extreme efficiency, even though in this individual the processing of visual information is extremely difficult. It seems as though, if there is any vision at all, this information becomes central to the child's organization of his environmental input regardless of how limited this sense avenue may be or how energy consuming its use may be.

As might be expected, this extremely efficient source of information, the visual sense avenue, is also the one with the widest range of controls. The eye can be moved in any direction and these movements have considerable extent. When the eye itself is moved, the combination of visual fields resulting will cover a little more than 180 degrees. Thus, all information lying in front of the plane passing laterally through the body is available. When eye movements are coordinated with movements of the head, this range of information can be extended to a full 360 degrees. Furthermore, the eye moves very rapidly, so that exploratory movements within this wide range can be made in quick succession.

MECHANISMS OF CONTROL

The direction in which the eye is pointed determines the particular visual information about the environment which will be received. As you read this page almost all of the visual information which you receive is composed of black marks on a white background, the letters on the page. If you raise your eyes from the book and look out the window, the visual information changes markedly. A wholly different section of the environment becomes the source of the visual input. By changing the direction in which the eye is pointed, we can alter the section of the environment from which the major concentration of information will arise. The nature of the visual information is therefore dependent upon the direction of gaze of the eye. Because of its flexibility of movement, the eye permits changes in information over very large portions of the environment in quick succession.

When you lift your eyes from this page and gaze out the window you have substituted one static source of visual information for another static source. Such alteration of the position of the eye is called *fixation*. The center of visual attention is constant and, upon movement, shifts rapidly to another center of concentration which also becomes constant. In addition to these changes of fixation, the eye permits another kind of control of information. The eye can sweep smoothly across a visual field producing a panoramic view of the whole. It can follow a moving object smoothly and continuously, keeping this object in the center of the visual field, and providing a direct correlation between the movement of the object and the perceptual alterations. Such an activity of the eye is called *pursuit*. It can give a continuous, temporally synchronized picture of the entire visual surroundings. Whereas a series of fixations is similar to a series of still pictures, a pursuit movement is similar to a moving picture when the camera is panning. Such pursuit movements are of vital importance in the development of a synchronized body of information about the environment.

The beginnings of control of the eye are found in the fixation reflex. The retina of the eye is divided into four quadrants with the *fovea,* or area of sharpest vision, at the center where the four quadrants intersect. The optic nerve is also divided into four parts, each part arising in one quadrant of the retina. Due to the decussation of the optic nerve and its division between the two hemispheres, the four parts of this nerve terminate in four separate areas of the cortex. Thus, the activity of each of the quadrants of the retina remains separate and is delivered to its own segment of the cortex (Fulton 1949, p 342).

Such an arrangement permits the eye to function similar to a bombsight. If, in an otherwise homogeneous visual field, a discrete source of more intense stimulation appears, the quadrant onto which this stimulus is projected will develop more activity than the other three. The cortex then senses an imbalance between the four segments of the optic nerve. Through a reflex mechanism, the extraocular muscles are readjusted until the stimulation is distributed evenly over the four quadrants. In the event of a single stimulus, such as we have been discussing, this readjustment serves to bring the projected image of the stimulus onto the point of intersection of the four quadrants, since only at this position will its resulting activity be spread evenly over all four. As we have seen, the fovea lies at the intersection of the four quadrants. The end result, therefore, is to project the image of the visual target onto the fovea where the greatest concentration of light sensitive cells lies. It is this foveal area which produces the clearest and most intense visual image and which, because of the intense concentration of cells, produces the most visual information. Because of its intensity, the foveal stimulation becomes the focus of visual attention.

The mechanism described above is the fixation reflex. It serves to bring most intense source of visual stimulation in the visual field into the center of visual attention. It is a reflexive response and is innate. At birth, or very shortly thereafter, the fixation reflex begins to function full-blown. No learning, other than the primitive activation of the reflex pattern, is required to bring it to optimum efficiency.

The fixation reflex serves to present the organism with discrete visual information. Certain important aspects of the visual environment, important because of their intensity, are "zeroed in on" so to speak, are delivered to the brain and are separated from their surroundings by virtue of the foveal-peripheral contrast. The concentration of cells in the fovea is very intense. This concentration diminishes in all directions with distance away from the fovea into the peripheral area of the retina. The gradient of concentration of such cells drops very rapidly as the boundary of the fovea is reached, then levels off and drops less rapidly until the extremes of the periphery are reached. An image projected on the fovea, therefore, stands out by virtue of its intensity like a little island in the visual sea.

The fixation reflex thus singles out and presents in an artificially isolated form the most intense source of stimulation in the visual field. Discrete visual contact with the environment is produced. Just like the initial motor contacts, however, this fixation induced contact is random from the point of view of the organism. It is dependent upon the momentary nature of the visual field and the relative intensity of parts of that field. All of these conditions are controlled by variables outside the organism and result in information which is, as yet, meaningless to the child. As with the initial motor contacts, the development of a meaningful body of information about the environment is difficult or impossible as long as the information-producing contacts are random and unsystematic. Such information-yielding contacts must be brought under the voluntary control of the child so that they can be related to the developing systematic body of information and so that their information can serve to integrate that body of information and augment its growth. As long as the contacts are random, the body of information is merely an accumulation of isolated experiences. If the contacts can be controlled, the body of information can become a system of information which presents to the child a complete and accurate picture of his environment.

Although the fixation reflex is primarily controlled by the involuntary nervous system, it is not entirely devoid of voluntary control. Visual fixation can be shifted at will. The tendency of the fixation reflex to center upon the most intense source of stimulation can be resisted while we attend, for our own purposes, to a less intense stimulus. The crux of the problem and the dilemma of learning lie in the phrase "for our own purposes."

Voluntary control means cortical control. Involuntary control, in general, means sub-cortical control. But cortical control depends upon an informational system in the cortex which will permit cortical attention.

As you read this page, there probably are many intense visual stimuli which surround you. Perhaps the lamp is reflected on the wall opposite you so that the amount of light from this glare source is greater than that from the page. At the moment your eye is held on the page because the information you are gathering from this source is important to you and your brain is directing most of its activity toward gathering and processing this information. This intense cortical attention is overcoming the tendency of your eyes to shift and focus on the source of intense visual stimulation. You overcome this reflexive response during reading, using the information to increase the strength of the voluntary control mechanisms of the eye. That such constant conflict for control goes on is evidenced by the increased fatigue in reading under conditions where intense stimulation external to the reading task exists. Harmon (1965) has investigated this phenomenon and has recommended a painting and decorating pattern for school classrooms designed to reduce the influence of such external visual factors.

You are able to overcome the influence of the fixation reflex as you read because you know what information you want and where in the visual field it is to be found. Such knowledge depends on a structured system of information which you are seeking to augment or confirm by your visual behavior. It is this structured system, however, which the child does not have and which he is seeking to build up. He does not know what information he needs or where to find it. Therefore, he has no basis for using the voluntary mechanisms available for control of the eye.

CONSISTENCY

The development of such a structured body of knowledge, as we have pointed out, depends on consistent inputs of information. It is very difficult when the input is random. But the fixation reflex provides information which, from the point of view of the organism, is random. A dilemma results. The control of the eye depends on a systematic body of visual information. Because the eye is not controlled, its information is random and hence the development of this systematic body of information is rendered difficult or impossible. The failure of this body of information, in turn, contributes to even less control of the eye. A vicious cycle exists in which lack of control prevents the establishment of a structure which might permit control.

The answer to the problem lies in the perceptual-motor match. The body of motor information has already begun to become structured when the development of the visual information begins. The first such control probably occurs when the child fixates his own hand. (*Gesell,* 1941) The gaze randomly lights upon the hand. It is probable that the double stimulation which results helps the child maintain the fixation. Kinesthetic stimulation tells him what and where his hand is. The visual information reinforces this kinesthetic information. He wiggles his fingers or shakes his wrist, thus creating intense kinesthetic stimulation. The visual information changes and intensifies accordingly. The summation of these two simultaneous stimulations creates a sufficiently strong cortical activity to hold the eye on the hand through the mechanisms of voluntary ocular control. (Held and Hein, 1963; Mikaelian and Held, 1964).

Thus the first ocular control has been established. A body of information has been built up which can utilize voluntary mechanisms to maintain visual fixation and accompanying consistency of visual information. When this simple structure has been firmly established, the infant can at will use it to permit voluntary shifting of fixation from another target to his hand. Now, instead of having to bring his hand into the line of sight and maintaining the resulting fixation upon it, he can hold up his hand and shift his eye over to it. He has learned to produce desired visual information at will. Visual data are no longer wholly random, but a point of reference, at least, can be depended upon. Such a point of reference can be used as the starting point for the development of a structured body of visual information. Since the eye can always be brought back to this reference point, the beginning of consistency in the gathering of visual data has been established.

When voluntary fixation of the hand is possible, then pursuit of the moving hand becomes the subject of experimentation. The child moves his hand and induces his eye to follow this movement. At first he probably makes use of the fixation reflex in this process. He moves his hand until its image is in the periphery of his visual field and then watches the reflex shift the eye over to fixate on it. As these fixations become more and more controlled, the brain begins to anticipate the visual movement and starts the eye movement in response to these anticipations. With greater precision of control, a smooth, uninterrupted pursuit movement develops which keeps the hand constantly in the center of the visual field throughout the movement.

When the body of visual information becomes adequate in extent and in consistency to act as its own control, the eye can act completely independently of the hand. The child now can explore with his eye and can generate as well structured and as consistent a pattern of information as he formerly did with his hand. The hand need be resorted to only when the visual information becomes complex or too ambiguous and additional data are required.

The eye must be brought under control both in its fixation activities and in its pursuit activities in order that consistent visual information can be obtained. In order for a systematic, structured picture of the visual environment to be built up, the input information must be consistent. No organized body of information can be built up if the data resulting from an experience with the environment are at one time one pattern and at another time a completely different pattern.

Consider how difficult it would be to read a passage if, when presented with the sentence "The mouse ran up the clock," the visual fixations involved were random. The child might then see— The m he clo se ra p the—et cetera. Actually, such erroneous fixations probably occur with all of us. We immediately correct them, however, because we recognize the inconsistency of the information. We exert control over the eye until its information fits the system and is consistent with it. The child must learn this kind of control of the visual input, and he is dependent upon consistency of the visual input to allow him to establish the system. Such essential consistency is possible if initial control of the eye is based on a system which is already consistent. In the case of the young child, this system is the motor system.

ESTABLISHING CONTROL

Some children will be found to have great difficulty establishing control of the eye. In the first place, the muscle systems involved in this control are among the most complex in the body. Their innervation comes from both the voluntary and the involuntary system; three pairs of muscles must work together in perfect synchrony; and two separate systems, the right eye system and the left eye system, must be perfectly congruent. Therefore, the sheer problem of coordination is staggering.

In the second place, the precision required in eye movements is among the most demanding in the organism. The fovea is only about two millimeters in diameter. Upon this minute area the image of the target must be accurately projected. This projection must be sufficiently precise to permit the child to sort out this one target for central fixation from among an intricate network of adjacent targets. Such precision is extremely demanding and it must be maintained over long periods of time. There are three basic problems which may lead to difficulty in the establishment of ocular control.

ANATOMICAL

In some cases deficits are present in the muscles themselves. One muscle of a pair may be too long, thus making it impossible to balance this pair. As a result the eye cannot be moved at all or cannot be moved to its full extent. This is a medical problem and the treatment usually involves surgical repair of the muscle.

PHYSIOLOGICAL

Sometimes one or more of the ocular muscles does not react properly. In popular terms it may be referred to as a weak or lazy muscle. This problem is also medical and treatment usually involves orthoptics, a system of exercises designed to strengthen ocular muscles.

EDUCATIONAL

The third problem is the one we have been discussing above; the purposeful control of the eye on the basis of the appropriateness of the information which it is delivering. This problem is an educational one and involves the matching of eye movements to the demands of a developing body of visual information about the environment.

It can be seen that there are two related problems involved in ocular control: the medical problem which answers the question, "Can the eye move?" and the educational problem which answers the question, "Why does the eye move?" In general, it is impossible to attack the educational problem until the medical problem has been solved. Therefore, whenever a child is found who shows a severe problem of ocular control, it is necessary to have a thorough medical examination before attacking the educational aspects of the problem. If no medical problem exists, the teacher can begin work on the problem of teaching the child to use his eyes for the purpose of maintaining consistent input information about his environment.

BINOCULARITY

One particularly thorny problem in ocular control results from the fact that our two eyes are set apart in our head. As a result the two eyes must work together but, because of their separation, they cannot work in a parallel manner. Each must retain its own posture but must do so in relation to the other. Depending on the distance and direction of the target, a complex set of covariant postures must be established and integrated.

In addition to the fixation reflex discussed above, there are three other reflexive mechanisms of the eye which are important to binocularity: accommodation, convergence, and fusion.

ACCOMMODATION

The lens of the eye is capable of changing its shape under the influence of the ciliary muscle. The result of such changes is to increase or decrease the amount of diffraction imposed upon the light rays as they pass through the lens. It is through this mechanism that a clear, sharp image of the target is focused on the retina regardless of the distance of the object from the eye.

CONVERGENCE

Because the eyes are separated in the head, the angle between the two lines of sight is different when the object is at a distance from what it is when the object is near at hand. When looking at a distant object, the two eyes are nearly parallel in the head and the two lines of sight nearly parallel to each other. When the object is near at hand, the two eyes must turn inward in order for each to point at the object, and the two lines of sight triangulate upon the target. You can observe this convergence function by holding a pencil upright in front of the eyes of a friend. Ask him to keep looking at the pencil as you move it toward his nose. You can see the eyes turn inward and triangulate on the target as the pencil moves toward his nose.

The convergence mechanism and the accommodation mechanism are interrelated to form the *accommodation-convergence reflex*. As a visual target moves nearer, the two eyes must increase their convergence; but at the same time each must increase its accommodation to keep a clear image focused on the retina. Thus these two functions are correlated. The nearer the target the more convergence *and* the more accommodation are required. The further the target, the less convergence *and* the less accommodation are required. This correlation is seen not only in the functions but in the mechanisms as well. The convergence reflex parallels the accommodation reflex. Thus, if accommodation is altered, as through the introduction of an eyeglass lens, convergence alters also to match the new accommodative status. These two mechanisms combine to produce a clear, single image of the object.

FUSION

The control of these complex mechanisms is provided by the *fusion reflex*. When the images are projected on exactly corresponding areas of the two retina, the central nervous system recognizes this fact and maintains this exact posture while the two images, being delivered to the brain from the two retina, fuse into one. The result is an impression of a clear, single object located in space.

You can observe this function if you set up a little experiment where the demand for fusion is low and hence the stimulus for the fusion reflex is weak. Look at a telephone wire silhouetted against the bare sky. You will probably note that the wire looks "fuzzy" and you may even experience a double image. You find this condition uncomfortable and you have the impression of visually "hunting around." Suddenly you see a clear, single image. The eyes now appear to "lock in" on that image; the searching stops, and your eyes seem to be "held in" by the fused images. Thus, fusion identifies and controls the exact alignment of the two eyes and provides true binocularity.

The stimuli for all these mechanisms, and especially for fusion, becomes much stronger when the information presented by the target becomes more meaningful. Voluntary clues to binocularity are added to and augment the stimuli which set off the basic reflexes. Partial or inadequate fusion can no longer be tolerated when the visual information becomes vital to the organism. However, the child must learn to apply these clues to the control of the two eyes. Frequently, the child cannot distinguish between information which is itself hazy and information which is hazy because of inadequate ocular control. Therefore, he ascribes the error to the wrong source and works on the wrong problem.

A ten-year-old boy was referred to a clinic because of difficulty in reading. As he was reading a test passage, the therapist noted that, when fatigue began to set in, his eyes lost their binocularity and each went its own way. On a hunch, the therapist asked, "By any chance, are you seeing two books?" The child replied, "Of course, I often see two books. Doesn't everybody?"

This child had no way of knowing that it was control of his eyes that was breaking down. He assumed, therefore, that the resulting breakdown in the information was natural and that it happened to everyone. He felt that he was just a poor reader who could not cope with the problem of disrupted information as well as the other children could. An explanation of his problem and a few simple procedures to teach him how to control visual information solved his difficulty in a few weeks and he became a normal reader.

As in the case of control of single eye movements cited above, two problems exist in the establishment of binocularity. The first is a medical problem of the intactness of the reflex mechanisms involved. The second is an educational problem of learning to use visual information to intensify and maintain such control. Because of the complexities involved, the establishment of binocularity is often a more difficult problem for the child to learn than is control of a single eye. Special attention frequently needs to be directed toward the teaching of binocularity both to aid the child in a difficult learning task which he has been unable to accomplish alone and because of the particular significance of the binocular function in so many classroom tasks.

EVALUATING OCULAR CONTROL

The evaluation of the child's ability to control his eyes involves an investigation of his performance in the two basic functions involved: fixation and pursuit. Complete procedures for such investigation are described in the Purdue Perceptual Motor Survey (Roach and Kephart, 1966).

FIXATION CONTROL

Hold a pencil twenty inches in front of the child's eyes and fourteen to sixteen inches to the left of center. Hold a ball-point pen with a colored top in the same position in front of the child but fourteen to sixteen inches to his right. Ask him to look at the erasure on the pencil, then shift and look at the top of the pen. (Any targets which include a small contrasting dot which can be fixated may be used.)

Observe what happens when the child fixates on the pencil. Can he "lock in" on the target promptly or is there considerable trial and error with the gaze bracketing the target with small movements before it can be accurately located? When fixation has been accomplished, can it be held? The child should be able to hold the gaze steadily upon the target for 10 to 15 seconds.

Now ask the child to shift his fixation to the pen. Can he shift promptly or is there a marked hesitation in starting the movement which would suggest difficulty in releasing the first fixation in order to move to the second? Can he fixate the second target promptly and hold this new fixation?

These questions cover the three phases of the fixation function: visual reach, grasp, and release. The child should be able to move his eyes promptly in the direction of the target thus indicating his awareness of how to contact it visually. He should "lock in" on the target promptly indicating that the fusion function operates efficiently. He should be able to maintain this fixation long enough to demonstrate that he can hold a fixation for the purpose of gathering necessary information. Finally, he should be able to release this fixation promptly upon demand in order to move on to the next.

Hold the two targets in the same plane as before in front of the child, but one above the other so that the direction of the eye movements must be vertical. Observe the same behavior of the eyes when they move vertically.

PURSUIT CONTROL

Using a common lead pencil with an eraser, hold the pencil upright before the child's eyes about 20 inches in front of his face. Ask him to fixate the eraser. Then say, "Now watch it, wherever it goes." Move the pencil about 18 inches to his right, following an arc of a circle with a radius of 20 inches of which the child is the center. Next move the pencil laterally to the child's left until it is 18 inches to his left.

By following the arc of a circle, the target is kept at a constant distance from the eye. If it were moved on a straight line, the distance to the eye would be greater at the extreme left and right extent of the movement and less in the center. Since a change of distance involves a change in accommodation of the eye (in which we are not now interested), we can eliminate this problem by moving the target in an arc, keeping the eye-target distance constant.

If the child moves his head instead of moving his eyes, ask him to hold his head still. Observe whether the movements are smooth or jerky. As has been pointed out above, eye movements are an extremely precise task. Therefore, the examiner must watch very closely; lack of control may be shown by extremely small spasms. The eyes should move as smoothly as ice cubes in a glass of water. Any jerking or unevenness is an indication of lack of complete control.

Watch the two eyes working together. Observe whether they maintain their relationship to each other or whether one wanders off the target. Such loss of relationship may be apparent only at the extremes of the movement or may come and go during the movement. Observe whether both eyes are following or whether one eye is leading and the other is simply being pulled along. This relationship can usually be observed by watching the timing of the two eyes. Does one get ahead of the other or do they stay together? In some cases, one eye will move but not the other.

Observe whether the child is always on target or whether he loses it from time to time. If he loses the target, can he regain it promptly or does he have to "look around" for it? Does he overshoot the target, and have to wait for it to catch up? Pay particular attention to the performance when the target crosses the midline of the child's body. Many children have trouble in crossing the midline and will reveal this fact by a slight jerk in the eye movement at this point.

Repeat the above procedure moving the pencil in a vertical arc. Observe the same responses as above. Watch carefully for a disruption of movement when the vertical midline is crossed.

Move the target in the two diagonal directions, from lower left to upper right and from upper left to lower right. Observe the responses by the child as indicated above. Particular care should be taken in observations when the target is moved in a diagonal direction. These diagonal movements are the last to appear developmentally and are the most difficult for the child. Difficulty is often shown in a "stair-stepping" movement. The eyes move laterally until they lose the target, then vertically to catch up, then laterally again, et cetera. In this way, the child can "follow" the target without making a diagonal movement of the eyes. This stair-stepping may be apparent over only a part of the total range of movement. It is most frequent at about the midline.

TRAINING ACTIVITIES

A number of ocular functions are required by common classroom activities. They will be discussed here in the probable order of their development in the child. In the training of any particular child who may be having trouble, it is well to observe these functions in order. Start with the simplest and, if the child shows no difficulty, move on to the next more complex function until the type with which he is experiencing difficulty is identified. More intensive training can begin at this point and proceed on through the series.

It is neither necessary nor desirable to drill on activities which the child can perform adequately. Nor is perfection in any function the goal. Classroom activities require a modest amount of facility in the functions described, but they do not demand extreme degrees of skill. When a level of performance has been attained which will permit the child to obtain a consistent input of visual information, it is more desirable to move on to other types of activity with which he needs help than to strive for high levels of skill in a given function which may not be useful in everyday tasks and problems. All training should be oriented, not to the training tasks themselves, but to their contribution to the child's overall performance. Therefore, training programs should move on to other problems as soon as a foundation has been provided which will permit such progress.

As with all other training tasks which have been discussed, those described below are only examples. In more difficult cases they will need to be augmented by the addition of other procedures. In all cases they will need to be varied and elaborated upon through the teacher's own ingenuity in order to assure generalization and transfer to other types of problem.

FIXATION

Hold a target directly in front of the child's eyes, about 20 inches away and directly at eye level. Ask him to look at the target. He should bring his eyes to the target quickly and surely and should "lock in" and hold the fixation for 10 to 15 seconds. Be sure both eyes are accurately aligned with the target. Ask him if he sees it clearly and singly. His report may not be accurate since, as illustrated above, he may not know when his perception is disrupted. If he can report trouble, he can verbally be encouraged to attack the problem. His work toward the solution of his own problem is the most potent training device which can be developed. If he experiences difficulty which he cannot report, the verbal question serves to direct his attention toward the source of the problem.

Initial targets may need to be quite gross, two to three inches in diameter. Such large targets decrease the precision required in the fixation function. The eyes can be slightly mispointed and still make contact with the target. They may slip slightly in attempting to hold and still not lose contact with the target. Large targets are thus easier to fixate than small targets.

In severe cases the intensity of the target stimulation may need to be increased. A useful device for this purpose is a toy sold around the fourth of July. It consists of a disc with a blue spiral painted on a white background. In the disc are a number of "windows" of red cellophane. When a plunger is pressed, the disc rotates rapidly. A flint behind the row of windows throws off sparks which become colored when seen through the cellophane.

This device provides a very strong visual stimulus. It has sharp color contrast, extreme brightness from the sparks, and movement both of the disc and the sparks. In addition, the plunger and the flint produce sound which adds an auditory stimulus to the visual stimuli. This device will be found very useful in cases where fixations are weak and visual attention is poor.

Since ocular control is established through matching the action of the eye to the movement of the hand, the hand should be brought into this training task. Ask the child to point to the target as he looks at it. Initially he may be permitted to follow the movement of his hand to the target as long as he "locks on" visually when the target is reached. Be sure, however, that he "looks" and does not transfer the entire task to his hand. In this type of response the reach and contact functions are being performed by the hand, and the eye is merely following the hand. The child should be encouraged to look at the target first and then point to it. In this case the eye should establish fixation and the hand should be brought in contact with the target quickly and surely.

If, in pointing at the target, the child misses, look carefully at the alignment of the eyes. One or both eyes may be off target. The effect of such an error in fixation is to shift the apparent location of the target in space. The child who misses when he points may be pointing to the location where he actually sees the target to be. His pointing error is then a reflection of his visual problem.

When the child moves his hand into the vicinity of the target and then explores with his hand to make contact, watch his eyes closely. Such performance frequently indicates an error in fixation as described above. The child points to where he thinks the target is and then seeks manual contact to correct the error. Such seeking is not visually guided and represents a suspension of vision, the task being completed by the hand. Obviously this suspension of vision in the face of a perceptual problem is what we are seeking to overcome by our training. This type of performance by the child should, therefore, be prevented. Require him to point directly at the target and do not allow him to make "blind" corrective movements.

The easiest fixation to make is one in which the target lies directly ahead. In this position the extraocular muscles are balanced. As the target is moved off center, the muscle pairs become more and more unbalanced and the position of the eyes is more difficult to hold. The next step is to present the target in different positions before the child. In addition to holding the target straight ahead, hold it to his left, to his right, above his line of sight, below his line of sight, et cetera. Remember that the further off center the target, the more difficult is the task. Therefore, start with small displacements and increase the angle as the child is able to perform.

At this point the child may turn his head toward the target rather than move his eyes. Such a procedure avoids the ocular task. Hold his head lightly so that it does not move and ask him to turn his eyes toward the target. Encourage him to perform without moving his head, and release your hold on his head and permit him to perform by himself as soon as he is able.

Fixation on a single target requires only one visual contact with the environment. In this respect it is similar to subjective space in which the child can use his own body as the point or origin of the localization. Many visual tasks in the classroom, however, require the child to shift attention from one point outside himself to another point outside himself without an intermediate reference to his own body. Such external shifts are more nearly similar to objective space and require the child to make visual response on the basis of an outside structure.

Hold two targets before the child, one to his right and the other to his left and approximately eighteen inches apart. Ask him to fixate on one and then, upon command, shift his gaze to the other. Be sure he shifts promptly and that he contacts the new target surely. When he has held the second target for 10 to 15 seconds, ask him to shift back to the first target. Have him shift his fixation from one to the other several times but *always upon command*. If he shifts targets before you command him, require him to return and maintain fixation until the command is given.

Use large targets and increase the intensity of the stimulation, if necessary, as you did when a single target was used. Do not permit the child to turn his head but require him to perform with his eyes alone. Ask him to point with his finger at the targets and be sure the movement of his eyes is matched to the movement of his hand.

When the child can perform with the targets relatively close together, gradually increase the separation until they are approximately 30 inches apart. This increase in distance between the targets increases the difficulty of the task in two ways. The eyes must shift to a sharp angle from the straight ahead position which increases the imbalance in the muscle pairs. In the second place, the target to which the gaze must be shifted lies well out in the periphery of vision at the instant when the command is given. Its strength and its stimulus effect are weaker when its image is thus far off the fovea. Therefore, the child who performs fairly well initially may experience difficulty when these longer excursions are demanded.

Classroom tasks require fixation movements in all possible directions. When the child can perform in the lateral direction used above, align the targets in other meridia. For example, hold one above the other so that vertical movements are required; hold them on a diagonal so that diagonal movements are required. Change the alignment of the targets frequently to avoid splintering in the learning.

Many classroom tasks require a shift of fixation from one distance to another. Such tasks are more difficult since, in addition to eye movement, the functions of accommodation and convergence are involved. All of these functions must be coordinated for successful performance.

Hold one target directly in front of the child and 10 inches away. Hold the second directly in front and 18 inches away. The far target will need to be held slightly higher so that it can be seen. Ask the child to look at the near target then, upon command, shift to the far target. Watch his eyes closely to see that they are working together and that the change of fixation can be made smoothly and decisively. Either fixation should be held for 10 to 15 seconds without difficulty.

When smaller targets are used the phenomenon *physiological diplopia* can be observed during this task. When the near target is fixated, a double image of the far target is seen. When fixation shifts to the far target, it appears clear and single, but now the near target is seen as less distinct and doubled. This doubling of images at distances other than the fixated distance is called physiological diplopia.

Frequently, if the child who is having trouble with binocularity can be taught to recognize this natural form of diplopia, it can help him to be aware of the existence of double images arising from inaccurate convergence. With this new knowledge, he can experiment with a visual task until the diplopia is conquered. Since he now knows what a clear, single image looks like and can contrast it with an inaccurate image, he can determine when his experiment is successful and observe the processes which led to the success. From such observations he can learn how to manipulate his binocular functions to produce more satisfactory information. In many cases this self teaching proves to be the most efficient type of learning possible.

When fixations can be accomplished in all target orientations and can be shifted in all directions, it is necessary to teach greater precision in the fixation function. For this purpose, the size of the target should be decreased. Use a series of targets decreasing in size by easy steps until the child can fix and hold targets about the size of a dime.

As the target is decreased in size, it may be necessary to increase its intensity in order to help the child gain more precise fixation ability. The use of bright colors in the target increases its visual stimulus intensity. Small quick movements of the target with excursions of four or five millimeters are effective since movement is a stronger visual stimulus than is a static target. A penlight, which is an intense source of light, may be used as an intense but small target. An increase of information may also increase target intensity. Thus a figured disc is more intense than a plain disc.

The great majority of classroom activities involve the recognition and manipulation of symbolic materials. It is well, therefore, to introduce symbols into visual training activities as soon as possible. Letters, numbers, and other symbols can be placed on the targets for the child to recognize and identify. Such symbols serve the twofold purpose of introducing a visual response to symbolic materials and also of establishing information as the primary purpose of the visual functions. Fixation practice is then not performed in isolation, but is tied to the information gathering function which, from the point of view of education, is its primary purpose.

VISUAL PURSUIT MOVEMENTS

In addition to the ability to fixate on a stationary object, the child needs to be able to maintain visual contact with a moving object. Pursuit movements are particularly important to education, since it is out of this skill that exploratory movements develop. Thus, following the perimeter of a figure, to investigate its shape, and similar visual explorations develop out of the pursuit function. A pursuit movement which can be systematically interrupted forms the basis for the visual following of a line of print. Whereas fixation permits the child to perform in a static visual task, pursuit movements permit him to perform in a continuous or changing visual task. Most classroom activities involve the latter type of task and hence smooth, accurate visual pursuit behavior is extremely important in the classroom.

STAGES IN OCULAR PURSUIT TRAINING

Stage 1.   In the initial approach to pursuit training, the testing techniques described in the Purdue Perceptual-Motor Survey (Roach and Kephart, 1966) are used as a training device. The teacher moves the same pencil target used in the testing procedure before the child's eyes in the principal meridia (lateral, vertical, diagonal, and rotary). However, instead of a single trial with a judgment of adequacy or inadequacy of performance, the target is moved repeatedly and the child is urged to increase the adequacy of his performance. As noted previously, lateral and vertical movements are easier than diagonal or rotary movements. Therefore, begin training with these easier movements and proceed, as the child is able, to the more difficult directions.

It is very important in ocular pursuit training that the child make progress readily in the training activity used. If he continues to follow the target with uncontrolled movement, he is in danger of merely practicing his errors and the training procedure defeats its own purpose. For this reason, the adult should be particularly alert for progress in control during the early stages of the training period.

If the child does not show observable improvement within a few trials (four to eight), it is doubtful that the training procedure used will be effective if continued. Therefore, in this early stage of training, be alert for improvement and if, within the first few trials, such improvement is not apparent, this training activity should be discontinued and the training should drop down to Stage 2.

Stage 2. Stage two is identical with stage one except that the target used is a penlight, a small pen-shaped flashlight such as those sold in drug and hardware stores. A penlight in which the bulb or a plastic shield for the bulb (which permits light to pass through) projects beyond the barrel of the light is desirable. With this type of light, the source of light is visible when the penlight is held in a vertical position at the child's eye level. The penlight target is moved in the principal meridia in the same manner as the pencil target in Stage 1. The same observations should be made, and the same procedure recommended in Stage 1 should be followed.

The purpose of Stage 2 is to increase the intensity of the visual stimulus. Whereas the pencil target was visible through reflected light and presented a relatively weak visual stimulus, the penlight presents its stimulus through direct light rays and is a much stronger visual stimulus.

As in Stage 1, observe carefully to note progress in the child's ability to control. If such progress is not noted within a few trials, then Stage 2 should be discontinued and training should proceed to Stage 3.

Stage 3. In this stage, the child is asked to point to the target and to follow it with his finger while he follows it with his eyes. The penlight target is used as in Stage 2 and the target is still moved in the principal meridia.

Following the moving target with the finger while it is followed with the eyes adds a kinesthetic clue to the visual clues used in Stages 1 and 2. As we said earlier, it is necessary to match the kinesthetic information from the extra-ocular muscles with the general kinesthetic pattern of the body in order to develop the desired ocular control. Such matching is made easier and more direct if a correlated kinesthetic stimulus is added to the visual stimulus. It is this correlation of kinesthetic and visual information which is achieved by the technique of this stage.

As in the earlier procedures, observe the performance of the child carefully. If he does not show demonstrable improvement within a few trials, this process is discontinued and the training moves on to Stage 4.

Stage 4. This stage is identical with Stage 3 except that the child is asked to place his finger on the light and move it in contact with the penlight as the light is moved. He is urged to offer a certain resistance to the movement of the light by saying to him, "Press down hard. Try to keep the light from moving." The light is then moved in the principal meridia as in the earlier procedures.

The purpose of Stage 4 is to increase kinesthetic stimulation. In Stage 2, the intensity of the visual stimulus was increased while in Stage 3 a coordinated kinesthetic and visual clue was presented. In Stage 4, the kinesthetic variable is emphasized while maintaining the kinesthetic-visual parallel. It is for this reason that the child is asked to press hard on the light and offer a certain resistance to its movement. This increased pressure and the development of resistance increases the tactual and kinesthetic information resulting from the activity. As before, the performance of the child is observed carefully. If no observable improvement is noticed within a few trials, the training moves on to Stage 5.

Stage 5. In this stage, the target is a ball. Begin with a large ball such as a beach ball or a playground ball. As training progresses and as the child's skill in the tasks improves, decrease the size of the ball. The teacher places both of his hands flat against the ball. The child places his hands flat against the other side of the ball directly opposite the hands of the teacher. Thus, the ball is held between the two pairs of hands. The teacher then begins to move the ball in the principal meridia carrying the child's hands along with him. The child is encouraged to watch the ball and to keep it in sight as it moves.

In this stage of training, the kinesthetic and tactual information is again increased. Both hands are used and, since the hands of the child are opposite the hands of the teacher, the teacher can produce as much resistance and as much kinesthetic information as he likes by simply pressing harder against the ball. At the same time, the visual stimulus is increased in strength by providing a larger target. Thus, in Stage 5 the child is given maximum information with which to develop his skill.

As before, the teacher watches very carefully to see how well the child is able to control his eye movement. Here again, if improvement is not observed within a few trials, the training is discontinued.

If the child does not show improvement at Stage 5, he should be referred to an eye specialist for help. If, at this stage of training, the child has not yet begun to show improvement, it is probable that a more severe problem than inadequacy in learning is present and that there is some neurological, physiological, or anatomical problem which must be solved before the learning problem can be attacked. These more severe problems require extensive treatment and their solution should be referred to a visual care specialist.

In beginning ocular pursuit training, work down through the stages described above until a level is found at which the child can start to learn. Once this level has been identified, use the activity of that stage as a training device, helping the child to achieve the desired degree of control through the activity. As soon as he has achieved control with one type of activity, move upward through the stages until, at the end of the training, he is able to follow adequately the pencil target prescribed in stage one.

As was pointed out earlier, some of the movements will be more difficult than others. The stage at which a child can perform will therefore vary from one meridian to another. A child may be found who can perform adequately in the lateral direction at Stage 1 but who, in a diagonal direction, must have the additional help provided by Stages 4 or 5. In the training of such a child, use whatever activity is appropriate for the particular movement which is being trained. However, move up through the stages as rapidly as possible until the child is able to perform at Stage 1 in all meridia.

PERCEPTUAL-MOTOR FUNCTIONING IN OCULAR PURSUIT

Occasionally, a child may have developed reasonable ocular control without adequate attention to the perceptual-motor match. This child has learned to control his eyes as a separate skill not related closely to the overall activities of his body. As a result he can move his eyes in the proper direction but cannot control his hand by visual monitoring in the same movement. Ocular control is here something of a splinter skill and cannot be used to determine or control the response.

Such a child has learned to manipulate perceptual variables. He has learned to balance perceptual stimulus against perceptual stimulus and even, in some cases, to manipulate the relationships between perceptual stimuli. These perceptual manipulations, however, show little relationship to his motor response. Such a child lives in two different worlds, a perceptual world and a motor world. Since these two worlds are not matched, constant confusion results. Such a child may read relatively well but write very poorly. He may recognize forms easily but be unable to reproduce them.

In order to be sure that the perceptual-motor match is being established always observe the child's performance in Stage 3, even though he may perform well in Stages 1 and 2. If the addition of the hand to the task *improves* the performance of the eyes, the perceptual-motor match is probably adequate and training can proceed to Stages 1 and 2 as soon as the child is able. If the addition of the hand does not alter the adequacy of the ocular performance or particularly if this addition deteriorates the performance of the eyes, it is probable that the perceptual-motor match is poor. In this event training should be concentrated in Stages 3, 4 and 5 until the hand and the eye are matched.

It is possible that during such eye-hand training, the performance of the eyes on the tasks of Stages 1 and 2 may deteriorate. A specific skill is being broken up and a more adequate skill is being substituted. During this process, performance may suffer temporarily. It is common knowledge that a typist who switches from the "hunt and peck" system to the touch system finds her typing performance deteriorating during the transition. If she persists, however, a new and more adequate skill is achieved and a new high in performance in finally achieved. Training in ocular control may follow a similar course if the original skills of the child were developed without reference to the perceptual-motor match.

It will be seen that these stages in the training of ocular control parallel the stages of development of the perceptual-motor match. In Stage 5, the hand is controlled and the eye is encouraged to follow. The control of the hand is reduced in Stage 4. In Stage 3, the eye leads the hand. Finally in Stages 1 and 2 the eye performs independently of the hand.

As mentioned above, Stage 3 of the training is always presented to the child, and his performance with the hand is compared to his performance without the hand. With this exception, evaluation starts with the presentation of Stage 1 and moves down through the stages successively until the stage at which the child can perform is found.

EXTENT OF MOVEMENT

It will be found that many children can follow the moving target adequately within a rather restricted range of movements. For example, the child may be able to follow the target with ease if it is moved two or three inches to the right or left. If, however, the movement of the target extends beyond this restricted range, the child may experience difficulty and his skill may break down. The further the movement toward the periphery required in either direction, the more difficult ocular control becomes. On the one hand, the child has had more incidental practice with restricted movements near the center of the line of sight than he had with wider movements near the periphery of the area of sight. On the other hand, all muscular control is more difficult as it extends toward the extremes of movement in any direction. For these two reasons, it should be expected that ocular control will become more difficult the further it is extended from the midline in any direction.

As stated earlier, we do not want the child to practice his own errors. Therefore, training procedures should begin by training movements in those areas in which the child can perform adequately. This may be a very restricted area near the center of the line of vision. As he becomes more proficient in this limited area, training will gradually move out in all directions, increasing the extent of the movement required. In this manner, the area within which he has control can be gradually expanded. It will be found, therefore, that broad movements will not be possible for many children, but restricted movements within a narrow area will be performed reasonably well. In such cases, the movement of the target will need to be restricted to the area in which the child can operate. Long excursions are given up and short excursions within the range in which the child performs are substituted. This range and the extent of the movements are gradually increased as the child becomes able to perform further from the center of his visual field.

At this point another problem frequently presents itself. As has been mentioned earlier, the kinesthetic-visual matching must be reversed every time the child crosses the midline of his body. This reversal in matching frequently causes the child difficulty in ocular control as well as in the eye-hand control which we have seen in other activities. Therefore, many children will have difficulty with the center of the visual field because they are required to cross the midline. Such children cannot be trained on one side of the midline alone since this would increase the difficulty which they are already experiencing.

With such children, therefore, it is necessary to give special practice in crossing the midline at the same time that we are attempting to extend the area over which they show control of eye movements. In the process of increasing the extent of control, the extent of movement in either direction is gradually increased. In so doing, however, the midline must be crossed in order to keep the movement balanced. When the midline is crossed the child has difficulty. In such cases, proceed as described above to increase the range of control, but at the same time give special help whenever he crosses the midline. It may be necessary to use a lower stage of training at or near the midline so that he is able to increase his midline control before the extent of movement can be increased. Since two problems are being attacked at once, the child frequently requires activities of a lower level of skill demand (lower stages of training) than will be necessary when either one or both of these problems begin to be solved.

KNOWLEDGE OF RESULTS

One difficulty encountered in ocular pursuit training techniques of young children is the problem of helping the child to know when he is performing adequately. Since he has little information regarding the operation of his eyes, he has no way of knowing when they are out of control. Since he has not established an adequate pattern of kinesthetic information from the extra-ocular muscles, he has no data with which to judge the smoothness of his pursuit movements. He will need to be given some information by which he can determine when he is "on target" and when he is not.

The purpose of pursuit movement is to keep the target centered on the fovea or central portion of the retina. This fovea is the area of clearest vision and when the image is adequately centered thereon, the child has a clear, sharp image of the target. If the image is centered on some portion of the retina other than the fovea, the image is less clear, less sharp, and less detailed. If the ocular pursuit mechanism is so far out of control that the image does not fall on the retina at all, the child has no image of the target; he "loses" the target. These facts concerning the image of the traget can be used to help the child determine when his pursuit movements are adequate.

Watch the eyes carefully to determine when they are pointed toward the target. If the child has lost the target, stop the movement of the target immediately and ask the child to re-fixate it. Such remarks as "Where is it?" "Where did it go?" "Look at it," will usually catch the child's attention and cause him to fixate the target again. When he has had a few such experiences and has learned that he should be able to see the target clearly and sharply at all times, ask him to use this information to determine the status of his control. Thus, he can be instructed to keep the target in view all the time or not to lose the target.

During all training activities be sure that the child's eyes are adequately centered on the target. Whenever they are not, training should stop and he should be requested to re-fixate the target. When he has re-centered on the target, training can begin again. It is essential that the child learn that it is possible to keep the target in view at all times and never to "lose" it. It is imperative that he learn how to maintain this type of control. If he is permitted to perform without the target adequately centered, we are permitting him to practice his errors and our training is doing no good and may be doing harm.

In some cases, when binocular training is being undertaken, one eye will lose its fixation while the other continues to fixate the target. In such cases, cover the eye which is fixating properly. The child is then left without a clear image of the target since the eye with which he is now looking is not adequately centered upon it. Then the statement "Where is it?" will cause him to re-fixate with the eye which has been "off target." The other eye can then be uncovered and training can proceed. At no time in binocular training should the child be allowed to follow with one eye while the other eye is not properly pursuing the target. Covering one eye will show him the problem and permit him to correct the error.

When the two eyes break apart in this fashion, diplopia or double image results. Older and more observing children are sometimes able to recognize that they are seeing two images. If such recognition occurs, it is a great aid to training, since the child can now recognize his errors and can help in his own training by trying to prevent or correct them.

If it is felt that the child might be able to recognize his diplopia, he should be encouraged to do so. Stop the target when the two eyes are out of line. Ask the child whether he sees two targets. Point out that one image will be sharper and clearer than the other. If he can identify the two images, ask him to point to but not touch one of them, then point to the other. In one case, he will point down the line of sight of the eye which is on target and hence point directly at the target. In the other case, he will point down the line of sight of the eye which is off target and hence will point to one side, above or below the target. Now ask him to touch the target and watch the two images come together. If his eyes do not line up when the finger contacts the target, ask him to press hard on the target or move it with his finger on it in short excursions until his eyes line up.

Although diplopia is probably the most obvious of the ocular control errors and the easiest for the child to recognize, other errors can also be recognized. Some children can come to recognize when their eyes have slipped off the fixation point and when they follow a target irregularly. When such recognition is possible, it should be encouraged. Thus, an eight year old boy in one classroom was having trouble maintaining visual fixation on a target. He learned that he was supposed to see the target at all times. Thereafter, when his eyes would slip off the target, he would exclaim "whoops" and maneuver his eyes back and forth until he regained contact. He was then able to learn quite rapidly how to return his eyes to the target when he lost fixation, and he soon expanded this learning to permit constant fixation. His awareness of his error permitted much more rapid learning.

BINOCULAR AND MONOCULAR TRAINING

In the normal course of development of ocular control in young children, the child develops control of a single eye first and, when control of each eye separately has been established, he integrates the two eyes together and establishes binocular control. For this reason we would expect, normally, that monocular control would come before binocular control. It is essential that the child develop the skills necessary to control each eye separately and that he integrate these skills for binocular control. Therefore, in helping him to gain ocular control we will want to follow the normal course of development. For this reason, we will wish to train him with the right eye alone, with the left eye alone, and with both eyes together.

In certain cases, children will be found in whom binocular control is superior to monocular control. These children will show apparently good control when tested with both eyes together. However, when tested with either eye alone, their control breaks down and they show considerable difficulty. If our statements concerning the development of ocular control are correct, cases such as these should not be expected. It is felt that such children have made an adaptation to the pressures of the environment surrounding them (which requires binocular responses) when they have not developed the necessary skills for these responses. As a result, they have developed an apparent binocularity which is achieved by simply tying the two eyes together rather than integrating the two control patterns. This apparent binocularity is not efficient and such children

frequently have difficulty with demanding visual tasks such as reading. The environment, however, continues to make binocular demands upon the child. We cannot suspend these demands while
monocular control of each eye is established. The activities of his
daily life continue to demand of the child binocular or pseudo-
binocular functioning.

It is not well, therefore, to train monocular control exclusively.
For such a child, each training session should contain some monocular work and some binocular work. Begin the session with training
of one eye, proceed to the other eye, and end the session with binocular training. This procedure will leave the child, at the end of
each session, as well prepared as possible to meet the demands of
his classroom and other environmental tasks.

FATIGUE

It will be found that children who have difficulty with ocular
control will become easily fatigued in these pursuit-training activities. It should be remembered that the control of the eyes is a very
complex neuromuscular problem. It must also be remembered that
the precision which we require in such training activities is extremely high. For these reasons, pursuit-training activities are easily
fatiguing and should not be carried on for long periods of time.

In addition to the problem of fatigue, the greatest amount of
learning in pursuit activities occurs while the child is adjusting the
neuro-muscular apparatus to the task. Therefore, the period of
most rapid learning is early in the training session and the amount
of learning per unit of time decreases as the session proceeds. It is
recommended that pursuit-training sessions be limited to approximately nine minutes. This time should allow roughly three minutes
for training of the right eye, three minutes for training of the left
eye, and three minutes for training of both eyes.

OCCLUSION

When monocular training is undertaken, it is necessary that
the eye which is not being trained be covered. For this purpose,
some kind of occluder or cover will be needed. A suitable device

can be made from a paper towel or a strip of felt. A hole is cut in the paper or felt so that when the strip is held up to the face one eye will be directly behind this hole; the hole should be large enough so that the child has unimpaired vision through it. A rubber band is broken in two and tied through small holes at the narrow edges of the strip so that it can pass over the child's head. The child then places this occluder over his face leaving one eye free to see through the hole, with the rubber band behind his head to hold the mask in place. When training is changed to the other eye, the child removes the occluder, turns it around, and replaces it with the opposite eye now in position behind the hole. Such masks can be made very easily and have been found satisfactory. Decorated to represent the Lone Ranger or other interesting characters, they also provide good motivational devices for the training.

CLASSROOM TECHNIQUES

The teacher, confronted with the problem of a large number of children in a classroom who must be kept occupied during the school day, will find it desirable to integrate these special training techniques with the regular activities of the classroom. Although some children will have problems so severe that they can be dealt with only in an individual setting, other children with less severe problems can be helped in small group situations. Also, as the children develop in the learning of pursuit skills, their training can shift from individual situations to a small group. As with many other neuro-muscular skills, a period of important initial learning is experienced. During this initial learning, great care must be taken to see that the child absorbs the fundamentals of the skill on which he is working. Also during this period, progress is rapid and performance improves markedly.

Following this initial spurt, however, there is a long period in which practice with repeated but less intensive training activities is required. This latter period serves to establish and fix the learning initiated in the former period. The period of "overlearning" of the skill is extremely important since the child must internalize the specific skills which he has learned and come to use them continuously in all the activities in which he engages. During this latter period, left to his own devices, he is apt to slip back into the poor habits which he had established formerly. Therefore, it is necessary that training be continued for a considerable period of time after the initial skills have been learned. During this long period of "over-learning," however, group activities and activities involving less of the teacher's time are possible.

ACTIVITIES IN SMALL GROUPS

When pursuit training has reached the level of Stages 1 and 2, training is possible in small groups. In the lower elementary grades the teacher usually establishes reading groups of six to eight children. Those children requiring additional training in ocular pursuits can be grouped together as one of the reading groups. The teacher can then arrange the children in a semi-circle around her chair, move the target before the children in much the same way as she would for a single child in training, and ask the children to follow the target. She can carry on much the same type of training activities recommended earlier for individual children in this small group situation. It is, of course, essential that she watch carefully the performance of the children and, should any child experience difficulty, remove him from the group and give him individual attention until his difficulty is overcome.

A complete series of pursuit-training activities, including right eye, left eye, and binocular, can be carried out in such groups. Small training groups substituted for all or part of the reading circle activity for these children have been used successfully in first grade classrooms in the public schools (Simpson, 1968).

During the later stages of pursuit training, and particularly during the period when skills are being internalized, it is possible to arrange for the children to assist in training each other. It has been found most practical to arrange the children in pairs. One child moves the target for the other child, observes his eyes as he follows the target, and in general performs most of the functions previously undertaken by the teacher in the more difficult stages of training. When the first child has been trained, the children reverse places and the first child now trains the second.

It will be found that children become very adept at helping each other. They watch each other's eyes very carefully and spot difficulties readily. This paired training has the additional advantage that the child who is performing the training is also receiving training himself, since he must move the target smoothly and therefore must exert neuro-muscular control similar to that required of the child being trained Under these circumstances, the child gets an even clearer concept of ocular control and what it can do than he obtains when the teacher is moving the target for him.

CHALKBOARD AIDS

Another activity which is very useful in training ocular pursuits and which can be adapted to use in the classroom involves the chalkboard. The teacher draws on the chalkboard a "road," using the flat side of a piece of chalk and drawing a strip about an inch to an inch and one-half wide. The child is given a plastic model of a vehicle which he is asked to "drive" by pushing it along with his hand on the road. Two-wheeled vehicles such as motorcycles have been found more satisfactory than four-wheeled vehicles such as automobiles since the former require more attention to keep them on the road. The two-wheeled models can be turned more easily, and as a result must be attended to more constantly to correct minor errors in direction. Begin with straight roads and proceed to curved and wavy roads which require considerable skill to negotiate. (Compare with Kirk and Johnson, 1951, p. 173.)

This type of pursuit activity can be used in the classroom either individually or in small groups. A series of roads can be constructed and, among a small group of children, each child can work on his particular road. Here again, pairs of children with one monitoring the other can be used. This technique can be extremely useful since it combines activity of the hand with activity of the eye.

PLAY ACTIVITIES

Many types of play activities are very useful in developing ocular-pursuit skills. Any game or sports activity which involves following a moving object and which requires the child to keep the moving object constantly in view can be used to aid in ocular control. Volleyball, basketball, kick ball, and similar sports are useful in this connection. It will be found that the child having difficulty with ocular control will gravitate to a position in these games where such control is not required. Thus, in football he will be found playing in the line; in baseball he will be found either as pitcher or catcher; he tends to avoid basketball but if he does engage in this game, he will play guard. Care must be taken, therefore, to see that the child enters into those phases of the activity which require following the moving object.

A number of commercially available toys which involve marbles or other objects that roll along a surface or down inclines may be used. Most of these toys are too small to provide the latitude of movement necessary for the training activities in which we are interested; however, they will be found very useful if they can be obtained in a suitable size.[1] It will be found that the children are fascinated by these devices and that they use them in a very specific manner for aid in their ocular pursuit problems.

THE MARSDEN BALL

A soft ball about the size of a tennis ball is suspended by a string from the ceiling or, if the technique is used outdoors, from an overhanging tree limb or similar support. The string can be attached to the ball by driving a small cup hook into the rubber and tying the string to this. When the opposite end of the string is attached to the ceiling, the ball swings like a pendulum. It can be swung laterally before the child, in a back and forth direction, or with a circular motion around him. By altering the length of the string, the timing of the swing can be slowed or made more rapid. Larger balls may be used initially for younger children or children having particular difficulty. As they become more adept, the size of the ball can be decreased (Marsden, 1953).

The child stands at one side about arm's length from the ball with the pivot line of the string directly in front of him. Pull the ball

---

[1]An effective rolling marble game may be obtained from Baugh and Reser Hardware, Inc., 432 Columbia, Lafayette, Indiana.

to one side and release it, letting it swing across in front of the child by its own weight. Do not throw or push the ball, but allow it to swing as a free pendulum. As the ball passes in front of him, the child is instructed to reach out and touch it with his finger. He must reach out and contact the ball directly in one movement. He is not allowed to thrust his finger into the path of the ball and wait for it to hit his finger.

He is given a starting point for his finger each time so that he thrusts out with a definite, prescribed movement. The first starting position will be the shoulder. The child is instructed to hold his hand beside his shoulder with his finger pointed ahead. When the ball passes, he is to thrust out and touch the ball. Other starting positions will be the eyes and the hip. He is always to thrust out in one steady movement, not to wander or search for the ball. He is to keep his head still and pointed foreward, following the ball with his eyes.

This technique requires that the child follow a moving target and respond in terms of the position of the target. It requires accurate timing and a synthesis between the visual system and the motor system. It aids the child in developing the vital translation between kinesthetic-tactual data and visual data. He must follow the ball with his eyes as though he were following it with his finger, and must learn to obtain the same information through this ocular following that he earlier received through manual following.

PRELIMINARY TECHNIQUES

Many children will be found who have difficulty in performing the above task. For them, it may be necessary to start with simplified versions of the task and gradually, as they gain skill, increase its difficulty. Thus, the child may need first to learn to reach out and touch the ball while it is standing still. With such a child, use a preliminary technique in which the ball is not swung but is allowed to hang motionless. Allow the child to position his finger within an inch or two of the ball before he thrusts at it. Then gradually, being sure he masters each stage before proceeding to the next, move the starting position back until he can thrust from his shoulder.

The ball may need to be swung through a very small arc at first to permit the child to succeed. Increase the length of the arc gradually until accurate following and anticipation are achieved. He may need to follow the course of the ball with his finger at first so that he can learn to match visual following with manual following. Later he can be asked to begin translating from one to the other by waiting until the ball starts swinging before he begins following it with his finger. He can thus be moved along until he can use visual data alone.

VARYING THE PROCEDURE

When the child has become adept at the task of hitting the ball, be sure that he is following it continuously and not just depending on a split-second awareness of the ball in a certain position to guide his aim. Certain children will learn how to avoid the demands of the swinging ball task by paying attention only to a small area directly in front of them. When they see the ball in this area, they thrust out. They have not followed the ball but have depended upon speed in a single perception for their performance. It is like looking for a single frame in a movie film instead of following the action. If a child has good perceptual speed, he may be able to perform well in the task by this method. He can be forced out of this restricted method by varying the procedure.

Instruct the child to thrust when you call out "Now." He does not know when you are going to give the signal, and he must thrust immediately when he hears you. Under these conditions, he is required to maintain readiness to respond at all times. Only by following the ball can he be ready at any time you may signal. It is well to insert this variation into the training procedure as soon as possible to insure that the proper method is being used. Be sure that he follows with his eyes and not with his head. He should be instructed not to move his head.

When the child has mastered the ball as it swings laterally to his body, we can move on to a fore and aft direction. In this procedure, pull the ball on a line directly in front of the child and let it swing. The ball then moves toward and away from the child. The child reaches out with his hand underneath the ball and with his finger pointed upward. He then moves his hand up so that his finger touches the ball from underneath. He should start in the prescribed starting position and execute the response in one continuous movement. He should hit the ball squarely from underneath, not position his finger and wait for the ball to swing into it. By paying attention to his thrusts, he can observe the direction and extent of his miss on each trial.

When the child begins to learn the task with his finger, he may be given a short bat with which to bunt the ball. It is desirable that these ball techniques be learned with the finger first. The tactual stimulation of the finger actually touching the ball, added to the visual stimulation, makes early learning more rapid and more thorough. When the bat is used, the child is encouraged to reach out and meet the ball, not to hold his bat out and let the ball hit it.

To train judgments over longer distances, the bat or a long, thin pointer can also be used with the ball swinging laterally. In this case, the child stands farther from the swinging ball and thrusts out with the pointer, touching the ball with its tip in the same manner that he formerly did with his finger. The pointer thus becomes an extension of the arm and the task requires spatial judgments beyond arm's reach. Here again, in the preliminary exercises the child should first experience tactual stimulation through the finger because of the value of this stimulation in the learning process.

The process of bunting the ball with the bat involves a spatial judgment and a process of following a target in the fore and aft direction in addition to the problems presented by the laterally swinging ball. Also, timing and rhythm are involved and the technique can be useful in the training of these factors.

TRAINING VISUAL PURSUIT

Ocular pursuit movements without accompanying gross muscle movement can be trained with the Marsden Ball by asking the child simply to watch the ball as it swings back and forth. He should be cautioned to hold his head still and follow the ball with his eyes alone. He should be encouraged not to lose sight of the ball at any time. For older children, we may paste cut-out letters of the alphabet on the surface of the ball.

As it swings, the child is asked to lie on his back on the floor and the ball is swung in a circular movement above him as he follows it with his eyes. During all of these procedures, watch the child's eyes to insure that the following movements are smooth and accurate. When movements are not smooth, encourage the child to "keep his eye on the ball." In these latter exercises, the swinging ball becomes the moving target of the earlier pursuit-training techniques and serves the same purpose. It has the advantage that the child can work alone and thus requires less constant supervision. Obviously, the gross problems of control must be solved before such relatively unsupervised practice can be effective.

SEQUENTIAL CONTROL

When visual following has been established through accurate pursuit movements, a continuity of space in relation to the self develops. No longer does a visual display extended in space appear as a mere collection of isolated relationships. The eye can now perform a "sweep" function which tends to tie the entire spatial extent together. Space now becomes a continuum which the controlled sweep of the eye holds together.

Once such a visual continuum is established, it can be interrupted for the purpose of gathering specific information. Such a disruption does not interrupt the overall continuum of information and, once the specific data have been obtained, the total visual performance can continue. Furthermore, the effect of this continuous preservation of the total impression serves to prevent the specific information from becoming isolated. It remains a part of the whole even though the effort expended on the specific may be relatively intense. The total visual field is molded into an overall impression, even though at no single instant of time can it all be seen at once. This totality becomes the overriding concern and any specific part, singled out for more intense investigation, preserves its relation to the whole while it is being dealt with individually.

Such a total visual process permits the child to deal sequentially with items of his environment while each item remains embedded in the total. The specific does not exist alone at any time, but its overall relation to the whole is always preserved. The ability to fixate sequentially without losing orientation to the total visual task is particularly important in reading. The visual task in reading demands a series of fixations. At each single fixation, certain specific information is gathered. Reading, however, requires that this single fixation not become separated from, but rather remains related to, those which occurred before and those which will come later. If the specific fixation breaks off from the series, not only is the visual task disrupted so that it cannot continue, but the continuity of the context is broken as well. Thus the child is left with no basis either neuromuscularly or cognitively for continuation of the reading process.

In the classroom, a child can frequently be observed who reads fairly well and who can call words from flash cards without difficulty. As he follows along the line of print, however, he appears, at some one fixation, to pick up the wrong clue. On the basis of this poor clue, he cannot recognize the word. Instead of exploring for a better clue, this child seems to "freeze" to the fixation he has. He appears unable to look back and forth over the word in search of a clue or clues which will stimulate recognition Instead, the whole process seems to stop while he desperately tries to recognize the word from a single clue. In extreme cases, even pointing or verbal prods are not sufficient to shift his visual attention. If he finally manages to read this one word correctly, he hesitates, appears not to be able to "get going" again, and frequently must be prodded to go on to the next word. When he does get started again, he frequently skips one or more words or sometimes a line. He may even go back and read a word that he has already read.

Such failures can be seen as a breakdown in sequential control. When difficulty or stress enters the task, the individual fixation loses its place in the series of fixations and comes to exist for itself alone. As a result, the child has "no place to go" if the particular clue he is getting proves inadequate. It has frequently been observed that such breakdowns occur on "easy" words which the child has read successfully many times as often as they occur on difficult words. This observation frequently puzzles teachers. Why should the child suddenly break down on a well-known word?

From the present point of view, it can be seen that the familiarity or difficulty of the specific word would have no bearing on the problem. When, by chance, the child picks up the wrong visual clue, it is as fatal to recognition of a familiar word as to any other. Such errors happen to all readers. The good reader, however, preserving the position of this fixation in a visual continuum, moves back and forth until the correct clue is found and then continues on. If the erring fixation breaks away from the visual-temporal continuum of fixations, however, such search becomes impossible.

The approach to such problems involves aiding the child in establishing a controlled series of visual events. Training involves the design of tasks in which the information from a single fixation is simple enough so that it does not present a problem. Attention can then be directed to the nature of the series and the place of each event within the series.

Lay out before the child a series of poker chips alternating red, blue, red, blue, et cetera. Ask the child to "read" the line of chips by looking at each, naming the color, then moving to the next. He should "read," "red, blue, red, blue" et cetera. Emphasize a smooth, regular progression with equal intervals between chips. Be sure that his eyes fixate on each chip in turn and help him establish a constant rhythm both with the eyes and with the voice. Be sure these two rhythms are synchronized so that he looks as he says.

It may be desirable to introduce a kinesthetic clue to aid him. Ask him to point to the chips as he "reads" them. Because of the eye-hand match, such pointing should directly reinforce the eye. Because of the relationship of motor rhythm to auditory rhythm, it should also reinforce the vocal response. Auditory clues can be added if the teacher reads the line of chips with the child.

Pay particular attention to the performance of the eyes. If the eyes do not move rhythmically or if the visual series is not apparent, the task cannot accomplish its purpose. Initially the hand may lead and the eye follow along. Later, however, the eye should begin to lead the hand. Finally, the eye should be able to perform independently of the hand.

When the child can maintain a continuous visual rhythm, more complex rhythmic combinations can be introduced. Tell the child that the red chips are long and the blue chips are short like the dashes and dots of Morse code. The line now reads r̄ed, blŭe, r̄ed, blŭe, r̄ed, et cetera.

At this point it may be found that the child has basic difficulty with rhythmic patterns. In this event it may be necessary to institute training in rhythm before continuing with the training of sequential visual control.

When rhythm patterns are introduced, it is important that the eyes perform in a rhythmic pattern also, and that this pattern be synchronized with the vocal pattern. Watch the child's eyes carefully to insure that this visual rhythm is present. It may help if the teacher points to the chips in proper order, the child being asked to follow her finger. He may point for himself and follow his own finger with his eyes.

More complex rhythm patterns can be introduced by grouping the chips by colors rather than simple alternation. Thus, blŭe-blŭe-rēd, blŭe-blŭe-rēd; or blŭe-rēd-blŭe-blŭe-rēd, blŭe-rēd-blŭe-blŭe-rēd are examples of more complex rhythmic series.

To bring the activity closer to the reading task, words printed on flash cards may be substituted for the poker chips. At first only one pair of alternating words should be used: as stēp hŏp stēp hŏp stēp, et cetera. Action words are best as they can be acted out to the same rhythm to which they are read. Ask the child to point to each word as he reads it while observing the rhythm marks.

A passage of poetry or nursery rhyme with a marked, sing-song rhythm can now be used. At first the passage should be copied on the chalkboard or laid out with flash cards so that the spaces between words or phrases are large enough to emphasize the visual movement involved. Ask the child to point to each word as he reads it, keeping his eyes and hand in rhythm with his voice.

Since the series of visual movements is the primary consideration, the passage should be read to the child a number of times so that he is thoroughly familiar with it. Do not worry that he may memorize it, as long as he points and looks at the word at the time he is saying it. It is desirable that the word recognition problem be reduced to a minimum so that attention can be concentrated on the series of fixations and the sequence of the process.

Emphasize the rhythm by marking the long and short syllables as before: thus   Mārў hăd ă lĭttlĕ lāmb
                                       Ĭts flēece wăs whīte ăs snōw
Encourage the child to read in a sing-song fashion so that the rhythm can pace his eyes as they move from fixation to fixation.

When this task can be accomplished from the large space available on the chalkboard, the child can be given a book with the same passages printed on a page. Enter the rhythm marks in the book to guide him. Ask him to point as he reads. Watch his eyes closely to be sure they are moving in a rhythmic series.

The additional clues can now be removed so that the child performs on his own. First remove the pointing so that the eyes must move under visual stimuli alone without kinesthetic reinforcement. Then remove the rhythm marks so that he generates his own rhythm from the context which is being read.

New material with which he is not familiar may now be introduced. Begin with sing-song verses which have a strong rhythm. If he has difficulty, ask him to mark the rhythm for himself by placing rhythm marks over the line of print as was done for him in the previous tasks. His attention is thus called to the rhythm and he can practice working out a visual rhythm and matching this to his reading rhythm. If he cannot analyze the passage for himself, read it for him to establish the rhythm pattern.

Group activities in which the children read in chorus or read with the teacher also help to establish this rhythmic flow. Be sure the children's eyes move with the rhythm. The children may also be asked to read in succession, one child reading the first line, another the second, et cetera. The teacher should begin so that the rhythm pattern is well established. Each child then carries on this pattern through his line. When another child is reading, the rest should read silently, making the same series of visual fixations which would be required in reading aloud and gathering the same information. In such an activity, the series is set up for the child and he can practice following along. Only occasionally does the entire task fall upon him. Thus while he is gaining control, he is not required to sustain this control for long periods without help.

Prose passages are more difficult since the rhythm is less regular. However, they can be approached in the same manner and can even be clued with rhythmic marks. It is important for the child whose sequential control is weak to have much experience reading material with which he is thoroughly familiar. It is, therefore, desirable for him to read the same passage a number of times or to repeat it after hearing it read. Do not hurry on to new or more difficult material until a fluent performance has been achieved.

Reading films are available in which the phrases are successively revealed. A window moves across the line hiding or fogging out all of the passage except that which appears behind a clear slot. This slot moves sequentially and rhythmically and can be paced to the speed of the child's level of performance. Teacher-made materials in which a slot is moved by hand across the line serve the same purpose. Such materials help to establish sequential fixations and teach the child to depend more on the sequence and less on the individual fixation.

SYSTEMATIC VISUAL SEARCH

Whereas sequential fixation functions to preserve the overall visual process and reduce the effect of the isolated fixation, visual search promotes an opposite function. In search, the child sweeps the field until the critical clue is encountered, whereupon fixation occurs and becomes the predominant function. When such search is random, success is closely correlated to the strength of the clue sought and its contrast with other items in the field. Thus to find one black marble in a group of white ones requires little search skill. To cross out the *e*'s in a line of letters requires a much more systematic approach. In this task the field must be searched in some kind of orderly fashion. A random search cannot insure that all the *e*'s have been found nor that the letters left untouched are not *e*'s. When each item must be considered and a decision made, search must become systematic to insure that no items are missed.

Classroom behavior frequently reveals the child's difficulty in systematizing visual search. In the common test item where a match to a standard item must be found among a series of items, it frequently is observed that the child has paid no attention to one or more of the comparison items. In picture analysis, when asked to find and point out a feature of the picture, he seems unable to find it but may end up describing an entirely different feature. It can be supposed that, in such tasks, this child is unable to search the visual field in an orderly fashion. Rather he ranges randomly over the entire field in a series of disconnected contacts. As a result, instead of dealing with what he wants, he must deal with what he gets. The result is failure and confusion in many types of school activity.

To teach the child more efficient visual search techniques, it is necessary to structure the task for him until he is able to structure it for himself. Lay out a row of five flash cards with pictures. Give the child a comparison card containing one of the pictures in the row. Ask him to find the one which is like the comparison, considering each card in order and indicating whether or not it matches. To be sure he is concentrating on each card and to provide additional clues to the search task, ask him to point to each card as he reports on it.

Guide the child into a systematic search. If he points randomly, misses a card, or considers a card twice, point with your finger as he points with his. Because of the conventional left to right orientation of the printed page and other visual displays, it is well to guide him into a pattern of left to right search. Point out that any orderly procedure is correct but the left to right, top to bottom method is preferred.

Move on to workbook materials with multiple choice matching items similar to that described above. Require the child to mark each item using one designation for an item which matches ($\sqrt{}$) and another ($\times$) for an item which does not match. This change from the usual procedure forces him to deal with each item. Watch his performance to see that he deals with them in order.

When left to right search techniques have been established, orient the items vertically on the page so that the child is required to search from top to bottom. This vertical direction of systematic search will be useful in many of the paper and pencil problems in arithmetic.

Visual search is more difficult when the units are arranged randomly than when they are arranged in rows or columns as in the previous tasks. Scatter ten to twenty poker chips of various colors randomly over the table top. Ask him to sort these chips by color, placing each color in a separate container. He must pick up and physically move each chip. Require him to deal with the chips in order, considering each as he comes to it and disposing of it in terms of its color. Do not permit him to proceed randomly but require a systematic procedure. Stress the left-right, top-bottom directions as being preferred.

Scatter the chips randomly again. This time ask the child to pick out the red ones and place them in the container, leaving the blue ones and white ones where they are. Require him to point to each chip in order and indicate how he will dispose of it. Do not permit random procedure and do not permit him to skip on to the next red chip. Be sure he considers each chip in order.

The search problem also becomes more difficult when the discrimination required is more complex. The color discrimination of the above tasks is a simple problem. The difficulty can be increased if pictured materials are used. Substitute for the poker chips pictures pasted on cards. Scatter these randomly and ask the child to pick out those which match a comparison card. Do not permit him to grab cards at random even though his choices are correct. Rather, emphasize the systematic search by requiring him to respond in some way to each card in turn. Emphasize the point that he must not only be sure a card he selects is correct but that he must also be sure he has not missed any matching cards.

When visual search is possible on the basis of perceptual variation in the items, ask for selection by categories. For example, from a random distribution of pictured objects, ask the child to select pictures of those items we eat or those we wear, et cetera. Stress the maintenance of a systematc procedure.

Symbolic materials can be used in the same manner. Scatter letters at random over a page. Ask the child to cross out all the *e*'s or all the vowels, or all the letters that occur in his name. Other symbolic materials such as geometric forms, words, and the like can be substituted for single letters. Stress orderly search and the maintenance of the order against the problems of difficulty of judgment on single items.

chapter 12

Chalkboard Training

SCRIBBLING

The earliest activity of the young child in any copying or drawing performance is that of scribbling. The very young child experiments with movement patterns and observes the traces which are left by these patterns on the paper, chalkboard, or whatever medium is being used. In the early stages, these movements are quite random and grow out of the child's experimentation with the basic movement patterns of his organism (Russell, 1956, p. 87; Gesell, 1940, p. 169; Bender, 1938, p. 7). He enjoys this new experience since it permits him to observe these movement patterns more accurately than he can when he moves merely for the sake of movement. Thus, his first approach to paper and pencil or any other writing or drawing medium is one of continued experimentation with the movement patterns which he has been carrying on for a long time. From this new experimentation he obtains two things: (1) additional experimentation with movement patterns and (2) observation of the pattern in the trace left by the activity.

PROBLEMS FOR THE SLOW LEARNER

Experimentation with basic movement patterns has frequently been restricted with the slow learning child. Being less quick in learning and less active in experimentation, he has failed to develop some of the basic patterns of the organism and, among those which he has developed, he has failed to complete the learning process. As a result, his knowledge of and ability with the kinds of movement which we find most useful in our culture are less adequate than that of other children. With this inadequate background, he is often forced into specific kinds of movement patterns by the school or by educational requirements of his culture. Thus, when he reaches the age of five or six, we set him down at a desk with a pencil and paper and require him to produce rather specific and highly skilled motor movements.

Such paper and pencil activities present difficulty to this child for two reasons: (1) because the size of the product is restricted and (2) because the patterns required are complicated. As we know from developmental psychology (Zubek and Solberg, 1954, p. 133), movement patterns begin in gross form using extensive muscle systems and, by a process of differentiation, are refined so that they can be produced in smaller size and with a less extensive musculature. This process of development requires time and careful learning. The slow learning child has been restricted in this learning process and, as a result, when we set him down to the small-size task required in the paper and pencil activities of the early grades, he is not ready to produce this refined and this specific a motor movement pattern. However, we insist that he perform in activities of this type. As a result, he very frequently breaks off a pattern of movement from his total movement pattern and develops this "splintered" pattern specifically for the purpose of solving the problem at hand. We frequently see a subsystem of movements designed for the paper and pencil task but unrelated to the total movement patterns of the child.

Adding to the problems created by size, the complexity of the movement pattern which we require of the child is greatly increased during early school experience. This complexity of movement, like the problem of size, puts the slow learner at a disadvantage. He has not absorbed these movement patterns as rapidly as other children have and he has not experimented as extensively. As a result, those patterns which he does possess are the simpler and less complicated ones. Now we throw him into a situation where extremely complicated patterns are required and, here again, he solves the problem in the only way he can. As far as possible, he reduces to simpler systems the complicated patterns which we require, distorting the tasks which we set for him in the interest of simplification.

Therefore, with slow learning children, we frequently have the problem of returning to basic motor movement patterns and permitting the child to recapitulate the process of development by which finer and more complex patterns are achieved. A difficulty, however, arises immediately. Because we have forced him to make certain adaptations in order to adjust to the situations in which we have placed him, these adaptations have become fixed and the uninhibited type of experimentation by which the normal child develops these higher degrees of skill becomes impossible for the slow learning child. We must break down these adaptations and find some method of getting the child back into the uninhibited experimentation which he requires to strengthen the basic skills needed in the learning process.

As an approach to this problem, chalkboard scribbling has been found a useful procedure. In this activity, the child is presented with a chalkboard and a piece of chalk. He is told to scribble, to make any sort of lines on the board which he would like to make. No restrictions are placed on the product which he is to produce but he is encouraged to experiment as broadly as he is willing to do.

"SPLINTER" MOVEMENTS

Very frequently we find these children, even on the chalkboard, maintaining the adaptations which they have learned in the paper and pencil situation. Thus, it is fairly common to find a child who will rest his wrist against the chalkboard and make all of his movements with his fingers and hand.

It is felt that this kind of behavior is a transition to the chalkboard of specific techniques developed to solve the problem of paper and pencil work in the early grades. It is felt that such children have developed a restricted motor approach in relation to a specific problem and that this motor pattern exists in isolation, "splintered off" from the remainder of their motor activity. As such, it has limited usefulness, being adequate for only one type of activity.

More important, this isolated response confuses the child since he is required to live with two basic sets of motor approaches. Since there is little or no connection between his two motor approaches, the complications of the environment to which the child is required to adjust are increased.

Our first attempts on the chalkboard will be to break down this limited approach and to encourage the child to approach the chalkboard task in terms of his total motor pattern rather than these specific patterns of hand and fingers. Therefore, we will want to move him away from the board so that he cannot rest his wrist against it. We will encourage him to move with his shoulder and elbow rather than with his hand and fingers. We will also encourage him to make his productions larger and to fill a larger space at the board.

TIGHT MOVEMENTS

We may find many children whose movements in the scribbling activity are tight and jerky. These children give the impression of being overcontrolled. It seems as though they are paying so much attention to the problem of controlling the movement that they have no attention left over for initiating the movement. Here again, it seems possible that many children of this type have been forced into conditions requiring precise control of a movement before they have had sufficient experimentation to understand the movement thoroughly.

With children whose movements are tight and jerky, our aim is to free the movement patterns. Encourage the child to move freely, not to be restricted, not to worry about where he is going or the form of the pattern which he is producing. We want his movements to be free-flowing and smooth.

In order to assist the child in freeing his movement patterns, it is often desirable to ask him to move away from the chalkboard so that his hand does not touch it. In this position, we ask him to make free-flowing movements without reference to direction or form. When he has achieved a smooth, free-flowing movement without the resistance of the chalk on the chalkboard, we can then move him up to the board and ask him to do the same thing on the chalkboard.

We can also aid him by using the auditory and tactual clues to smooth-flowing movement that are produced by the friction of the chalk as it moves over the surface of the chalkboard. We encourage him to observe the rhythmical sounds which result from smooth-flowing curved movements and the rhythmical feel of such movements. We may even take a piece of chalk ourselves and point out these rhythms, asking him to imitate our rhythm as he produces his pattern.

In all chalkboard training that features scribbling, the teacher should be alert for jerky, rough, or tight movement patterns. Do not permit the child to persist in these patterns, to practice the errors which he is already making. Encourage him to smooth out and free these movement patterns. The first and perhaps most important value of this training procedure is that it teaches the child free-flowing movement.

OBSERVING THE "TRACE"

The chalkboard permits us to observe the movement patterns of the child and the freedom with which they are being produced. By observing the marks which he leaves on the board, we can see irregularities and tensions in his performance. By adding this information to our direct observations of his movements, we can help him learn initiation and control of major movement patterns.

However, in addition to what the chalkboard shows us, it also shows something to the child. Through the marks which he leaves on the board, he can observe the movement pattern which he has produced in a manner in which he is not able to observe it otherwise. When he simply makes a smooth movement in free space, this movement remains a series of activities in time. He progresses through the movement pattern and, as one phase is completed, the next phase is begun. At no point can he observe the total pattern all at one time. He must be content with the portion of the pattern which he is negotiating at any given instant in time. When the chalk leaves a mark on the board, however, this mark becomes a trace of the movement pattern itself. The trace remains permanent through time. By observing the trace, the child is able to observe the total movement pattern at one time. By this method, he has translated a movement pattern which was a series of activities in time into a simultaneous presentation in space. By observing this trace, the child can see the whole process of the movement pattern instead of being concerned with only fragments of it as it progresses through time.

This observation of the trace left by a motor movement pattern is very important in the development of the young child. He uses it for the purposes described above, to observe a pattern in a more permanent fashion. Such observation is one of the reasons for the young child's fascination with scribbling as a play activity. Just as it is important to the development of the normal young child, it is important to the development of the slow learning child. With his confusion among movement patterns and his inadequate elaboration of movement patterns, it is particularly important that the slow learning child be able to observe these patterns as total processes.

Therefore, in this scribbling performance we will want to call the child's attention to the trace left as a result of his movement. We will want to make sure that he carefully observes this trace and that he identifies it as a permanent record of a movement. When he has produced a pattern and when we know that he is aware of the movement which produced the pattern, we will ask him to stand off from the board and look at the mark which he has made. We may even ask him to trace portions of his pattern so that he can observe the manner in which a pattern on a chalkboard can "stand for" a pattern of motor movement.

In this manner, he can be taught that marks on a piece of paper or a chalkboard symbolize movement patterns. Such knowledge increases the richness of the symbolic information conveyed by such marks and helps him to gear the whole symbolic field into his total pattern of activity. We can therefore use the activity of scribbling on a chalkboard for two basic purposes: (1) to help the child smooth out and free motor patterns and (2) to help the child stabilize these movement patterns in time and recognize symbolic visual patterns as permanent motor movement patterns.

THE MOTIVATIONAL PROBLEM

Of course, with older children we will find difficulty in obtaining free scribbling movements because of the motivational problem.

Many of these children will consider this type of activity "baby stuff." The ingenious teacher will be able to find many methods of motivating the child and modifying the activity in the interest of motivation while still ensuring that the two basic results to be obtained from this training procedure are retained.

FINGER PAINTING

Finger painting frequently can be used as a substitute for chalkboard scribbling in cases where motivation is a problem. In the use of finger paints, we must direct our attention away from the product which the child achieves and toward the process by which he manipulates the materials. We will therefore use the finger paints as a scribbling technique. We will be interested in how the child moves his hands and fingers and how he observes the results of these movements.

Finger paints, like the chalkboard, can be used to free the movement patterns and to produce smooth-flowing, free movements. Here again, we must pay attention to the activities of the child rather than to the product. We encourage the child to experiment with all kinds of movements, placing emphasis on smooth movements *vs.* unsmooth movements. We also encourage him to observe the differences in the traces resulting from these movement patterns. In this manner, we do the same thing with finger paints that we were able to accomplish with chalkboard scribbling. It is essential that the finger paints be an experimental medium in which the child can experiment freely with his movement patterns without relation to any product which might result.

One definite advantage of finger paints in this connection is the possibility of using two hands. Since he can get both hands into the paint, he can experiment with movement patterns of two hands simultaneously. This permits him to observe the difference between the same movement in both hands and the opposite movements in both hands. He can observe the difference between parallel movements on the two sides and contrary movements on the two sides. Here again, we are interested in experimentation. Encourage the child to make smooth, flowing movements simultaneously with both hands. Point out any differences between the patterns in the two

Through constant experimentation and observation, marks (which are the traces of movement) come to stand for the movement which produced them. (Courtesy of Nothman from Monkmeyer).

hands (such as size, shape, smoothness of movement, etc.) and help him to experiment with these patterns until they are matched. The possibility of observing both hands operating simultaneously is a marked advantage of the finger painting medium.

CHALKBOARD (DIRECTIONALITY)

The teacher stands at the chalkboard beside the child. He places a dot at random on the board. The child places his chalk on the dot. The teacher then places another dot at random on the board and the child draws from the first to the second dot. The teacher then makes another dot and, without lifting his chalk from the board, the child draws from the second dot to the third. The game is continued in this same manner, the teacher always waiting until the child has drawn his line before placing the next dot.

PURPOSE

The purpose of this technique is to aid the child in establishing and maintaining directionality and changes of direction. For this reason, the dots are placed at random and in such fashion that the child must change the direction of his movement each time.

This technique is somewhat similar to the connect-the-dot puzzle commonly encountered in which the dots are numbered and the child connects them in series. The present method is felt to be superior for training purposes since it can be used with children who have not yet learned to count and also because the presence of so many dots is often distracting to the child and he cannot perform the task.

SPECIAL PROBLEMS

For children who have difficulty with this activity, use shorter lines and permit the child to pause after drawing each line before he is given the new direction. Some children will have difficulty in establishing the direction in which they should draw and will start off in the wrong direction. Aid the child by calling his attention back to the target dot, as by calling, "Here," and tapping the dot with the chalk. If necessary, guide his hand to help him get started.

Other children will start in the right direction but will be unable to maintain this directionality until they reach the target dot. As a result, their line will "wander" toward the target. Encourage the child at all times to "draw nice straight lines." Shorter distances do not require the child to maintain his directionality for so long a period and hence are easier. If he has trouble, start with short distances and increase their length as the child's skill increases.

Some children can initiate a movement successfully but then have difficulty stopping. Such a problem will result in the child's "overshooting" the target dot. We can aid him by guiding his hand with ours or by providing a cardboard stop at the target dot against which he can bump his chalk. We can give him a stronger stimulus for the stopping response by using larger dots or colored chalk which will produce a dot of a contrasting color to the line he is drawing. We can also help him with the anticipation of his stop by chanting a rhythmic phrase such as "Hit the *dot.*" This phrase should be spoken with distinct rhythm and with a marked accent on the last word. The child can then move in rhythm with the chant and by following the rhythm anticipate when he is to stop. Rhythm also helps him maintain his attention on the problem of stopping during the entire act.

The technique should start with short lines and a marked pause at each target dot. As the child gains skill, the teacher should place his dots at greater distances and increase the tempo of the game. Be sure, however, that the child comes to a full stop on each dot.

At first the child will be distracted if he must cross a line that he has already drawn to reach the next target dot. Therefore, at first, we will place our dots so that he is never required to cross a line he has previously drawn. When he becomes more skillful, we can cross and recross previously drawn lines. Do not attempt to produce a meaningful drawing as an end product of this game but use the technique only to aid the child with the problem of changing the direction of lines. At all levels of difficulty of this task, we should work toward a smooth, continuous movement.

CROSSING THE MIDLINE

As we have discussed in earlier chapters, the problem of maintaining direction while crossing the midline may give some children difficulty. For this reason, at early stages of the game, the dots should be kept on one side of the midline, preferably the side of the dominant hand. As the child increases in skill, we can begin to cross the midline. These crossings should be limited in the early sessions. Thus, the child will be asked to cross the midline only for an inch or two. As he gains skill with the specific problem of crossing, we can increase the extent of the movement across the midline so that eventually we can ask him to draw from full arm's length in one direction to full arm's length in the opposite direction. Watch the child closely during these activities. Be sure that he does not avoid the midline problem by walking back and forth in front of the chalk-board (thus moving his midline with him and avoiding crossing) or by pivoting his body at the hips so that the midline is thrown at various angles in such a way that he is not required to cross it (see Roach and Kephart, 1966, pp. 47-58).

THE CLOCK GAME

In the directionality training described previously, we have required the child to orient on one point in space and perform a motor movement which will bring his hand to that point. In this simple activity, it was only necessary that he determine the direction of a single point. This he could accomplish by a sighting or aiming type of activity. When he had determined a single direction, it was only necessary for him to move his hand in this predetermined direction.

As we have seen before, the child must learn to orient his whole body toward the concept of direction. Since the two sides of the organism are in some respects opposite to each other, the directional orientation required by each side is somewhat different from that required by the other. It is therefore desirable that some training procedure be used in which the child is required to orient both sides

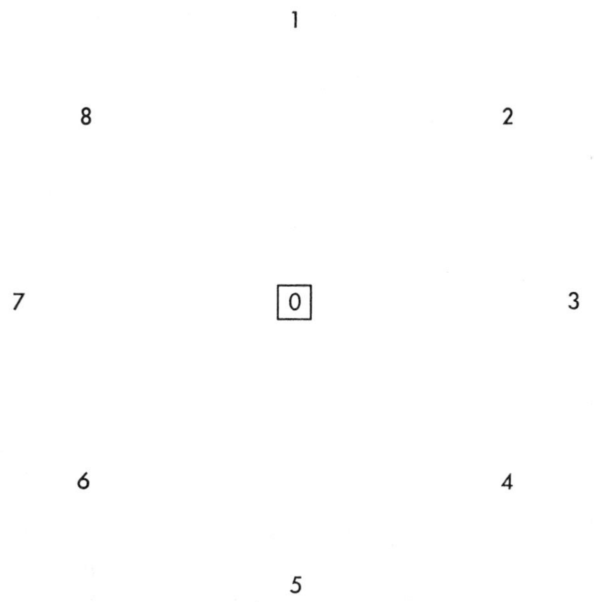

FIGURE 11. Chalkboard positions used in the Clock Game

of his body simultaneously in a given direction or toward a given set of directional commands. We would like him to be able to orient directionally with both sides simultaneously. Therefore, we would like an activity in which both sides must be oriented independently and must perform a directional movement simultaneously. In this manner, we can be assured that the child is orienting directionally with his organism and not with a single part or group of parts. He must also learn to control the interaction of the two sides of his body toward a common goal or toward separate but predetermined goals. In this manner, he can learn to use his two sides in an integrated fashion. The "reciprocal interweaving" of Gesell (Gesell, 1928) can be perfected and its results observed.

On the chalkboard locate eight numbered points equally spaced around the circumference of a circle approximately eighteen inches in diameter (see Figure 11). The points should be so arranged that points 1 and 5 determine a vertical axis, points 7 and 3 determine a horizontal axis, and points 6 and 2 and 8 and 4 determine two diagonal axes. In the center of the imaginary circle, place a square box labeled *O*. This box is the goal for all movements terminating in the center of the circle.

Instruct the child to place the right hand on one of the numbers and the left hand on a second. Then ask him to move the left hand to a prescribed number and the right hand to another prescribed number which you call out for him. He should move both hands simultaneously and they should arrive at their respective goals at the same time.

There are a number of combinations of movements which we will want to investigate with this procedure.

1. OPPOSED MOVEMENT

a. *Toward the Center.*   In this pattern of movement, the child is started with his two hands on the circumference of the circle and asked to bring them both toward the center. Thus, in the simplest movement we start him with his left hand on the number 7 and his right hand on the number 3. He is then asked to bring both hands to the center box *O* simultaneously. Watch closely to see that both hands move at the same time, that they move at the same rate of speed, and that they arrive at the center box at the same time. If the child is having difficulty with this type of movement, it is probable that his first approach to the problem will be to move one hand first and, after this movement is completed, move the second hand. If we allow him to continue according to this method of procedure, we will not teach him the patterns which this technique is designed to aid. Therefore, in our instructions and in the practice sessions, we will want to call his attention to such errors and ask him to correct them. He must start the movement of the hands simultaneously and continue them at the same rate of speed so that they reach the goal at the same time.

The pattern of movement presented by this subsection is perhaps the simplest of all possible patterns. In the first place, it seems probable from studies of developmental movements that movements from outside in are easier than movements from inside out. This subsection presents all patterns in the order outside in. In addition to this fact, in this pattern the child is required only to sight on a single goal, the zero box. During the initial instructions, he may change his visual fixation from 7 to 3 as frequently as he wishes and may take as much time as he needs to locate his hands on 7 and 3. He may attend to his right hand until it is on 3 and then, leaving it there, he may attend to his left hand until it is on 7. He is not required to coordinate the two sides until the performance actually begins. At the command "Bring your hands to zero," he has only to fixate on the zero box. If his only method of orientation is by sighting or aiming, he has a single point at which to aim. The aiming process can be completed in one activity, and he has only to orient his movement systems to this single control.

The simplest movement is the horizontal one starting at 7 and 3 and proceeding to zero. The next movement is the vertical movement starting at 1 and 5 and proceeding to zero. More complicated, as we have seen before, are the diagonal movements starting at 6 and 2 or 8 and 4 and proceeding to zero. A tabulation of the possible movements in this subpattern in approximate order of their difficulty is presented in Table 1 under 1(a).

b. *Movement Away from Center.* In this pattern, the child begins with both hands at the center box and upon command moves out to numbers designated by the teacher. Thus, with both hands located at *O*, he is asked to move his left hand to 7 while he moves his right hand to 3.

This pattern is somewhat more difficult than the previous pattern. Here the child is required to determine the directionality of the two hands independently. He must either look at 7 and retain this directional clue in memory while he looks at 3, or he must be able to look at the center of the circle and with the periphery of his vision be aware of the location of 7 and 3 at the same time. In pattern 1(a), we only required him to coordinate the two sides of his body toward a single directional clue. In the present pattern, we require him to orient to two directional clues at the same time and to orient the two sides of his body to these clues respectively.

TABLE 1

Clock Game

Movement Combinations in Approximate Order of Difficulty

LEFT HAND		RIGHT HAND	
Start	Stop	Start	Stop
1 (a) Opposed movement toward center			
7	0	3	0
1	0	5	0
5	0	1	0
8	0	4	0
6	0	2	0
(b) Opposed movement away from center			
0	7	0	3
0	1	0	5
0	5	0	1
0	8	0	4
0	6	0	2
2 Parallel movement			
7	0	0	3
0	7	3	0
1	0	0	5
0	1	5	0
5	0	0	1
0	5	1	0
8	0	0	4
0	8	4	0
6	0	0	2
0	6	2	0
3 (a) Movement with cross meridia			
Movement toward center			
7	0	1	0
7	0	5	0
1	0	3	0
5	0	3	0

TABLE 1 (Continued)

LEFT HAND		RIGHT HAND	
Start	Stop	Start	Stop
8	0	1	0
8	0	3	0
8	0	5	0
6	0	1	0
6	0	3	0
6	0	5	0
8	0	2	0
6	0	4	0
7	0	2	0
7	0	4	0
1	0	2	0
1	0	4	0
5	0	2	0
5	0	4	0
(b) Movement away from center			
0	7	0	1
0	7	0	5
0	1	0	3
0	5	0	3
0	8	0	1
0	8	0	3
0	8	0	5
0	6	0	1
0	6	0	3
0	6	0	5
0	8	0	2
0	6	0	4
0	7	0	2
0	7	0	4
0	1	0	2
0	1	0	4
0	5	0	2
0	5	0	4
4 (a) Cross movement—cross meridian			
Movement left to right			
7	0	0	1
7	0	0	5
7	0	0	2
7	0	0	4
8	0	0	3
8	0	0	5
8	0	0	1
8	0	0	2
6	0	0	3
6	0	0	1
6	0	0	4
6	0	0	5

TABLE 1 (Continued)

LEFT HAND		RIGHT HAND	
Start	Stop	Start	Stop
(b) Movement right to left			
0	7	1	0
0	7	5	0
0	7	2	0
0	7	4	0
0	8	3	0
0	8	5	0
0	8	1	0
0	8	2	0
0	6	3	0
0	6	1	0
0	6	4	0
0	6	5	0

In the early stages of training, we permit him to look back and forth from 7 to 3 as frequently as he wishes in order to determine the directions demanded. It is desirable, however, that he be able to maintain visual fixation at O and at the same time be aware of 7 and 3 with peripheral vision. Many children, in tasks involving difficulty or stress, reduce the area of their peripheral vision (Kephart and Chandler, 1956). Their visual field "tunnels down" so that the only material of which they are aware is that which lies straight ahead of them. Obviously this restriction of visual field reduces the awareness on the part of the child of many clues which would be helpful in the solution of his problem. We are interested in counteracting this tendency on the part of the child, and the present technique can be used for this purpose if we encourage him to fixate on the center of the circle and be aware of the periphery at the same time.

In this pattern, as in the previous one, the teacher must be sure that the child starts with both hands at the same time, that he proceeds at the same rate with both hands, and that he arrives at the two goals simultaneously. In activity of this type, some children will be found who give all their attention to the dominant hand and permit the non-dominant hand to take care of itself. Such children should be encouraged to pay attention to both hands at the same time and to be aware of the movement of both hands simultaneously.

As in the previous pattern, the lateral direction is the simplest, the vertical direction is next, and the diagonal directions are most difficult. A tabulation of the various combinations in their approximate order of difficulty is given in Table 1 under 1 (b).

2. PARALLEL MOVEMENT

Here we require the hands to move parallel to each other. Thus, the child is asked to begin with his left hand on 7 and his right hand on *O*. He is then asked to move his left hand to *O* and his right hand to 3. Both hands are moving in a left to right direction and are moving over the same distance.

Again, the teacher should observe whether the child moves both hands simultaneously, whether he moves them at equal rates, and whether he arrives at the two goals at the same time. As in the previous patterns, it is desirable that the child pay attention to both hands and he should be encouraged to be aware of the movement of both hands at the same time. As in pattern 1(b), the present pattern can be used to aid the child in maintaining peripheral awareness during a difficult task. This is done by encouraging the child to maintain visual fixation on the center box while the movement is taking place.

We want the child to learn parallel movements in both directions (that is, right to left and left to right) and in all meridia. A table of the various combinations of movements is presented in Table 1 under 2.

3. MOVEMENT WITH CROSSED MERIDIA

In this activity, one hand is required to move in one direction while the other hand moves in another direction. Thus, the child may be asked to place his left hand on 7 and his right hand on 1. At command, he is asked to bring both hands together at *O*. In order to do this, one hand must travel in a lateral direction while the other hand is traveling in a vertical direction.

In order to accomplish this activity, the child must do two things. (1) He must be able to move one side of his body in a given direction while the other side is moving in another direction. There must be enough independence of the two sides that they do not need to move in bilaterally symmetrical relationships. (2) He must be able to evaluate spatial relationships on the lateral axis according to the same scheme with which he evaluates them on the vertical axis. Thus, the distance from 7 to O must appear to him the same as the distance from 1 to O. If one of these axes appears longer than the other, the two hands will not meet in the center simultaneously We therefore present, with this pattern, a considerably more difficult task for the child to accomplish.

As before, the teacher should observe the beginning of the movement, its speed, and whether the final goal is reached simultaneously with both hands. Again, the child should pay attention to both hands equally so that both sides of his body are under control at the same time. Attention to both sides is more necessary for the solution of the task in the present pattern than in either of the previous two. Here again, the child should be encouraged to maintain visual fixation on the O center box.

The two overall directions of movement described above are possible in the present pattern also. Thus, the movements can be set up in such a way that both hands are moving toward the center or they can be set up so that both hands are moving away from the center. As in pattern 1, the movement toward the center is easier than the movement away from the center. Also, as we have seen before, movements in a lateral direction are easiest, vertical movements are more difficult, and diagonals are most difficult. A tabulation of the various possibilities in approximate order of their difficulty is given in Table 1. In this tabulation, movements toward the center have been presented first [section 3(a)] and movements away from the center second [section 3(b)].

4. CROSS MOVEMENT — CROSS MERIDIA

a. *Left to Right.*   In this pattern, the hands are moving in opposite directions and at the same time are moving in opposite meridia. Thus, the child is asked to begin with the left hand at 7 and the right hand at O. He is then asked to move his left hand to O and his right hand to 1. These patterns are an extension and a more difficult combination of the patterns in number 3 above. The same observations and cautions are pertinent here that were described there. In the first group of patterns, the general direction of the movement is left to right.

b. *Right to Left.* These patterns are similar to those of number 4(a) above except that the general direction of movement is right to left. We will want to give the child practice in both of these directions of movement since we want him to have a complete and integrated concept of direction and of movement in a given direction when these are signaled by a visual stimulus. The various movements in this pattern as well as those of pattern 4(a) are tabulated in Table 1 under 4(a) and 4(b).

When the child has become reasonably proficient with the activities described above, a circle of larger diameter can be substituted for the eighteen-inch circle. This larger circle should be approximately thirty inches in diameter. On the one hand, a larger circle requires greater skill of the child since the movements are longer and must be maintained over a longer period of time. On the other hand, it requires awareness of clues at a greater distance into the periphery of vision when the teacher requires the child to maintain fixation on the *O* center box while the task is being performed. In general, the further a stimulus lies from the center of vision the more difficult it becomes to recognize it or to use it as a control for general behavior (Feinberg, 1949). The larger circle is particularly desirable for increasing the aid which we provide the child in keeping his peripheral visual field operative during a stress-producing task. The same general procedure is used with the large circle that was used with the smaller circle.

For children who cannot read or who have difficulty recognizing the number symbols, substitute pictures, colors, or other materials with which the child is familiar for the numerals around the circumference of the circle. It is desirable that the child perform the task with chalk rather than with his finger or by moving his finger in the air in front of the chalkboard. The line resulting from his movement helps us and the child to determine how well he has performed.

Some children will not maintain a high level of motivation in the drawing tasks described here. For such children, other devices may be substituted to solve the motivational problem. One teacher, for example, gives the child small toy cars which he drives into the garage (the *O* center box) or which he delivers, two at a time, to customers' homes (numerals on the circumference of the circle).

CHALKBOARD (ORIENTATION)

Ask the child to stand before the chalkboard with a piece of chalk in each hand. Ask him to perform circular motions with both hands simultaneously. Note the direction of the movement in each hand. Then ask him to bring the chalk in contact with the board so that he is drawing circles with each hand simultaneously. He should be asked to continue drawing pairs of circles, each pair on top of the previous pair. He should continue the motion, not stopping after each circle is drawn, until he produces a series of retraced circles, one set with the right hand and one set with the left hand.

Normally we expect the child to draw his circles clockwise with the left hand and counterclockwise with the right. If he begins with these directions, we ask him to change and draw counterclockwise with the left hand and clockwise with the right. When this movement has been established, we ask him to make his hands move parallel to each other, going clockwise with each hand. When he has established this movement, we ask him to shift and go counterclockwise with both hands. In this manner, we let him experience all combinations of direction of movement with the two hands, both those in which the movements are opposed and those in which they are parallel.

We want the child to observe the difference between movements in different directions and between different combinations of movement on the two sides of the body. Therefore, we will want to call his attention to the movements and the difference in the way they "feel." We can direct his attention to the movements by asking him to shift abruptly during a movement pattern. Instead of asking him to move left clockwise, right counterclockwise, and then stop, completing this task, and then asking him to move left counterclockwise, right clockwise, we will ask him to shift in the middle of the pattern. Thus, while he is moving in the left clockwise, right counterclockwise pattern, we will call, "Change direction." At this signal, he is to shift direction as rapidly as possible without interrupting the movement. In like manner, ask him to shift from opposed to parallel patterns in the midst of the activity, and to change the direction of the parallel patterns without interrupting the activity.

At the same time that we are showing him the difference between the movement patterns, we want him to observe that the results are circles irrespective of the directions with which they were produced. Therefore, we will want to direct his attention to the product of his movement during the entire activity. His attention can be called to the trace on the board by asking him to produce good, round, smooth circles.

In most cases, a change in movement will result in a disruption of the pattern which will in turn result in a distortion of one or both of the circles. Ask the child to correct the distortion (by watching the circles he is drawing) and to smooth out the movement as rapidly as possible. When a reasonably accurate, smooth circle has been achieved, give the signal for a change of movement pattern.

Remember that the learning in this activity results from the change of direction and the reorientation of the process. As soon as the child has established correct patterns in the new direction, little further learning takes place. Therefore, little is gained by having the child continue a direction after he has mastered it. We gain more by asking him to change and readjust his perceptual-motor process. Long periods of training are not indicated; short periods with frequent changes are more effective.

Remember, however, that unless the child establishes an adequate perceptual-motor response after each change (achieves a reasonably round, smooth circle), he has not learned the relationships that we are trying to teach him. Therefore, he must be helped to achieve an acceptable (although not necessarily perfect) production at each step. If certain patterns are too difficult for him and he cannot achieve an adequate production, drop back to simpler patterns or help him by guiding the hand, tracing over heavy circles drawn previously on the board, and so forth.

THE LAZY EIGHT

An appreciation of direction of movement and of form independent of direction of movement can also be aided by use of the "lazy eight." With one continuous line, draw on the board a figure 8 lying on its side. The figure should be approximately twenty-four inches wide and approximately ten inches high. Ask the child to trace over and over this figure with one continuous line without taking his chalk from the board. When he has achieved a smooth, free movement which is reasonably accurate, ask him to reverse directions without removing his chalk from the board or interrupting the activity.

This figure is particularly helpful since the direction of movement in the left-hand loop is the opposite of that in the right-hand loop. In spite of this difference in direction, the visual counterparts of these movements are the same when drawn or traced on the chalkboard. Such a form permits the child to observe relationships between different motor acts and perceptual products within the same figure.

The child should be asked to trace this figure in both directions with the right hand and also in both directions with the left hand. By experiencing both hands in this task, he can observe the differences and similarities between movements on one side of the body and on the other. He should be asked to stand so that the entire figure is to the right of the center of his body in some trials and so that the entire figure is to the left of his body in other trials. At other times, he should be asked to stand so that the center of his body is directly in front of the crossing point between the two loops. By varying the position of his body in all of the above combinations, we can present to him the fact of laterality related to direction of movement and perceptual products. Present all combinations of hand, direction, and body position so that the child's experience may be as diversified as possible.

As in the earlier exercises, the learning in the lazy eight exercise occurs during the adaptation to a new direction, hand, or position of the body. To continue practice after this adjustment has been made results in a decreasing rate of learning. Therefore, short periods of training with numerous changes in method are most rewarding.

DRAWING AND COPYING

In the scribbling activity which we described earlier, we presented the child with a problem in which motor activity was predominant. The child was encouraged to experiment with motor patterns and to observe the visual counterparts of these patterns as they developed in the form of marks on the chalkboard. In scribbling, the motor element was predominant and the perceptual element was secondary. The child's attention was directed from the motor to the visual.

In directional activities, as in the dotting game or the clock game, we have imposed a single visual control upon the motor activity. In these games, the child was required to make a visual orientation toward a goal. He was then required to initiate a motor pattern which would bring his hand in contact with his goal. This sort of activity requires a visual control over the initiation of the action. It involves aiming or sighting behavior and guiding a motor movement toward the sighted goal. This is, as it were, a single visual control over a motor activity. After the sighting has been accomplished and the orientation to the goal has been established, visual control may be no longer necessary. The child, in effect, establishes his perceptual control first and performs the motor movement second. Such activity is analogous to an open system of control (Brown and Campbell, 1948, p. 2), wherein the visual controls are established before the action is initiated and their control function is completed before the action takes place.

When we ask the child to draw or copy a form, we set a new task for him. We require him to exert a constant visual control over the motor movement pattern. In copying, we require him to set up a visual control which is operative throughout the motor activity. Visual control now becomes dominant and motor activity is secondary to perceptual activity. With copying, it is not possible to set up the control ahead of time. The child must constantly keep in mind the visual information and use this information to guide the motor activity at each instant of the performance. When he is copying from an actual model, the visual data are physically present. When he is drawing, he is presumably copying a mental image in which the visual data are present in memory. In either event, the perceptual data must exert a constant control over the motor activities.

It will be seen, of course, that what we have been discussing in the past few pages is the skill which has frequently been called eye-hand coordination. In the scribbling stages, we were concerned with the hand primarily and the eye only secondarily and as a means of observation. In the dotting and clock game activities, we inserted a single control over the hand by the eye. In our present drawing and copying activities, we will now attempt to bring the hand under constant control of the eye. We are attempting to set up a visual-motor feedback (see page 112; also Strauss and Kephart, 1955, pp. 2-5) in such a way that visual data can be used as a constant, closed-system control of the total activity.

THE CIRCLE

Gesell and others (Gesell, 1940; Bender, 1938; Goodenough, 1926) have shown that the first form to be reproduced by the young child is that of the circle. Our current intelligence tests place the drawing of the circle at a lower age level than the drawing of any other form (Terman and Merrill, 1937; Wechsler, 1949). The circle is the simplest form operationally since it involves a constant direction and a constant rhythm. In order to complete a circle, it is only necessary that the child set up a movement in a constant curved direction and maintain this movement until closure is made. In like manner, the rhythm of the movement is not interruped in the process of completing the circle. We will therefore want to start our training in drawing and copying with this simplest of all forms.

MOVEMENT

Our first problem is to teach the child the circular movement itself. For this purpose, the teacher may stand in front of the child and describe a circular movement with her hand and arm. The child is asked to imitate this movement. If he experiences difficulty, we may guide his movement by asking him to touch his finger to the teacher's. As the teacher moves around in the circular motion, the contact of the finger guides the child's arm in a similar movement. By this method, some of the difficulties of the child's movement pattern can be eliminated.

Many children will have greater difficulty than can be removed by this simple method. These children will need additional tactual and kinesthetic clues to help them form a circular motion. These clues can be supplied by the use of *templates*. A template is a pattern cut out of cardboard or similar material.

The form to be studied is cut out of a sheet of cardboard. The template is then the cardboard sheet with the cut out portion in its center. Thus, in the case of the circle, we would have a sheet of cardboard with a circular hole in its center. The child inserts his finger in this circular hole and runs it around the circumference of the circle. Through this activity, he gets tactual clues regarding the movement pattern from the contact of his finger with the edges of the template. In like manner, the template forces his hand into a prescribed motion. Whenever this forcing takes place, the muscular tensions and tonuses are changed from those which occur when he is making the incorrect motion. Kinesthetic end organs produce sensations indicating these changes in muscle tension. These kinesthetic clues, added to the tactual clues, form a strong picture against which to compare his movement.

If the child has particular difficulty, the teacher may ask him to press hard against the template. This pressure increases both the tactual and the kinesthetic clues. When he begins to have less difficulty, the teacher may suggest that he press lightly against the sides of the template. In this manner, she can reduce the tactual and kinesthetic clues as the child becomes able to perform on his own with less and less assistance from these additional sets of clues.

TEMPLATES

When the child begins to develop an idea of the circular motion, we will want to bring this activity under visual control. Our first approach to this problem involves the use of templates held against the chalkboard. The first activity at the chalkboard is a continuation of the development of the circular movement pattern discussed above. The template is held firmly against the board by the teacher. The child is asked to place his finger inside the cut out circle and to run it around the edge of the form. Here he is obtaining tactual and kinesthetic clues to the required movement, as previously described. In addition, he is getting further tactual information from the contact of his finger with the surface of the chalkboard as well as with the edge of the template. The teacher should encourage the child to watch his finger as it runs around the circumference of the circle.

The child is then given a piece of chalk which he is asked to place inside the template. He is then asked to run the chalk around the edge of the template in the same way in which he ran his finger around its edge. This activity results in the drawing of a circle. Here again, the task is made easier by the kinesthetic information provided by the template and the tactual information provided by the contact of the chalk with the board and with the edges of the template. When a circle is completed in this manner, the template is removed from the board so that the child can see what he has drawn.

At this point, we are introducing visual clues which we will later want to make the dominant factors in the child's control of his performance. Therefore, it is very important that at this early stage we begin to call his attention to the visual factors involved. After each attempt, the teacher will therefore remove the template from the board so that the child can see what he has drawn. He will also want to call the child's attention to the drawing and to make sure that he observes this visual trace left by the activity.

TRACING

We are now ready to introduce the problem of visual data as a guide and control for motor activity. We do this by asking the child to trace over a representation of the form which we are trying to teach. We will want to introduce this problem in stages since it represents a major learning task for the child, and we cannot ask him to jump immediately from a tactual and kinesthetic control to a visual control. We must interpose intermediate steps to help him.

a. *Visual-Tactual-Kinesthetic.* At the first stage, we will simply add visual information to the tactual and kinesthetic information which the child has already learned to use. For this purpose, we will draw a circle on the board which can be enclosed with the template. The child is then asked to place his chalk inside the template and to draw over our visual circle. To aid him in this activity, he has the tactual information from the chalk on the board and the edges of the template and the kinesthetic information from the template. At the same time, we will call his attention to the visual data and encourage him to use these visual data as a guide in the process, depending as little as possible upon the tactual and kinesthetic clues.

At this early stage, we will want to make the visual information as strong as possible. Therefore, the circle which we ask him to trace will be made with very broad, heavy lines. The circumference should be drawn an inch to an inch and one-half wide and the chalk should be heavy and obvious. It is desirable, if possible, to use colored chalk to increase the strength of the visual clues. Red is most suitable since it is more striking than any other color.

By using a heavy line we do two things: (1) we increase the strength of the visual stimulus by increasing its quantity, and (2) we decrease the demand for precision in the child's movements. By using bold strokes with the chalk, we increase the strength of the visual clue by increasing the brightness contrast between the circumference of the circle and the surrounding chalkboard area. If we use colored chalk, we further increase the strength of the visual clue by adding a color contrast to the brightness contrast. By these means, we make the visual data as striking, as strong, and as predominant as we possibly can. By using a wide line, we decrease the precision demands of the task. If the circumference of the circle is one inch to one and one-half inches wide, the child can make a reasonably large error and still be successful in performance. Since we are introducing visual control, we are more interested at this stage in type or quality of performance than we are in precision of performance.

b. *Visual-Tactual.* In (a) above, we presented the child with three clues to the copying task: visual, tactual, and kinesthetic. Since we want him to be able eventually to perform this task on the basis of visual clues alone, we will want to remove the additional tactual and kinesthetic clues as rapidly as possible. Here again, however, we cannot remove these abruptly; we must remove them in a series of intermediate steps.

The first clue which can be removed is the kinesthetic. We do this by removing the template in the activity in (a) above. We now ask the child to trace with his finger over the circle which we draw on the board. This circle is drawn with a wide line and the visual clues are made as strong as possible. By using his finger for this tracing activity, the child obtains a maximum amount of tactual information. As it rubs over the surface of the chalkboard, his finger gives him constant and strong tactual data at the same time that he is obtaining visual data from our drawn circle. If necessary, we can increase the tactual information by asking him to press hard against the board with his finger. As he is able to perform more readily, we will want to decrease the tactual information by asking him to press more lightly. During all this activity, we want to call his attention constantly to the visual data by asking him to watch what he is doing and to stay on the circle. Since the circle has been drawn with a very broad line, the precision required to stay on its outline is reduced.

c. *Visual-Minimum Tactual.* When the child is able to perform adequately by tracing with his finger on the chalkboard, we will want to reduce this tactual clue and further reinforce the visual clue. This we can do by asking him to trace around our circle with chalk. The tactual information resulting from the chalk as it rubs against the surface of the board is less intense than that resulting from his finger when it rubs along the same surface. At the same time, a new set of visual information is introduced. The line produced by the child as he draws with his chalk is added to the visual data represented by our circle on the board. He is encouraged to observe this line while he is producing it and to compare it with ours. Here again, we are still using the circle made with broad and heavy lines so that the visual information is at a maximum and the precision required is at a minimum.

Be sure that the child maintains a smooth, free movement during the tracing. Do not permit him to slow down and tighten up his movement. Some children will move very slowly and in short spurts, checking each spurt after it has occurred. Such children are not using the visual information to guide a movement pattern. They are splitting off the motor aspects of the task from its perceptual aspects. The motor movements (spurts) are not under visual control but are produced by purely motor activity. After each spurt, the child compares his product with the model by a vision-to-vision match. Such procedures avoid the problem of perceptual-motor control and the monitoring of movement patterns by perceptual data. They are not aiding the development of a closed system of control. We will therefore want to discourage such approaches to the tracing activity since they do not result in the type of learning which we are trying to achieve.

d. *Visual.* When the child can perform with a minimum of kinesthetic and tactual clues, we can remove the tactual clue entirely and ask him to perform the task under visual guidance alone. This we do by asking him to trace the circle in the air. The child is asked to hold his finger up to the copy of the circle but not quite touching the chalkboard. He is then asked to trace the circle in the air over the copy but in front of the chalkboard. The teacher should watch carefully to see that he stays on the line even though his finger is not touching the board. Visual clues are still at a maximum since the copy we give him is still made with broad, heavy lines.

e. *Reduced Visual Clues.* Since we want the child to be able to perform the tracing task with a normal set of visual clues, we will want to remove the artificially strong visual data which we have been using up to this point. Here again, we cannot move abruptly to tracing a circle in which the circumference is drawn with a normal stroke but must move toward this goal with intermediate steps. This can be done by gradually reducing the strength of the visual clues which we offer.

The first step is to remove the color clue, drawing the broad, heavy circumference with ordinary chalk. We can then begin reducing the width of the line which we use in our copy. Thus, we may cut it down from an inch and one-half to an inch, then to three-quarters of an inch, then to one-half inch, et cetera, until we can draw a circle in which the circumference is made with a chalk line of normal width and which the child is still able to trace over with his chalk.

Do not forget that, as you reduce the width of the line, you are not only reducing the strength of the visual clues, but you are also increasing the precision of movement required of the child. Therefore, the process of reducing the width of the line is determined both by the child's ability to use reduced visual clues and by his ability to make more precise movements.

COPYING

When we ask the child to copy a circle, we have introduced a new variable which was not present in the task of tracing a circle. In the task of tracing, the visual data were constantly present at each instant of the performance. As he traced around the circle, at any instant, the visual data required to guide the next instant of performance were immediately before him. When he is asked to copy, however, the visual data are in one position on the board and his production is in another position. He must therefore introduce mental images of the visual data to serve as immediate guides to his performance. The copy supplies the general set of visual data, but its application must be accomplished through the use of memory information.

The difficulty interposed by this memory requirement is frequently seen in the trouble which the child has in achieving a closure. The end of his circular motion does not meet the beginning. As a result, his production is not closed but there is an overlap or a gap in his circle between the starting point and the ending point. In order to close his circle in the copying task, the child must remember his beginning point and must keep in mind the total movement pattern so that previous activities are remembered and have an effect on present activities.

In the tracing performance, as soon as the child has traversed a portion of the circumference, he can, if he wishes, forget all about this portion and simply continue his activity guided by the copy which lies directly in front of him. When he is required to copy, however, this immediacy of response is inadequate. Past activities must continue to influence present activities so that the child keeps the starting point always in mind and, upon completion of the activity, comes back to it. Only in this way can a closure be achieved. In copying, no instant of activity can remain independent but must be integrated with remembered previous activity and anticipated future activity.

We can help the child to achieve closure by calling special attention to the beginning and ending point of his activity. Thus, we may make a large bold X on the board. We ask the child to begin his circle at the X and to end it at the X. As he progresses with his activity, this strong stimulus helps him to keep in mind the point at which he began and the point at which he must end. We can also aid him by verbally calling to his attention the starting X and the ending X. Thus, we add auditory and verbal clues to the visual clues. As he becomes more proficient, we will want to reduce these artificial clues until he can operate without them. Obviously we can reduce the clues by reducing the number of verbal hints which we give him and by gradually reducing the size of the X which we give him as a clue.

REPRODUCTION

When the child can copy a form, we want him to be able to reproduce it from memory. Thus, we want to be able to say to him,

"Draw a circle," and we want him to be able to reproduce an adequate circle from this verbal clue alone. In this activity we have inserted a further demand upon his performance. In tracing, we gave him continuous visual clues as a guide to his activity; in copying, we required the substitution of remembered clues for part of the visual clues. Since he could look back and forth to the copy, we offered him help whenever his memory clues weakened or failed him. When we ask him to reproduce a circle on verbal instructions alone, however, we ask him to guide his total performance on the basis of a mental image or a set of remembered data. In this performance, all of the guiding of the motor movement must result from memory images. Thus, reproduction of the circle represents the highest type of performance where all of the control of the activity has become cortical and intellectual.

VARIATION

All of the activities discussed above have been very specific and could be applied to a specific circle. We want the child to develop a generalized concept of a circle rather than a specific concept of a given circle. Therefore, if we go through the stages of chalkboard activity with a particular circle, we are in danger of teaching the child how to reproduce a *particular circle* but failing to teach him the generalized concept of the circle. Therefore, we will want to vary the activities described above in terms of the variables in the circular form itself. There are a number of these variables, and in our activities we will want to use circles varying in all of the aspects with which we want the child to become acquainted.

a. *Size.* The child must learn that the characteristic aspect of a circle is its shape. Therefore, we will want to vary the sizes of the circles which we offer him as examples. In all of the activities above, we should present circles of varying sizes. Do not use the same size circle in all sessions or in all activities of one session. Sometimes present small circles, sometimes large circles, and sometimes intermediate sizes. These variations should, however, be kept within a reasonable range. Obviously we do not wish to give the child a circle so large that he cannot comprehend all of its parts at one time. On the other hand, if we make the circles too small, we may drive him back into the "splinter" type of activity discussed in our description of scribbling techniques.

b. *Speed.* The child must learn that the circle is drawn with a constant rhythm (as opposed to squares and other forms in which the rhythm must be interruped). Again, we want him to realize that the constancy of rhythm (Piaget and Inhelder, 1956, p. 65) is the important factor and not the rhythm itself. Therefore, we should vary speed in our activities just as we varied size. Sometimes we will ask him to draw circles rapidly, sometimes we will ask him to draw them slowly, et cetera.

c. *Solid vs. Outline Figures.* The child must learn how to see a form as a figure on a background. This is more difficult in the case of outline forms than in the case of solid or colored-in forms. In the case of the outline form, the area enclosed by the contour is objectively similar to the area lying outside the contour. If form preception is adequate, the child disregards this similarity and the area within the contour comes to stand out and appear different from the area outside the contour (Kephart, 1958). In this way, he develops the concepts of figure-ground. With many children, however, this figure-ground relationship does not arise spontaneously We will want to help these children develop the figure-ground relationship. If we do not pay attention to this problem, we are in danger of teaching them how to reproduce the contour of the figure without seeing or responding to the figure as a form.

Therefore, we will want in the course of chalkboard training in drawing to incorporate training in figure-ground relationships. This can be be done by coloring in the area bounded by the figure. When the form is colored in, the inside area stands out against the outside area since it is different in either brightness, color, or both. Such additional clues aid the child in developing the figure-ground relationship.

For this reason we will want, in teaching the child the drawing of a circle, to vary the figure-ground relationship. Part of the time we will ask him to color in the circle, and part of the time we will ask him to draw it in outline. The coloring-in problem presents some of the same difficulties that we have discussed in terms of outline drawing. Thus, we will want to provide the child with templates so that tactual and kinesthetic clues can be added to his performance, and we will want to offer him increased visual clues by the use of broad lines and strong visual data just as we did for his outline-drawing performance. In all of the types of activity discussed above, we will sometimes ask him to draw in outline and sometimes ask him to color in. Here again, always call attention to what he has done. Ask him to step away and look at the product which he has made when he has finished it.

d. *Direction.* We want the child to know that a circle is the same thing if you draw it in a clockwise direction as it is if you draw it in a counterclockwise direction. Therefore, in training, we will want to vary the direction in which the child draws. Sometimes we will ask him to draw counterclockwise, sometimes clockwise. Again, call his attention to the fact that the circle is the same regardless of the direction in which it is produced.

e. *Hand.* We also want the child to know that a circular motion produced by the right hand is the same thing as a circular motion produced by the left hand. Therefore, we will want to vary the hand which we ask him to use. Sometimes we will ask him to draw or trace with the right hand, and sometimes with the left hand. Again, we call his attention to the fact that the product is the same regardless of the hand which is used.

We will also want to present all of the combinations of direction and hand. As we have seen earlier, a clockwise movement with the right hand is different from a clockwise movement with the left hand. The motor patterns presented by these two movements differ. We want the child to know the different ways in which he can produce a circular motion and to recognize that regardless of how it is produced it still is a circle. Therefore, in our activities, we will ask him sometimes to draw clockwise with the right hand, counterclockwise with the left hand, sometimes the reverse. In this manner, we present all of the combinations of movement patterns of the hands which result in a circular product.

f. *Other Body Parts.* We also want the child to know that the circular movement remains circular independent of the body part with which it is produced. Thus, in addition to asking him to produce circles with his hands, we will ask him to draw circles with his toe in sand or other soft material. We may ask him to hold a pencil or crayon in his teeth and draw a circle with his head. Many children do not appreciate the circular pattern as applied to parts of the body other than the hand. It is important that the child realize that a circle is a generalized pattern and can be produced by any body part which is capable of a circular motion.

VERBAL COMPONENT

Throughout all our activity in drawing and copying, we will want to be sure that the child attaches the verbal symbol to the production which he is making. Language and communication demand the use of a verbal symbol which must stand for a motor pattern, an image of a motor pattern, or the data from motor patterns particularly as these are combined with sensory elements to form perceptions (Piaget and Inhelder, 1956, p. 453). Therefore, we will want from the beginning to increase the symbolic value of the verbal symbol by attaching it to all experiences in which it is applicable. Therefore, in drawing a circle we will want to attach the word *circle* to all of the activities that we can. Thus, in our instruction, we will use the word *circle;* in calling attention to the production of the child, we will use the word *circle.* In like manner, we will ask him what he is going to draw, what he has drawn, and what the production which he has made is called. In this way, we keep the verbal symbol constantly in relationship to the child's activities.

OTHER FORMS

We have seen that the simplest form for the child to reproduce and the one which appears earliest in the development process is the circle. Other simple geometrical forms appear characteristically later in the development process. Table 2 is adapted from Gesell (Gesell, 1940) and indicates the order of appearance of these forms as he has observed from his research. From this table, it will be seen that the order of appearance of ability to copy the various forms is as follows: circle, cross, triangle, diamond. Gesell does not list the ability to copy a square in this table, since he found extreme variability depending on the method of duplication which the child used. From his further observations and those of other workers (Bender, 1938; Terman and Merrill, 1937), however, it would seem that the square appears at approximately the four-year level.

TABLE 2

Age of Appearance in Developmental Sequences of Ability to Copy Simple Geometric Forms (Adapted from Gesell, 1940).

Age	Ability
36 months	: Copies circle
48 months	: Copies cross
60 months	: Copies triangle
66 months	: Prints a few letters
72 months	: Copies diamond

In helping the child to develop drawing and copying ability, we will want to follow the order of forms represented by this developmental sequence. We will therefore wish to present forms in the order in which they appear in Table 2. We have already discussed the circle as the simplest form. The next form would be the cross.

THE CROSS

The cross involves three principles which were not present in the circle: (1) the construction of a vertical line, (2) the construction of a horizontal line, and (3) the problem of bisecting a line. We should help the child with each of these problems separately.

THE VERTICAL LINE

In his spontaneous scribbling, the child normally produces vertical lines before he produces horizontal lines. Gesell (1928) places imitation of a vertical stroke at the twenty-four to thirty month level, imitation of a horizontal stroke at the thirty-six to forty month level. Most frequently the direction of these vertical lines is from top to bottom. Ask the child, therefore, to copy the vertical leg of the cross first. If he has difficulty, begin with the problem of drawing a vertical line.

In helping the child construct a vertical line, we can use many of the devices which we have used previously in helping him draw a circle. Thus, the initial step would become that of establishing the concept of a straight, vertical line. Again, as in the case of the circle, ask him to move his hand up and down in a vertical direction, establishing the vertical movement. If he has difficulty, we can guide his hand or ask him to keep the tip of his finger in contact with our finger as we describe a vertical motion.

His first vertical performances on the chalkboard can be aided by the use of templates. In this case, the template consists of a straight line. A straight narrow groove is cut out of the template material so that when the chalk is placed inside the groove and moved in a vertical direction a straight line results. This pattern is frequently overlooked in the construction of templates. However, the teacher will find the use of a straight-line template very rewarding.

When the child can produce a straight line with a template, in which erroneous movements to either the right or the left are prevented, he is given a ruler or straight edge in which only erroneous movements in one direction are prevented. Thus, we can increase the difficulty of the task by easy stages.

When he is able to produce a straight line with the ruler, we can then remove these supports and ask him to produce a straight vertical line without external aids in a free situation where he must develop all of the control himself. As a further aid at this latter stage, we may give him a broad, heavy colored line to trace over. In this manner, we can increase the tactual, kinesthetic, and visual relationships.

THE HORIZONTAL LINE

The horizontal line is taught in the same manner as the vertical line. Ask the child to copy the horizontal leg of the cross. If he has difficulty, help him in the same manner as before. Present first a complete template, then the ruler or straight edge, then the strong visual clues, and finally free copying.

Most children will show a preference for horizontal lines drawn in the left-to-right direction. The child should be encouraged to experiment with horizontal lines drawn in both directions. He must learn that a horizontal line is the same regardless of the direction in which it is drawn. However, since many of our cultural activities proceed from left to right, we will want, when we are sure that he has the complete concept, to encourage the child's preference for the left-to-right direction.

AVOIDING DIAGONALS

The cross used in this exercise is one in which the arms are vertical and horizontal. Do not rotate this cross so that the arms are diagonal. As we will see later, this diagonal orientataion is much more difficult. The cross with which we are concerned here is a plus sign, not an "X." The point of intersection of the two lines is such that each is bisected. Thus, all four of the arms of the cross are of the same length. Again, the cross is like a plus sign not like a "T."

DEVELOPING CONCEPTS OF LENGTH

Many children who can adequately produce the vertical and horizontal lines alone will be found to have difficulty orienting these two lines to each other in the proper relationship. Thus, the horizontal line may be placed too high or too low on the vertical axis or the horizontal line may be too long either on the left or, more frequently, on the right. These deviations indicate that the child is having difficulty with the problem of the relationships between the parts of this figure and particularly with the problem of bisecting a line. In certain cases, where one section is drawn markedly longer than its counterpart, he may also be having difficulty stopping. The problem of stopping will be dealt with in more detail in our discussion of the square.

The problem of bisecting involves the concepts of "longer," "shorter," and "equal" as these apply to linear lengths. These concepts are a more difficult type of generalization than we usually consider them. The child requires a great deal of information on the basis of which to develop such concepts.

"Long" v. "Short." We begin with the concept of "long" versus "short." We want the child to appreciate the difference between two unequal lines in three areas: kinesthetic, tactual, and visual.

Draw two horizontal lines on the chalkboard, one longer than the other. We give the child kinesthetic information by asking him to "bound" the lines with his hands. In this procedure, the child is asked to place his left hand at the left end of the line and his right hand at the right end. He is then asked to transfer to the short line and perform the same operation. His attention is called to the difference between the position of his hands when he bounds the short line and when he bounds the long line. We point out to him that when his hands are closer together the line is shorter and when they are farther apart the line is longer.

We may wish to increase his kinesthetic information concerning lengths by asking him to compare in a similar "bounding" manner various objects about the room. We will also want him to experiment with lines of different lengths rather than with a single pair of lines so that he will generalize his information rather than learn specifically the difference between two lines of a specific pair.

We can increase his tactual awareness of length by asking him to trace over the lines which we have drawn. Tactual information in such an activity is related to time. With the longer of the two lines he gains tactual information over a longer period of time, whereas with the shorter of the two lines he gains the same tactual information for a shorter period of time. Ask the child to trace at an even rate over the longer line and then at the same rate over the shorter line. Then ask him to compare these two experiences pointing out the difference between the two. His appreciation of this difference can be increased by adding auditory stimulation to the tactual and kinesthetic stimulation. Thus, we may count or chant as he traces the length of a line. Here again, we are increasing the awareness of the time over which the tactual stimulation is operative. Counting or chanting serves to structure the time interval and provides an additional basis for comparing the tactual stimuli.

During all of the above activities, we encourage the child to look at the lines while he is experimenting with them. We want him eventually to be able to make the comparison of length on the basis of the visual stimuli alone. When we have helped him to compare by adding kinesthetic and tactual stimuli to the visual, we can ask him to make his judgments on the basis of the visual stimuli alone. In this case, we will ask him to look at the two lines and tell us which is the shorter. He can then check his judgments by the tactual and kinesthetic methods which he has previously learned. Here again, we will want to present a wide variety of different pairs of lines, beginning with those in which the difference in length is less marked. Only in this way can we assure generalization of the concepts which we are attempting to develop.

The Concept of Equality. When the child has become aware of "longer" and "shorter," he can move on to the concept of "equal," which is neither longer nor shorter. His concept of equality in length can be aided by the same procedures which we used to increase his concept of "long" versus "short." Bounding of two lines with his hands and observing that he need not change the position of his hands when he goes from one to another will help him to appreciate equal lengths in lines. In like manner, tracing with his finger and observing that the same amount of time is consumed in tracing one line as in tracing the second line will help him to establish the concept of equality.

He can then be asked to make a line which is the same length as one which the teacher has placed on the board and check his product by the tactual and kinesthetic methods. He can also be asked to divide a line in two parts so that the left part will be equal to the right part. Here again, he can be asked to check his visual judgment with kinesthetic and tactual judgments. We can then ask him to copy the cross in such a way that the vertical line will divide the horizontal line in half and the horizontal line will divide the vertical line in half.

EQUALIZING THE TWO LINES

Many children will be found who are able to produce a cross in which both lines bisect but in which the vertical sections are longer than the horizontal or vice versa. Although the relationships within the figure have been properly reproduced, the vertical and horizontal relationships are not equal. Such a production frequently indicates that the child has not matched vertical length to horizontal length. A visual stimulus in a vertical orientation does not appear to be the same length as that same stimulus when it occurs in a horizontal orientation. For this child, visual clues to length are unequal when they are in different meridia.

To aid such a child, we must teach him how to compare vertical length with horizontal length. In this problem, we can use the same techniques which we used in teaching him "long" versus "short." Thus, we may ask him to bound a vertical line with his hands and then perform the same operation with a horizontal line, comparing the two kinesthetic patterns. In like manner, we can ask him to trace over a vertical line and subsequently to trace over a horizontal line and compare the tactual stimulation. It may require several such experiences before the child is able to make a judgment of equality between a horizontal and a vertical line. He should experiment with lines of different lengths in the different orientations and also with lines of the same length in the different orientations. As soon as he is able to make judgments, we encourage him to make predominant use of the visual data. We can increase the significance of the visual data by asking him to make his judgments on the visual information first and subsequently to check it by kinesthetic or tactual information.

THE SQUARE

The square adds a new element with which the child has not previously had experience, namely, corners. Executing a corner involves two additional types of activity. The first of these is stopping a movement at a prescribed point, and the second is changing the direction of a movement. The child must learn first to stop at a corner and then to turn a corner.

THE PROBLEM OF STOPPING

As we have seen earlier in this discussion, the problem of stopping a movement is as difficult as the problem of starting a movement. The activities involved in stopping are essentially the same as those involved in starting and demand a repatterning of the neurological impulses guiding muscular activity. The child must not only reverse this neural patterning, but reverse it at a given time and at a given place. The stimulation for such stopping behavior is not strong and is only in part a direct perceptual stimulation. The child must learn to stop where he wants the corner to be. This point is determined in part by perceptual data from the paper itself and in part from anticipated data concerned with the length of the line which he desires to produce. Thus, the stopping point or stimulus for stopping is very weak and is a combination of perceptual data and imagery. In most children, we find the difficulty arising primarily from this latter problem. The child is able to stop but he is not able to anticipate the point of stopping. He does not get a sufficiently strong stimulus for the stopping activity.

We can help the child with the problem of stopping by increasing the number of clues which are available to him. Thus, we can increase the visual clues by providing a wide, heavy, and preferably colored line as a stopping point. On the right side of the chalkboard draw a heavy line approximately an inch and one-half to two inches wide. Have the child place his chalk about eighteen inches to the left of this line. Ask him to draw to the line and stop before he crosses it. If he still has difficulty in stopping, place a ruler or straight edge along the right-hand side of the broad line as a "stopper." The child then draws his line until the ruler prevents him from going further. He is encouraged to stop before he hits the ruler and to stop on the broad, heavy line. Motivation may be increased by asking the child to imagine that his chalk is an automobile. He is asked to drive his car onto the street but not across the street. He must not hit the "curb" (ruler) on the other side of the street. As the child becomes more adept, the ruler is removed and the width of the line is decreased.

THE PROBLEM OF TURNING

When the child is able to stop within a reasonable distance, we can shift our attention to the problem of turning the corner. In this task, the child must change the direction of a movement without completely terminating the task. He must alter direction in a movement which is a part of a total motor activity and, in the process of changing direction, must not lose sight of the total activity.

In this problem also, we can help him by increasing the clues to the new direction. Again draw a broad, heavy colored line on the right-hand side of the chalkboard. Ask the child to place his chalk about eighteen inches to the left of this line. Then ask him to draw over to the line and go down in the new direction without getting off the line. If he has difficulty, again use a ruler as a "stop." The child then draws over to the ruler and proceeds down its length. If he still has difficulty, provide two rulers, one on each side of the broad, heavy line. The child then draws over to the line and proceeds down between the two rulers.

When the child begins to develop some skill in turning this corner, we can first remove the rulers and then decrease the width of the line. Eventually we can ask him to execute this corner without these additional clues. By this activity, he can be taught to draw a corner (which is one of the elements of a square) by himself. During the learning process, when the wide line is in use, motivation can be provided by asking the child to imagine that his chalk is a car, as we did before. The child then drives his car over to the road, turns, and drives down the road without getting off.

STRENGTHENING FORM PERCEPTION

The execution of the square also presents a greater demand for form perception than was required by either the circle or the cross. As we have seen earlier, form perception develops by differentiating out of a globular mass elements of a form which are subsequently recombined into an integrated or constructive figure. The elements of the square, as Hebb (Hebb, 1949, p. 83) would suggest, are the lines and the angles. We have previously helped the child to execute each of these elements. We must now call his attention to the presence of the elements in the square form, helping him to differentiate them out of the globular mass and to reintegrate these elements into a constructive figure.

To help the child differentiate the elements out of the globular figure, we call his attention to the corners. This can be done with a template or a square cut from wood or cardboard. To the visual information regarding the corners, we add tactual and kinesthetic information by asking the child to feel these characteristics of the form. We want him to feel these, in order, around the contour of the figure so that he is aware that there are four such elements in a certain relationship to each other. We may also add auditory information by asking the child to count the corners or to give an auditory signal when he arrives at a corner.

We can help the child preserve the relationships between the elements by asking him to complete the total square figure. This he does by establishing a temporal order of events which corresponds to the spatial simultaneous order of events represented by the copy figure. Thus, we ask him to draw a square. We encourage him to complete this figure with one continuous line and we call attention to the order in which the elements appear. We call attention to each corner as he approaches it and point out its relationship to the previous element and to the next element.

SUPPLYING ADDITIONAL CLUES

As in the case of the circle, we will need to aid the child in this drawing behavior by supplying additional sensory clues. Kinesthetic clues may be supplied by the use of the template, tactual clues by the activity of tracing, and increased visual clues by the use of broad, heavy colored lines. We will use these clues in combination and remove them in order as the child's ability increases. Thus, we will want to use with the square the same general series of activities outlined above for the circle.

GENERALIZING THE CONCEPT

As in the case of the circle, we want the child to generalize the concept of square, and therefore we will alter the size, the rhythm or speed, the direction, and the starting point. In order to increase the figure-ground relationship, we will sometimes ask him to color in the square form and sometimes ask him to draw the contour of the form. Thus, we will carry him through the several stages: tracing with a template, tracing with the finger, tracing with chalk, copying, and reproducing.

AVOIDING DIAGONALS

Care should be taken to keep the square form always in the vertical and horizontal orientation, never in the diagonal orientation. If the square is rotated through 45 degrees, its sides become diagonal lines instead of vertical and horizontal lines. As we shall see, the reproduction of diagonal lines is much more difficult and occurs much later in the developmental process than the reproduction of horizontal and vertical lines. We will want, therefore, to avoid the diagonal directions during training with the square form. Diagonal directions will be important in the drawing of triangles and diamonds and should be postponed until these figures are introduced.

THE RECTANGLE

The rectangle introduces another new problem for the child, that of disproportion of size among the various sides. The child must learn that opposite sides of the rectangle are parallel and that two of these parallel lines are longer than the other two. Furthermore, he must learn that the differences between the length of the sides are proportional.

DEVELOPING THE CONCEPT OF "PARALLEL"

The problem of parallelism between opposite sides of the figure becomes more important in the case of the rectangle than it was in the case of the square. Although opposite sides of the square were also parallel, this parallelism could be achieved in large part by merely paying proper attention to the length of the sides. If the sides are of equal length and the corners are right angles, parallelism is assured in the case of the square. In the case of the rectangle, this parallelism is not so easily accomplished. Since the sides differ in length, the concept of parallel lines is much more useful in the reproduction of the rectangle than in the reproduction of the square.

It is therefore desirable that we help the child with the concept of "parallel" when he reaches the rectangle. Here again, we can help him if we can increase the clues to parallelism. The visual clues can be enhanced by the addition of tactual and kinesthetic clues. In this procedure, we will ask the child to trace with his finger the two opposite sides of the rectangle simultaneously. Thus, he will trace one side with his right hand and one side with his left hand. Call his attention to the fact that his hands remain the same distance apart during the entire tracing activity. Draw an angle on the board and ask him to trace the two sides of the angle simultaneously. Call his attention to the fact that in the case of the angle (nonparallel lines) his hands come together or grow wider apart, whereas in the case of the parallel lines they remain the same distance apart. Ask him to try this tracing activity on the two long sides of the rectangle and also on the two short sides. Call his attention to the fact that the same parallel relationship is present between the two long sides that is present between the two short sides.

THE PROBLEM OF PROPORTIONALITY

We have already described techniques by which we can help the child observe differences in the length of lines (see the cross above). These same procedures can be used again to help him to observe the difference between the long side of the rectangle and the short side.

In the case of the rectangle, however, another problem is presented. Not only are the sides different in length but the difference in length is proportional. It is not sufficient to observe that one side is long and the other short. The length of the two sides must be proportional. A failure to recognize this proportionality leads the child to draw highly elongated rectangles in which the long side is disproportionately longer than the short side. Such attempts have been observed by any teacher in the elementary grades. The child must recognize that the nature of the rectangle is due to the proportionate differences in length rather than to differences in length per se. This problem of proportionality has been discussed at length by Piaget and Inhelder (1956).

We can help the child to observe the problem of proportionality if we can teach him to use the additional clues, which we have previously given him to judge differences in length, as measuring devices. Thus, we may ask him to bound with his hands the short side of the rectangle and, without moving the position of his two hands, lay this distance along the long side of the rectangle. If the rectangle is, for example, twice as long as it is high, he can observe that he lays his hands out twice along the long side. We can then call his attention to the fact that the long side is "twice as long" as the short side. The same procedure can be used with the tactual stimulation of tracing with the finger. He can observe that it takes him twice as long to trace the long side as it does to trace the short side. Here we have helped him to establish subjective measuring units by kinesthetic and tactual information.

GENERALIZING THE CONCEPT

We will want to use similar rectangles of various sizes. Thus, we might present a figure six inches by twelve inches. At a later point, we would present the same figure, but nine inches by eighteen inches. Both of these figures are similar rectangles since they are twice as long as they are high. However, they differ in absolute size and the objective measurements are different. We want to call the child's attention to the fact that these figures are similar even though their overall lengths are different. We want him to observe that the basic concept of the rectangle is the proportion between the two sides and not the absolute length of the two sides. We will need, therefore, to present a large number of figures, some of which are similar and some of which are dissimilar, and ask him to observe the similarities and dissimilarities, pointing out that these are a function of the proportionate differences between the sides.

In this connection, we will also want to present the rectangle in the two primary orientations, one in which the long side is horizontal and one in which the short side is horizontal. Here again, we want the child to come to appreciate the general concept of a rectangle. We must therefore present it in both orientations so that he learns that a rectangle is the same figure regardless of which side becomes the base.

STRENGTHENING FORM PERCEPTION

As with the square, the child must learn to differentiate the elements of the rectangular figure and to reintegrate these elements into a constructive form. Here again, we will want to call his attention to the elements of the figure (lines and angles) and to the relationships between these. We will want to use the same series of procedures which we used in the case of the square and the circle. Ask him to trace with his finger around a template, to trace with chalk around a template, to trace a broad heavy line with his finger and with chalk, to copy the form, and to reproduce the form. In all of these activities, call particular attention to the sides and angles. This can be done auditorily by chanting, as well as tactually and kinesthetically. If the child produces a sound or a word in connection with each side, and if the word or sound associated with the long side occupies a longer period of time than in the case of the short side, this auditory information can be added to the visual, tactual, and kinesthetic information to help him keep the elements of this figure separate and to keep their relationships in mind.

Since we are attempting to teach the general concept of "rectangle," we will want to vary the size and the proportions of the figures which we present him. We will also want to help him establish the figure-ground relationship by asking him sometimes to color in the figure and sometimes to draw its contour.

FIGURES WITH DIAGONAL LINES

As we have seen so often previously, the production of diagonal lines is more difficult than the production of either vertical or horizontal lines. It would appear that diagonal movements occur later in the developmental process than other types of movement. (Gesell, 1940). Bender found that vertical lines were copied approximately correctly at five or six, whereas oblique lines were not copied correctly until nine or ten years (Bender, 1938). The age levels quoted by Bender are somewhat higher than those quoted by Gesell owing to differences in the complexity of the tasks which they presented to the child. However, there is general agreement between these two workers regarding the order in which directional lines are achieved. Piaget and Inhelder, on the other hand, were unable to observe a difference between the age of acquiring verticals and the age of acquiring horizontals (Piaget and Inhelder, 1956, p. 400). However, they found diagonals developing later than either verticals or horizontals (*ibid.*, p. 74). We will therefore not present the child

with figures involving diagonal lines until he has learned to reproduce figures involving horizontal and vertical lines. Among the
common geometrical forms involving diagonal lines are the triangle
and the diamond.

Since the new problem in these figures is the diagonal direction,
we will want to give the child special help with this movement. As
in previous activities, we can use templates and tracing techniques
to increase his awareness of the diagonal. It will be found desirable
to present the child first with a diagonal line alone. Ask him to draw
across the chalkboard in a diagonal direction. If he is unable to
accomplish this drawing adequately, we may increase the visual
clues by providing him with a wide heavy line which we ask him
to trace. If he still has difficulty, we can add a ruler or a template
as a guide, thereby adding tactual and kinesthetic clues to the visual
clues. We can then help him to learn the diagonal movement by
the same techniques which we used to help him learn the circular
movement.

THE TRIANGLE

When the child has mastered the diagonal movement itself, we
can present him with the triangle. It will be easiest if we first present
him the triangle with its base down and its apex up. This would
appear to be the most natural orientation for this figure and the one
which the child appreciates most readily. Helping him with the triangular figure will follow the same steps outlined above in our discussion of the square. First, we can provide him with templates and
a broad, heavy line, giving him maximum clues. As he is able to
perform in this situation, we can remove the template, reducing the
clues to visual and tactual. Later, we can reduce the intensity of the
visual clues until he is tracing in a normal fashion. From this stage,
he can proceed to copying and reproduction.

As with the other forms discussed, we want to be sure that the
child gains the concept of "triangle" rather than learning the reproduction of a specific figure. For this reason, we will vary the size
of the triangle and, to aid him in his figure-ground relationship, we
will sometimes ask him to color in the figure and sometimes trace
around its periphery. When the child has begun to learn the tri-

angle in its upright orientation, we will present it in the opposite orientation with the apex down. He should recognize that the triangular form is the same regardless of its directional orientation.

THE DIAMOND

The most difficult of the common geometrical forms for the young child is the diamond. Reference to Table 2 will indicate that the normal child does not copy this form until he is seventy-two months of age. It can be seen that the diamond form magnifies the difficulties of diagonal movement which we first encountered in the triangle. In the case of the diamond, the child must at each point in the form transfer from one diagonal direction to another. All of the elements of this figure represent diagonals. Frequently we see the child displaying difficulty when he changes direction from one diagonal to another. Thus, as he approaches a corner of the diamond he may make a number of false starts and, only after he has started the movement, recognize that it is proceeding in a wrong direction. Through this experimental motor activity, he produces "ears" on his form, a problem which will be recognized by any elementary school teacher.

The steps in teaching the diamond are the same as those in teaching the square and the triangle. Begin first with maximum clues, using templates, a broad, heavy line, and maximum tactual stimulation. As the child progresses, gradually reduce these clues, removing first the template and then reducing the strength of the visual stimulus. Finally, ask the child to copy the form and then to reproduce it from memory.

As always, we will want to present the diamond in various sizes. We will also present it in both orientations: first with its long dimension vertically and then with its long dimension horizontally. It will be found that ability to produce this form in one orientation does not guarantee ability to produce it in the other orientation. It will be found frequently that when the diamond is rotated through 90 degrees, the child will appear to be presented with an entirely new task and the steps in teaching the form in its original orientation will need to be repeated in whole or in part in this new orientation.

In the diamond figure, as in other forms, we will want to help the child with his figure-ground construction by asking him to color in the form part of the time. He should also learn that the diamond is the result of two triangles with their bases together. We can aid in the development of these relationships by drawing a line bisecting the diamond figure and asking him to reproduce the two halves separately, pointing out that they are triangular figures. In like manner, we can give him cutouts of triangles which, when placed base to base, form the diamond figure.

It will be noted that both the order of presentation of simple geometric forms and the stages in teaching these forms follow very closely those recommended by Jolles (1958).

COMPLEX FORMS—LETTERS AND WORDS

When the simple geometrical forms discussed above have been learned by the child, he has all of the basic patterns required for the reproduction of more complex forms. Now such figures as the Maltese cross, the divided rectangle, and similar forms, either symmetrical or asymmetrical, can be understood by the child. He will still need help in organizing the elements of these more complex forms into adequate wholes, but the basic patterns for their recognition and reproduction are now present.

LETTERS

Among such complex forms are the twenty-six specific figures which we know as the letters of our alphabet. It therefore follows that at this stage the child can begin to learn the reproduction and recognition of letters. If, in some of the more complicated letter forms, he continues to have difficulty, we can help him by techniques similar to those used to present the more simple geometrical forms. Thus, templates and tracing can be used to help the child learn to reproduce single letters. It should be borne in mind that we are here teaching the child the problem of form in the individual letters. We are not concerned at this point with teaching the alphabet or with individual letters as a prelude to reading. Our concern is wholly with the ability of the child to recognize the form of the letter. It is felt that such forms cannot be fully appreciated until they can be reproduced and until the visual data represented by the letter on paper come to have meaning in terms of the movement patterns of the child's organism.

WORDS

Like letters, words represent complex forms. Therefore, at this stage the child can learn to reproduce and recognize simple words and phrases. Here again, we are interested in the child's development of a full appreciation of the form represented by the word. It is felt that this can best be accomplished by using as many clues to the development of this form as possible. Therefore, just as with simple geometric forms, the child should trace the word either with or without templates, depending upon his ability, should then copy the word, and finally reproduce it. After he has learned to reproduce a word, he should be able to recognize it on paper or on the chalkboard. If he has difficulty in recognizing the word as produced by someone else (reading the word), we can aid his recognition by using the process of reproduction as a clue to recognition. Thus, for the word which is not recognized, we would ask the child to trace over it or to reproduce it on the chalkboard. Such procedures are recommended by Fernald and have been found very useful in early stages of teaching reading (Fernald, 1943).

Throughout all of the activities described above, one of the factors toward which we have been working is the use of these concepts of form and pattern in the later activities of reading. Reading involves the association of a verbal and auditory pattern with the visual pattern. For this reason, we want to encourage the child to verbalize during all of the drawing and copying processes. We want to encourage him continually to associate a verbal pattern with the motor activity in drawing and copying. For this reason, it is desirable to call the child's attention to the verbal association in all of the training activities in this area. Thus, we may use the word *square* in association with his production of a square; we can ask him what he is drawing, and when he has finished, we can ask him what he has drawn. It will be found helpful at all stages in learning to draw a square to associate continually the word *square* with the process of producing the figure and also with the figure when it has been produced. This verbal component becomes particularly important when we reach the stage of letters and words. Here we are coming much closer to the reading process itself and we will want to establish the habit of associating verbal components with such activities. We will therefore ask the child to say the letter or word as he is writing it. When he has completed his writing, we will ask him to read what he has written (Fernald, 1943).

FROM CHALKBOARD TO PAPER

All of the activities which we have been describing have been carried out on the chalkboard. The chalkboard differs from paper and pencil in two fundamental ways: (1) it is oriented vertically, and (2) the sizes are consistently larger. However, our final goal is the reproduction of these forms and figures on paper at a table or desk.

The table or desk represents a different orientation from that of the chalkboard. On the chalkboard, the orientation was vertical and the top of the chalkboard was "up." In like manner, the top of each of the forms which the child reproduced on the chalkboard was a vertical "up." When we pass from the chalkboard to the horizontal orientation of the desk, however, the top of the paper changes from a true vertical "up" to a conventional "up" which is a direction away from the child. The child needs to learn that the orientation on the desk is a conventional one and he must learn to make the transition from the true "up" of the vertical orientation to the horizontal "up" of the horizontal orientation. Most elementary school teachers have observed the child who, when asked to put a mark on the bottom of the paper, turns the paper over and puts his mark on the backside. He has translated the concept "top" and "bottom" in terms of the vertical orientation and has not learned to appreciate the conventional orientation of paper on a desk (see Strauss and Kephart, 1955, p. 179).

In order to help the child make this transition, it will be found useful to bridge the gap by degrees. Thus, if the chalkboard is one which can be tilted, we can move it toward the horizontal orientation a bit at a time and let the child work his way through from the vertical "up" to the "up" of desk and paper. Thus, we would ask him to perform with the chalkboard vertical, then we would tilt it ten degrees toward the horizontal and ask him to perform again, then tilt it twenty degrees, et cetera, until it becomes horizontal.

In like manner, the size of the reproductions which we ask the child to make on paper are considerably smaller than those which we ask him to make on the chalkboard. He must learn to translate the movement patterns that he has established into the more precise and less extensive patterns required to produce smaller figures. At the same time, he must not lose these patterns as a part of the total motor system.

We can help him in making this size transition by approaching it through easy stages. At first, the teacher may want to use large sheets of newsprint on a table, permitting the child to reproduce his figures in approximately the same sizes that he used on the chalkboard. We can move from the large newsprint and crayons to paper of letterhead size and pencils. We can also carry him gradually from large figures covering the entire sheet to small figures of the size we desire, reproduced in order on the page.

When he has made this transition and is ready for letters and words, we can provide him with primary tablet paper. This paper has spaces between the lines which are approximately twice the size of the normal ruled tablet paper. We can then ask the child to fit his letters into these wide spaces. When he has been able to reproduce at this primary size, we can provide him with ordinary tablet paper and ask him to reduce the size of his figures again until they will fit within the lines of such paper. We must be careful at each of these stages to see to it that the new size of drawings develops out of the total motor pattern which we began to establish on the chalkboard and continued to encourage on the large sheets of paper. Smaller drawing and copying tasks should not be entered into as a new type of activity which is accomplished by a new and unrelated series of motor performances. These finer and more precise patterns must develop out of and remain related to the more gross movement patterns.

chapter 13

Training Form Perception

DIFFERENTIATION OF ELEMENTS

Frequently we see the child in whom the differentiation process in form development has not been completed. Such a child has not differentiated the elements of the form out of the global mass or has not carried this process of differentiation far enough to permit him to make necessary distinctions between forms. For this child, training should begin by increasing the degree of differentiation within forms. A number of technques can be used to call attention to and emphasize elements so that their differentiation out of the mass is encouraged.

FORM RECOGNITION

A particular form can be recognized by virtue of the presence of qualities which it possesses or elements which are unique to it. These qualities or elements are emphasized when recognition of the form is required. If particular attention is drawn to the factors essential for recognition, these particular aspects of the form are given special emphasis for the child.

As has been pointed out, form recognition does not necessarily imply constructive form perception. The earliest approach to the problem of identification by the child is the isolation of "signal qualities" which can be used for identification. In the final stages of the development of form perception, such dependence on signal qualities must be discouraged in the interest of the development of the more efficient "emergent qualities" of the constructive form. At the beginning stages of development, however, where the child is differentiating from the initial global mass, such signal qualities are an integral part of his problem. It is through such learnings that he will be encouraged to differentiate a sufficient number of elements to make constructive form possible.

Form recognition, therefore, is a poor indicator of form perception. It guarantees only the initial phases of development. When training needs to be directed at these initial phases, it may prove a highly useful training technique. When form perception develops more fully and when constructive form becomes the object of training, however, this technique will need to be abandoned in favor of techniques which more directly encourage more complex form manipulations.

Recognition training should begin with concrete objects and overall qualities; thus, color and size are frequently used as beginning differentiations. Present the child with two blocks of contrasting color. Use primary colors and do not try for fine discrimination of shade. Color as a quality of an object rather than fine color distinctions is the object of the training. Ask the child to hand you a block of the color you name. The problem can be complicated by presenting the child with four or five blocks of different colors and asking for a specific color. Reverse the problem by handing the child a block and asking him to name the color.

When size is used as the quality, present the child with two blocks, one of which is markedly larger than the other. Ask the child to hand you the larger (or smaller) of the blocks. Permit the child to manipulate the blocks so that tactual and kinesthetic information is permitted and so that the match between visual and tactual-kinesthetic information is structured. This task can be made more difficult by decreasing the size difference between the blocks.

Numerosity is frequently used as an identifying quality, especially in connection with beginning numbers. Present the child with two objects, one of which has more parts than the other. For example, using the wheel of a Tinker Toy, attach one spoke to it. Take a second wheel and attach two spokes. Ask the child to give you the one with more spokes. Be sure he understands the language which you are using.

At this stage, do not press for numerical concepts. Do not ask the child for a wheel with two spokes. The problem in the present exercise is to present numerosity as an identifying feature of a form, not the number system or the identification of quantities. In like manner, do not stress counting. The child needs to learn to differentiate differences in quantity before he can learn to identify or refine these quantitative differences.

One of the most important identifying qualities is shape. Present the child with a round block and a square block. Ask him to hand you the one you name. Here again, the child initially will identify through a signal quality. Thus, he will differentiate between the circle and the square on the basis of the presence or absence of a corner. In the differentiation stage of the development of form perception, however, this signal quality is the critical learning task. More refined recognition on the basis of constructive form can come later. Such constructive form cannot be developed, however, until a large number of elements have been differentiated as signal qualities. These elements can then be integrated into the constructive form. Therefore, it is desirable at this initial stage to call the child's attention to the identifying element or elements. Thus, the corner of the square should be pointed out to the child as the important element to be noted.

The problem of identification on the basis of elements of shape can be made more complex for the child in three ways. (1) The critical element can be made more similar to other elements so that its differentiation is more difficult. Thus, a square and a rectangle might be paired. As the sides of the rectangle are reduced nearer and nearer to the size of those of the square, the problem of differentiation becomes more difficult. (2) The number of elements can be increased so that the number of differentiations required is increased. Thus, the choice between a hexagon and an octagon is more difficult than that between a square and a triangle. (3) The critical element may be buried among one or more extraneous elements. Thus the choice between a red square and a red rectangle is easier than that between a red square and a green rectangle. The choice between a plain square and a plain rectangle is easier than the same choice when the surfaces of the forms are patterned with "noisy" figures.

The preceding discussion has dealt with the identification of concrete items. When the child has begun to develop differentiation of elements and when he can begin to recognize these elements visually, tactually, and kinesthetically, he can be encouraged in increasing dependence upon visual data. At this stage, the child can be introduced to pictured representations of objects.

Begin with pictures of familiar objects such as those found in children's story books. These pictures are designed to simplify the differentiation task and to present critical elements in as uncluttered a form as is practical. They are, therefore, very useful in aiding the child in the differentiation of such elements. Read the story to the child and ask him to point out in the picture those aspects described in the story as you read it. First stress total figures — the boy, the dog, et cetera. Then stress parts of figures—the boy's arm, the dog's tail, et cetera. Finally stress elements which suggest action or movement—the boy running, the dog jumping, et cetera.

When the child can deal with pictured representations of familiar objects, symbolic materials can be presented. He can be asked to choose between or to name geometrical forms. As these forms become more complex, letters and numbers can be introduced and he can be asked to name these. At this stage, attention should be called to those elements which are important to the differentiation, and the child should be helped to identify on the basis of these signal qualities.

MATCHING

Another technique which can be used to emphasize the elements of the figure and the differentiation of these elements out of the global mass is that of matching. In the initial stages, matches should be required which are based on very simple elements or qualities and where the critical element is well identified. As the child begins to develop more adequate differentiation, the tasks can be made more complex by increasing the number of elements to which he must attend or by decreasing the differences between elements. Since the interest in these exercises is in perceptual differentiation, the matches will be based on perceptual elements rather than on conceptual or categorizing elements. When necessary, the child's attention should be called to the critical element and he should be aided in noting this critical element as the signal quality required for the choice.

CONCRETE OBJECTS

Matching exercises should begin with the use of concrete, three-dimensional objects where manipulation and tactual kinesthetic information can be added to visual information. Present the child with two objects. Hold up an object identical with one which was presented to the child. Ask the child to point out the one of his objects which is identical with the one you are holding. Initially the match should be based on a single quality of the total object: color, form, numerosity, et cetera. Later the match can be made on the basis of elements within a form: square versus rectangle, a cup with a handle versus a cup with no handle, et cetera. Such matching can be combined with other activities in the classroom. Thus, if the child is required to pile Lincoln Logs according to size, he is required to identify each piece in terms of a quality, length. He can also be asked to pack blocks of various shapes into boxes. If the boxes are designed so that only blocks of a certain shape fit, he is required to identify these particular blocks from among the mass and pack them in the box, rejecting those which do not match.

Sorting is also a form of successive matching. The child is given an object and is requested to find all of the objects similar to a given object from among a group. As he deals with each object in turn, he is required to match it to the comparison object.

When the concern is with perceptual differentiation, the basis of the sorting should, of course, be a perceptual differentiation. Sorting can also be used in categorizing or concept formation. In these more advanced activities, however, the basis of the sort is a more complex generalization. Thus, sorting by color, size, shape, and the like are perceptual activities and demand attention to perceptual elements. Sorting out foods, transportation vehicles, clothing, and the like are conceptual activities and are considerably more advanced. In the present exercises, sorting should be limited to those activities which are based on the identification of perceptual elements.

The sorting activity can be more meaningful if the child is asked to identify those objects within the room which are similar in one or more qualities to a comparison object. Thus, he might be asked to point out all of the red objects within the room, or to pick up all the books on the children's desks so the teacher can store them in the cupboard. Such activities can add realism to the child's perceptual differentiation. Now he is differentiating for a purpose, permitting him to perform a useful task rather than merely satisfying the teacher. In like manner, these activities form a bridge between the type of matching which permits complete manipulation of objects to the less concrete manipulations required in the recognition of symbols and the like. When he is searching for matching objects around the room he is either not permitted to manipulate the object (as when he sits in his seat and points out the object) or he is permitted to manipulate the object only for the purpose of verification (as when, having made a mistake, he is permitted to go to the object and correct his mistake).

Parents and others can aid the teacher in the development of such perceptual differentiations. At home, parents can ask the child to point out certain objects and to recognize familiar objects in his environment. Games in which the child is asked to identify all of the objects of a certain type within the room or the play area can be used in out-of-school hours by parents to aid such perceptual differentiation. The child can be given sorting and matching tasks within the home situation. Thus, he can put the dishes away after the dishwashing task, sort out the plates by size, sort out cups from saucers, sort knives from forks, et cetera.

The process of perceptual differentiation is a long one and requires much experimentation by the child. The generalization of such differentiation requires experience with perceptual elements in a large number of different situations. For these reasons the assistance of the parents in after-school hours can broaden, both quantitatively and qualitatively, the experiences which the child is provided in the field of perceptual differentiation and which are extremely important to the child's education. The teacher should encourage parents to help with this task and should provide information which will make their assistance maximally useful.

PICTURES OF FAMILIAR OBJECTS

When the child has learned to identify similar elements in concrete objects, he can be taught to deal with these elements in pictured representations of objects. These should begin with familiar objects and situations. When the child is dealing with concrete objects he has a maximum of information: tactual, kinesthetic, visual, auditory. When he deals with symbolic presentations such as letters and words he is limited primarily to visual information for the differentiation of the necessary perceptual elements.

Representations of familiar objects can be used to make the transition between these two extremes. The child has had a wealth of information about the object, much of which remains in his memory. When he is presented with the visual representation of this object he can call upon much of the past information to help him in making the necessary perceptual differentiation. Therefore, representations of familiar objects should be introduced before the more symbolic materials.

Present the child with two pictures: for example, one of a boy and one of a dog. Show him the picture of a boy identical with the one he holds. Ask him to indicate which of his two pictures is like yours. Initially, the choice should be based on rather gross perceptual elements, such as the difference in form and shape between a boy and a dog. Later the differentiation can be based on more and more precise perceptual elements, such as the choice between a picture of a boy with a hat on and a boy with no hat on.

Many paper and pencil materials are available which require this type of matching. The left-hand side of the sheet shows a comparison figure. On the right-hand side a number of figures is given, one of which matches exactly the comparison figure. The child is required to mark that figure on the right which exactly matches the one on the left. For training in perceptual differentiation those materials should be chosen for which the matching is done on perceptual rather than conceptual or categorizing characteristics.

Such activities can be combined with common classroom techniques. Thus, the child can construct a scrapbook in which he cuts out and pastes in matching figures. He can look through magazines or other similar materials and select pictures of a given object to paste into his scrapbook. The task can be made more difficult by defining more rigidly the figures which will be included. Thus, in the initial stages the child might be required to select pictures of boys. In later stages he might be required to select pictures of boys playing baseball. The latter task requires attention to a larger number of perceptual details than does the former.

It is important that the child learn to identify perceptual elements for the purpose of recognition not only in situations in which the elements themselves are presented but also in situations in which he is required to develop through memory or imagery the necessary identifying elements. Thus, when the child is presented a picture and is required to find one like it, the perceptual elements on which the choice is made are present during the entire task time. He can compare back and forth at any time to check his element against the element of the comparison figure. If the element used as the basis of the choice is presented verbally, however, the child is required to develop a memory or image of the element, differentiate it out of the choice figure, and compare this differentiated element with the memory or image. This latter task is more difficult and requires greater facility in the manipulation of perceptual elements. On the other hand this is a more natural task and is the type of perceptual differentiation which he will more frequently be asked to perform. It is, therefore, desirable that the comparison figure for the matching activity be presented verbally when the child has reached the stage of differentiation which permits him to deal with this type of presentation. The child is presented with the picture of the boy and the picture of the dog. He is asked verbally "Give me the picture of the boy." Again, as the child's ability increases, the differentiations are made more complex.

At this point, training in perceptual differentiation can be combined with language arts training. A story can be read to the child. The child can be asked to select from a group of pictures the one which best illustrates the story or a part of the story. He can be asked to point out in a picture that part which is being discussed in the story. This story procedure is particularly useful in pointing out to the child those elements of the figure which suggest movement or action.

Here again, the parents can be extremely helpful in the education of the child. The teacher should encourage the parent to read to the child at home and to ask the child to point out in pictures what is being read to him. The teacher should suggest or supply to the parent suitable reading materials with adequate pictures and should tell the parent how to use such reading activities for the development of perceptual differentiation.

GEOMETRIC FORMS

The symbols of our written language are elaborations and combinations of simple geometric forms. The basic geometric forms are the circle, cross, square, rectangle, triangle, and diamond. The child should become thoroughly acquainted with these simple forms before moving on to the more complex combinations represented by letters and numbers.

Matching activities with geometric forms begin with the manipulation of concrete objects. Forms cut from wood, plastic, rubber, and other materials are available. The child should be given practice in matching and sorting these objects. The procedures outlined above for matching concrete objects can be used.

When the child has had experience with the matching of concrete forms, he can be introduced to drawings of simple forms on paper. Workbooks and similar materials are available presenting such matching tasks. The child is given a comparison form on one side of the page and a series of forms on the other side. He is asked to indicate the one among the series of forms which matches the comparison form. As before, help should be given the child in identifying the element or elements necessary for the identification. He should be aided in differentiating this element out of the initial global mass.

When the child has developed some facility with these basic forms, he should be asked to identify these forms as they occur in familiar objects about the room. He should learn to recognize that the door is a rectangle, that the light fixture is a circle, et cetera. Ask him to see how many circles he can find about the room, how many squares, et cetera. Be sure that he recognizes that a rectangle in a vertical orientation, such as the door frame, is the same form as a rectangle in a horizontal position, such as a desk top.

SYMBOLS

The letters of our alphabet and the numbers of our numerical system represent symbols very important for the child to learn to identify. These figures, however, are complex and the perceptual elements required for their recognition are difficult. Therefore, the child will need considerable facility in dealing with the less complex forms before he attacks these symbolic materials. When he is ready to attack these more complex symbols, however, he will need extensive practice in this particular activity to permit him to differentiate sufficient perceptual elements and to manipulate these elements with sufficient flexibility to permit the rapid and precise recognition required by our use of these symbolic figures. Matching activities in the symbolic area should begin with concrete objects. Letters cut out of wood, plastic, and other materials are available. The child should learn to identify these figures through the use of all available information: visual, tactual, kinesthetic, auditory. The child must learn to identify the figure on the one hand and to attach the proper name to it on the other hand. For the first of these problems the matching technique is very useful.

Follow the suggestions outlined above for the matching of concrete objects in providing experiences for the child in the matching and sorting of cutout letters. Since the naming of these letters is such an important part of the manipulation of the symbol, it is desirable to attach continuously the verbal name for the letter to the activity. Thus, the child might be given an A and a B. The teacher might hold up an A and ask him to match it. The teacher should then say "This is an A. Find me one like it". When the child has made the correct choice he should be asked to name the letter. In this way the verbal designation for the form is kept constantly before the child.

When the child has developed sufficient facility with concrete cutout letters, paper and pencil matching can be introduced. There are many excellent materials available for this purpose. An example of a workbook of this type is Wilson and Rudolph's *My Alphabet Book*. This workbook contains a large number of matching exercises. The exercises begin with letters in which the critical element of the form is relatively well defined. It continues with more difficult combinations until the child eventually is asked to deal with the matching of confusion letters in which the critical element is difficult to locate (such as *X* versus *K*, *E* versus *F*, and the like). The child is required to select, from a group of letters, the one which exactly matches the comparison letter.

For children who have difficulty making the transition from the cutout letters to letters on a page, additional information may be helpful. Such information can be supplied, for example, by "sandpaper letters." These letters, the surfaces of which are covered with sandpaper, are shown on a sheet of paper. Flocking and other materials may be used instead of sandpaper to provide a textural surface. The child is able to explore the surface of the letter and obtain additional tactual information which he could not obtain from the letter printed on the paper alone. Such materials are frequently useful in the transition stage from concrete objects to symbolic representations.

From letters, the child normally advances to the matching of short words. Practice in such simple word matching is normally provided in the workbook materials. Thus, after a series of exercises involving matching of single letters, the workbook frequently proceeds to exercises requiring the matching of simple word forms.

Also helpful at this stage are the picture matching cards. A series of simple line drawings of familiar objects and situations is provided. Each drawing appears on two cards. The child is asked to pair the cards so that the pictures match. Either on the back of the picture card or on separate cards a word designating the picture is written. The child is then asked to turn the cards over and match them by comparing the words. He has now matched symbolic materials. In the final stage, the child is asked to match a picture on one card to the proper word on the other card. He has now matched the picture to its symbol.

These picture-word cards can be very useful in encouraging the differentiation of perceptual elements. The matching of the pictures helps the child differentiate the elements in familiar pictured materials. The matching of the words helps the child in the differentiation of elements important to the written symbols of the language. Finally, matching of the word to the picture leads into prereading and reading activities.

MISSING PARTS

Another method by which a perceptual element can be emphasized is to omit the element. The child is presented with a figure in
which one of the elements has been left out. He is required either
to point out what is missing or to supply the missing part. If he has
difficulty, clues are supplied. It may be suggested verbally that a
part serving a certain function may be missing. His attention may
be directed to an area of the figure in which he should search for
the missing part. If he has difficulty identifying the part from
memory or image, he may be given a complete figure which he is
asked to compare with the incomplete figure.

Such activities can be provided with concrete materials. Thus,
a puzzle, such as a manikin puzzle, can be put together with one
part missing. The child is then asked to identify the missing part
and to finish the construction of the figure. Block constructions can
be finished except for a part or parts, and the child is asked to finish
the construction. A figure may be constructed on pegboard with
one element omitted. Thus, three sides of a square may be constructed by the teacher. The child is then asked to finish the square
by constructing the fourth side.

Paper and pencil exercises requiring the child to complete an
incomplete figure are frequently found in readiness and prereading
workbooks. In general, these exercises deal with symbolic materials
and are useful when the child reaches the stage where he is able
to deal with such complex figures.

The Frostig materials (Frostig and Horne, 1964) involve a
series of exercises for figure completion which serve a similar purpose. Pictures of familiar objects are presented with one part omitted. The child is asked to indicate verbally what part is missing or,
if he has efficient motor control, to draw in the missing part.

In the final exercises in this series, the parts of a figure are given
at the top of the page. The child outlines these parts with different
colored crayons. He then looks at the complete figure at the bottom
of the page and outlines on this figure each part in the same color
that he has used at the top of the page.

Such activities and exercises draw attention to and emphasize
elements of a figure. The child is aided in observing critical percep-

tual elements and in differentiating them out of the initial global mass.

TRAINING CONSTRUCTIVE FORM

Constructive form perception involves the combination of the elements of a figure into a new and integrated form. It is obvious that training in the differentiation of the elements of a figure is essential before training in constructive form perception is begun. Unless the child is aware of and able to perceive the elements of a form, he cannot combine them into an integrated total.

When he is ready to begin combining elements into figures, he needs experience with forms in many situations and under many different kinds of conditions. He will need practice in the manipulation of total forms and parts of forms and in the manipulation of one form in relation to another.

MANIPULATION OF TOTAL FORM

FORM BOARD

The most common method of presenting the child with experience in the manipulation of total forms is the form board, many types of which are available commercially. The common geometric forms are cut out of wood or similar material. A board is supplied with depressions into which the forms fit. The child is asked to place the forms in the proper depressions in the board.

Form boards vary from simple boards with few figures (circle, square, triangle) to complex ones with many figures which have complicated shapes. Boards are available with simple figures each presented in a number of sizes. Such boards aid the child in the recognition of form as independent of size. Split form boards present forms that have been cut into parts. The parts must be assembled before they are placed in the appropriate depression.

The child with a weakness in form perception may counter his problems with the form board by using elements of the figure. Thus, the child may fit the apex of the triangle into the proper depression and manipulate this angle until the form falls into place. He has given all his attention to the angle and has shown little if any awareness of the remainder of the form. Such a child is taking the signal element to solve his problem. It is likely that for this child the remainder of the form remains global and undifferentiated during this task. The form board task will contribute to the development of constructive form perception only insofar as the child deals with the total form rather than a single element.

In using the form board, therefore, the child should be encouraged to deal with the form as a whole. If he pays undue attention to a single detail for recognition and depends on random manipulation to fit the form into the depression, he should be stopped and asked to start again. His attention should be drawn to the total form and away from the single element. He should be encouraged to select the proper form before he begins manipulation, to line the total form up with the depression, and then to insert it quickly and surely. If he makes a mistake, he should be encouraged to stop and start again rather than depend upon random manipulation to solve the problem.

Such form boards provide an excellent introduction to manipulation of total forms. For the child whose manipulative ability is limited, the movements required are relatively gross and little precise fine motor control is involved. When the form is properly placed, it "locks in" by virtue of the fact that it falls into the depression. The child then has immediate knowledge of results in every successful performance.

GROSS FORM

The child needs to explore form in large figures which require gross motor manipulation. He should be provided experience with figures of sufficient size that he is required to walk around them. A square box for example, might illustrate a square form. The child walks around the box exploring the elements of the form as he goes. The box should be of sufficient size so that he can get inside it and explore the inner elements of the form as well as the outer elements. He should be encouraged to deal with the total form rather than the individual elements. Thus, he should anticipate the end of each side and the corner. Anticipation of what is coming is possible only insofar as he begins to put together the elements of the form in an integrated fashion.

Forms can be drawn on the floor with chalk or laid out with tape or strings. The child is then asked to walk around the form anticipating the elements as he goes. Again he should be encouraged to consider the total form rather than the single elements.

As he begins to develop some degree of integration, certain elements of the form can be omitted. Thus, in the square form only the corners may now be marked on the floor and the child is asked to walk around the square, filling in the sides through memory or visual imagery as he goes. Eventually, it should be possible for him to walk in a square pattern without any of the elements being supplied for him, but depending entirely on his image of the form to direct his movement.

These gross activities give the child a more total experience with form than is possible with the small objects or paper and pencil reproductions which are customarily provided. The necessity to walk around the form emphasizes the relationship between form and space. Since the whole body is involved in the manipulation, a greater amount of information is supplied through such activities. In addition to these factors, time is involved in locomoting around a figure. This involvement of time in the pattern is related to the characteristics of proportion in the length of the lines. When a corner is encountered, the activity is interrupted in time and begins again. We have seen how important the relationship between time and space becomes in the reproduction of forms. Gross activities such as the above provide an excellent method of laying the groundwork for these time-space relationships.

SIMPLE PUZZLES

Simple puzzles can be constructed for the child which encourage him to manipulate forms as wholes. The most satisfactory puzzle consists of a simple picture from a magazine. The picture should present a single form or a very limited number of forms. The figure should stand out sharply against a relatively undetailed background. The figure-ground relationships should be strong. Paste this picture on cardboard or heavy paper backing. Cut a straight horizontal line through the middle of the card so that the upper half is exactly equal in size to the lower half. Ask the child to assemble the two halves of the picture. Since the two halves are identical, if he tries to match edges, he finds that he can match the two cut edges together but also he can match the top edge to the bottom edge. One of these solutions is correct and one is in error. Therefore, in assembling the puzzle, he is forced to pay attention to the picture as opposed to the details of the card. The correct solution is indicated only by the completion of the figure. This task can be made more complicated by cutting the card into four or more equal pieces, by making straight cuts properly spaced horizontally, vertically, or both.

This simple type of puzzle will be found very useful. It can be used with picture materials as described above. As the child becomes more proficient, it can be used with outlined drawings of simple geometric forms and, when the child has progressed sufficiently, with letters and figures as outlined by Strauss and Lehtinen (1947, pp. 176-177).

MODELING

Clay, putty, and similar pliable materials represent media in which the child can experiment with total form through modeling. In modeling, the child begins with a formless mass. By manipulating the pliable material he molds this mass into a form. If too much attention is given to a single detail or a single element, the overall form becomes distorted. Therefore, modeling is an excellent activity for permitting the child to deal with total characteristics of form. Such modeling activities should be simple and directed toward the basic geometric forms. Thus, the child might be asked to model a ball, a brick, a cylinder, and similar simple forms.

Similar to modeling is stamping. The child can roll out a flat disk of clay. With a cookie cutter he can then stamp out forms from the clay. The stamping process involves production of the whole form in one operation and hence provides experience in the manipulation of total forms. The child should pick out the stamped out form from the clay. Be sure that he has paid attention to the total form and recognizes it. He should then manipulate this form in some manner which will emphasize its total shape—such as laying out rows of similar shapes, sorting shapes, and the like.

Simple forms are preferable to more complex forms, and those with pronounced signal qualities should be avoided. Thus, the simple animal forms easily obtained in variety stores are useful.

MANIPULATION OF ELEMENTS

In addition to the manipulation of total forms, the child will require practice in the manipulation of the elements of a form. In such exercises the elements are presented as units. The child is then asked to put these units together into a constructive form. Since the elements of a form are lines and angles, these units will be various representations of lines which the child puts together to form angles and complete forms. Each element is manipulated as a whole, but each element is also independent and must be chosen from a group and placed in the proper relationship to elements already selected.

In such activities the element is provided and already differentiated out of the mass. The task for the child emphasizes the relationship between these elements. These relationships can be manipulated without altering or destroying the element. If the child works on paper and pencil or chalkboard, he draws a line with his pencil or chalk. He has thus constructed an element. When he constructs the next element, however, he must also obtain the proper relationship between the two elements. If he does not, the only way in which he can manipulate this relationship is to remove one of the elements and start over. In the present exercises, however, the elements are permanent, and can be manipulated in any manner without destroying them. Such exercises, therefore, provide the child with direct experimentation with relationships without his worrying about alteration or destruction of elements in the process. In the development of form perception, many children need a great deal of experimentation of this kind in which they can free their attention from the elements themselves and apply it to the relationships between elements.

STICK FIGURES

PICK-UP STICKS OR MATCH STICKS

Match sticks (with heads removed) can be used to construct simple geometric figures. The teacher will find it desirable to prepare a series of forms in which the elements (sticks) are glued to a piece of wood or cardboard. Prepare the forms illustrated in Figure 12. Give the child thirty match sticks with which to construct his figures.

In figures of this type, elements of the form (lines) are broken down and presented to the child separately as sticks. He is required to supply the integration of these elements, all of which are alike, which will result in a product representing accurately the figure presented to him. He must develop and execute for himself the constructive aspects of the forms. The task does not require the coordination demanded in drawing or copying but, at the same time, emphasizes the constructive aspects of form perception while demanding less attention to the elements themselves. A series of tasks, increasing in difficulty, will be found helpful in the use of such materials to aid form perception. For a discussion of the developmental variables in the match stick task, see Piaget and Inhelder (1956).

A. Task 1 (square).

   1. Lay the square pattern before the child on a desk or table. Be sure that it is centered directly in front of him and far enough away so that he can work between the pattern and the front of the table. Say, "Make one just like this." The pattern is in full view of the child and laid flat on the table in the same orientation as his production. Observe the order in which he places his sticks. If he does not begin at once, ask, "Can you go right around, this way?" Outline with your finger a continuous counterclockwise progression around the contour. If he is still unable to begin, ask him to run his finger around the contour of the model. Call special attention to the corners and the change of direction at each. To ensure that he does not learn this order as a specific task element but learns the concept of continuity of direction,

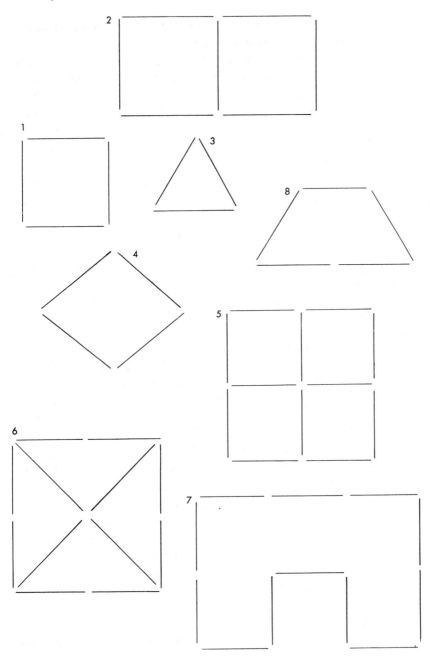

FIGURE 12. Match stick forms.

require him to go sometimes clockwise, sometimes counter-clockwise, in a random order.

2. Hold the pattern vertically before the child. Say, "Now make one like it." If he fails, lay the pattern horizontally and let him feel around the contour. Then have him make one. Now raise the pattern at a 10 degree angle to the horizontal. Have him make one. If he is successful, raise the pattern to 20 degrees and repeat. Continue until he can reproduce from the vertically oriented pattern.

3. Remove the pattern from the child's view. Say, "Now make one like it." If there is an error, show him the pattern again and let him correct his error.

4. With the pattern out of sight, ask him to make one twice as large. If there is an error, reintroduce the pattern and ask, "Is yours just like this?" If he recognizes the error, help him correct it. If he does not recognize the error, ask about the specific point or points of error. Then help him correct his form.

B. Task 2 (rectangle).

1. Repeat steps A(1), A(2), A(3), and A(4), using the rectangular form. If the child has difficulty with the rectangular shape (for example, produces a square instead of a rectangle), ask him to run his finger over the long edge of the pattern and then over the corresponding edge of his figure and compare these two movements. Then ask him to correct his figure. In order to relate this comparison to total form rather than only one element (side), ask him to run his finger around the square pattern, then around the rectangular pattern, and compare the differences in total contours. Introducing an auditory rhythm (as 1, 2, turn; 1, turn; 1, 2, turn; 1, turn) may aid him in observing the differences in length and long-short relationships of the four sides.

2. Present the pattern rotated 90 degrees so that one of the short sides is nearest the child. Repeat steps A(1), A(2), A(3), and A(4) in this rotated position.

3. Show the child the pattern with a long side on the base. Say, "This is the way the figure looks when it is right side up."

Rotate it 90 degrees. Say, "Now I have turned it on its side. You make me one that is right side up."

4. Repeat A(4) with figure rotated 90 degrees.

C. Task 3 (triangle).
   1. Present the triangle with its base toward the child. Repeat steps A(1), A(2), A(3), and A(4).
   2. Repeat B(2) and B(3), only rotate the triangle 180 degrees so that its apex is toward the child.

D. Task 4 (diamond).
   1. Repeat steps A(1), A(2), A(3), and A(4).
   2. Repeat steps B(3) and B(4) with the diamond rotated 90 degrees.

E. Task 5 (divided square).
   1. Repeat steps A(1), A(2), and A(3).
   2. Show the square form of task 1. Ask, "Can you find this figure in the one you have made?" If he answers "No," ask him to run his finger around the contour of item one. Then run his finger around one of the small squares of item five. If he still cannot see the small square in the large square, pull it out by removing these four sticks from the total figure. When he can recognize task one in this context, put it back into item five. Let him run his finger around it again. Repeat until he can recognize task 1 in one of the squares of item five. Continue until he sees that there are four small squares combined in task five.

F. Task 6 (diagonals).
   1. Repeat steps A(1), A(2), and A(3) using the square form with two diagonals.

G. Task 7 (irregular rectangle).
   1. Repeat steps A(1), A(2), and A(3) using the irregular rectangle.
   2. Repeat step B(2) with pattern rotated 90, 180, and 270 degrees.
   3. Repeat step B(3) with pattern rotated 90, 180, and 270 degrees.

4. Repeat step E(2). Ask, "Can you add one more stick and make one like this (small square) in the one you have (irregular rectangle)?" Help him find all three possibilities.
5. Repeat step G(4) using the rectangular form of task 2. Help him find both possibilities.

H. Task 8 (trapezoid).
1. Repeat steps A(1), A(2), A(3), and A(4) using the trapezoid.
2. Repeat step G(2).
3. Repeat step G(3).

USE OF THE BODY AS AN ELEMENT IN A FORM

In order to develop the form perception generalization, the child needs to experience form in many situations. As we have seen repeatedly, the body and its activities form the point of origin for all interpretations of the outside environment. For this reason, a very helpful series of exercises will be found in those involving the use of the body and its parts as elements in the construction of a form.

The common circle game in which the children join hands and form a circle is an example of an activity in which the body is used as an element in a form. The child must be aware of the overall figure and must adapt his posture to the requirements of this figure. He is, therefore, required to construct the form and to integrate his body as one of the elements in this form.

Such circle games can be expanded to present more complex forms. Thus the child can use his body in the formation of a square in at least three ways.

(1) Four children stand upright, one at each corner of the square. Each child holds his arms out horizontally at the shoulders so that they form a right angle and so that he touches the fingers of the child on either side of him. The four pairs of arms thus form the sides of a square. A larger square can be formed by positioning another child between each of the original four. Each of these new children holds his arms out parallel to the

shoulders so that they form a straight line. Each additional child now represents an extension of one side of the square.

(2) A child sits on the floor at each corner of the square. Each child positions his legs so that they form a right angle at the hips and so that they just touch the foot of the child on either side. The four pairs of legs now form a square figure.

(3) A child lies on the floor in the supine position with his body straight. The next child lies on the floor at right angles to the first child with his head touching the feet of the first child. The third child lies in a similar position with reference to the second child and so on until the square form is completed by the bodies of the children.

(4) A child sits upright on the floor with his legs out straight in front of him. The next child sits at right angles to the first child with his back touching the feet of the first child. This is continued until the square form is produced. The activity can be varied by having the second child position himself with his back to the side of the first child. The third child then positions himself with his feet touching the feet of the second child. The fourth child touches the back of one child and the feet of another. The square can be made larger by interposing additional children on each side.

Rectangular forms can be constructed by interposing additional children on two sides of the square but not on the other two. Triangular figures can be developed by using three children instead of four.

In this method of constructing forms, each child, as he takes his position, is encouraged to be aware of the total form. He then manipulates his body into the position of one of the elements in the form. During the manipulation process, however, he is encouraged to retain the total form since no other clue is given which will permit him to determine the proper position of his own body.

When such a figure has been constructed, one of the children can be asked to leave the form. Another child is then asked to take his place. This child is also given experience in the integration of form. He must construct the total form, identify the missing element, and position his body in terms of that element. The form is again the clue to the proper position.

LARGE LINCOLN LOGS

Another task in which elements must be integrated into a form involves Lincoln Logs and similar construction materials. In Lincoln Logs, structural elements equivalent to the lines of a figure are combined to produce forms. These materials differ from "Leg-o" and similar construction materials in which items are combined to form elements. These latter materials are useful at a later stage in training but are too difficult for the present phase in which elements are to be manipulated as a whole and the child is not required to construct or analyze them into parts.

In addition to the commercially available Lincoln Logs, larger sets can be constructed from plywood. The small materials are useful but the larger materials permit the child to manipulate the element not only from outside the form but from inside as well, since they permit him to produce constructions which he can get inside of and climb on. These larger materials, therefore, permit more extensive experimentation and more gross manipulation. They do not require the precise motor control which is needed to manipulate the smaller materials. For these reasons, they will be found more useful at earlier stages in the child's experimentation with the elements of a form.

Three-quarter inch plywood panels are cut into strips four inches wide. The strips are then cut into various lengths. A useful set, all cut from one 4' x 8' sheet of plywood, includes the following pieces:

16 pieces 36 inches long
16 pieces 24 inches long
34 pieces 12 inches long

Each piece is notched on each side one and one-half inches from each end. The notches are 1 inch deep and ¾ inches wide. (See Figure 13.) This permits the logs to lock when laid at right angles to each other.

The children use these materials in construction. Most of the projects are, of course, representations of a house or modifications of such representations. In order to complete the construction, the child must maintain the overall form of his project and manipulate each element to fit it. Each element must be properly positioned with the one which has gone before or it will not "lock."

When the construction is built up with several layers of logs, the resulting product is large enough to get into and to observe orientation from both the inside and the outside. When only one layer of logs is used, the elements form the contour or perimeter of the figure and can be used in much the same way that stick figures

FIGURE 13. Notching of large size "Lincoln Logs"

are used. The provision of doors, windows, and the like in the construction permits the child to experiment with the development of figure by the omission of elements or parts of elements. The construction of figures in this manner permits experimentation with integration of elements when the normal figure-ground relationships are reversed.

MANIPULATION OF ITEMS

The elements of a form can be further broken down into items. In this situation, the child is supplied with a large number of undifferentiated units from which he is required to construct a figure. These units are such that they can be combined into lines and angles. The child uses the units to produce the elements of the form and, by manipulation of the units, simultaneously deals with the element and the total form. Thus, in constructing a line with the units, he must maintain an awareness not only of the nature of the line (the element) but of its direction and its orientation to other lines (position in the form).

The manipulation of items to construct a figure is thus more difficult than the manipulation of elements. The child's attention must be distributed over a wider area of the task and a weakness in form perception leads to errors which are more difficult to correct. The figure is artificially broken down into units more discrete than the elements which are ordinarily the final breakdown with which he is asked to deal. He must organize this mass of discrete units into an integrated pattern. A weakness in constructive form perception makes the task very difficult. On the other hand, when form perception is sufficiently advanced to permit the child to deal with such complexities, the manipulation of units offers him excellent practice in the manipulation of constructive form. Out of this practice, he can develop a more highly integrated and more flexible form perception.

THE PEGBOARD

The pegboard is a modification of the Strauss Marble Board (Strauss and Lehtinen, 1947; Strauss and Kephart, 1955). It serves the same functions and provides the same activities as the earlier equipment, but it will be found easier to use since the pegs remain more firmly in the board than do the marbles. The pegboard consists of a square board in which rows of holes have been drilled. It will be found desirable to use a relatively large board (at least twelve by twelve inches). It will also be found desirable to ensure that the holes are not soo small (one-eighth of an inch in diameter has been found adequate) and that the holes are not too close together (one-half inch between centers). A square piece of acoustic ceiling tile will make a very adequate pegboard. Select a square in which the holes are arranged in straight vertical and horizontal rows. Tile of this kind has twenty-two holes in each direction and provides adequate space and an adequate number of holes for rather elaborate forms to be laid out.

The device will be found to work better if the pegs are relatively large. Pegs of extremely small diameter and extremely short pegs require too much manipulative ability from the child and distract

Important figure-ground relationships can be learned with pegboards.
(Courtesy A. Devaney, Inc.).

him from the problem of form. It will be found that golf tees make excellent pegs for use with ceiling tile. Clip off one-half inch from the sharp end of the tee so that there will be less danger of the child's hurting himself and so that the length will be more adequate. Golf tees have an additional advantage in that they have a relatively large head. When these tees are set in a row in the pegboard, the heads of adjacent tees come close together. By bringing the units of the form (pegs) closer together, the form problem is made simpler since the units are not as distinct. Such a simplification can only be accomplished with heads on the pegs since bringing the shafts of the pegs closer together to decrease the intervening space increases the number of units in the form and also increases the manipulative problem.

Difficulty of the Task. It will be seen that the pegboard presents a somewhat more difficult form perception problem than either of the two techniques previously described. In the case of puzzles and form boards, it was only necessary to match one form to another. The child could solve the problem by matching the block to the cut out depression in the board. With the match stick problems, the elements of the form were maintained intact. The elements in this problem are lines and each line is represented by one stick so that the number of pieces in the completed product is no greater than the number of lines in the form. In the case of the pegboard, however, the elements themselves (lines and angles) are broken down into units (pegs). Thus, in completing the pegboard task, the child is required to build up elements of the form from homogeneous units.

The pegboard, therefore, offers a difficult form perception problem for two reasons. In the first place, the form is broken up into a large number of units. The number of units is larger and the form is more completely broken up than is normally the case. The child must hold the form against an exaggerated distraction of units. In the second place, the task is elongated in time. It requires more time to place pegs in a pegboard than it does to place match sticks or to draw lines with a pencil or crayon. For this reason, the spatial-temporal translation problem is increased with pegboard materials. The child must hold the form over a longer period of time and in the face of greater temporal distractions than is the case with other materials.

For these reasons, it will be found that pegboards are very useful in helping the child develop form perception. They represent a difficult task and permit us to offer more difficult types of training. When form perception has begun, it can be solidified and can be "over-learned" through such training. This "over-learning" can operate as a margin of safety for the child in his daily activities. If form is extremely solid, we can be sure that it will consistently emerge and will be available in normal activities. It is obvious, however, that the pegboards will be found too difficult for the child who has little form perception or only the beginnings of form perception. The more simple activities (copying and match sticks) should be used first to ensure that the child has enough form perception to be able to handle the pegboard tasks. For a discussion of the relationships between pegboard activities and mental ability, see Werner and Strauss, 1939; Werner, 1944; Crain and Werner, 1950.

Stages of Training.   Two boards and two sets of pegs are provided, one for the child and one for the adult. The pegs should be of a color contrasting with the background. In this way, the form can be made to stand out more sharply against the background and the difficulty of the task is kept reasonable. On his board, the adult outlines a simple figure (square, rectangle, triangle, etc.). This figure is then shown to the child and he is asked to make one like it on his board.

There are two stages in the training activity. In the first stage, the board with the model figure on it is left in full view of the child. He may consult it whenever he has difficulty and he may constantly compare his production with the model. In the second stage of training, the model figure is shown to the child only briefly. When the child begins to work, the model is removed and the child is asked to complete the activity with no further reference to the model.

With any individual form (such as a square), it will be desirable to move from the first stage to the second stage as rapidly as possible. The child who has little form perception will tend to attack the problem of the pegboard on the basis of the units themselves. Thus, he will, by counting holes, determine the placement of the first peg. He will then orient the second peg to the first peg or, in some cases, he may resort to counting holes again to locate the second peg. In this peg-by-peg fashion, he will proceed around the form. It will be seen that this type of activity can be carried out with little reference to the total form itself. The child can deal with each peg independently and can produce a reasonable replica of the model without having seen or attended to the total form. He can achieve a production without integrating the units or constructing the form. Obviously it is undesirable for him to proceed in this fashion since the training which is desired is not being achieved. Such a unit-by-unit solution becomes much more difficult when the model is removed from view. Therefore, by moving from the first to the second stage as soon as possible, the child is forced out of the disconnected unit approach and is encouraged to construct the form and use it as a basis of his procedure.

The order of difficulty of simple forms on the pegboard follows roughly the order of difficulty discussed earlier in connection with chalkboard drawing. We saw in the earlier discussion that the circle was the simplest form to draw or copy. On the pegboard, a circle represents specific difficulties because of the placement of the holes. Therefore, it should not be used in pegboard activities or, if it is used, should be introduced very late in the process. In pegboard activities, the straight line replaces the circle as the simplest type of form.

Maintaining Form against Background. Some children will have difficulty holding the form represented by a straight line against the distraction represented by the large number of additional holes in the pegboard. Thus, they may start to construct a straight line of pegs and be drawn off into slanting or angle lines. It should be remembered that the structure represented by the holes in the pegboard is much more obtrusive than the structure represented by normal background materials. Therefore, the child may need help in overcoming the distraction represented by this structure which he would not need in drawing or other activities where the background is less highly structured. He can be given aid in maintaining form against this background by the use of a template for a straight line as described under chalkboard training. A cardboard or plastic template is prepared in which a long, narrow opening representing a straight line has been cut out. This template is laid along the pegboard in the prescribed direction, and the child places his pegs within the cut out area of the template. As a result of this activity, he is able to construct a straight line which he can then observe and evaluate. When he has learned to construct a straight line with the maximum assistance represented by the template, remove the template and lay a straight edge such as a ruler across the pegboard. Under these conditions, the child is required to maintain the straight line form against distraction in one direction but is given help in overcoming the distraction in the opposite direction. This intermediate step may help him to make the transition between the straight line produced with the template and a straight line produced by free activity on the pegboard.

Constructing Lines. The child should learn to produce a straight, horizontal line completely across the pegboard. He should also learn to produce a straight, vertical line extending over the length of the pegboard. He should learn to produce these lines in various positions on the pegboard. Straight lines near an edge are easier since the edge represents a guide. Straight lines near the center of the board are more difficult because the guiding effect of the edge of the board is further removed. Do not use diagonal lines at this stage of training since they are considerably more difficult and it will be found that the simple square and rectangle form can be presented and learned as soon as a straight line can be achieved. The use of these simple straight line forms will make the problem of the diagonal less difficult at a later stage in training.

When the child has learned to construct a straight line, he must learn the problem of achieving a line of a given length. This problem involves the same difficulty of stopping which we discussed earlier in connection with chalkboard activities. In the pegboard, the row of holes extending ahead of the point at which he is working tends to draw the child on, so that the problem of stopping becomes more severe in pegboard activities. The child has a tendency, when he has learned to follow a row of holes, to follow it on to the edge of the board.

He can be given aid in learning to stop by being presented with a line shorter than the length of the board. When he has begun his production in the proper position, lay a ruler or other device in the opposite direction at the point where he should stop. He then follows the row of holes until he comes to this obstacle and stops there. The ruler then presents a strong stimulus for the act of stopping. When he has learned to stop with a ruler, place the last peg in the row for him. He then follows along the row of holes until he comes to the pre-placed peg. This peg then represents a stimulus for stopping. It will be found useful to outline the line which he is to construct by placing beforehand the first peg and the last peg. The child is then asked only to fill in the intermediate pegs. He should be encouraged as soon as possible to learn to stop when his line is of the prescribed length without these additional clues.

Constructing Squares and Rectangles. When the straight line has been mastered, a square can be presented for reproduction. With this new form, the child may again become distracted by the structured background. It may therefore be necessary again to provide him with a template so that the distraction of the background will be partially overcome. He should be encouraged to dispense with the template as soon as possible. It will also be found useful in helping him overcome the background problem if a solid square constructed by filling in the entire square area with pegs is presented. This form with its mass in contrast with the background is a stronger figure-background combination than an outline form in which only lines contrast with the background. It may be found that the child can perform more easily with these solid squares than with the outline square. They will therefore represent a valuable intermediate step in the training process. The square models should be varied in size as in chalkboard training to ensure that the child develops the concept of "square" rather than learning to reproduce a specific figure.

When the square has been mastered, the rectangle can be presented. The same problems discussed in chalkboard construction of a rectangle should be considered in the pegboard construction of a rectangle. The rectangle should be presented in both orientations, one with the long side as the base and one with the short side as the base. The problem of proportionality within the rectangle will need to be considered also.

The Problem of Orientation.   The pegboard presents two background problems. The board itself is a background and, as we have seen, is a structured background. In addition, since the board is relatively small in relation to the total visual field, it constitutes a secondary form on a background represented by the table top and the rest of the visual surroundings. Therefore, the child should learn to deal with the pegboard as an intermediate background situation. For this reason, he should pay attention to the orientation of his production in relationship to the board itself. Ask him to construct a figure where the model has been placed in the upper left-hand corner, in the lower center portion of the board, et cetera. Ask the child to make his figure just like yours, not only in terms of the form itself, but in terms of the position of the figure on the board. The first problem of the form board is the construction of the figure itself. Therefore, pay attention to this problem first and be sure that the child is able to construct the figure. Then move on to the problem of orientation of the figure on the board and ask him to orient his figure to the pegboard in the same way that yours is oriented.

Constructing Diagonals.   At this stage in the training process, the diagonal line may be introduced. It will be found that all of the problems encountered in the learning of the horizontal or vertical line will be encountered again when the diagonal line is presented. As we have seen frequently before, diagonals are more difficult than verticals and horizontals. It will therefore be expected that the child will have difficulty in constructing diagonal lines. In addition to these problems, the construction of the pegboard is such that the diagonal line is more difficult with this device. The alignment of the holes on the diagonal are farther apart on the pegboard and the space relationships of holes on the diagonal are different from the space relationships on the horizontal or vertical. In many cases, it will be found necessary to return to the straight-line template or to the ruler as aids in helping the child to construct diagonal lines. The problem of stopping may occur again and can be aided by the same methods used with horizontal and vertical lines. When the diagonal line has been mastered, the triangle and diamond figures can be presented.

After these basic, simple forms are learned, more complex forms involving extensions and combinations of the simple forms can be presented. If it is felt desirable, a series of complex forms can be devised and even letters and numbers can be designed for use on the pegboard (see Jolles, 1958).

Multiple Forms.   When single forms have been mastered, the form perception problem can be increased in difficulty by presenting two forms on the board at once. Begin by constructing two figures which lie adjacent to each other. That is to say, one or more pegs of the second form are adjacent to one or more pegs of the first form (see Figure 14). This arrangement of forms presents a further difficulty for the child. When he is engaged in completing one of the forms, the second form represents a distraction and he may be carried off in a wrong direction by the stimulus of the second form. Observe whether, in his work with adjacent forms, the child completes one form first and then moves on to the second form. Such a procedure indicates that he has seen this design as two independent forms adjacent to each other. If he constructs one line of the first form and then a line of the second form or splits his approach in some similar manner, it may be suspected that he has not seen or dealt with these two forms as separate wholes. Encourage him to

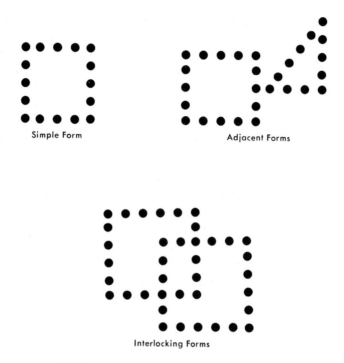

Simple Form   Adjacent Forms

Interlocking Forms

FIGURE 14. Illustrations of Pegboard figures.

recognize each form and to deal with each separately. It may be found that kinesthetic information will aid in separating the two forms. Ask the child to run his finger around the square form (Figure 14). If necessary, guide his hand so that he will not be led off by the distraction of the triangular form. Then ask him to reproduce this square. Next ask him to run his finger around the triangle and reproduce that figure. When he can perform with this kinesthetic help, ask him merely to look at the square, name it, and reproduce it. Then have him look at the triangle, name it, and reproduce it. Finally, ask him to look at the total figure, name the two forms, and reproduce each in proper orientation for himself.

Interlocking Forms. A further complication can be introduced by the use of interlocking forms. In this design, one form includes a portion of the second form (see Figure 14). With interlocking forms, it is desirable that the child again complete each form separately. Many children work their way around the outside edges of the two forms and fill in the central common area later. This procedure would indicate that they have dealt with one form involving complications rather than two forms interrelated with each other. The child should be encouraged to complete one form and then the other. In this way, we can be sure that he understands that two forms are present and we can be sure that he is able to manipulate the relationships between these two forms. The same intermediate steps recommended for adjacent forms will be found useful with interlocking forms.

In all training activities involving two forms either adjacent or interlocking, it is desirable that the second stage of training, where the model is shown the child but is removed while he is constructing his forms, be used as soon as possible. Because of the difficulty of this task, children have a tendency to look back and forth from their construction to the model, checking each line or each peg. This type of behavior indicates a concern with elements or detail rather than with the total form. The child should be encouraged to dispense with this method as soon as possible and care should be taken to see that he is required to deal with the forms as wholes. Such encouragement can be provided by removing the model and by noting carefully the method of construction which he uses. Examples of methods of construction based on reproduction of elements rather than total forms can be found in Strauss and Lehtinen (1947, pp. 33-34).

BUILDING BLOCKS

The child can be set to the task of constructing elements of form through the use of building blocks. He is given a supply of one-inch cubes such as those available from school supply companies. With these materials, he is asked to build a form. He must construct the form by first combining the blocks into a line or angle and then building up the next element in proper orientation to this first one.

As with the pegboard, two phases of training can be used: one in which he is given a model to follow and one in which he is shown a model and required to construct the form from memory.

In the former, the teacher builds a form which is placed in front of the child. In the latter, the child is shown a model which he is allowed to inspect but which is taken away when he begins to build. It is desirable to move into the second phase as soon as possible since it is in this phase that the child deals with the form and not simply with the items or the elements.

If the cubes are all one color, the elements of the figure are well defined. If various color cubes are used, color becomes a confusion variable which must be overlooked in the interest of form. Often the child will find the variation in color so distracting that he cannot maintain attention on the form. It is well, therefore, to start with blocks of a single color and introduce color variation as the child becomes able to withstand this distraction. The independence of color and form as well as the dominance of form over color, however, is encouraged when cubes of various colors are introduced. Therefore, the teacher should work toward the stages in which the child can construct a form with blocks of a number of colors.

As in the case of the pegboard, a solid form gives more figure-ground contrast than an outline form. Thus, a solid square in which the entire form is constructed with blocks is more contrasting than one in which only the perimeter is built up with blocks. Therefore, it is desirable to start with solid figures and progress to outline figures.

The construction of adjacent and interlocking figures is possible with blocks just as it was with the pegboard. The same considerations outlined for the pegboard apply to the construction of these figures with blocks. The method by which the child proceeds should be watched and the teacher should be sure that he is dealing with the forms themselves and not merely the orientation of elements with little reference to the total.

When figures are constructed on the pegboard, the items are positioned in predetermined points. The holes on the pegboard are arranged in straight rows and columns, and the child has only to select the correct hole. When he is building a line, the line will be straight by virtue of the arrangement of the holes as long as he selects a hole in the correct row. With blocks, however, control over the element as it is being built does not exist. The line which the child is building may slant or zigzag. The child is required to control the elements as he builds. Block construction is, therefore, more difficult than pegboard construction since it requires not only control of the item but simultaneous control of the elements as well.

The child who is experiencing difficulty in this control can be aided by outline figures. The figure to be constructed is outlined on a large sheet of paper which is laid flat on the table top. The child then builds up his block construction on this sheet following the outlined figure. If a solid square figure is being constructed, it is drawn on the sheet and shaded in. The child then covers the shaded area with blocks. Be sure that he uses a consistent method in placing the blocks and does not merely put them down at random until the figure is covered. He should follow the configuration of the form in such construction. He might fill in the figure by rows, working either up or down one row at a time. He might fill in the figure by columns, working either from left to right (preferably) or from right to left, one column at a time. He might outline the perimeter of the figure first, following the edges of the drawing, and then filling in the center.

If an outline form is being constructed, a line drawing of the the perimeter in an organized fashion and not place blocks at random. He should proceed from one element to the next adjacent element and not deal with elements at random during the construction. figure is presented on the sheet. The child should proceed around

There are two problems involved in the control required to construct forms in this manner. The first of these is perceptual control. The child has difficulty monitoring his motor performance on the basis of perceptual information. In this case the perceptual information is related to the developing form rather than to the perceptual data directly (as in perceptual-motor matching). Such monitoring control can be aided by supplying additional data concerning the form as outlined above. The qualities of the total form are emphasized by the drawing on the sheet. These form qualities can then be used for control of the elements of the form.

The second problem of control involves the control of the motor activities involved in the construction. Either because of a weakness in fine motor ability or in the perceptual-motor match, the child cannot control his hand adequately to permit construction.

He knows what he wants to do with the element of the form but he cannot get his hand to perform with sufficient accuracy to accomplish it. The cerebral palsied child with an involvement of the arm or hand offers an example of such a failure of motor control.

For such a child, more direct motor aid is required than that provided by an outline of the form on a sheet of paper. For him, frames or templates can be supplied. A template of reasonable thickness so that it will resist uncontrolled motor movements is laid on the table top. The child then constructs his figure within the template either outlining it or filling it in. The frame of the template serves to control the motor manipulations. The child's use of form in this task is revealed by his method of procedure. He should proceed systematically with his construction both in terms of the blocks themselves and of the order of the elements which he builds up from the blocks.

The large building blocks available from school supply houses can be used in the same fashion to permit the child to experiment with the building of forms from items. These blocks are either square or rectangular, approximately 12 inches wide, and may be fabricated either from wood or a reinforced cardboard.

These large blocks can be used in the same manner as the small cubes. Either outline or solid figures can be constructed by laying the blocks out on the floor just as the cubes were laid out on the table top. These large forms have the advantage that the child can walk around them, get in them, or climb over them. He can thus learn the form principle in more gross kinds of activity. Such variation is important in the development of the form perception generalization. Too often the child is given experience with form only in small figures. He fails, therefore, to generalize to large figures where the spatial extent of the form is greater and the exploration of the form involves extensive movement through space (with attendant problems of space structure) and through time (with attendant problems of temporal sequence).

In addition, the large blocks present the advantage that their manipulation takes more time. The child is thus required to maintain the form quality over a greater period of time and to resist the distraction of more complex manipulations during the construction. One of the major purposes of manipulation of items in form perception is to give the child practice in maintaining the form principle while he manipulates the item and in resisting the distraction represented by such manipulation. With the large blocks, the mechanics of their manipulation takes considerably longer. In addition such manipulation is considerably more distracting since it involves major movements through space and neuro-muscular activities which are spread more widely throughout the body. One of the major purposes of the activity is therefore emphasized by the use of these materials.

The large building blocks can also be used to construct three dimensional forms. By piling the blocks up in an integrated fashion, forms can be constructed which the child can explore from both outside and inside. Such overall exploration adds to the generalization of the form perception principle. It also permits manipulation of form in a vertical as well as a horizontal plane.

CONSTRUCTION SETS

Tinker Toys, Mechano, Leg-o, and similar construction sets are commercially available and present various types of units from which the child constructs forms. A booklet usually accompanies such sets in which objects for construction are diagrammed. For the child with weakness in form perception, these prepared diagrams frequently will be found to be too complicated. Too many items are required for the completion of the task and the child cannot keep in mind the relationships between so many units simultaneously. As a result, the task frequently becomes one of merely joining one unit to the next, carefully following the directions, with little concern for the overall production. Such an overly complex task forces the child away from experimentation with the form into a routine manipulation of the units where the emphasis is on precision of movement rather than integration of parts into a constructive whole.

The teacher may, therefore, find it necessary to simplify the construction as these are described in the materials accompanying the set. Such simplification can be accomplished in either of two ways: (1) new designs can be prepared in which a fewer number of units are required and in which the number of elements necessary for the total form are less or where the organization between these elements is less complex; (2) the teacher may construct a part of the form giving it to the child to complete. Be sure that the elements which he is required to complete are intimately related to the total form and not just tangential parts added for decoration or additional realism. Thus, if the structure is a windmill, do not complete the figure and ask the child to add the vanes on the wind wheel. Rather, complete the wheel yourself and ask him to complete the frame. The frame is a basic and necessary part of the windmill. The vanes are unique to the windmill and hence more obvious to us. To the child, however, they are much less vital to the overall structure. By asking him to construct the frame, which is more basic to the form of the structure, we encourage him to deal with the basic form rather than elements in isolation.

Just as the prescribed designs may be too complex, so the materials in these construction sets may require too precise a manipulation, especially for the child who may have, in addition to his form weakness, a difficulty in fine motor control. In this event, the child has so much trouble with the mechanics of manipulating the materials that he has little energy or attention left over for the form perception problem. The task then becomes one of fine motor coordination rather than constructive form perception. It may, therefore, be necessary to select among these materials in terms of the manipulative ability of the child.

Materials will be found appropriate or inappropriate for certain training activities depending upon the relationship between the material, the child, and the task. Thus, Tinker Toys may be used to train eye-hand coordination. The task is to insert the peg in the hole. If we give the child a construction task, he is forced, because of his inability to get beyond the eye-hand problem, to change the prescribed task from one of constructive form to one of eye-hand coordination. Therefore, regardless of how we set up the task or of the instructions we use, the activity will become one of eye-hand coordination and fine motor control. At a later stage in development when eye-hand coordination has become more precise, the child is free to use the Tinker Toy materials for experimentation with form. Now the task will involve form perception and, although the materials are the same, the activity and learning of the child are quite different. The child has changed in the interum and, therefore, his relationship to this material has also changed.

From this illustration, two points regarding the use of training materials become apparent. (1) The same material can serve different training purposes at different stages in the development of the child. The task presented by the material will either become changed to meet the needs of the level of training appropriate for the child's stage of development or it may be altered deliberately by the teacher to meet these needs. The latter method of alteration is obviously preferred.

(2) No material is specific to a given training activity. The fact that a given material was carefully designed to serve a certain training purpose is no guarantee that that purpose is the one which will be served or that, for a particular child, any purpose at all will be served by the material. The child's behavior toward the material must be observed and the function of the material must be determined from this observation. Materials serve different purposes and become, in fact, different things depending upon the child's relationship to them.

CHILDREN AS UNITS

The children in the classroom can themselves be used as units out of which forms are constructed. At times when the children change rooms, one child can be asked to place the others in a straight line. The child can place the other children around the perimeter of a square or a circle. Any activity in which the group needs to be arranged in a pattern can be used to train form perception by asking one child to manipulate the others into the prescribed pattern. Many common classroom activities require such patterned grouping of children.

The use of children as units in a pattern permits the child to see the form problem from two angles. At one time he is outside the figure and manipulates the children into position. At another time he is inside the figure as one of the units. This reversal of roles serves to stress the pattern or integration aspects of form construction. These aspects are particularly important when the children move in pattern, as in marching around a circle. Here the child must maintain his relationship to the child in front of him but also must maintain this relationship in terms of the overall circular pattern of the movement.

If the children have difficulty maintaining such a moving figure, they may first be asked to hold hands as they move around the figure. In this activity the arms become the elements of figure and the problem is similar to that of manipulation of elements. When they have become more proficient, they can be asked to release their hands and maintain awareness of the form on the basis of the pattern of the individual units.

UNIT FIGURES

Materials are available in which simple outline forms are presented in a series of points. Most common among such materials are sewing cards and numbered dot drawings. In the former of these, a very dim outline of a figure is perforated at intervals. The child, by sewing from perforation to perforation, completes the outline with colored thread or yarn. Each element of the figure is broken down into arbitrary units (stitches) and the child builds up the elements by adding unit to unit as he proceeds.

In the numbered dot drawing, a simple figure is outlined. Each change of direction is indicated by a dot. The dots are numbered consecutively and the child draws from dot to dot. In this activity, the elements of the form are broken down into units although the breakdowns are less regular and are more closely related to angles rather than lines as was the case in previous materials. The child completes the form by proceeding in order from dot to dot.

Such materials permit experimentation with the construction of form by the summation of units in order. It is important to call the child's attention to the overall form. Ask him, before he begins, to guess what the picture is. As he proceeds, stop him from time to time and ask him to again guess what the picture is. Such a procedure continues to emphasize the integrated form throughout the activity. The child is encouraged to use what units he has already constructed to help him predict what type of pattern is developing.

In like manner, the child's attention should be called to the elements of the form upon which he is working. If he can guess what the picture is or if he has been told what it is, he can be asked what part he is now working on. It is well to stop him periodically and ask him what parts (elements) of the picture he has finished, what parts he is now working on, and what parts he has still to do. His attention is thus called to the parts of the figure and how he is combining units into elements and eventually elements into the total form.

If the child does not direct his attention to the overall form or show persistent interest in the picture which he is constructing, it is likely that these activities are not, for him at this stage, related to form perception. It is probable that he is merely proceeding from unit to unit and little more than eye-hand coordination will be involved. If, on the other hand, the child is using these activities to promote form perception, he will continue to show more interest in the picture which is developing than in the manipulations which he is using.

MANIPULATION OF SUB-FORMS

Another activity permitting experimentation with constructive form involves the manipulation of parts of a form in which the parts are logical divisions of the whole. Thus, the child might be presented with materials to build a house. He would be given the frame of the house and such parts as chimney, windows, doors, et cetera, which he is to paste on or otherwise assemble into a completed product. Note that the parts are true sub-forms. They can be treated by themselves and have form qualities and meaning independent of the house. On the other hand, they are parts of a house and belong logically to the total construction. Certain commercial jigsaw puzzles have meaningful parts, such as a piece cut in the shape of a dog. However, the shape has nothing to do with the picture which is being put together and has no logical relation to the scene. Such pieces represent confusion forms rather than subforms. They are not suitable for the present purposes.

Where the part is a true sub-form, however, it serves to call attention to subdivisions of the total form. Since the child needs experimentation with the integrative aspects of form, such separation of complete parts encourages him to attend to their integration within the whole, both with reference to each other and with reference to the overall form. The situation is thus set so that the integrative aspect of the parts is emphasized. Where, in other situations he might overlook these parts because of his difficulty in organizing them in the total, he is here prevented from simplifying the problem in this way and is forced to deal with the part in terms of its relation to the whole.

TRAINING FIGURE-GROUND RELATIONSHIPS

In the preceding discussion we have dealt with the question of form perception *per se*. Intimately related to form itself, however, is the problem of figure-ground differentiation.

The difficulties which the teacher encounters in developing such concepts as "on top," "under," "above," and "below" may frequently be related to weakness in the figure-ground relationship. Such concepts involve, on the part of the child, an ability to manipulate figure-ground relationships. These manipulations, in turn, involve an awareness of the figure versus ground and various relationships between these two. Thus, when we say to the child, "Put the book *on* the table," the book must become figure and the tabletop must become ground. Furthermore, the figure must overlay the ground. At the same time, the child must maintain the awareness that the ground is continuous under the figure even though it cannot be seen in the area covered by the figure. He must also be aware that the figure can move across the ground without altering the characteristics of the ground. Many children with weaknesses in figure-ground relationship behave as though they were not aware of the continuity of the ground below the figure. Thus, for these children the book, as it lies on the tabletop, appears to interrupt the ground, as though it fit into a hole in the tabletop. To move the book would involve alterations in the ground as well as in the position of the figure. The ground beneath the figure ceases to exist.

When we say to the child, "Put the book *under* the desk," we ask him to maintain an awareness of the figure while it is hidden by the ground. Again, for the child with weakness in figure-ground relationship, the figure may appear to lose its existence when it is obstructed by the ground. The child must learn to maintain the desktop as ground even though it is the only aspect of the figure-ground relationship which is visible. He must also maintain awareness of the figure and its location in space even though there is no visual information concerning this relationship.

Concepts such as "on top of" and "underneath" become difficult when the child is unable to establish this figure-ground relationship and to manipulate it. These concepts depend upon a relationship between figure and ground. Without such a relationship there is no "on top of" and there is no "underneath." The concepts signify a certain relationship between figure and ground, and if the figure-ground concept is weak, the manipulation of such relationships will prove difficult.

As the child develops, these figure-ground relationships become more complex. Now, instead of a figure which lies in a single plane and a ground which lies in another single plane, the child may be confronted with figures which lie in various planes in space and with a ground which extends through space, which he must structure into one of a number of planes as conditions require. The figure-ground relationship now becomes more flexible so that the child ranges over a continuum of space, selecting now one object, now another, in various spatial relationships as figure, the remaining objects moving into the ground. Problems of directed attention, of task versus surround, of sequential manipulations of parts of tasks, and the like are all related to such flexible manipulations of the figure-ground relationship.

TRAINING BASIC POSITION CONCEPTS

BODY PARTS AS FIGURE

Training may be begun in such concepts as "over" and "under" by using body parts as a figure. By this means tactual and kinesthetic information is available as to the existence of the figure and the position of the figure even though the visual information is altered. Thus, the child might be asked, "Put your hand on the table." In this case, visual information indicates the existence of the hand and its position above the tabletop. Tactual information from contact of the hand with the table surface indicates the same relationship. Kinesthetic information maintains awareness of the existence of the hand and some indication of its location in space.

Now ask the child, "Put your hand under the table." The visual information changes and no longer indicates the existence or location of the hand. However, tactual information from contact with the bottom surface of the table still indicates the existence and location of the figure. Kinesthetic information now indicates the existence of the hand and an alteration in location since he now must push up to maintain contact with the table surface, whereas formerly he had to push down to maintain such contact. The visual information has undergone radical change. Tactual and kinesthetic information, however, have undergone less change. These latter can therefore be used to aid in maintaining the figure-ground relationship which may have become disrupted by the radical visual change.

OBJECTS AS FIGURE

When the child can maintain awareness of the body part as figure under these figure-ground alterations, he can be taught constancy of objects as figure under similar alterations. Ask the child to place an object on the table. Ask him to manipulate the object so that he maintains tactual and kinesthetic contact with it. Ask him to lift up the object and feel with his hand underneath it, observing that the ground is continuous under the figure. Now ask him to place the object under the table pressing it up against the table surface. Again, ask him to manipulate the object so that he gets tactual and kinesthetic information similar to that which he received when he placed his hand under the table.

Obtain an object such as a form board figure. Attach adhesive material to the back of the object. Ask the child to place the object under the table pressing against the table surface with the adhesive side of the block so that it adheres to the underneath surface of the table. Ask him to manipulate the object as before and to make the same observations as before. Then permit him to crawl under the table and look up at the object adhering to the undersurface of the tabletop. He can now check visual information, which remains correlated, with tactual kinesthetic information.

Place the object on top of the table and ask the child to make the same manipulations, crawling under the table and looking up, observing that only the ground and not the figure can be seen from this position. Such activities permit the child to compare the more constant tactual and kinesthetic information with the varying visual information.

FIGURE-GROUND DIFFERENTIATION

Materials

Three background boards 12 x 12 inches cut from cardboard, each covered with material of a different texture: white gloss paper, sandpaper, black felt.

Figure variations

Form	Size	Color	Texture
circle	3″ x 3″	white	gloss paper
square	2″ x 2″	red	sandpaper
cross	1″ x 1″	black	felt

Figures cut from cardboard presenting all combinations of the variations listed. Thus, there will be circles of three sizes. For each size there will be three colors and for each color, three textures — a total of 81 figures.

Give the child one of the background boards and a figure which varies from the ground in both color and texture. Instruct the child to examine each piece. Insure that he examines the piece visually, that he manipulates it kinesthetically, and that he feels it tactually.

Place the figure in the center of the ground. Instruct the child to:

a. Feel over the entire board noting the difference as he passes over the perimeter of the figure.

b. Feel over the figure as though he were coloring with his finger, again noting the difference which occurs at the edge of the figure.

c. Feel over the background as in coloring in, noting the difference at the edge of the figure.

d. Run his finger around the perimeter of the figure using tactual differentiation as well as visual differentiation to establish the border of figure and ground.

In order to develop the figure-ground generalization, repeat this experience using various sizes, various colors, and various textures except that color and that texture which matches the background.

When the child can identify the figure-ground relationship under these conditions of contrast, then the task can be increased in difficulty. Present figures in the same way as above, but use figures which match the background in texture. In this activity the color variable remains contrasting, but one of the variables previously used to differentiate figure and ground is now constant between the figure and background. Next present figures having the same color as the background. Now color becomes the variable which cannot be used for differentiation. Use the same activities outlined above (manipulating the object, feeling the ground under the object, et cetera) to help the child differentiate the figure-ground relationship.

At the most difficult stage figures can be used which match the background in both color and texture. The child must now differentiate on the basis of the differences which occur at the boundary of the figure. Use the same manipulations outlined above to establish this differentiation.

CONSTANCY OF GROUND

Give the child a background board with a figure which varies in both color and texture placed in the center of it. Instruct the child to examine the figure and the ground as before. Be sure that he examines this relationship visually, kinesthetically, and tactually. Now have him lift the figure and feel the ground underneath it. Point out: (1) that the ground continues *under* the figure; and (2) that the figure is *on top of* the ground. In order to aid in the development of generalization, repeat this procedure varying the figure in color and texture. Point out that although the figure varies, the ground remains constant.

Now ask the child to select a figure and place it *on* the ground. Repeat the activities outlined above stressing the constancy of the ground and the figure *on* the ground as the figure-ground relationship. Ask him to repeat this observation with a number of figures varying in texture and color. Permit him to make the selection so that the qualities of the figure are strong for him. Be sure that the child notes that the ground does not change as the figure is altered and that the ground *underneath* the figure remains present and unaltered regardless of the alterations in the figure.

Present the same variations of figure using another background board. Point out what happens when the figure matches the ground in one or more variables. Repeat the experiments with the background board in a vertical instead of an horizontal position. Point out that the figure-ground relationships remain the same irrespective of the orientation of the materials. Alter the position of the figure on the ground. Thus, instead of presenting the figure always in the center of the background, present it to one side or in a corner. Note that the figure-ground relationship remains the same regardless of the position of the figure on the ground.

CONSTANCY OF THE FIGURE

Present the child with two of the background boards. Give him one of the figures which contrasts in both color and texture with the two backgrounds. Instruct him to place the figure on the first board, then pick it up and place it on the second board. Observe that the figure remains the same when the background is altered. The child should check this by tracing around the figure with his finger. Repeat these observations using all combinations of the three background boards.

Repeat the above steps using all variations of color, size, and texture. Observe particularly what happens when the figure matches the ground in one or more variables. Be sure that the child notes that, although the differentiation problem alters markedly when figure and ground match, the figure-ground relationship remains the same and the figure remains constant.

COMPLEX FIGURE-GROUND RELATIONSHIPS

Present the child with one of the background boards and a large figure contrasting with the ground in color and texture. Place on the board a small figure contrasting with both the large figure and the ground. Ask the child to note the relationship of the two figures on a single ground. He should observe that the ground remains constant in both cases.

Now ask him to pick up the small figure and place it on top of the large figure. Now he has developed a complex figure-ground relationship. The small figure is a figure on a ground represented by the large figure. The large figure in turn is a figure on a ground represented by the background. Have him observe that all the figure-ground relationships previously learned are maintained in this complex figure-ground situation.

Have him place the large figure on top of the small figure. Have him note that the small figure cannot now be seen. Have him pick up the large figure and find the small figure beneath it. Point out how a large figure covers and hides a small figure just as the small figure covered a portion of the large figure or a portion of the background. Permit the child to experiment with these figure-ground relationships using all variations of figures and grounds.

CUTTING AND PASTING

Having experimented with situations in which the figure-ground relationship is flexible and can be manipulated, the child should now move to relationships which are more formal. Whereas the figures used in the above exercises could be moved about on the ground and the ground beneath the figure could be investigated directly, such is not the case in a picture on a page. Here the figure is fixed on the ground and the overlap of figure-ground must be imagined or assumed. Intermediate between these two extremes are the activities of cutting and pasting.

In the cutting activity, the figure is embedded in the ground. A physical separation of figure from ground is then achieved. In the pasting activity, the figure is placed on a ground and this placement is made permanent by the paste. Thus a rigid figure-ground relationship (a "picture" on a page) has been destroyed by the cutting and another rigid figure-ground relationship has been created by the pasting. In maneuvering the cutout picture onto the new ground, the figure-ground relationships, investigated in the earlier exercises, can be observed again and the child can see how the relationships are made rigid but are not destroyed during the process.

CUTTING

If the child has marked difficulty with fine motor control or eye-hand coordination, this task should not be used. Such a child will need to give so much attention to the mechanics of cutting that he will not be able to observe the figure-ground relationships which are the objective of the lesson. For such a child, scored figures which can be torn easily from the ground should be provided. If such scored materials are not available, the teacher should cut out the figures for the child and then proceed to the pasting activity.

Select a picture to be cut out in which the figure-ground relationship is emphasized. The picture should be a simple subject presenting a mass of figure rather than a maze of details. The contour should be simple and the boundary lines of the contour should be strong and easily identified. Broad, heavy contour lines are preferred. The figure-ground relationship should be as nearly that of a single figure on a single ground as possible. A figure-ground relationship should be suggested by the picture (such as a running boy). This relationship should be one that has been experienced by the child in concrete experience and is of interest to him. The principles for selecting pictures for cutting and pasting follow:

1. High color contrast between figure and ground.
2. Strong boundary between figure and ground.
3. Minimal detail within figure which might confuse or complicate the figure-ground relationship. Avoid a figure which has figure within it so that there is a figure on a ground which is itself on a ground.
4. Avoid figures with complex or detailed contours. Such figures stress eye-hand control and distract attention from figure-ground relationships.
5. Select figures which suggest movement (running animal, floating balloon, et cetera) so that flexibility of figure-ground is suggested. (A running animal, for example, *suggests* a figure moving over a ground.)
6. Select pictures of objects that are within the child's experience and which are of interest to him.

If the child's manipulative ability is poor, a frame can be drawn around the picture. The child is then asked to cut out around the frame rather than around the contour of the figure. This procedure simplifies the mechanics of the cutting and leaves the child freer to observe the figure-ground problems.

Ask the child to cut out the picture. He should observe that the figure is separated from the ground. He might hold the picture up with his hand (as nearly as possible a figure with no ground). He might maneuver the figure across a ground. Thus he might hold a picture of a running boy vertically and push it across the table top. Here the normal orientation of a figure to the ground is preserved. He might place a sheet of paper vertically behind the figure as he pushes it across the table top so that the figure moves across a ground. He might lay the sheet of paper on the table and place the figure flat on top of it. He has now produced the conventional representation of figure-ground (a picture on a page). He might then move the picture across the paper, as a boy might appear to run under conditions of the conventional representation.

PASTING

Pasting permits the child to experiment with figure-ground until a desired relationship has been achieved and then to solidify the relationship which he has produced. Guidelines can be inserted into the ground which suggest a certain relationship. The child is then asked to maneuver the figure until the suggested relationship appears. Figure-ground differentiation is simplified since only the figure can be manipulated.

In the simplest phases, the child is asked to mount a figure on a ground. Thus, he might be given a blue sheet of paper and a series of brightly colored circles representing balloons. He is to create a picture of balloons floating in the sky. He manipulates the circles until he has them properly positioned and then pastes them down. He should observe that the figure is *on* or *in front of* the ground and by feeling over the sheet observe the separation of figure and ground.

In the next phase, details can be added to the ground. Thus, instead of a plain blue sheet, he might be presented with a sheet on which there is a horizon line so that sky is separated from land. He must then paste his balloons in the sky. The child is now required to differentiate the ground; it is no longer homogeneous. He must locate his figure according to aspects of this differentiated ground. He is required to construct a *figure to ground* relationship. Such differerentiations of the ground should be kept as simple as possible. Begin with only two variables, such as earth and sky. More complex differentiations can be introduced as the child progresses. Be sure that the child responds to the differentiation and not merely to the pictorial elements. Thus, be sure that he separates the ground into earth and sky and does not merely locate his figure in terms of the *line* of the horizon.

Finally, other figures can be introduced into the ground. Thus, the child might be presented with the sheet on which sky is separated from land. However, there might be added a picture of a man selling balloons and holding in his hand the strings to which the balloons should be attached. The child is then asked to paste his circles on the ends of the strings. Now he is required to construct not only a figure to ground relationship but also a *figure to figure* relationship. He must orient his figure both to the ground and to other figures. He must maintain an overall figure-ground relationship so that he can orient his figure to both of these variables at once.

These pasting activities can be made more complex as the child's ability increases by adding more detail to the ground so that it becomes more distracting. The difficulty can also be increased by increasing the complexity of the relationships between figures. Thus, adjacent figures or overlapping figures may be used.

SCANNING

If one searches for a particular object among a group of objects, he selects one or more qualities of the object in question. As his attention runs over the group of objects, the specific quality is encountered. That object immediately becomes figure and the remainder of the objects become ground. The object under consideration is clear and sharp while the rest are dim and vague. The selected object can then be examined for all qualities necessary for discrimination and then be retained or rejected on the basis of this examination.

If, however, figure-ground relationships are poor, the object in question does not emerge from the ground for examination or does not thus emerge strongly enough or long enough to permit accurate examination. As a result, the child with weak figure-ground may experience difficulty in systematically searching for an object or a piece of information. Frequently such children are accused of being inattentive and disorganized.

In like manner, a difficulty in maintaining a figure-ground relationship may result in a child's holding on to a stimulus when he should go on to examine the next object. The object which he has examined does not recede into the ground when he has finished his examination and, hence, he does not free his attention for the next object. The child is, therefore, unable to continue his search or scanning but seems frozen to the immediate object of regard.

SORTING

Sorting exercises are frequently helpful in aiding the child to develop a figure-ground ability which will permit systematic search.

In the initial phases, the figure-ground relationship should be strong. Thus, the child might be presented with a box of blocks or marbles all of the same color. He might then be given one block of a different color and asked to place it in the box. He then looks away for a few seconds, after which he is asked to find his block again. In this activity, the child has created his own figure-ground relationship as he placed his block in the box. His attention should be called to how his block stands out from the rest. He is then asked to react to the figure-ground relationship which he has created when he finds his block again.

The task can be made more complex by using in the box a variety of objects which vary in a number of qualities. The child's object should be the only one possessing that quality which is being used for discrimination. Thus, the child may have a red block. The objects in the box vary in size, color, and shape, but his is the only red one. In this case, the conditions of the ground are more complex and there are more stimuli presented which can distract him. He must learn to keep these many stimuli in a ground relationship so that he can search systematically for his figure.

In the exercises above, the child created his own figure-ground since he himself put his object in the box. In the next phase, the child learns to react to a figure-ground created by someone else.

Now the teacher places the figure block in the box and asks the child to find it. The child can either be shown the figure block before it is placed in the box and asked to remember it during the search or he can be given an identical block and asked to find one like it in the box. The former procedure is more difficult.

Emphasize a certain and prompt response. The purpose is to encourage the child to construct a figure-ground relationship with the key object as figure. If such a relationship is going to develop, it will develop relatively promptly. Therefore, the child's response should be prompt. If it is not, he is probably hung up on an extraneous stimulus or he is aimlessly wandering from object to object. In either event, the construction of the desired figure-ground relationship is being hampered rather than furthered. If a prompt response does not occur, the child should be stopped, asked to look away, and then asked to start over again.

This task can be made more difficult by increasing the complexity of the ground as was done in the previous exercise. It is the figure-ground relationship, not perceptual discrimination *per se*, that is being taught at this point. Therefore, care should be taken to see that, when the complexity of the ground is increased, the perceptual discriminations required are not made finer or more difficult. Thus, if the child is to find the red block, it would not be desirable to include among the ground objects some in varying shades of red. To so do, would be to shift the emphasis from the figure-ground problem to a problem of color discrimination.

The child can now be asked to find more than one object. He can be given a box of objects which includes two red blocks and asked to pick out *all* the red blocks. The number of key blocks included in the box can then be increased to about half the total number of objects. Here the child is asked to manipulate the figure-ground relationship. When he selects the first key block it becomes figure while the second key block remains a part of the ground. When he selects the second key block, that which was formerly ground now becomes figure.

Present the child with a box of blocks half of which are red and half of which are green. Ask him to sort out the red blocks. In this case each object must be assigned to either figure or ground depending upon its color. The distinction between figure and ground is based on the presence or absence of a key quality. This sorting task can be altered using other qualities as the basis for the sort, for example, size and form. The task can be made more difficult by varying qualities other than the key quality as in the earlier exercises. Care must be taken not to increase the difficulty of the perceptual differentiation as the complexity of the task is increased.

When the child has developed sorting ability with such concrete objects, paper and pencil sorting tasks can be introduced. Such paper and pencil sorting tasks can be found in many readiness and beginning reading workbooks. They involve a number of figures on a page. The child is asked to mark those figures which match a comparison figure. Avoid pages with too many figures so that the page is cluttered with material. Such pages are too difficult for the child whose figure-ground is weak. Begin with only a few figures and increase the number as the child progresses. As an activity more directly preparatory to reading, letters and short words can be used as the figures after the child has demonstrated his ability with less complex figures.

COLORING

The child with a weakness in figure-ground frequently has difficulty with coloring. Coloring involves dealing with a figure on a ground and being particularly aware of the boundary between figure and ground. Normally, that portion of the page lying within the boundary of the figure appears different from the remainder of the page. It appears to stand out by virtue of its status as figure. If the figure-ground relationship is weak, however, this characteristic of the figure may be limited or it may fade in and out. As a result the area to be colored is not clearly marked and its separation from the ground, which is the clue to stop coloring, is not sharply defined. If practice in coloring is continued without regard for the child's figure-ground problems, he may learn only to "color to the line" rather than learning to color in a form.

Coloring can be approached through cutting and pasting; when the child has cut out a figure, ask him to color it. Be sure he colors all of the figure but do not be concerned if he colors outside this area as long as his coloring is oriented to the figure. When he lifts up the figure, his mistakes are eliminated and he can see the figure without error. Ask him to observe this figure against various grounds as in the pasting exercises, and finally ask him to paste it down permanently upon a ground. Call his attention to the integrity of the figure under all these conditions.

To encourage the integrity of the boundary of the figure, cut the form to be colored out of stiff paper or cardboard. Mount it on a disc so that it stands 1/2″ to 3/4″ above the surface of the paper. Now ask the child to color the figure. Be sure that the background sheet contrasts in color with both the cutout figure and the crayon which the child is using. As he approaches the boundary in his coloring he receives tactual and kinesthetic clues in addition to the visual clues, since the crayon runs off the raised figure. When the coloring is completed, ask the child to observe the figure-ground relationship. Then remove the disc and proceed as in pasting.

The integrity of the boundary can also be encouraged by the use of cut out templates. A template of some transparent material such as clear plastic is best so that the separation between figure and ground is not so artificial. Place the template on the sheet and ask the child to place his crayon inside the cutout figure. He should draw around the boundary first to emphasize the contour and then proceed to color in the form. Be sure all of the figure area is colored. The template will limit the child's mistakes. When the coloring is complete, remove the template and call the child's attention to the figure-ground relationship which he has created.

When the child has begun to solidify the figure-ground relationship, he can be introduced to the more formal type of coloring activity found in the customary workbooks and work sheets. Begin with those tasks in which the figure-ground relationship is more simple. Choose a page which has only one figure on the page and where the boundary of the figure is uncomplicated (see principles of selecting figures for cutting and pasting). Emphasize the boundary of the figure with a broad, heavy line to aid the child with the figure-ground separation.

FROSTIG WORK SHEETS FOR FIGURE-GROUND PERCEPTION

When the child has achieved a basic awareness of the figure-ground relationship, the Fostig Program for the Development of Visual Perception will be found useful. This program includes a series of 69 exercises in the area of Figure-Ground Perception. These materials are paper and pencil tasks concerned with the more complex aspects of figure-ground. Therefore, it is well that they be preceded and accompanied by more concrete examples. The activities described above might well precede the Frostig exercises. Responses to three dimensional objects, such as finding a prescribed object in a room, sorting concrete objects, picking out objects from a box containing many different objects, and the like should accompany the paper and pencil exercises.

References

Abbott, W. *The Theory and Practice of Perspective*. London: Blackie and Son, 1950.

Andrews, G. *Creative Rhythmic Movement for Children*. Englewood Cliffs, N.J.: Prentice-Hall, Inc., 1954.

Asher, E.J., J. Tiffin, and F.B. Knight. *The Psychology of Normal People*. New York: D.C. Heath and Co., 1946.

Bannatyne, A.D. The Color Phonics System, in J. Money and G. Schiffman (eds.), *Disabled Reader*. Baltimore: Johns Hopkins Press, 1964.

Bartley, S.H. *Principles of Perception*. New York: Harper & Brothers, 1958.

Bender, L. *Psychopathology of Children with Organic Brain Disorders*. Springfield: Charles C. Thomas, Publisher, 1956.

Bender, L. *Visual Motor Gestalt Test and Its Clinical Use*. New York: American Orthopsychiatric Association, 1938.

Bexton, W.H., W. Heron, and T.H. Scott. "Effects of Decreased Variation in the Sensory Environment," *Canad. J. Psychol.*, 8 (1954), 70-76.

Binet, A., and T.H. Simon. *The Development of Intelligence in Children*. Baltimore: Williams & Wilkins Co., 1916.

Birch, H. *Brain Damage in Children — the Biological and Social Aspects*. Baltimore: Williams & Wilkins Co., 1964.

Birch, H., and L. Belmont. Auditory-visual integration in normal and retarded readers. *Am. J. Orthopsychiat.*, 34 (1964), 851-61.

Blom, G.E., G.K. Farley, and C. Guthals. The concept of body image and the remediation of body image disorders. *Jr. Learning Disabilities*, 3, 1970, 440-47.

Brown, G.S., and D.P. Campbell. *Principles of Servomechanisms*. New York: John Wiley and Sons, Inc., 1948.

Bush, W.J., and M.T. Giles. *Aids to Psycholinguistic Teaching*. Columbus: Charles E. Merrill Publishing Co., 1969.

Carton, A.M. *Relationship of Auditory-Motor Rhythm to Reading Achievement.* Unpublished M.S. Thesis, Purdue University, 1963.

Chaney, C.M., and N.C. Kephart. *Motoric Aids to Perceptual Training.* Columbus: Charles E. Merrill Publishing Co., 1968.

Coghill, G.E. *Anatomy and the Problem of Behavior.* Cambridge: Cambridge University Press, 1929.

Craik, K.J.W. *The Nature of Explanation.* Cambridge: Cambridge University Press, 1952.

Crain, L. and H. Werner. "The Development of Visuo-motor Performance on the Marble Board in Normal Children." *J. Genet. Psychol.,* LXXVII (1950), 217-29.

Cratty, B.J. *Movement Behavior and Motor Learning.* Philadelphia: Lea & Febiger, 1964.

Cruickshank, W.M., and G.O. Johnson (eds.). *Education of Exceptional Children and Youth.* Englewood Cliffs, N.J.: Prentice-Hall, Inc., 1958.

Dunsing, J.D. *Reading Achievement: Its Relationship to Perceptual and Motor Activity.* Allegheny County (Penn.) Schools, 1963.

Dunsing, J.D., and N.C. Kephart, Motor Generalizations in Space and Time, in J. Hellmuth (ed.), *Learning Disorders,* Volume I. Seattle: Special Child Publications, 1965.

Dusser de Barenne, J.G. The Labyrinthine and Postural Mechanisms, in C. Murchison (ed.), *Handbook of General Experimental Psychology.* Worcester: Clark University Press, 1934, pp. 204-46.

Early, F. New Uses for the Old Template. *Academic Therapy,* 4 (1969), 295-298.

Early, G.H. Developing Perceptual-Motor Skills: Overburdened Cognitive Processes. *Academic Therapy,* 5 (1969), 59-62.

Early, G.H. *Perceptual Training in the Curriculum.* Columbus: Charles E. Merrill Publishing Co., 1969.

Ebersole, M., N.C. Kephart, and J.B. Ebersole. *Steps to Achievement for the Slow Learner.* Columbus: Charles E. Merrill Publishing Co., 1968.

Eccles, J.C. *The Neurophysiological Basis of Mind.* Oxford: Clarendon Press, 1953.

Einstein, Albert. *The Meaning of Relativity,* 5th ed. Princeton, New Jersey: Princeton University Press, 1955.

Feinberg, R. "A Study of Some Aspects of Peripheral Visual Acuity." *Amer. J. Optom.,* LXII (1949), 62.

Fernald, G.M. *Remedial Techniques in Basic School Subjects.* New York: McGraw-Hill Book Company, 1943.

Fishback, W.T. *Projective and Euclidean Geometry,* 2nd ed. New York: John Wiley and Sons, Inc., 1969.

Fisher, M.D., and R.V. Turner. The Effects of a Perceptual-Motor Program upon the Academic Readiness of Culturally Disadvantaged Kindergarten Children. Accepted for Publication, *J. Learning Disabilities.*

Flavell, J.H. *The Developmental Psychology of Jean Piaget.* New York: D. Van Nostrand Co., Inc., 1963.

Foster, Josephine C., and Marion L. Mattson. *Nursery-School Education.* New York: D. Appleton-Century Company, 1939.

Freeman, F.N. *Psychology of the Common Branches.* Boston: Houghton Mifflin Co., 1916.

Frostig, M. *Marianne Frostig Developmental Test of Visual Perception.* Palo Alto, Calif.: Consulting Psychologists Press, 1961.

Frostig, M. *Movement Education: Theory and Practice.* Chicago: Follett Educational Corp., 1970.

Frostig, M., and D. Horne. *The Frostig Program for the Development of Visual Perception.* Chicago: Follett Educational Corporation, 1964.

Fulton, J.F. *Physiology of the Nervous System,* 3rd ed. New York: Oxford University Press, 1949.

Gale, R.M., (ed). *The Philosophy of Time.* Garden City: Doubleday & Company, Inc., 1967.

Gelb, A., and K. Goldstein. "Analysis of a Case of Figural Blindness," in W.D. Ellis (ed.) *A Source Book of Gestalt Psychology.* New York: Harcourt, Brace and Co., 1938.

Gesell, A. *Infancy and Human Growth.* New York: The Macmillan Co., 1928.

Gesell, A. *The First Five Years of Life.* New York: Harper and Brothers, 1940.

Gesell, A. and C.S. Amatruda: *Developmental Diagnosis,* 2nd ed. New York: Paul B. Hoeber, 1947.

Gesell, A., F.L. Ilg, and G.E. Bullis. *Vision — Its Development in Infant and Child.* New York: Paul B. Hoeber, 1941.

Gibson, E.J. "Improvement in Perceptual Judgements as a Function of Controlled Practice or Training," *Psychol. Bull.,* L (1953), 401-31.

Gibson, J.J. *The Perception of the Visual World.* New York: Houghton Mifflin Co., 1950.

Gibson, J.J., and E.J. Gibson. "Perceptual Learning: Differentiation or Enrichment," *Psychol. Rev.,* LXII (1955), 32-41.

Gillingham, A., and B. Stillman. *Remedial Reading Training for Children with Specific Disabilities in Reading, Spelling and Penmanship.* Bronxville, New York: the authors, 1956.

Godfrey, B.B., and N.C. Kephart. *Movement Patterns and Motor Education.* New York: Appleton-Century-Crofts, 1969.

Goodenough, F.L. *The Measurement of Intelligence by Drawings.* Yonkers-on-Hudson: World Book Co., 1926.

Gottschaldt, K. "Uber den Einfluss der Erfahrung auf die Wahrnehmung von Figuren 1: Uber den Einfluss Gehaufter Einpragung auf ihre Sechtbarkeit in Unfassenden Konifigurationen," *Psychol. Forach.,* VIII (1926), 261-317.

Graham, C.H. "Visual Perception," in S.S. Stevens (ed.) *Handbook of Experimental Psychology.* New York: John Wiley and Sons, Inc., 1951, pp. 868-920.

Guyton, A.C. *Textbook of Medical Physiology,* 3rd ed. Philadelphia: W.B. Saunders Co., 1966, p. 653.

Hall, D. *Pentatonic I, Orff Schulwerk, Music for Children.* Mainz: B. Schott's Sohne, 1960.

Harlow, H.F. "Thinking," in H. Helson (ed.), *Theoretical Foundations of Psychology.* New York: Van Nostrand, 1951.

Harmon, D.B. *Restrained performance as a contributing cause of visual problems.* Norman, Okla.: Optometric Extension Program, 1965.

Hebb, D.O. *The Organization of Behavior.* New York: John Wiley and Sons, Inc., 1949.

Held, R. and A. Hein "Movement — produced stimulation in the development of visually guided behavior." *J. Comp. and physiological psychol.,* 50 (1963), 872-876.

Hurlock, E.B. *Child Development.* New York: McGraw-Hill Book Co., 1942.

Ismail, A.H., and J.J. Gruber, *Integrated Development: Motor Aptitude and Intellectual Performance.* Columbus: Charles E. Merrill Publishing Co., 1967.

Itard, J.M.G. *The Wild Boy of Aveyron.* New York: Appleton-Century-Crofts, Inc., 1932.

Jacobson, E. *Progressive Relaxation.* Chicago: University of Chicago Press, 1938.

Jersild, A.T. *Child Psychology.* Englewood Cliffs, N.J.: Prentice-Hall, Inc., 1960.

Johnson, D.J. and H.R. Myklebust. *Learning Disabilities.* New York: Grune and Stratton, 1967.

Jolles, I. "A Teaching Sequence for the Training of Visual and Motor Perception." *Amer. J. Ment. Def.,* LXIII (1958), 252-55.

Jones, E., E. Morgan and G. Stevens. *Methods and Materials in Elementary Physical Education.* Yonkers-on-Hudson: World Book Co., 1957.

Kagerer, R.L. The Relationship between the Kraus-Weber Test for Minimum Muscular Fitness and School Achievement. Winter Haven, Florida: Winter Haven Lions Club, 1958.

Karnes, M.B. *Helping Young Children Develop Language Skills.* Arlington, Va.: Council for Exceptional Children, 1968.

Katz, Joseph J. and Ward C. Halstead. *Protein Organization and Mental Function.* Comp. Psychol. Mongr., 20 (1), (1950), 1-38.

Kephart, N.C. "Visual Behavior of the Retarded Child." *Amer. J. Optom.,* XXXV (1958), 125-33.

Kephart, N.C. and R.E. Chandler. Changes in the Visual Field in a Pursuit Tracking Task. *Optom. Weekly,* XLVII (1956), 507-9.

Kirk, S.A., and G.O. Johnson. *Educating the Retarded Child.* New York: Houghton Mifflin Company, 1951.

Kirk, S.A., J.J. McCarthy, and W.D. Kirk. *The Illinois Test of Psycholinguistic Abilities.* Urbana: University of Illinois Press, 1968.

Koffka, K. *The Growth of the Mind.* New York: Humanities Press Inc. 1951.

Kounin, J. "Experimental Studies of Rigidity. The Measurement of Rigidity in Normal and Feebleminded Persons," *Character in Personality*, IX (1941), 251-73.

Kounin, J. The Meaning of Rigidity: A Reply to Heinz Werner," *Psychol. Rev.*, LV (1948), 157-66.

Krech, D. and R.S. Crutchfield. *Elements of Psychology*. New York: Alfred A. Knopf, Inc., 1958.

LaDue, F., and J. Normon. *This is Trampolining*, 2nd ed. Cedar Rapids, Iowa: Nissen Trampoline Co., 1956.

Lewin, K. *Principles of Topological Psychology*. New York: McGraw-Hill Book Company, 1936.

Lorente de No, R. *A Study of Nerve Physiology*. New York: Rockefeller Institute for Medical Research, Vols. 131, 132, 1947.

Lotz, R.H. *Mediciniscke Psychologie oder Physiologie der Seele*. Leipzig: Weidmann'sche Buchandlung, 1852.

Lowder, R.G. *Perceptual Ability and School Achievement*. Available from Winter Haven Lions Club, Winter Haven, Florida, 1956.

Luneburg, R.K. *Mathematical Theory of Optics*. Berkeley: University of California Press, 1964.

Lynn, R. *Attention, Arousal and the Orientation Reaction*. Oxford, England: Pergamon Press, 1966.

Mabbott, J.D. Our Direct Experience of Time. *Mind*, 60, 1951.

Marsden, C.D. "The Marsden Ball," in *Visual Training at Work. Optometric Extension Program Papers*, 25 (8) (1953).

McCulloch, W.S. "Why the Mind is in the Head," in L.A. Jeffries (ed.), *Cerebral Mechanisms in Behavior*. New York: John Wiley and Sons, Inc., 1951.

McTaggert, J.M.E. *The Nature of Existence, Vol II*. Cambridge: Cambridge University Press, 1927.

Mikaelian, H., and R. Held. "Two types of adaptation to an optically rotated visual field. *Am. J. Psychol.*, 77 (1964), 257-263.

Mountcastle, Vernon B. (ed.) *Medical Physiology*, Volume II. Saint Louis: The C.V. Mosby Company, 1968.

Neilson, N.P. *Physical Education for Elementary Schools*, Rev. Ed. New York: The Ronald Press Company, 1956.

Oppenheimer, J. *All About Me*. Available from the Glen Haven Achievement Center, Fort Collins, Colorado.

Paterson, D.G. *Physique and Intellect*. New York: Century House, Inc., 1930.

Pavlov, I.P. *Conditioned Reflexes*. Oxford: Humphrey Melford, 1927.

Pavlov, I.P. *Lectures on Conditioned Reflexes*. New York: International, 1928.

Penfield, W., and L. Roberts. *Speech and Brain Mechanisms*. Princeton: Princeton University Press, 1959.

Phillips, John L., Jr. *The Origins of Intellect Piagets Theory*. San Francisco: W.H. Freeman and Co., 1969.

Piaget, J., and B. Inhelder. *The Child's Conception of Space*. London: Routledge and Kegan Paul, 1956.

Pimsleur, P., and R. Bonkowski. Transfer of Verbal Material across Sense Modalities, *J. Ed. Psych.,* 52 (1961), 104-107.

Plenderleith, M. "Discrimination Learning and Discrimination Reversal Learning in Normal and Feebleminded Children," *J. Genet Psychol.,* 88, 1956, 107-12.

Potter, M.C. "Perception of Symbol Orientation and Early Reading Success." New York: Teacher's College, Columbia University Contributions to Education, No. 939, 1949.

Riesen, A.H. "The Development of Visual Perception in Man and Chimpanzee," *Science*, CVI (1947), 107-08.

Roach, E.G., and N.C. Kephart: *The Purdue Perceptual-Motor Survey*. Columbus: Charles E. Merrill Publishing Co., 1966.

Robinson, H.M., M.C. Letton, L. Mozzi, and A.A. Rosenbloom. "An Evaluation of the Children's Visual Achievement Forms at Grade 1, "*Amer. J. Optom.*, XXXV (1958), 515-25.

Russell, D.H. *Children's Thinking*. Boston: Ginn and Company, 1956.

Schilder, P. *The Image and Appearance of the Human Body*. New York: International University Press, 1935.

Seguin, E. *Idiocy and Its Treatment by the Physiological Method*. New York: Columbia University Press, 1907.

Senden, M. *Raum-und Gestaltauffassung bei Operierten Blindgeborenen vor und nach der Operation*. Leipzig: Barth, 1932.

Sherrington, C. *Man On His Nature*. Cambridge: Cambridge University Press, 1951.

Sherrington, C. *The Integrative Action of the Nervous System*. New Haven: Yale University Press, 1948.

Shinn, M.W. *The Biography of a Baby*. Boston: Houghton-Mifflin Co., 1900.

Simpson, D.M. *Learning to Learn*. Columbus: Charles E. Merrill Publishing Co., 1968.

Small, V.H. "Ocular Pursuit Abilities and Readiness for Reading." Unpublished Ph.D. dissertation, Purdue University, 1958.

Stern, C. *Children Discover Arithmetic*. New York: Harper & Brothers, 1949.

Stevenson, H., and E. Zigler. "Discrimination Learning and Rigidity in Normal and Feebleminded Individuals," *J. Person.*, XXV (1957), 699-711.

Strauss, A.A., and N.C. Kephart. *Psychopathology and Education of the Brain Injured Child, Vol. 2: Progress in Theory and Clinic*. New York: Grune & Stratton, Inc., 1955.

Strauss, A.A. and L.E. Lehtinen. *Psychopathology and Education of the Brain Injured child*. New York: Grune & Stratton, Inc., 1947.

Street, R.F. *A Gestalt Completion Test*. New York: Teacher's College, Columbia University Contributions to Education, No. 481, 1931.

Terman, L.M., and M.A. Merrill. *Measuring Intelligence*. New York: Houghton Mifflin Company, 1937.

Vernon, M.D. *Backwardness in Reading.* Cambridge: Cambridge University Press, 1957.

Vernon, M.D. *A Further Study of Visual Perception.* Cambridge: Cambridge University Press, 1952.

Vinacke, W.E. *The Psychology of Thinking.* New York: McGraw-Hill Book Company, 1952.

Wechsler, D. *Wechsler Intelligence Scale for Children.* New York: Psychological Corp., 1949.

Welch, L. "The Transition from Simple to Complex Forms of Learning," *J. Genet. Psychol.,* 71 (1947), 223-51.

Wellman, B.L. "Physical Growth and Motor Development and Their Relationship to Mental Development in Children," in C. Murchison (ed.), *A Handbook of Child Psychology.* Worcester: Clark University Press, 1931.

Wepman, J. *Auditory Discrimination Test.* Chicago: The Language Research Associates, 1958.

Werner, H. *Comparative Psychology of Mental Development.* New York: International Universities Press, 1948.

Werner, H. "Development of Visuo-motor Performance on the Marble Board Test in Mentally Retarded Children," *J. Genet. Psychol.,* LXIV (1944), 269-79.

Werner, H. "The Concept of Development from a Comparative and Organismic Point of View," in D.B. Harris (ed.), *The Concept of Development.* Minneapolis: University of Minnesota Press, 1957, pp. 125-148.

Werner, H. and A.A. Strauss. "Types of Visuo-motor Activity in Their Relationship to Low and High Performance Ages," *Proc. Amer. Assoc. Ment. Def.,* XLIV (1939), 163-8.

Wiener, N. *Cybernetics.* New York: John Wiley and Sons, Inc., 1948.

Wilcox, J.C., and E. Wilcox. A Neurophysiological view of the neurologically handicapped adolescent. *Academic Therapy,* 5 (1970), 271-275.

Woodworth, R.S., and H. Scholsberg. *Experimental Psychology.* New York: Henry Holt & Co., Inc., 1954.

Zubek, J.P., and P.A. Solberg. *Human Development.* New York: McGraw-Hill Book Company, 1954.

Zuk, G.H. Perceptual Processes in Normal Development, Brain Injury and Mental Retardation, *Amer. J. Ment. Def.,* 63 (1958), 256-59.

Name Index

Subject Index